SHAKESPEARE
AND THE MAKING OF
AMERICA

SHAKESPEARE
AND THE MAKING OF
AMERICA

KEVIN J. HAYES

AMBERLEY

For James Crowley

First published 2020

Amberley Publishing
The Hill, Stroud
Gloucestershire, GL5 4EP

www.amberley-books.com

British Library Cataloguing in Publication Data.
A catalogue record for this book is available from the British Library.

ISBN 978 1 4456 8806 0 (hardback)
ISBN 978 1 4456 8807 7 (ebook)

1 2 3 4 5 6 7 8 9 10

Typesetting by Aura Technology and Software Services, India.
Printed in the UK.

Contents

Acknowledgements

Many people deserve thanks for making this work possible. I am especially grateful to Connor Stait at Amberley Publishing for encouraging me to undertake this project. I have assembled the research materials over a period of several years, often while working on other projects simultaneously. I would like to thank the librarians at many institutions across the nation: Boston Athenaeum; Boston Public Library; John D. Rockefeller, Jr Library, Colonial Williamsburg, Inc.; New York Public Library; Firestone Library, Princeton University; the Library Company of Philadelphia; Albert and Shirley Small Special Collections Library, University of Virginia; and Virginia Historical Society.

While researching an earlier project, *Thomas Jefferson in His Own Time*, I received a research fellowship from the Robert H. Smith International Center for Jefferson Studies at Monticello, Virginia. This fellowship is the gift that keeps on giving. As a fellow, I have received access to the library's research databases, which have greatly facilitated the research for the present book. I would like to thank those who helped me locate information in places I did not have the opportunity to visit, including Samantha Dorsey at George Mason's Gunston Hall and Maria Zapata at the Robert B. Haas Family Arts Library, Yale University. I would also like to thank Jeremy Dibbell for his work on the Legacy Libraries section of LibraryThing, which I often check when I get stuck for ideas.

My wife Myung-Sook nudged me toward this project. Her positive attitude and unending enthusiasm, as always, kept me going. Finally I thank James Crowley. While we were in graduate school together at the University of Delaware, Jim coached me as I studied for my doctoral examinations in Shakespeare and the English Renaissance. Memories of those late-night study sessions often returned as I wrote the present work. I dedicate this book to him.

Preface

The best professional conferences cast magic spells over their participants. 'George Washington Goes to War', a weekend symposium held at Mount Vernon a few years ago, had that effect on me. The organisers invited me to the symposium to deliver a talk on Washington's field library. Best of all, they provided me and my wife Sooki with complimentary lodging on the grounds. After the last session of the symposium, we walked from the lecture hall in the visitor centre back to our room, making a slight detour to stroll past Mount Vernon in the moonlight. Though hesitant to break the symposium's magic spell after we returned to our room, I eventually switched on my laptop and re-established contact with the outside world, something I had avoided throughout the weekend.

My inbox contained an email from the editor of a historical magazine asking if I would review the latest biography of George Washington. I had been trying to write fewer book reviews to make time to write more books, but the editor caught me at a good time. The symposium left me eager to continue my study of all things Washington, so I accepted his invitation to review the book. A few days after we got home I received my review copy in the mail and started reading. I remember being disappointed with the author's treatment of Washington's intellectual life. She wrote that Washington almost never read for pleasure and, for proof, asserted that his published papers contain few literary references. They don't? Off the top of my head I could recall allusions to five different Shakespeare plays in Washington's writings: *Henry V*, *Julius Caesar*, *Othello*, *The Tempest* and *Twelfth Night*. As I wrote my review, I told the author to take Cole Porter's advice: 'Brush up your Shakespeare!'

This historian's neglect of Shakespeare is not unusual. The increasing compartmentalisation of academic study means that historians sometimes don't read literature and, conversely, that literary professors don't read history. One day a friend of mine from the history department walked past my office and saw me with my nose stuck in a book. He asked what I was reading. '*The New Inn*,' I told him. 'It's a play by Ben Jonson.' Showing him the book, I mentioned seeing the Royal Shakespeare Company perform *The New Inn* at the Swan Theatre in Stratford-upon-Avon in 1987, the first time the comedy had been staged since it opened in 1629. I offered to loan him the book, a generous offer given that my copy was the official programme to *The New Inn* I had acquired in Stratford, which contained the complete text of the play.

'I don't read plays,' my historian friend responded. His response was not unexpected. A few months earlier I had offered to lend him my copy of Tom Mead's *Killers of Eden*, an Australian novel that had come up in conversation, whereupon he had replied, 'I don't read novels.'

My friend's refusal to read either novels or plays reveals much about his attitude toward the written word. He seemed to divide writing into two basic categories: history and fiction. This either / or distinction neglects all the subtle gradations between the two. I did not say anything at that moment, but his refusal to read fiction seemed like it might hobble his understanding of history. How can a historian who doesn't read fiction recognise the fictions in history?

Compartmentalisation has also hindered the study of literature in recent decades. As literary studies have become more and more specialised, professors of English have ignored everything outside their areas of expertise. Specialists in American literature neglect British literature. Specialists in nineteenth-century American literature neglect colonial American literature. And, sad to say, specialists in early American literature neglect the literature of the colonial South.

I had the great fortune to study at the University of Delaware in the late eighties. At that time Delaware was arguably the best place in the world to study American literature, but it also had a strong programme in British literature. While reading early American literature with J. A. Leo Lemay, I also read Shakespeare with Jay L. Halio. One year Prof. Halio taught an experimental seminar, 'Hamlet and Lear'. We devoted the first half of the semester to *Hamlet*, the second to *King Lear*, giving us time enough to delve into the textual, critical and cultural history of both plays. The seminar went so well that Prof. Halio wrote a pedagogical essay about it for *Shakespeare*

Quarterly. While keeping the names of me and my classmates secret, he applauded our enthusiasm, hard work, intellectual curiosity and daring ideas. The present work has its roots in my concurrent graduate study of Shakespeare and early American literature at the University of Delaware.

To study Shakespeare's impact on colonial American history requires an in-depth study of colonial American literature, one that recognises its geographic breadth. Understanding Shakespeare's American influence also requires a knowledge of cultural history, performance history, political history, social history and the history of the book, a wide-ranging field that encompasses the history of libraries, reading practices and the social uses of books.

There have been some good efforts devoted to the subject of Shakespeare's influence on eighteenth-century America. The first and, in many ways, the best has been Edwin Eliott Willoughby's essay, 'The Reading of Shakespeare in Colonial America', which appeared in 1936. Chief bibliographer at the Folger Library in Washington, Willoughby assembled numerous references from early American literature to show that colonial Americans did read and enjoy Shakespeare.

As the single fullest essay on the subject to appear to that time, Willoughby's article became the standard work in the field. As such, it forms an example of a phenomenon I call the Obstinance of Ingrained Information. Though Willoughby located much new material, he perpetuated some errors of others and added some of his own. Once his article became the standard, professors who have taken up the topic of Shakespeare and America have largely devoted their attention to the nineteenth and twentieth centuries, relying on Willoughby for their information about colonial America. They have not only perpetuated his errors, they have also neglected to search for more information about Shakespeare in colonial America. If Willoughby did not find it, they seem to think, then it is not worth finding.

Complicating matters further, some who have discussed the topic of Shakespeare's influence on eighteenth-century America have often ignored the work of other scholars in the field, a neglect that can be quite frustrating, as Tennessee Shakespearean Alwin Thaler discovered. Thaler found a reference to *Othello* in Benjamin Franklin's correspondence and published his findings in a leading scholarly journal only to see his article ignored. Twenty years later the author of an essay about Shakespeare's influence on the leaders of the American Revolution in *Shakespeare Quarterly* asserted that Franklin made no known references to Shakespeare. Thaler wrote an angry note to *Shakespeare Quarterly* to lament the author's neglect of his research.

From the final third of the seventeenth century, when the first known copy of a Shakespeare folio can be located in colonial America, the story of his influence on the making of America is a rich and varied tale showing how people read Shakespeare, appreciated his art and let his words and ideas shape their thought. Shakespeare held a prominent place in eighteenth-century American libraries. Reading Shakespeare, colonial Americans immersed themselves in a world of art and ideas that transcended the times in which he wrote his plays. Studying Shakespeare's impact on early American readers, writers and thinkers, the present work takes the story through the ratification of the Constitution in 1788, when Shakespeare's words were brought to bear to persuade American citizens to accept the Constitution as their form of government. *Shakespeare and the Making of America* tells a story that reveals for the first time the profound influence England's greatest writer had on the creation of the United States of America.

Kevin J. Hayes
Toledo, Ohio

1

Mr William Shakespeares Comedies, Histories, and Tragedies

The James River, the heart and highway of colonial Virginia, brought hogsheads of tobacco downriver on the first leg of the journey to Britain and crates of essential supplies upriver on the last leg of the journey home. The Virginia planters whose stately mansions lined the river ordered a huge variety of goods from London to adorn their homes, operate their farms and please their families. Perhaps no imports were more important than books: objects that let them recreate European learning and culture in the New World. At Westover, the Palladian mansion he built on the James in Charles City County, William Byrd assembled an extraordinary library, the best one in colonial Virginia. Over the course of his life, Byrd obtained books by the finest authors in the finest editions, including what is arguably the greatest book in the history of English literature, *Mr William Shakespeares Comedies, Histories, and Tragedies*.[1]

William Byrd, the second of that name, was the first born in Virginia. His father William Byrd, who had been born in London in the mid-seventeenth century, accepted an uncle's invitation to emigrate to the colony and become his heir. The invitation let him break free from his lower-class upbringing and establish himself as part of the landed gentry in the New World. Once his uncle died in 1671 and he inherited the plantation, Byrd proved himself a resourceful and hardworking tobacco planter and fur trader. In 1673 he wed Mary Horsemanden, who gave birth to their son and his namesake on 28 March 1674.[2]

The colonial Virginia gentry usually sent their sons to England for their education. The Byrds were no exception. In the early 1680s the elder Byrd sent young William to Felsted Grammar School in Essex, England, where he would receive an excellent classical education that stuck with him all his life. As an adult, Byrd habitually read Greek,

Latin or Hebrew every morning. Once his formal schooling ended, he spent a few years learning the mercantile trade in Rotterdam and London but then entered the Middle Temple to read law, becoming a licensed attorney in 1695.[3]

His fellow students at the Middle Temple included two men who would turn their attention from the bar to the boards: William Congreve and Nicholas Rowe. Congreve would establish himself as the foremost comic dramatist of his age. His comedies, especially *The Way of the World*, would delight London audiences for decades. Congreve's comedies probe love and marriage with wit and sympathy. Rowe took to tragedy, writing such works as *Jane Shore*, dramas that feature tragic female protagonists, victims with the strength to suffer and the character to evoke awe and pity. In short, Rowe became the leading tragic dramatist of his age, challenging stage conventions to create more subtle and sympathetic protagonists.

Rowe enhanced his literary standing by associating himself with Shakespeare. The full title of *Jane Shore*, to continue the example, is *The Tragedy of Jane Shore Written in Imitation of Shakespear's Style*. Not only is its plot based on a suggestion from *Richard III*, but *Jane Shore* also follows Shakespeare's poetic form, being written in blank verse, well, mostly. Rowe did use rhyme in spots to the consternation of some discriminating theatre-goers. Thomas Morris, a fashionable dilettante and drama critic before he came to America as an infantry officer during the Seven Years' War, heaped curses on Rowe for lapsing into heroic couplets at inappropriate moments in *Jane Shore*.[4]

The prologue to the tragedy, which Rowe also wrote in rhyme, contains a brief tribute to Shakespeare. In retrospect, the couplet celebrating Shakespeare's greatness may be the most memorable part of the play: 'With rough, majestick force he mov'd the heart, / And strength and nature made amends for art.'[5] This couplet encapsulates the critical stance toward Shakespeare that would prevail through the eighteenth century: Shakespeare's natural genius, not his knowledge of stagecraft or dramatic theory, is what makes his plays great.

Publisher Jacob Tonson, who had shrewdly bought the copyrights to Shakespeare's plays, approached Rowe to edit a multivolume edition. Since Shakespeare was appreciated mainly for his tragedies in the early eighteenth century, Tonson selected a popular author of tragedies as editor. Rowe's hand in the new edition would help Tonson market it. Tonson would apply a similar marketing strategy with the subsequent editions of Shakespeare he published.[6]

Rowe brought his stage experience to the task of editing Shakespeare. For his edition, which first appeared in 1709, Rowe made Shakespeare more accessible. The seventeenth-century folio editions like the one Byrd owned, could be difficult to read, burdened with obsolete spellings and textual errors but lacking scene divisions, stage directions and lists of *dramatis personae*. Using the Fourth Folio of 1685 as his base text, Rowe cleaned up the plays, correcting errors, resolving inconsistencies, differentiating scenes and adding scene localities. He also modernised the texts, a practice that remains part of editing Shakespeare.

Rowe's editorial efforts significantly broadened Shakespeare's reading audience. His biographical research also helped make Shakespeare more accessible. Rowe assembled more facts about Shakespeare than anyone before him. He prefaced his edition with 'Some Account of the Life etc. of Mr William Shakespear', the first biography of its subject. Rowe's life would remain the standard biography for decades, and most eighteenth-century editions of Shakespeare's works would reprint it in full or in part.

The extent of Byrd's friendship with Rowe and Congreve is unknown, but his passion for the stage may partly reflect their influence. Byrd briefly returned to Virginia after completing his legal studies, but by mid-1697 he was back in London, where he would remain until 1705.[7]

Byrd is best known to posterity as the author of two parallel narratives that relate in different ways the story of his 1728 survey of the boundary between Virginia and North Carolina: *The History of the Dividing Line* and *The Secret History of the Line*. The *Secret History* reflects his contact with the Restoration stage, especially in its use of typenames to indicate the defining traits of many memorable characters. Byrd named himself Steddy, and assigned other members of the expedition such names as Astrolabe, Firebrand, Merryman and Meanwell.

Another sobriquet – the Samuel Pepys of American literature – emphasises Byrd's lifelong practice of keeping a shorthand diary. Though he apparently maintained his secret diary throughout adulthood, no diaries from the 1697-1705 period survive to chronicle his life as a young man in London. If his later behaviour is any guide, Byrd attended the theatre many times a week and saw all the best productions. Surviving letters reflect his in-depth knowledge of the London stage. The first week of September 1703, for example, he informed a correspondent of the death of leading actress Susanna Verbruggen. Byrd's involvement with the theatre extended to play-writing, according to local tradition. Robert Bolling, the Virginia poet who recorded the anecdote, said that when Byrd was in London he and some friends got together and wrote *The Careless Husband* for Colley Cibber.[8]

Byrd's letters do supply evidence of a few plays he saw during the 1697-1705 period. Writing to Lady Betty Cromwell in 1703 he mentioned attending Bartholomew Fair, where he saw two actor-managers perform, Thomas Doggett and William Penkethman. According to his letter, Byrd was more interested in the casts that Doggett and Penkethman assembled, which he calls 'a frightfull collection of nymphs for actresses'. At Bartholomew Fair that year Penkethman starred in one comedy called *Jeptha's Rash Vow*, and Doggett starred in another, *The History of Bateman*. A third play produced at Bartholomew Fair that year was *The Famous History of Dorastus and Fawnia*, which was based on *Pandosto*, Robert Greene's popular prose romance. *Pandosto* is best known as Shakespeare's principle source for *The Winter's Tale*.[9]

Byrd also followed the controversies surrounding the English stage. The Rev. Jeremy Collier spearheaded the fullest attack, critiquing the theatre's obscene language, sexual innuendo and general moral decay. Collier developed his argument in *A Short View of the Immorality and Profaneness of the English Stage*, which sparked a fierce pamphlet war, turning the morality of the English stage into a political firestorm and lending literary criticism an adversarial quality, which it retains to the present.[10]

In *Short View*, a work Byrd added to his personal library, Collier identified a degenerate streak in the theatre that extended back to ancient Greece and continued through the English Renaissance to the Restoration. He observed: 'As for Shakespear, he is too guilty to make an evidence: But I think he gains not much by his misbehaviour; he has commonly Plautus's fate, where there is most smut, there is least sense.' Byrd collected several published responses to Collier, including James Drake's *Antient and Modern Stages Survey'd*.[11]

Shakespeareans love the Drake, who trounced Collier's *Short View*. In a marginal gloss adjacent to his discussion Drake observes that Shakespeare is 'prefer'd to all the rest of the English dramatists'. Though Drake thought Shakespeare lacked both Ben Jonson's artistry and the sparkling wit of the playwriting duo of Francis Beaumont and John Fletcher, his plays had sufficient beauties to make amends for their defects. Drake especially enjoyed the moral excellence of Hamlet's plot: 'Here was a murther privately committed, strangely discover'd, and wonderfully punish'd. Nothing in antiquity can rival this plot for the admirable distribution of poetick justice.'[12]

During the 1697-1705 period, Byrd had the opportunity to attend many Shakespeare plays: *Cymbeline*, *Hamlet*, *Henry IV*, *Henry VIII*, *King Lear*, *Macbeth*, *Othello*, *Richard III* and *The Tempest*. Most, if not all, of these productions dramatised Shakespeare with a twist. *The Tempest* was Shakespeare turned into an opera by Thomas Shadwell. *King Lear* was Shakespeare as altered by Nahum Tate (Lear survives). *Richard III* was Shakespeare as adapted by Colley Cibber, who cut several characters and several hundred lines from the play to emphasise the eponymous hero, a part Cibber played himself. And, to name just one more example, *Henry IV* was Shakespeare as altered by Thomas Betterton, who established his acting reputation in the role of Hotspur.

The performance of *Macbeth* at Drury Lane on Saturday, 27 November 1703, gave Jeremy Collier the opportunity to renew his attack on the theatre. It coincided with the Great Storm of 1703, which had brought damaging winds and rain to London the previous day. By Saturday night the storm had lessened but had not quite dissipated. Carving a path of destruction through London, it toppled some two thousand chimney stacks. Collier and his fellow reformers took a traditional view of the violent storms, seeing them as a punishment God inflicted on sinners. When Drury Lane Theatre opened on Saturday night to present *Macbeth* as scheduled, Collier was downright indignant, especially since this particular play begins with a fateful thunderstorm followed by destructive winds in the second act. Arriving at Macbeth's castle, Lennox informs him: 'The night has been unruly: where we lay, / Our chimneys were blown down.'[13]

In the play the violent storm outdoors parallels Macbeth's concurrent murder of Duncan inside his castle. The audience at Drury Lane that Saturday night recognised the parallel between Lennox's words and the recent storm damage. After the actor playing Lennox mentioned the chimneys being blown down, the audience gave him an ovation. Collier was aghast. Why, the London theatregoers saw the Great Storm of 1703 as little more than a delightful coincidence that enhanced the make-believe of *Macbeth*. From his viewpoint the audience ignored divine providence altogether: dangerous behaviour in the face of an angry God.[14]

Learning of his father's death two years later, Byrd returned to Virginia to inherit his lands. After settling into the life of a Virginia planter, he met Lucy Parke, the feisty daughter of Daniel Parke, the governor of the Leeward Islands. In a double ceremony on 4 May 1706, Byrd wed Lucy, and John Custis wed her older sister Frances. Establishing a home of his own, Byrd rebuilt his father's more modest house at Westover into a luxurious brick mansion. No proper eighteenth-century gentleman's home, he knew, would be complete without a library. William Byrd I deserves credit for establishing the library at Westover, but his son brought it to greatness.

William Byrd II designed and built a separate structure to house his books during the summer of 1709. The library Byrd built was one long spacious gallery which would eventually house twenty-three walnut bookcases with up to seven shelves each. A great space for entertaining, the library was large enough for ten couples to dance simultaneously. On rainy days when he could not exercise outdoors, Byrd used to pace through the gallery. To keep it as roomy as possible, he furnished the library sparsely, but it did contain a couch. In his secret diary the randy Byrd recorded giving Lucy a 'flourish' on the library couch.[15] Byrd's connotation for the word 'flourish' is apparently original. To be sure, he did not get it from Shakespeare, not unless he heard fanfare while giving his wife a flourish.

In the summer of 1710 Byrd thoroughly reorganised his library, putting the books into the basic order they would retain the rest of his life. He arranged them by subject, devoting individual bookcases to history, law, medicine, belles lettres, divinity, classics and other subjects. Within each bookcase, the lower shelves held folios while the upper ones held progressively smaller books – quartos, octavos, duodecimos.[16]

Though only a fraction of Byrd's library survives, its organisation is known by a manuscript catalogue that Williamsburg bookbinder John Stretch compiled. Stretch listed the books as they were shelved at Westover, creating a *de facto* blueprint of Byrd's mind. Stretch catalogued the books by their spine titles, which roughly coincided with their title pages. *Mr William Shakespeares Comedies, Histories, and Tragedies* is listed as 'Shakespear's Plays'.[17]

The fact that Byrd shelved the volume on a lower folio shelf narrows its identification to four possible seventeenth-century editions. Willoughby argues that Byrd's copy was the Fourth Folio of 1685, which he presumably obtained while living in England during the late seventeenth century. Others have dated Byrd's acquisition more precisely, asserting that he had obtained it by 1696, the year he returned to Virginia.[18]

The late seventeenth-century dates make sense, but they remain conjectural. Byrd's Shakespeare does not survive, or, if it does, it survives without his engraved armorial bookplate. Like other early American bookplates, Byrd's used to have more value than many of the books it adorned. Collectors often removed bookplates and, with them, all evidence of a book's ownership. The Fourth Folio of 1685 is the most likely edition Byrd owned, but he could have owned the First Folio of 1623, the Second Folio of 1632, the Third Folio of 1663 or a separate reissue of any of these editions, none of which were impossible to find in the second-hand bookshops of Byrd's London.[19]

Rumours about other Shakespeare folios in colonial Virginia have circulated for years. Earl Gregg Swem, the librarian at the College of William and Mary, told Alfred Westfall that the family of a former William and Mary student owned a copy of the Fourth Folio, which had been brought to America in the seventeenth century. All Swem's efforts to find the folio were unsuccessful. He never could trace the volume beyond the rumour.[20]

Happily, new evidence now places a Shakespeare folio in seventeenth-century Virginia. Major Edward Dale's copy of Juvenal's works, which survives at the Folger Library, contains some exciting manuscript evidence partway through the volume. Onto the blank leaf facing page 46, Dale's son-in-law Thomas Carter and his grandson, godson and namesake Edward Carter recorded their inventory of Dale's library, dated 16 February 1695 – exactly two weeks after his death. Theirs is more detailed than other contemporary inventories. Besides authors' names and short titles, the Carters recorded formats and publication dates. Dale's copy of *Mr William Shakespeares Comedies, Histories, and Tragedies* was the Second Folio of 1632. In short, Dale owned the earliest known Shakespeare folio in colonial America.[21]

Dale's Shakespeare reflects his English background. Like many royalists, he emigrated to Virginia in the early 1650s, that is, after Charles I was executed and Oliver Cromwell came to power. Dale settled on the north side of the Rappahannock River in Lancaster County. Establishing himself as a prominent local citizen, he received a commission as clerk of the county in 1655 and later became sheriff, a justice of the county court and a representative in the House of Burgesses. A man of strong opinions, he frequently dissented from the decisions of other members of the county court. Overall, Dale became a model of the Virginia gentleman, though in one instance he violated Virginia's renowned hospitality.

According to family tradition, a stranger passing through Lancaster County stopped at the Dale home one day around dinnertime. The family stabled the stranger's horse and invited him to dinner, which was just being served. When everyone was seated, the stranger bowed his head and offered a long puritanical prayer, blessing Oliver Cromwell and cursing King Charles II. The stranger's prayer so incensed Dale that he ordered him from the table, sent for his horse, and told him to hunt for his dinner elsewhere.[22]

Dale's anger is understandable. Though he had settled into the life of a Virginia gentleman, he still retained a fondness for the England he knew. The dates of his books show that he acquired many of them while living in Virginia, but some he may have brought with him when he emigrated in the early 1650s. Besides Shakespeare's Second Folio, Dale also owned Thomas Lodge's English translation of Josephus's *Workes* (1609) and John Donne's *Eighty Sermons* (1640). Dale's library suggests that he sought to recreate the England he knew on the banks of the Rappahannock. No wonder he was angry when a Cromwellian showed up at his dinner table.

On a much grander scale Byrd's library at Westover let him recreate his London intellectual life. Nestled between Beaumont and Fletcher and Ben Jonson, his copy of of *Mr William Shakespeares Comedies, Histories, and Tragedies* stood on the second shelf from the bottom of the eighth bookcase: 'Entertainment, Poetry, Translations etc.' The three-volume cluster links all four authors, then considered the finest dramatists of the English Renaissance. Laden with several other big, beefy folios, the shelf was the most distinguished one in the Westover library, at least in terms of literary history. It held the collected works of Francis Bacon, Sir Thomas Browne, Geoffrey Chaucer and Edmund Spenser. The third shelf from the bottom was sized for octavos. It contained a copy of Lord Lansdowne's *Four Plays*, which included *The Jew of Venice*, as he titled his altered version of *The Merchant of Venice*. Two books away from *Four Plays* and directly above *Mr William Shakespeares Comedies, Histories, and Tragedies* stood Collier's *Short View* and the responses to it.[23]

Byrd read other critical discussions about the stage, few more influential than those in the *Tatler*. On 8 July 1710, he recorded in his diary, 'I unpacked several things in the afternoon and then gave my wife a flourish and then read in the *Tatler*.'[24] Byrd would record reading the *Tatler* several more times: enough to indicate that he read the entire collected edition. Founded by Richard Steele, the *Tatler* reflects the coffee-house culture of early eighteenth-century London. Many of its articles are dated from Will's Coffee House: a regular haunt for Byrd when he lived in London. Reading the *Tatler* in Virginia, he could vicariously re-experience his life in London.

The *Tatler* contains numerous references to Shakespeare, who is mentioned more than any other author.[25] For this periodical Steele assumed the persona of Isaac Bickerstaff, a fictional character Jonathan Swift had created. In the *Tatler* Bickerstaff often quotes memorable passages from Shakespeare and sometimes incorporates critical discussions of his work. In one episode Mr Truman, a friend who has read a draft of a play Bickerstaff is writing, approaches him with some advice. Truman criticises Bickerstaff's emphasis on his hero's pomp and grandeur: 'The man is to be expressed by his sentiments and affections, and not by his fortune or equipage.' Truman recommends

Shakespeare's *Julius Caesar* for example. Shakespeare does not depict Caesar commanding all the powers of Rome but instead displays him in his nightgown. Avoiding the showy methods of portraying Caesar's greatness, Shakespeare depicts him debating the subjects of life and death with his most intimate friends.[26]

The attitude Truman displays in his discussion with Bickerstaff reflects Steele's attitude toward Shakespeare throughout the *Tatler*. Steele and his contributors – Joseph Addison, most importantly – stress the aspects of Shakespeare's characters that reflect nascent democratic values. The critical discourse in the *Tatler* parallels the political discourse of the times. Though it contains much literary discussion, the *Tatler* was more a social and political journal, manifesting Whig philosophy, especially in its pragmatic moderation and quest for consensus.[27]

Byrd's secret diary sometimes illustrates the social use of books in his family. Like any good bibliophile, he enjoyed perusing the libraries of friends and neighbours. While visiting the Custises that month, he examined John Custis's library. Though far smaller than the Westover library, which would swell to over three thousand volumes, Custis's four-hundred-volume library was among the largest in colonial Virginia.

On one shelf Byrd noticed a book he and Custis had in common: Collier's *Short View*, which he read aloud to the others by way of entertainment. Like Byrd, Custis had travelled from Virginia to England in his boyhood to study. He received a good classical education and also learned the mercantile trade.[28] Custis grew interested in the stage and its controversies while living in London during the 1690s. Besides obtaining a copy of Collier's *Short View*, he also acquired a volume with the spine title 'Collier Answerd', perhaps a bound volume of pamphlets responding to Collier's *Short View*.[29]

Custis may have had some Shakespeare in his library when Byrd examined it in late 1709, the year Rowe published his edition. When John Custis died in 1749, his son Daniel Parke Custis inherited the library. Daniel died less than ten years after his father, having done little with the library, which would descend to his son John Parke Custis, then a young child. Upon his death Daniel Parke Custis's library was inventoried. The inventory lists 'Shakespeare's Works', a spine title too vague to identify the precise edition.[30] When Martha Dandridge Custis – Daniel's widow – remarried, her new husband made arrangements to transport the Custis library to their home. Martha's new husband, of course, was George Washington, their home Mount Vernon.

Before moving the Custis collection to Mount Vernon in 1759, Washington catalogued it and, in so doing, preserved John Custis's shelf organisation.[31] One title towards the end of the inventory stands out: 'Shakespeare – 1 volume'. Gauged solely by the title, this volume could be either a Shakespeare folio or one volume from a multi-volume set. Washington listed it next to another broken set: a single octavo from the two-volume *Sportsman's Dictionary*. The inventory thus suggests that the Custis Shakespeare was also an octavo, not one of the library's folios, which Washington listed separately.[32]

After Washington had the Custis books transported to Mount Vernon, he combined them with his own library, retaining Custis's organisation. Washington inventoried the whole Mount Vernon library in 1764, by which time his cataloguing skills had greatly improved. He now recorded more specific details about what title and which volume of Shakespeare was in the Custis collection: 'Shakespears Works – 1st V.'[33] Being an octavo, the adjacent book – Aphra Behn's *Lover's Watch* – reinforces the likelihood that the Custis Shakespeare was the first volume of Rowe's edition, a volume of comedies.

Other private libraries in William Byrd's Virginia also contained copies of Shakespeare. His friend Edmund Berkeley had much in common with both Byrd and Custis, though less is known about his life. Born in Virginia in the early 1670s, Berkeley may have visited London in the late 1690s and enjoyed the theatre there. He served with Byrd on the council, Virginia's upper legislative house and general court. Byrd found him 'a very good, humoured man' and recorded in his diary a number of visits to Berkeley's home. The diary does not say whether he examined his library as he had Custis's, but Byrd did note that Berkeley's Gloucester County home was 'very neat', indicating that he looked around enough to see how his host decorated and maintained the home.[34]

Berkeley had a good library. Half the size of Custis's, it contained approximately two hundred volumes. The number is approximate because the people – taking a library inventory was a two-person job – who inventoried the library were lax when it came to recording the number of volumes for each title. Berkeley's copy of Shakespeare is listed as 'Shakespeare's Works'.[35] This spine title does not provide enough information to identify the edition more precisely. It could indicate a folio edition, one volume of Rowe's edition or Rowe's six-volume edition with the total number of volumes omitted.[36]

Arthur Spicer was another Virginian who, like Byrd, Custis and Berkeley, apparently encountered Shakespearean drama on the London stage and also added Shakespeare to his library. Spicer was a friend of William Byrd I, whose 1689 correspondence mentions that he had recently arrived from London. Spicer established himself as the foremost lawyer in the Northern Neck, a huge swath of Virginia real estate located between the Potomac and the Rappahannock rivers. Upon joining the Virginia gentry, Spicer accepted more and more local responsibilities, becoming a justice of the peace and being elected to the House of Burgesses.[37]

Beyond his legal vocation and official positions, little else is known about Spicer. He was a good host: passing through the Northern Neck on their way to Williamsburg in November 1697, two Maryland travellers stayed with him one night and noted Spicer's hospitality. In his will he stipulated that his son John be sent to England for his education: nothing too unusual. What is unusual is that Spicer stipulated which school he wished John to attend: Charterhouse. Many people considered Charterhouse the finest school in England. It was founded on the site of the old Carthusian monastery in Charterhouse Square. The original location still affected the students: Charterhouse alumni are known as Old Carthusians. John Washington – George Washington's great grandfather – was an Old Carthusian. Spicer's desire to send his son to Charterhouse reflects his love for the boy as well as his dedication to learning.[38]

The historical document that reveals the most about Arthur Spicer's personality is the catalogue of his books prepared after his death in 1699. Much as William Byrd perused the libraries of friends and neighbours to understand their minds, historians can peruse surviving library inventories to understand people of the past. The books we own tell others who we are.

As a practising attorney, Spicer used his law books hard but did not always take the best care of them. Neither did he keep up with the latest legal literature once he settled in Virginia.[39] The people who compiled the inventory listed all the legal titles but valued Spicer's entire collection of law books at a measly five pounds. Following the list of law titles in the inventory, a note says that the foregoing books were 'old, broken and damnified'. The rest of his books reveal that Spicer was well rounded, open minded and intellectually curious. The inventory lists such works as Francis Bacon's *Advancement of Learning*, Sir Thomas Browne's *Religio Medici* and a copy of *Macbeth*.[40]

Macbeth first appeared in print as part of the First Folio of 1623. The play was neglected until William Davenant brought it back to the London stage around 1664. The leading theatrical manager of his day, Davenant benefitted from the patronage of the Duke of York. The theatre Davenant established at Lincoln's Inn Fields became known as the Duke's Theatre. Instead of staging *Macbeth* as Shakespeare wrote it, Davenant revised the play. Besides altering its plot, he enhanced its theatricality by giving the witches greater prominence and adding some musical numbers. Davenant's *Macbeth* was a great success on the Restoration stage.

After Davenant's death in 1668 *Macbeth* continued to be performed. Capitalising on the play's theatrical success, Shakespeare's *Macbeth* was issued separately in a quarto edition in 1673. The title page reads *Macbeth: A Tragedy Acted at the Dukes-Theatre*. The title is imprecise. It was not Shakespeare's text that was performed at the Duke's Theatre, but Davenant's. The text of Davenant's version appeared in print the following year under the title *Macbeth, A Tragedy: With All the Alterations, Amendments, Additions, and New Songs as It's Now Acted at the Dukes Theatre*. Spicer's inventory does not list the author of *Macbeth*, which is no surprise. Neither the 1673 Shakespeare text nor the 1674 Davenant text named the author on their title pages.

In his *Intellectual Life in the Colonial South* Richard Beale Davis identifies Spicer's copy as 'the first quarto of *Macbeth* of 1673'.[41] Eager to dispel the image of the barefooted, loose-limbed, slack-jacked Southern hick who can barely read or write – already a stereotype in colonial times, as Byrd's *History of the Dividing Line* shows – Davis is quick to locate a copy of Shakespeare in seventeenth-century Virginia: a little too quick. Spicer's *Macbeth* could have been Shakespeare's, but it could have been Davenant's instead. Actually, Davenant's is more likely. Davenant's *Macbeth* was republished in 1687 after the debut of a new production. A theory: Spicer attended a performance of Davenant's *Macbeth* on the London stage and obtained a copy of the play before coming to Virginia in 1689.

The possibility that Spicer's *Macbeth* could be either Shakespeare's or Davenant's provides an opportunity to contrast the two texts to see how Shakespeare was altered for the Restoration stage. Davenant greatly expanded two roles, Macduff and Lady Macduff. In his hands Macduff becomes a major character that actors enjoyed performing. Davenant created a balanced drama, weighing the ambition of the Macbeths against the compassion of the Macduffs. Whereas the world in Shakespeare's *Macbeth* tends toward disorder, in Davenant's *Macbeth*, the Macduffs' prominence keeps a sense of cosmic order in place.[42]

Davenant's changes to individual lines further reflect the quest for order. Two lines from the opening scene exemplify his revisions. As Shakespeare's *Macbeth* begins, the three witches materialise in a thunderstorm. After discussing where and when they should meet

Macbeth, the three end the scene speaking in unison: 'Fair is foul, and foul is fair, / Hover through the fog, and filthy air.' Disliking the irregularity of these lines, Davenant supplied some extra words to turn them into a heroic couplet, the fundamental building block of Augustan verse: 'To us fair weather's foul, and foul is fair! / Come hover through the foggy, filthy air.'[43]

Like others who adapted Shakespeare for the Restoration stage, Davenant reflects the general philosophy of Augustan verse. As Alexander Pope would say in his *Essay on Criticism*, 'True wit is nature to advantage dress'd.' The poet should follow nature yet enhance it. Augustan poets and playwrights saw in Shakespeare a great natural genius but one whose works left room for improvement. Pope, who would edit Shakespeare himself, observes in the preface to his edition: 'The poetry of Shakespear was inspiration indeed: he is not so much an imitator, as an instrument, of Nature; and 'tis not so just to say that he speaks from her, as that she speaks thro' him.'[44]

For the sake of regularity Davenant sacrificed much. The extra words he added to the first line diminish its meaning. Shakespeare's antithetical statement – 'Fair is foul' – is universal. With his initial prepositional phrase, Davenant limits the idea solely to the witches. Davenant reduces a metaphysical pronouncement to a weather report. As Shakespeare puts it, the witches' words convey a central theme of the play and, indeed, of the human condition: the ambiguity of evil and the ease with which good and evil can be transposed.[45]

The revisions Davenant made to the next line clarify that it is something the witches say to one another before they exit, which Davenant's stage direction makes more dynamic. In Shakespeare's *Macbeth* the stage direction for the witches says, 'Exeunt'. In Davenant's *Macbeth* the stage direction says, 'Ex flying'.

Shakespeare's witches are not all that hover through the filthy air. So do the concepts of foul and fair. The fog obscures the distinctions between the two, reinforcing their ambiguity. Furthermore, Shakespeare's conjunction makes the fog and filthy air two different elements. One is natural; the other implies human action: someone has dirtied the air. Changing the fog from a noun into an adjective, Davenant minimises the complexity of Shakespeare's conjoined pair. For Davenant the 'foggy, filthy air' is all one element.

Once Davenant brought his *Macbeth* to the London stage, it became the only version theatre-goers would see for decades to come. Davenant's *Macbeth* was the play Drury Lane staged after the Great Storm of 1703, and it was Davenant's *Macbeth* that William Byrd saw when he returned to London in the second decade of the eighteenth century. Byrd attended at least two performances of *Macbeth*, one on 15 May 1719 and another the following season, on 19 September 1719. Though a contemporary advertisement for the September performance emphasises that the play was written by Shakespeare, make no mistake: Byrd saw Davenant's *Macbeth*. The rest of the advertisement provides confirmation, mentioning that the play would be performed 'with all the musick, dances, and other decorations proper to the play'.[46] The description makes *Macbeth* sound more like musical comedy than serious tragedy. In Byrd's day people attended *Macbeth* to see the pageantry, not the pathos. Remember what the fashionable lady sitting next to Addison asked before the curtain rose on a performance of *Macbeth* one night: 'When will the dear witches enter?'[47]

Byrd had returned to London in 1715 for financial reasons. Daniel Parke's governorship of the Leeward Islands had ended in disaster. In 1711 the Byrds and the Custises had received the news that angry planters had stormed the government house and slain Parke, who willed his Virginia lands to his daughter Frances. John Custis realised they would have to sell nearly all his father-in-law's holdings to pay off his debts. Byrd agreed to receive Parke's Virginia lands in exchange for assuming his debts: a disastrous financial decision he would regret for years to come. Byrd had to visit England to start untangling Parke's hairy finances. He would also act as Virginia's unofficial London agent to counteract the improprieties of Lieutenant Governor Alexander Spotswood. Though Byrd left his wife Lucy behind, she followed him to London in the summer of 1716. Sadly, she contracted smallpox and perished that autumn.[48]

By mid-December 1717, when his surviving London diary begins, Byrd was searching for a new Mrs Byrd. He set his sights on Mary Smith, the daughter of a wealthy Londoner who lived in his neighbourhood. Byrd often encountered Mary at the theatre, which gave him all the more reason to attend regardless what was playing. On 26 December 1717, for example, Byrd visited Lincoln's Inn Fields Theatre, which staged *Cymbeline* that evening. He did not pay close attention to the performance, as his diary reveals: 'I went to the play in Lincoln's Field, where I had the pleasure to sit next to my dear Miss Smith and talked pretty much to her and she was not shy.'[49]

Lincoln's Inn Fields was then one of two licensed theatres in London, the other being the Theatre Royal Drury Lane adjacent to Covent Garden. When Byrd's diary mentions which of the two theatres he attended, the plays he saw can be discerned. On Saturday, 8 February 1718, for instance, Byrd recorded that he 'went to the play in Covent Garden'. That evening Drury Lane staged a production of *Othello*, with Barton Booth in the title role. Though best known for playing the Ghost in *Hamlet*, Booth had made several other Shakespearean roles his own. Besides Othello, he also excelled playing Lear and Banquo. The night Byrd saw *Othello* Colley Cibber played Iago with Hester Santlow as Desdemona. Recognised by many contemporary theatre-goers for her dancing as well as her acting ability, Santlow chose her roles carefully. For the most part she avoided playing evil women. When it came to Shakespeare's female roles, she preferred to play such idealised characters as Cordelia and Desdemona.[50]

Byrd's interaction with Mary Smith and other women in the audience show that for him attending the theatre was more social activity than intellectual pursuit. On 1 November 1718, for example, *Julius Caesar* was one of two possible plays Byrd could have seen, but his diary makes no mention of it: 'After dinner I put several things in order and had just light enough to read a little English and then went to Will's Coffeehouse and from thence to the play, where I found indifferent women.'[51]

Though the sentence is frustrating for its refusal to record the title of the play that evening, it beautifully contrasts the two ways Byrd came in contact with Shakespeare's work: reading and theatre-going. Alone in his London apartment, Byrd took advantage of the waning daylight to enjoy a favourite activity. With night coming on, he continued to read as long as he could make out the words on the page. Light would return once he entered the theatre. Hanging coronas with dozens of candles typically drenched the London stage with light. While illuminating the action on stage, the lights would cast shadows into the seating gallery, deepening the darkness and masking the action in the audience.

Unlike Samuel Pepys, Byrd seldom recorded critical comments about the plays within his diary. On 20 December 1718, for instance, he comes as close as he would ever come to recording an appreciation. *Hamlet* was one play he could have seen that evening. He wrote, 'About 6 o'clock I went to the play, where I was diverted very well.' His entry for 30 March 1719 is more typical. That day he attended one of two possible Shakespeare plays, either *The Tempest* at Drury Lane or *Hamlet* at Lincoln's Inn Fields. He did not name the play but did mention two women he met at the theatre. He sat with one but went home with the other.[52]

In late 1719 Byrd returned to Virginia to take care of his plantations. Edmund Berkeley had died in his absence. Berkeley's executors had the estate inventoried as they settled his affairs. The inventory is what provides the evidence that he owned a copy of Shakespeare. Often listing books title by title, estate inventories reflect the substantial monetary value that books held in colonial America. Since bookbinders' spine titles represent bibliography at a bare minimum, it sometimes requires considerable detective work to identify inventoried books more precisely. Once identified, the book titles offer crucial clues for reconstructing early American intellectual life.

When it comes to putting library inventories to biographical use, they have one major drawback: they can only identify what books people owned at the time of their deaths. The inventories do not reveal when people acquired individual books. Berkeley owned a copy of Shakespeare when he died in 1719. How long had he been reading Shakespeare? Did Berkeley discover Shakespeare in 1709 when so many others did with the release of Rowe's edition? Or did he discover Shakespeare in his teens when the Fourth Folio appeared? Without supporting documentation – letters, diaries, reminiscences, financial accounts, surviving books with evidence of ownership – these questions must go unanswered.

Even within the limits imposed by incomplete evidence, many generalisations are possible. Listed with all his other books, Berkeley's copy of Shakespeare helps paint a vivid picture of his literary life. His edition of Shakespeare's works was not the only volume of plays in his library. He also owned the works of prominent Restoration playwright Thomas Southerne. And he may have had a Shakespeare quarto, as well. A bound volume of separately issued plays apparently contained a copy of *Julius Caesar*.[53]

Making big conclusions from small evidence is always dangerous, of course. Thomas Macnamara, an attorney in early eighteenth-century Maryland, would seem from his library inventory to be a hardworking lawyer well versed in case reports, statute law and legal theory who also possessed a lively interest in history and literature. His library contained two major editions of English drama, a multi-volume edition of Beaumont and Fletcher's *Works* and Rowe's six-volume edition of Shakespeare.[54]

Fine literary tastes do not always reflect upstanding morals. Macnamara turned out to be the most despicable blackguard in colonial Maryland. Born in County Clare, Ireland, he came to the New World shortly before the start of the eighteenth century and bound himself to Charles Carroll, who is known to history as Charles Carroll the Settler to distinguish him from the similarly named members of his distinguished Maryland family. In 1704 Macnamara was brought up on charges for 'biting off one of the ears of Matthew Beard of Annapolis'.[55] He was acquitted of the charges, but his subsequent behaviour reflects his chronic brutality.

Carroll retained him as a law clerk. Macnamara took advantage of his generosity and insinuated himself in the Carroll family, a staunchly Roman Catholic family, it should be added. Macnamara raped Carroll's niece Margaret. Having impregnated her, Macnamara agreed to marry Margaret – with disastrous consequences. By 1707 she fled from him and appealed to the Maryland council to sanction their separation because of the 'cruel, barbarous inhuman treatment of an unnatural husband towards her'. She appeared before the council 'so battered, bruised, and inhumanly beaten in most parts of her body, that had she not been of a constitution more than ordinary strong she could hardly have recovered it'. Finding Macnamara to have 'a mad, turbulent, furious, and ungovernable temper', the court granted her a legal separation to save her life and ordered him to pay an annual fifteen pounds sterling alimony.[56]

Macnamara went to Pennsylvania around 1709 to practise law but was soon disbarred and returned to Maryland. In 1710 he went on trial for murdering a local merchant. He pleaded 'homicide by chance medley', that is, death by accident, but the provincial justices raised the charge to manslaughter and ordered his hand branded with the letter 'M'.[57]

While practising law in Maryland, Macnamara was often disbarred, but, inexplicably, the colonial authorities kept letting him return to his practice. In 1712 he was charged with attempted buggery, whereupon he was suspended from practising law until he was cleared of the charges. The charge of buggery was dismissed, but he was convicted of assault. Afterwards, remarkably, he served as clerk to the Lower House of the Maryland Assembly and, even more remarkably, was elected mayor of Annapolis![58]

Reading, especially reading great literature, is typically considered an elevating activity, but, as the case of Thomas Macnamara demonstrates, it did not necessarily work that way. For other Shakespeare enthusiasts in the colonial South – Berkeley, Byrd, Custis, Dale, Spicer – reading apparently did work to improve the mind and elevate the soul. Byrd, the only one who left sufficient evidence to trace his reading activities, must serve to represent the rest, all of whom had the opportunity to see Shakespeare performed on the London stage and read Shakespeare at home in Virginia.

The impact of the London stage on the colonial American interest in Shakespeare has largely been ignored. One recent study neglects how many and how often colonial Americans of taste and intellect travelled to England for reasons of education and business, theorising that American interest in Shakespeare during the eighteenth century developed independently from British interest in Shakespeare.[59] Such theories ignore the transatlantic context of early American intellectual life. Colonial Americans typically attended the theatre when they visited London. Reading Shakespeare upon returning to America let them relive their London life, but, in so doing, it let them appreciate Shakespeare not merely for entertainment, but also as a fount of art and ideas.

Byrd's personal experience suggests that attending the London stage was a social experience, a time to speak with the men and flirt with the women, but not to pay close attention to the plays. Reading Shakespeare at home, on the other hand, was a much different experience. Reading there among house guests could be a social activity, as Byrd's experience with Collier's *Short View* indicates, but nowhere in his surviving diaries does he record reading Shakespeare aloud. After all, his copy of *Mr William Shakespeares Comedies, Histories, Tragedies* – an unwieldy folio – was hardly a book to hold open and read with guests. Rather, it was a volume for him to open on his library table, letting him read Shakespeare's text slowly and deliberately to enjoy everything it had to share.

2

Benjamin Franklin and the Governors

During his first few years as an apprentice in the Boston printshop of his brother James, Benjamin Franklin learned all the skills necessary to run the shop, everything from editing text to composing type, printing books and writing newspaper copy. Given what was about to happen to James, it was a good thing Benjamin had mastered all these skills. In June 1722 James Franklin, the first investigative journalist in American history, reported in his newspaper, the *New-England Courant*, that local officials had colluded with some pirates. Offended by the report, the Massachusetts Assembly imprisoned him. Benjamin Franklin, at sixteen, assumed the management of the *Courant* during his brother's incarceration.

Benjamin took advantage of the opportunity to run the newspaper himself, trying everything he could to improve it. Hard pressed to fill the columns of the *Courant* the first week of July, he looked around the printshop for inspiration and found a clever way to fill half a column: he would catalogue the newspaper office's library. Franklin introduced the catalogue with a headnote, which informed readers: 'We are furnish'd with a large and valuable collection of books; which may be of vast advantage to us, not only in making indexes, but also in writing on subjects, natural, moral, and divine, and in cultivating those which seem the most barren.' After this statement, Franklin supplied a partial catalogue of the *Courant* office library.[1]

Leo Lemay has identified the catalogue as a crucial document for understanding Franklin's early intellectual development. It lists many important books Franklin would read and remember.[2] Among the titles toward the bottom of the list and thus, by convention, shelved toward the top of the bookcase, is 'Shakespear's Works'. Since

Franklin grouped this title with other small format books, it most likely represents Rowe's edition.

Franklin's headnote reveals how he read Shakespeare as a newspaperman. The edition was a reference work he and his brother could put to practical use in the business of writing newspaper articles. It offered a good stimulus, providing text to read, ponder and use for moral reflection. Acknowledging that the *Courant* office owned a copy of Shakespeare, Franklin revealed his knowledge of great literature and thus reinforced the newspaper's cultural and intellectual authority.

That Franklin's earliest published writings and his first serious attention to Shakespeare coincided means that verbal echoes may occur throughout the body of Franklin's writing. In the first number of 'Silence Dogood', the essay series he published in the *Courant* that same year and, incidentally, the first newspaper essay series in American literature, Franklin discusses the importance readers place on an author's personality. They want to know 'whether he be poor or rich, old or young, a schollar or a leather apron man'. Franklin's words recall the opening scene of *Julius Caesar*, in which two tribunes of the people accost a carpenter, wondering why he is out in public without wearing a sign of his profession. They ask him where his leather apron is.[3]

Of course, Franklin did not need to read Shakespeare to learn about leather aprons. Many tradesmen and craftsmen in colonial Boston wore them, but *Julius Caesar* reinforces the garment's symbolic value as a sign of the wearer's profession. Typically seen as a symbol of the lower class, the leather apron achieves higher status in Franklin's hands. His conjoined pair – 'a schollar or a leather apron man' – puts the university-educated man and the tradesman on an equal footing.[4]

Franklin's use of the phrase in 'Silence Dogood' may come closer to Shakespeare's use of it elsewhere. In *Henry VI, Part II*, Jack Cade's rebels discuss how his rebellion will give England new life. When George complains, 'Virtue is not regarded in handicraftsmen,' Nick replies, 'The nobility think scorn to go in leather aprons.' George adds, 'Nay, more, the King's Council are no good workmen.'[5] Like Benjamin Franklin's, George's words make the leather apron not just a sign of a profession, but a badge of honour. The nobles are such lousy workmen they don't deserve to wear the leather apron.

The *Courant* office was not the only place in early New England where Shakespeare could be found. Despite the animosity toward stage plays among the Puritans, by the mid-1680s many New Englanders had begun discussing the possibility of establishing a local theatre and performing plays. Increase Mather put the kibosh on these these discussions. He reminded people that the theatre was the Devil's temple, stage plays the Devil's lectures and actors the Devil's agents. People who attended plays effectively abandoned their faith in Christ and became servants of the Devil.[6]

Just because the Puritans were against performing plays does not mean they were against reading them. The long-held notion that Increase's son Cotton Mather owned a Shakespeare First Folio has now been debunked.[7] But dramatic literature could be found elsewhere in colonial New England. John Josselyn, who first came to New England in 1638 for a fifteen-month stay and returned in 1663 to stay for eight years, revealed his familiarity with the writings of Ben Jonson in *An Account of Two Voyages to New-England*, which he published in 1674.

Josselyn spent much of his time in Black Point (now Scarborough), Maine, where he studied the natural history of New England. After a lengthy botanical description in *Account of Two Voyages*, Josselyn conveys some uncertainty about his readers by quoting two pieces of scatalogical humour from *The Masque of the Gypsies*, Jonson's most ambitious and popular masque. Josselyn says, 'I have finished now my relation of plants, etc. I have taken some pains in recollecting of them to memory, and setting of them down for their benefit from whom I may expect thanks; but I believe my reward will be according to Ben Jonsons proverbs, Whistle to a jade and he will pay you with a fart, Claw a churl by the britch and he will shit in your fist.'[8]

Though no New England copies of Shakespeare's plays can be dated as early as Josselyn's Jonson, Shakespeare was not unknown among Puritan divines. Boston bookseller Samuel Gerrish found a copy of a seventeenth-century folio edition in the library of one New England preacher, either the Rev. Rowland Cotton, pastor of Sandwich, Massachusetts, or the Rev. Nathanael Rogers, pastor of the church in Portsmouth, New Hampshire. Cotton had died in 1722, Rogers the following year.

After their deaths, Gerrish obtained the libraries of both men, combined the two collections, catalogued them and put them up for auction. Since Gerrish did not stipulate which books had belonged to whom, it is unclear whether the Shakespeare folio had belonged to Cotton or Rogers. More is known about Cotton. His ear for language and the dramatic flair of his sermons gave him two reasons to study Shakespeare.[9]

Regardless which preacher owned the Shakespeare folio, its presence in early eighteenth-century New England refutes the stereotype that says Puritans did not read plays. Dramatic literature could be read for what it had to teach. Both Increase and Cotton Mather brushed up their Latin by reading the racy comedies of Plautus and Terence.[10]

Shakespeare had great moral value for his readers. His works could be read in the manner Benjamin Franklin suggests, that is, as a starting point for meditation and contemplation.

More open-minded, the next generation of Puritan preachers would quote Shakespeare alongside Scripture. Jonathan Mayhew, for one, graduated from Harvard College in 1744. Three years later he was ordained and took a position with the West Congregational Church in Boston. The earthquake that shook New England in November 1755 inspired him to deliver a sermon, 'Of the Dissolution of All Things', which he based on a verse from the Second Epistle of Peter. Explaining how the world would be destroyed, Mayhew observes:

> This is the predicted fate and destruction, at least of that globe which we inhabit; and where vain, foolish, and worldly minded men imagine, that even 'their house shall continue forever, and their dwelling places to all generations; where they call their lands after their own names', and set up pillars and monuments to eternize their memory! All these things shall be dissolved; reduced to cinders, ashes and smoke; and pass away —
>
> The cloud-capt towers, the gorgeous palaces,
> The solemn temples, the great globe itself,
> Yea, all which it inherit, shall dissolve,
> And, like the basely fabrick of a vision,
> Leave not a wreck behind![11]

The first quotation in this passage comes from the Book of Psalms; the second comes from *The Tempest*.[12] Specifically, the lines of verse comes from something Prospero says to Ferdinand and Miranda in the fourth act once the wedding masque he had created for them has finished. Mayhew's textual errors suggest that he was quoting the passage from memory. The word 'basely' makes no sense. In the original Shakespeare says, 'like the baseless fabric of this vision'. In addition, Mayhew substitutes 'wreck' for Shakespeare's 'rack'. The word 'rack', which means a wisp of fog or mist, was largely obsolete by Mayhew's day. Eighteenth-century usages of the word were largely references to Prospero's speech. Mayhew's 'wreck' emphasises the violence of the world's dissolution.

Harvard College, founded primarily to educate new generations of preachers, had the six-volume octavo edition of Rowe's Shakespeare in its library, which was shelved in Bookcase 23. Instead of being arranged by subject as William Byrd organised his library, the Harvard books were shelved in the order they were processed. The exquisitely detailed library catalogue lists the bookcase number, shelf number and shelf placement for each volume. Despite its details, the catalogue did not make it any easier to locate books in the Harvard library. Finding a specific book required scanning the catalogue page by page.[13]

The catalogue's details do make it possible to envision how the books were shelved at Harvard during the early eighteenth century. Reading the catalogue now, one can almost picture how the library looked then. The Harvard librarian added new bookcases as needed. When the catalogue was published in 1723, the library had twenty-three bookcases, each about five feet wide and seven or eight feet tall.[14] Since it was shelved in the last bookcase, Rowe's Shakespeare was among Harvard's most recent acquisitions. Bookcase 23 had eight shelves altogether. The first two from the bottom were folio shelves. The third combined folios and quartos. Shelves four through seven each contained a combination of quartos and octavos, though octavos predominated. The top shelf held quartos. The Harvard Shakespeare formed the first six volumes on the sixth shelf.[15]

Franklin lampooned the students of Harvard College in 'Silence Dogood', but his precise contact with the campus remains uncertain. There is no evidence he ever used its library or perused its catalogue, but he might have. Years later Franklin would similarly organise his own library according to bookcase number, shelf number and shelf placement, but he innovated his catalogue to make it easy to locate individual books.[16]

The 1723 Harvard library catalogue is not the only evidence to show what its students were reading. As Harvard librarian Hugh Amory explains, the volumes that survive from students' personal libraries suggest a wider range of intellectual interests than the college library catalogue. Samuel Browne, a student from a prominent family of merchants in Salem, Massachusetts, attended Harvard during the mid-1720s, graduating in 1727. Browne's student library contained several plays, including two that stem from Shakespeare. Browne owned Lord Lansdowne's *Jew of Venice* and *The Tempest: or, The Enchanted Island*, the operatic version of Shakespeare's play written by John Dryden and William Davenant.[17]

James Franklin scarcely appreciated his little brother's contributions to the *Courant* during his imprisonment. He scarcely appreciated anything his brother did and often beat him mercilessly. Tired of James's cruel treatment, Benjamin made plans to break his indenture and secretly sail from Boston to New York. His friend John Collins agreed to help. Together they devised a clever ruse.

Collins told Captain Arnout Schermerhorne, skipper of the New York sloop *Speedwell*, that his friend got some 'naughty girl' pregnant and needed to leave town fast. Franklin hoped to sneak aboard the *Speedwell* without being seen. Captain Schermerhorne was willing to help him escape trouble – provided he could pay for his passage. Franklin raised the money by selling some of his books: a sacrifice that shows how desperate he was to escape. On 25 September 1723 Franklin was safely aboard the *Speedwell* as it left Boston harbour. Unable to find work in New York, he continued south to Philadelphia, where he took a position as a journeyman printer with Samuel Keimer.[18]

One day Keimer and Franklin looked out the shop window to see Sir William Keith, the governor of Pennsylvania, walking toward them. Assuming Governor Keith wished to see him, Keimer hurried to answer the door. To Keimer's chagrin, the governor asked to speak with his youthful employee. Flabbergasted, Keimer introduced Keith to Franklin, whereupon the governor invited him to a nearby tavern to enjoy the double pleasure of conversation and madeira.

Despite Franklin's youth, Keith recognised in him a potentially powerful ally. This meeting was the first of many. Keith cultivated a friendship with the ambitious journeyman, encouraging Franklin to start his own printshop. With a printer on his side, Keith would have a forum and a platform for his administrative policies. Occasionally he invited Franklin to his home. Keith also facilitated Franklin's membership to the Tiff Club, a social organisation for skilled craftsmen the governor had established to strengthen his power base. Philadelphia's influential Quaker merchants disliked the idea of working men becoming a political force. Isaac Norris, for one, saw lower class involvement in the political process as ridiculous and irresponsible.[19]

Though Keith himself never recorded the story of his friendship with Franklin, he was a good writer who left some general comments that can enlighten their interaction. *Observator's Trip to America*, a pamphlet Keith would write two years later, shows his dramatic flair and offers an inkling of what it was like to visit his Philadelphia home. Keith structured *Observator's Trip to America* as a set of dialogues between Observator and Roger, two figures who both represent Whig political philosophy. Observator is witty and urbane; Roger is a plain-speaking man and thus forms a good comic foil.

In one dialogue Observator relates his visit to the governor's mansion, where he goes about seven o'clock one morning to deliver a package. A jolly servant with a rubicund visage welcomes him inside, has him sit down and says the governor will appear shortly. Less than three minutes later Keith comes downstairs dressed in his nightgown. (Perhaps it is not coincidental that Keith depicts himself adorned in the same manner that Shakespeare depicts Julius Caesar.) Keith shakes hands with Observator and has him take a seat. Shortly after they start talking Keith offers his guest an eye-opener in the form of a fine cordial, which he accepts. Before Observator leaves, Keith expresses his willingness to do what he can for him.[20]

Written to cast its author in a positive light, *Observator's Trip to America* cannot be taken as too close an approximation of reality. According to one modern reader, the work reveals Keith's unbridled vanity, but that criticism may be too harsh.[21] Keith's attractive writing style mirrors his personal charisma. As a set of dialogues, the pamphlet also reflects Keith's interest in dramatic literature, which a Shakespearean allusion reinforces. A common man who represents democratic values, Roger asks a rhetorical question: 'Can any man tell me who is or can be a better judge of the peoples good, than they are themselves?'

Roger answers the question himself, but, as Jeanne Malloy observes in her excellent study of early American dialogues, Roger's answer echoes Shylock's most famous speech from *The Merchant of Venice*. Identifying the similarities between Jew and Christian, Shylock asks if the Jew is not 'fed with the same food, hurt with the same weapons, subject to the same diseases, healed by the same means, warmed and cooled by the same winter and summer as a Christian is? If you prick us do we not bleed?' In *Observator's Trip to America*, Roger compares 'us poor country folks' with his supposed betters, observing, 'We are made of the same flesh and bones, and after the same manner with themselves, so that our sense and feeling of happiness and misery, justice and injustice, good fortune and ill fortune, are much the same in us all.'[22]

Keith's interest in dramatic literature resurfaces in *An Essay on the Education of a Young British Nobleman*, a book of educational advice he wrote that jibes with Franklin's personal philosophy. Young men, Keith recommends, should continue to study after they leave school. He does not mention Shakespeare, but what he says about reading comic drama applies. Keith observes:

> Men of rigid study in learned societies ... are apt to place a greater value on a trifling criticism in language and orthography, than upon a great and manly thought; and have a higher ambition to correct and explain an obscure, or perhaps an obscene passage in Plautus or Terence, than to eradicate a vice out of human society. Such men may become useful

> drudges in the affairs of literature, but a great genius can never satisfy himself with mere speculation; he presses forward with eagerness, until he has reduced his enquiries into some useful practice.[23]

Much of Franklin's reading would follow the pattern Keith recommends, that is, to channel literary study into useful ways to improve society. Franklin's earlier headnote to the *Courant* office library catalogue had said as much.

Encouraging him to start his own printshop, Keith said that if Franklin could secure his father's support, then he would also contribute to the venture. Toward the end of April 1724 Franklin returned to Boston to ask his father for the money to set up a printing business of his own. Josiah Franklin balked at the idea. Benjamin had also come to Boston to retrieve his personal belongings, which mainly consisted of books he had left behind. The precise contents of Franklin's library at this time in his life is unknown. What is known is that his collection was substantial enough to impress the captain of the sloop that took him back to Philadelphia.

When the sloop reached New York, the captain told William Burnet, the governor of New York and New Jersey, about this bookish teen. The son of Bishop Gilbert Burnet, Governor Burnet had had a scholarly upbringing. William Smith, whose *History of the Province of New-York* reveals much about colonial New York's leaders, called Burnet 'a man of sense and polite breeding, a well read scholar, sprightly, and of a social disposition. Being devoted to his books, he abstained from all those excesses, into which his pleasurable relish would otherwise have plunged him.'[24] Upon learning about young Franklin, Burnet asked to meet him. Franklin would describe their meeting in his autobiography: 'The governor treated me with great civility, show'd me his library, which was a very large one, and we had a good deal of conversation about books and authors. This was the second governor who had done me the honour to take notice of me, which to a poor boy like me was very pleasing.'[25]

The catalogue of Burnet's library suggests topics he and Franklin could have talked about that day. Containing 1600 titles totalling approximately 3000 volumes, Governor Burnet's was among the top private libraries in the colonies. Prepared by John Wilcox, a London bookseller who specialised in auctioning large private libraries whom Franklin would befriend the next year, Burnet's is the most detailed catalogue of a private library to survive from the colonial American experience. A bibliographer's dream, the catalogue makes it possible to identify the specific editions of books Burnet owned.

Given his superior literary tastes and the general excellence of his library, it is unsurprising that Burnet had a complete edition of Shakespeare at the governor's mansion. He owned Rowe's edition of Shakespeare's *Works*, not the six-volume 1709 octavo edition but the nine-volume 1714 duodecimo edition, the last volume of which contained 'Venus and Adonis', 'Tarquin and Lucrece', Shakespeare's miscellaneous poems and some critical essays on Shakespeare by Charles Gildon.[26]

Perhaps the most important aspect of Franklin's encounter with Burnet is the deference the governor paid to this young tradesman. Franklin's library let him surmount otherwise insurmountable class barriers. A substantial library had given this teenaged printer and son of a tallow chandler the opportunity to talk books with a colonial governor and son of a bishop. Knowledge of books, Franklin realised, offered an entry to society.[27]

Burnet was one in a series of governors of New York and New Jersey with literary inclinations. Robert Hunter, the previous governor, had moved in London's finest social and literary circles before he came to New York to assume the governorship. Hunter's service as aide-de-camp to the Duke of Marlborough during the War of the Spanish Succession was his path to preferment. He also befriended some of London's leading authors. William Smith, who called Hunter 'a man of wit and personal beauty', also mentioned his 'intimacy with Mr Addison and others, who were distinguished for their good sense and learning'. Richard Steele, another man of letters Hunter befriended, welcomed his contributions to the *Tatler*, so Hunter contributed some poems to the periodical.[28]

Appointed governor of New York and New Jersey – a dual position that would not be split until 1738 – Hunter reached New York in 1710. His governorship proved highly successful. Far from impairing his literary interests, it gave him the raw material for a play he would write in office, *Androboros*. The first published play in American literature, *Androboros*, which means 'man-eater', is a political satire spoofing many local politicians. It endeared Hunter to the reading public.[29]

Set in an insane asylum managed by the Keeper, the character representing Hunter, *Androboros* dramatises the story of its author's political opponents. The character named 'Tom of Bedlam' serves as clerk of the provincial senate. This name occurs frequently in English literature to indicate a harmless madman or simpleton, but the character type extends further back in literary history. The behaviour of Tom of Bedlam in *Androboros* recalls the tricky servants in the comedies of Plautus.[30] The character is not necessarily a reference to Tom O'Bedlam, the identity Edgar assumes in *King Lear*. But it could be. Given Hunter's use of Shakespeare elsewhere in *Androboros*, his use of the name Tom of Bedlam may very well come from *King Lear*.

Hunter is not the only early American writer whose words recall Tom O'Bedlam. Franklin himself echoes the character's catchphrase – 'Tom's a-cold' – in *An Account of the New Invented Fire-Places*, the pamphlet he wrote to advertise the stove he invented. In the pamphlet Franklin observes: 'I suppose our ancestors never thought of warming rooms to sit in; all they purpos'd was to have a place to make a fire in, by which they might warm themselves when acold.' Lois MacLaurin has identified the parallel between *King Lear* and Franklin's *Account*. Though the reuse of a single word with a folksy one-letter prefix may not seem like a strong enough peg on which to hang a source study, MacLaurin demonstrates that from the mid-eighteenth century most usages of the increasingly obsolete term 'a-cold' were deliberate echoes of *King Lear*.[31]

Another passage elsewhere in Franklin's work confirms his debt to *King Lear*. After Lear has given away the kingdom to his ungrateful daughters, the Fool teaches him some lines of didactic verse, which begin:

> Have more than thou showest,
> Speak less than thou knowest,
> Lend less than thou owest,
> Ride more than thou goest,
> Learn more than thou trowest ...

Franklin echoes these lines in *Poor Richard's Almanack* with the following piece of advice: 'Proclaim not all thou knowest, all thou owest, all thou hast, nor all thou canst.'[32]

The character of Tom O'Bedlam in *King Lear* especially appealed to the early American imagination. Accused of plotting against his father, Edgar must change identities to escape. From colonial times a fluid identity has been a defining trait of the American character. The idea that people could come to America and redefine themselves had been part of American promotional rhetoric since the founding of Jamestown. Though Edgar changes his identity to become Tom O'Bedlam, he does not make himself invulnerable. Far from it. Divesting himself of his clothing, he casts off his old identity but, in so doing, subjects himself to harsh treatment at Nature's hands. Surviving the cold takes on the quality of an endurance contest in the wilderness. Those who succeed emerge with a new attitude and subsequently treat the cold with contempt, not fear. The phrase 'Tom's a-cold' changes from a complaint to a boast. Tom O'Bedlam is the prototype of the American Adam, a man cast from paradise who must remake himself in the wilderness.

Solemn – one of the few sane characters in *Androboros* – is based on Lewis Morris, Hunter's closest and most trusted friend in New York. Morris was a politician and a man of letters in his own right. He would serve as the first governor of New Jersey after the position was split from the governorship of New York. He also enjoyed dramatic writing. Like Governor Keith, Morris tried his hand at writing conversation. He may have helped Hunter write *Androboros*, and he drafted two similarly titled works, 'Dialogue on Trade' and 'Dialogue Concerning Trade'. Morris enjoyed debate so much that, according to Franklin, he would encourage his children to argue against each other for his diversion while sitting at the table after dinner. These two dialogues combine his passion for the Socratic method with his interest in dramatic literature. Both dialogues, as Malloy observes, build upon realistic expository scenes, using incident to spark conversation.[33]

Solemn's love of reading and knowledge of Shakespeare in *Androboros* may reflect Morris's. In the second scene of the third act, Solemn is seated at a table piled high with books as Androboros, in a 'pensive mood' enters in 'doleful dumps'. Tom, Solemn and the Keeper have convinced Androboros that he is dead and visible only to Solemn. The situation gave Hunter the chance to indulge his talent for slapstick. While under the delusion, Androboros gets knocked off a chair, covered with floor-sweepings, sprayed with water and blinded with snuff.[34]

Androboros had begun the scene with a long-winded emotional speech, which devolves into tears. Once Androboros bawls himself to incoherence, Solemn delivers a speech of his own:

> How painful, yet unprofitable are all the deeper ways of art? The vulgar undisturb'd, frequent the silent shades, and quietly enjoy the pleasure of soft recess or balmy slumbers, whilst I whom science has rais'd so far above them, have not a peaceful hour. If at any time I would see into futurity, I must take my talisman, and then all ghosts or spectres which chance at that time to crowd the ambient air, become visible to me, and to me alone. Not dreaming of any search into the intellectual world, but by meer chance, I grasp'd my talisman thus, when streight (Takes a tobacco-stopper out of his pocket. Starts up wildly.) Angels and all the ministers of grace, defend me. Be thou a spirit of health, or goblin damn'd! Bring with thee airs from heav'n, or blasts from hell, though com'st in such a

questionable shape, I'll speak to thee. Thanks good Hamlet for this again, I'll call thee General. Valiant Androboros, O speak.[35]

Solemn's speech to Androboros brilliantly echoes the moment when Hamlet sees the ghost of his father in the opening act of *Hamlet*.[36] Hunter uses two of Hamlet's speeches to construct it. Solemn begins by echoing his soliloquy in the second scene of Shakespeare's play: 'How weary, stale, flat and unprofitable, / Seem to me all the uses of this world!' By the time he finishes, Solemn is quoting almost verbatim from one of Hamlet's speeches in the fourth scene. He even acknowledges his source, varying Hamlet's words only to place Androboros in the position of the ghost.

Solemn's speech in Androboros anticipates Mark Twain's Shakespearean spoof in *Huckleberry Finn*, which draws on the same two speeches from *Hamlet* and incorporates snippets from other plays. Twain's editors trace the humorously mangled Shakespearean soliloquy back to the early nineteenth century.[37] *Androboros* shows that Shakespearean spoofs entered American literature at least a century earlier.

Subscribers' lists in eighteenth-century English books can be rich sources of information about who owned what. Once Jacob Tonson announced his plans to issue a lavish edition of Shakespeare edited by Pope – the most widely respected poet of the Augustan age – many distinguished English readers subscribed to it. The first volume of Pope's Shakespeare contains a list of subscribers, a prestigious set of names that includes the following: 'His Excellency William Burnet, Esq., Governor of New-York and New-Jersey'.

Since Burnet owned a perfectly good reading copy of Shakespeare, his subscription to Pope's Shakespeare may stem less from intellectual curiosity and more from social prestige. Pope's Shakespeare, a six-volume edition handsomely printed in a large quarto format that sold for five guineas, was the product of good bookmanship. Its presence on a library shelf was a sign of taste. Perhaps nothing about Pope's Shakespeare reveals its value as a class marker more than the list of subscribers. The king of England is listed at the top. The rest of the subscribers are listed alphabetically. Within each letter of the alphabet, the names appear according to social status. Governor Burnet's name comes fifth in the B-section, after one duke, one duchess and two earls.

Besides the social status it represents, Pope's Shakespeare indicates Burnet's desire to keep current his knowledge of the latest literary scholarship. Londoners often looked down their metropolitan noses at the colonials, seeing them as backward in taste and culture. In *The Dunciad*, for example, Pope calls the British colonies 'ape-and-monkey climes', a derogatory phrase that would become a proverbial epithet for colonial America.[38] Pope suggests that the American colonists preferred the writings of Grub Street poetaster Ned Ward over more respectable writers. With a copy of Pope's Shakespeare in the governor's mansion Burnet could demonstrate that he was *au courant* when it came to London's latest books.

Pope brought Shakespeare to the Augustan age, making the plays amenable to eighteenth-century tastes. Questioning Shakespeare's authorship of some vulgar passages, Pope banished them from the text and relegated them to footnotes. The most infamous passage Pope removed concerns the Porter in *Macbeth*. Macduff still knocks at the gate in *Macbeth*, but no longer is the Porter there to answer. Not only did Pope cut the Porter's long speech upon hearing the knock, he also omitted his exchange with Macduff, in which the badly hungover Porter discusses how drinking affects a lecher: 'It makes him and it mars him; it sets him on, and it takes him off; it perswades him, and disheartens him; makes him stand to, and not stand to.'[39] In Pope's Shakespeare nothing tumesces, and the only thing that detumesces is the size of the font as he transfers salacious passages to footnotes.

On his quest for decorum Pope ignored what the Porter's speech adds to the drama. Despite their playfulness, the Porter's words have a serious purpose. Paralleling the drunken lecher's sexual equivocation with Macbeth's uncertainty, they reinforce the parallel between Macbeth and the Porter and thus bring Macbeth's crime from the larger-than-life realm of high tragedy into the realm of the everyday. The Porter's account of drink-induced venereal difficulties anticipates yet parodies the ineffectual behaviour Macbeth will demonstrate through the remainder of the tragedy.[40]

Pope's editorial process differed significantly from Rowe's. Rowe approached Shakespeare as a dramatist: he started with the Fourth Folio and used his stage experience to clean up its text. Though Pope started with Rowe's text, he approached Shakespeare as a bookman: he diligently assembled many early editions of separately published Shakespeare plays, good quartos and bad, comparing variants and using his best judgment to reconcile cruxes and make emendations. Pope let eighteenth-century tastes affect some of his changes – he occasionally altered Shakespeare's word order for greater metrical regularity – but many of his textual emendations are quite thoughtful.

Take *Othello* for example. Asked how he enchanted Desdemona in Pope's edition, Othello explains that it was his own personal story of exciting adventures – 'hair-breadth 'scapes' – that attracted her most: 'My story being done, / She gave me for my pains a world of sighs.' Whereas the first quarto had said 'a world of sighs', the folio text had inadvertently changed 'sighs' to 'kisses'. Unaware of the quarto text, Rowe retained the word 'kisses' from the folio. Restoring the earlier version, Pope explained his emendation in a footnote: 'It was *kisses* in the later editions. But this is evidently the true reading: the lady had been forward indeed, to give him a world of *kisses* upon the bare recital of his story.'[41]

Pope emphasised outstanding passages with sets of inverted commas in the margins. In *Macbeth* he designates a ten-line section from the speech that Macbeth makes upon learning of his wife's death. The passage ends with the memorable lines:

> Life's but a walking shadow, a poor player,
> That struts and frets his hour upon the stage,
> And then is heard no more! It is a tale
> Told by an ideot, full of sound and fury,
> Signifying nothing!

And in *Othello* Pope highlights Iago's statement on the value of reputation:

> Who steals my purse steals trash, 'tis something, nothing;
> 'Twas mine, 'tis his, and has been slave to thousands;
> But he that filches from me my good name,
> Robs me of that, which not enriches him,
> And makes me poor indeed.

This passage would become a favourite among early American readers. Philalethes, to take a pseudonymous contributor to the *Virginia Gazette* for example, would quote these lines as an epigraph to a powerful essay critiquing people who spread malicious falsehoods about others for the sake of self-interest or self-aggrandisement. Such liars are vipers that destroy whomever they bite. With no reputation themselves, they try to bring everyone down to their level. When their listeners believe their lies, they take great pleasure in seeing others ruined.[42]

Far from simply repeating memorable passages that Rowe, Steele and others had already identified, Pope used his critical acumen to mark these 'shining passages'. His edition highlights notable passages others had found in Shakespeare and identifies many previously unrecognised passages Pope thought worthwhile. Upon finishing his edition, he had doubled the number of memorable passages in Shakespeare.[43]

Though Pope's Shakespeare initially appeared in a six-volume quarto edition, some early American library catalogues list the edition in seven volumes. Here's why. After Tonson issued Pope's edition of Shakespeare's plays, Dr George Sewell prepared a quarto edition of Shakespeare's poetry to piggyback atop Pope's edition. Sewell titled it *The Works of Mr William Shakespear: The Seventh Volume*. In light of this unauthorised supplement, Pope attacked Sewell in 'Fragment of a Satire', along with Lewis Theobald, who had savaged Pope in *Shakespeare Restored: or, A Specimen of the Many Errors, as Well Committed, as Unamended, by Mr Pope in His Late Edition of This Poet*. Pope wrote: 'Yet ne'er one sprig of laurel graced these ribbalds, / From sanguine Sew——— down to piddling T———s.' Pope would ridicule Theobald at much greater length in *The Dunciad*, making him the 'King of Dulness'.[44]

Aware that controversy sells books, Jacob Tonson recruited Theobald to edit his next edition of Shakespeare. Theobald's Shakespeare appeared in seven volumes in 1733, eight volumes in later editions. In his preface Theobald renews his critique of Pope's approach to Shakespeare: 'He has attack'd him like an unhandy slaughterman; and not lopp'd off the errors, but the poet.' When he got to *Macbeth* in his own edition, Theobald put the Porter back in and restored his speech about how drink can make the lecher 'stand to, and not stand to'.[45]

Theobald's Shakespeare would go through nine editions by 1773, making it the most popular version of Shakespeare's work in eighteenth-century England. The experience of early American readers bears out its popularity. Theobald's Shakespeare would be the most popular version in colonial America as well. It shows up in numerous estate inventories and library catalogues.

In 1727 Burnet was transferred to the governorship of Massachusetts to make room for Colonel John Montgomerie to take over as governor of New York and New Jersey, a reward for his loyal service to the Prince of Wales, who became King George II that year. Montgomerie chose the governorship of New York and New Jersey over Jamaica. Robert Hunter, who had taken the Jamaica position, sustained his interest in the mainland colonies. With Montgomerie's appointment, Hunter wrote to James Alexander, a member of the New York and New Jersey council, urging him to assume the role of advisor to the inexperienced Montgomerie.[46]

Burnet packed his books and went to Boston, but the shelves of the New York governor's mansion were not empty for long. Colonel

Montgomerie's intellect has only been recognised recently. William Smith misunderstood his life and mind, asserting that he was 'little acquainted with any kind of literature'.[47] Montgomerie's library belies Smith's assertion. He had an excellent collection of books, which he brought with him to America. His library was rich in dramatic literature. He had the collected plays of the leading dramatists of both the Renaissance and the Restoration stage: Beaumont and Fletcher, Congreve, Dryden, Jonson, Otway and Shakespeare. Like Burnet, Montgomerie was one of the original subscribers to Pope's Shakespeare. Montgomerie's interest in Shakespeare extended beyond Pope's edition. He also obtained Sewell's unauthorised supplement.[48] During the late 1720s, in short, colonial governors from Boston to Kingston were reading Shakespeare.

Montgomerie did not have a major impact on New York or New Jersey, mainly because his tenure as governor was so short. He died unexpectedly in 1731, just three years after he had arrived in New York. His library made a more lasting impact than his presence in New York. Montgomerie died intestate, so his books were auctioned off in the summer of 1732: the greatest book auction New York had ever seen so far. The record of the auction survives complete with a list of buyers, which reads like a who's who of colonial New York. Practically all the leading members of the city's new generation of political leaders attended.[49]

John Avery was one New Yorker present. A mysterious figure, Avery has almost escaped history. Contemporary documents identify him as a gentleman. He was sufficiently respected to receive the freedom of the city in 1731. At the auction of Montgomerie's library Avery purchased sixteen volumes: Dryden's English translation of *Plutarch's Lives*, an eight-volume edition of the *Spectator* and Pope's six-volume Shakespeare, with Sewell's unauthorised supplement.[50]

The knowledge of books and literature Benjamin Franklin gained during his apprenticeship in Boston served him well after he left the city. It gave him common ground with men in power. He learned that information gleaned from books was not just useful in itself; it also had social and political value. His passion for reading brought him into the most powerful circles in colonial America and helped advance his career. Shakespeare was one author the office library of the *New-England Courant* and the governor's mansion in New York had in common. Literary knowledge opened doors for Franklin: the name 'Shakespeare' became an open sesame.

3

Franklin Redux

Upon returning to Philadelphia from Boston in 1724, Benjamin Franklin told Governor Keith that his father had refused to supply him with the capital to purchase the printing equipment he would need to establish his own shop. Keith sloughed off the bad news. He reassured Franklin, letting him know that he would still support his business enterprise. The two continued seeing one another. Whenever Franklin visited the governor, Keith would speak of their joint venture as a 'fix'd thing'.[1]

London became central to Keith's plans for Franklin's future. The governor told his protegé to start planning a business trip across the Atlantic. In London Franklin could obtain all the equipment and supplies he would need: a printing press, type, paper, everything. Not only did Keith promise to write letters of introduction to his London friends, he also promised Franklin a letter of credit sufficient to cover his equipment costs. Franklin loved the idea of going to London. Besides pursuing his business plans, he hoped to enjoy all the cultural, intellectual, literary and social activities the city had to offer. For one, he would have the opportunity to attend the theatre and see many Shakespeare plays performed on the London stage.

In terms of theatre-going the experience Franklin would have in London was not dissimilar to that which other London-bound Americans enjoyed during the early eighteenth century. Many took the opportunity to attend the theatre or, at least, to immerse themselves in the literary culture of the metropolis. After William Byrd returned to Virginia from London in 1719 but before Franklin arrived in 1724, a notable American named Samuel Johnson went to London, where he familiarised himself with English drama, if not at the theatre, then in the bookshops.

Born in Guilford, Connecticut in 1696, Samuel Johnson was a precocious youth. At fourteen he entered the Collegiate School (later, Yale College). When colonial agent Jeremiah Dummer sent a huge collection of books to Yale in 1714, Johnson took advantage of it. All at once, according to his autobiography, he had 'the vast pleasure of reading the works of our best English poets, philosophers and divines'.[2]

Though Johnson listed Shakespeare as one of the authors he read at the time, he misremembered. Shakespeare was not among the authors whose works Dummer sent to Yale. Ben Jonson was. Dummer also sent a copy of Elkanah Settle's *Defence of Dramatick Poetry*. Besides being a theatrical polemicist, Settle was a dramatist in his own right. He had already adapted *Midsummer Night's Dream* as *The Fairy-Queen, An Opera*. In his *Defence of Dramatick Poetry* Settle refutes Collier's *Short View of the Immorality and Profaneness of the English Stage*. The presence of Settle's *Defence* at Yale verifies that Puritan strictures against the stage were relaxing.[3]

Johnson worked as a tutor after graduating from Yale in 1714, but he resigned in 1719, by which time he had begun to question his training as a Congregational minister. He wondered whether he should take holy orders in the Anglican Church instead. Doing so would require him to visit England and be ordained by the Bishop of London, who had jurisdiction over British North America. To track his intellectual development during this time of spiritual uncertainty, Johnson kept a list of the books he read from one birthday to the next. A devoted bookman, Johnson would maintain his reading log for the next thirty-seven years. When he went to London in 1722 he brought the log with him.[4]

His time in the metropolis broadened Johnson's literary tastes. There is no evidence to say whether he attended the theatre, but he could have: the books he read in London reflect his burgeoning interest in English drama. He read several plays, including Joseph Addison's *Cato*, a tragedy that would capture the *Zeitgeist* of Revolutionary America, and *Irene*, a blank verse tragedy by a more renowned man named Samuel Johnson.[5] (To avoid confusion we're going to have to call him 'Dr Johnson'.) Ordained a deacon and a priest, the Rev. Samuel Johnson was appointed missionary to Stratford, Connecticut by the Society for the Propagation of the Gospel in Foreign Parts (SPG).

Occasionally Johnson would take a break from his pastoral duties in Connecticut and divert himself by reading other plays. In May 1724, for example, he read Richard Steele's comedy, *The Conscious Lovers*. Toward the end of that year he read some additional comedies by the same author.[6] Though the switch from *Cato* to comedy may seem like a big leap, *The Conscious Lovers* exemplifies the Augustan literary aesthetic: to delight and instruct. Even as it dramatises a playful story of two lovers separated by confusion and intrigue but ultimately reunited, *The Conscious Lovers* never forgets its didactic purpose, inculcating upright moral values even as it keeps audiences laughing. *The Conscious Lovers,* as Henry Fielding would say, contains 'some things almost solemn enough for a sermon'.[7]

In May 1730 Johnson reread *Cato*, after which he read some additional plays: *The Wonder, A Woman Keeps a Secret*, a Susannah Centilivre comedy; *The Mourning Bride*, William Congreve's only tragedy, which is best known for its opening line, 'Music has charms to sooth a savage breast'; *Lady Jane Grey*, in which Nicholas Rowe dramatises the life of another renowned tragic female protagonist; and Rowe's *Tamerlane*, a tragedy using the story of Tamerlane as a thinly-veiled retelling of the life of King William III. Posterity may remember Rowe's *Tamerlane* best for his eloquent definition of death: 'the last sad adieu 'twixt soul and body'.[8]

In 1731 Johnson read *The Libertine*, Thomas Shadwell's take on the traditional story of Don Juan, which draws upon Molière's *Dom Juan*. The following year Johnson embarked on the greatest series of plays he would read since he started his reading log. In August 1732 he picked up one volume from a multi-volume set of Shakespeare and read it cover to cover. This first volume inspired him to read others. Before September ended Johnson would read three additional volumes of Shakespeare's plays.[9]

Since Johnson read entire volumes of Shakespeare's works, he did not record the titles of individual plays. Neither did he record which edition he read, but in 1732 there were only two possible multi-volume editions: Rowe's or Pope's. A decade later Johnson would return to Shakespeare. In this instance he did record one play title, *Henry VIII*. Reading *Henry VIII* Johnson was not alone. Many colonial American readers would enjoy the play and recognise parallels with current events.[10]

Despite its apparent thoroughness, Johnson's reading log does not list everything he read. The bookish references in his correspondence offer supplemental information. Besides reading Shakespeare for himself, he shared his plays with others. In 1744 Johnson promised to send his son William a Shakespeare volume from his library, but he wanted to reread it first. He told William: 'I will finish Shakespeare if I can so as to send it by the first opportunity.'[11]

When he went to London in 1722 Johnson did not go alone. He went with some Yale friends, who were also disaffected from the

Congregational church and wished to be ordained in the Church of England. Similarly, Franklin went to London with his friend James Ralph, a young man with literary ambitions whom Franklin had met in Philadelphia. Little is known about Ralph's background. He and Franklin became friends mainly because they both loved to read. Before they left, Governor Keith seemed strangely reluctant to give Franklin specific details about the connections he had arranged for him in London. Franklin trusted the governor and followed his plan.

Perhaps Franklin should have grown suspicious, but he left Philadelphia for London believing the governor would keep his promise. Surely, no one would send a friend across the Atlantic empty-handed. Less naïve than Franklin and more familiar with man's capacity for underhanded double-dealing, Ralph could have cast some doubts about Keith, but Franklin kept the governor's role in his business plans a secret. Ralph did not pry; he was keeping the reason for his trip to London a secret as well.

Since Ralph had a young wife and a new baby, Franklin, who would later say, 'A good wife and health, / Is a man's best wealth', found it strange that Ralph would leave them for a lengthy overseas trip. As Franklin originally understood the situation, Ralph was going to London to establish an importing business. Ralph's business plans were a ruse. Once they reached London, Ralph revealed that he had come to England expressly to abandon his young American wife and their child. He had no intentions of returning to Philadelphia. Shocked by Ralph's selfishness, Franklin nonetheless remained his friend.[12]

Governor Keith undermined Franklin's trip to London, not by writing a bellerophonic letter, but by writing no letters, neither the promised letter of credit nor the letters of introduction. Franklin suddenly found himself stranded in London with his ambitious business plans destroyed. The width of the Atlantic separated him from home with insufficient funds to return. Ralph was useless. Having spent all his cash for the passage, he was hoping Franklin would support him in London. Learning that skilled printers were sometimes hard to come by, Franklin sought a position with a London printing house, which would provide an invaluable experience he could put to use upon returning to Philadelphia.

In less than a week Franklin found work with Samuel Palmer, a master printer who owned and operated a printing house situated in a part of the converted Lady Chapel of the Church of Saint Bartholomew-the-Great in East Smithfield. As a former chapel, it had a high ceiling with large windows all around, which admitted great shafts of light. According to a contemporary description, the shop was light and roomy, 'strong and airy'.[13]

Whereas Franklin quickly found a position with Palmer, Ralph had more trouble finding employment. His job search was hopelessly unrealistic. Fancying himself an actor, he sought to become a stage performer. Ralph did have a natural eloquence: Franklin had never known a 'prettier talker'.[14] Seeking work as an actor at Drury Lane, Ralph approached Robert Wilks, the theatre's manager and one of its busiest actors. All Ralph's pretty talking could not convince this would-be employer to hire him. Wilks bluntly told Ralph that it would be impossible for him to succeed on the London stage.

What little pocket change Franklin had left after paying for the necessities of shelter and sustenance, Ralph helped him spend at the theatre, which became a frequent diversion for them. Ralph especially admired Lincoln's Inn Fields: 'The theatre is beyond dispute a masterpiece, and tho' as simple as 'tis possible, both in design and finishing, fruitful in beauties, and affording the spectator the highest satisfaction.'[15]

Franklin does not name the plays he and Ralph saw together in his autobiography – but he thought about it. His outline for the book mentions attending the performances of both Robert Wilks and Colley Cibber.[16] Whereas Wilks had a more natural acting style, Cibber's was more affected. Strangely, their contrasting styles complemented one another, and the two often performed together. Both appeared in Shakespearean productions while Franklin was in London.

During the 1724-25 season, Franklin and Ralph could have seen several Shakespeare plays – comedies, histories and tragedies. Ralph considered Shakespeare 'the father of the English stage'. Praising his talents, Ralph observed: 'Having a soul as noble as his genius was comprehensive, he was equally superior to vanity, peevishness, avarice and envy – He could give place to Marlowe, as a better performer than himself, on the stage – He could take even Johnson by the hand, without being shock'd by his pride or aw'd by his learning – He could leave his works, like the Sybils leaves, to provide for their own immortality.'[17]

The first week of January 1725 Franklin and Ralph had the opportunity to see *King Lear* at Drury Lane, starring Barton Booth in the title role with Wilks as Edgar. Of course, the *Lear* they saw was Tate's version, which ends with Lear's kingdom restored and Edgar and Cordelia in a clinch. Lincoln's Inn Fields staged *The Merry Wives of Windsor*. This production had opened months earlier, but the January performance incorporated new costumes, scenery and innovative special effects. The *Weekly Journal* reported that it featured 'the boldest piece of machinery that ever yet was seen upon the stage'.[18]

The performance of *The Merry Wives of Windsor* that Franklin and Ralph could have seen starred James Quin as Falstaff. Quin had a quick wit and a ready supply of amusing anecdotes, but his conversational skills did not necessarily transfer to the stage. Thomas Morris, who was quite young when he saw Quin perform, found him 'a perfect reciter of verse'. Quin was a little pompous, perhaps, but his manly tone enhanced his acting style. Theatre-goers agreed that Quin reached the pinnacle of his abilities as Falstaff in *The Merry Wives of Windsor*.[19]

Hamlet, *Henry IV*, *Henry VIII*, *Julius Caesar*, *Macbeth*, *Measure for Measure*, *Othello*, *Richard III*, *The Taming of the Shrew*, *The Tempest*, *Timon of Athens*: Franklin and Ralph had the opportunity to see all these plays during their first winter in London. Among Shakespeare's works, *Julius Caesar* was performed most often that season. Shakespeare became an enduring passion for Ralph. He later acquired Thomas Hanmer's six-volume edition of Shakespeare's works, which he held onto the rest of his life.[20]

Given Hanmer's willingness to smooth out Shakespeare's sometimes irregular verse, his edition came under attack upon its publication. William Warburton, who would prepare an edition of his own, critiqued Hanmer's regularisation of Shakespeare's verse: 'He hath tricked up the old bard, from head to foot, in all the finical exactness of a modern measurer of syllables.'[21] Despite Warburton's critique, Hanmer's edition found favour with early American readers. It shows up frequently in library inventories throughout the colonies. Handsomely printed, Hanmer's edition may be more notable as an example of fine bookmaking than as an exemplar of textual editing. Hanmer based his text on Theobald's and ignored the earlier editions.[22]

Franklin's London writings suggest his ongoing attention to Shakespeare. *A Dissertation on Liberty and Necessity, Pleasure and Pain*, a philosophical treatise he published anonymously in 1725, incorporates a favourite Shakespearean phrase, 'sleep of death'. In the To-be-or-not-to-be soliloquy, Hamlet finds something positive in the 'sleep of death', which ends the 'heartache and the thousand natural shocks / That flesh is heir to'. Owen Aldridge, who first identified Franklin's use of this Shakespearean phrase, explains that everyone receives equal amounts of pleasure and pain according to Franklin's theory. Echoing Hamlet in terms of both phrase and sentiment, Franklin also sees something positive in death, which puts an end to pain: 'During the course of life we are ourselves continually removing successive uneasinesses as they arise, and the last we suffer is remov'd by the sweet sleep of death.'[23]

Gauging by references in his later writings, *Othello* would become Franklin's favourite Shakespeare play. With Barton Booth as Othello and Colley Cibber as Iago, the performance he and Ralph could have seen at Drury Lane was not dissimilar to the one William Byrd had seen the previous decade, though Desdemona was now played by Sarah Thurmond, whose broad dramatic range made her a good utility player. During Thurmond's dozen or so years at Drury Lane, she added numerous roles to her repertory, including Lady Macduff.[24]

Shakespeare's work influenced other plays performed on the London stage that season. Dryden's blank-verse tragedy *All for Love: or, The World Well Lost* was inspired by *Antony and Cleopatra*. The production at Drury Lane starred Anne Oldfield as Cleopatra, Barton Booth as Antony and Colley Cibber as Alexas. After Susanna Verbruggen's death in 1703, Anne Oldfield had taken over several of her roles, which marked the start of her long and prolific career on the London stage. Franklin and Ralph had the opportunity to see her when she was at the peak of her powers.[25] *All for Love*, perhaps the finest tragedy of the Restoration stage, ideally suited Oldfield's acting abilities. Though formal and artificial compared with *Antony and Cleopatra*, *All for Love* exemplified eighteenth-century tastes and proved quite popular.

After William Congreve's six-volume edition of *The Dramatick Works of John Dryden* appeared the following decade, Ralph acquired the set for his personal library. When Ralph's books were sold upon his death, Franklin attended the auction and purchased his old friend's copy of Dryden's *Dramatick Works*.[26] Besides *All for Love*, the edition included two other plays adapted from Shakespeare, *The Tempest: or, The Enchanted Island* and *Troilus and Cressida: or, Truth Found Too Late*. Reading Dryden's Shakespearean adaptations from the comfort of his Philadelphia home in the coming years, Franklin could relive the times he and Ralph spent together attending performances on the London stage.

Partway through the eighteen-month period Franklin spent in London during his first visit to England, he and Ralph went their separate ways. Ralph tried his hand at poetry. Franklin relates his friend's initial attempts at verse in his autobiography, but the story goes far beyond what Franklin says. In 1728 Ralph published his second book of verse, *Night: A Poem, in Four Books*, which he followed with an attack on Pope, *Sawney: An Heroic Poem Occasion'd by the Dunciad*. In *Sawney* Ralph defends the Grub Street writers whom Pope had ridiculed in *The Dunciad*.[27]

Pope had not mentioned Ralph in the first edition of *The Dunciad*, but he struck back in the second, *The Dunciad Variorum*, a revised text with extensive footnotes. In the poem's text Pope famously refers to Ralph's *Night*: 'Silence, ye wolves! while Ralph to Cynthia howls, / And makes night hideous – answer him, ye owls.' In his footnotes Pope identifies his allusion to Hamlet's speech to the Ghost in the opening act: What may this mean / That thou, dead corpse, again in complete steel, / Revisits thus the glimpses of the moon, / Making night hideous.'[28]

Before he is finished with Ralph, Pope mentions Shakespeare again. Pope identifies Ralph as a 'low writer', who is 'wholly illiterate and [knows] no language not even French'. Pope's poem repeats an anecdote that was circulating around London. It concerns Ralph's recent efforts to write a play. When someone advised him to study the rules of dramatic poetry before he began, Ralph, comparing himself to his ideal, replied, 'Shakespear writ without rules'.[29]

After he and Ralph separated, Franklin moved closer to Lincoln's Inn Fields, but he could have continued attending performances at Drury Lane. Since the previous season, the theatre at Lincoln's Inn Fields had made some improvements. On Friday, 24 September 1725, it staged a production of *King Lear*. That night the improvements were more notable than the acting. The *Daily Journal* reported, 'The gilding, painting, scenes and columns of pier glass [i.e., mirrors], rais'd for the better illuminating the stage and other parts of the house, gave a general surprize and satisfaction to the spectators.'[30]

Though Lincoln's Inn Fields had a flashy new decor, Drury Lane had a stronger Shakespeare schedule that season, holding performances of *Hamlet*, with Wilks in the title role and Booth as the Ghost; *Henry IV*, with Wilks as Prince Hal and Booth as Hotspur; *Julius Caesar*, with John Thurmond in the lead role; *Macbeth*, with the versatile John Mills in the starring role, Wilks as Macduff and Booth as Banquo; and *Othello*, with the same leading cast as the previous season. Not to be outdone by Lincoln's Inn Fields, Drury Lane staged its own production of *King Lear* that season. Booth starred as Lear, and Wilks played Edgar.[31]

The theatrical calendar for the 1725-26 season shows how important his tragedies were to Shakespeare's early eighteenth-century reputation. In addition, it reflects the comparative value tragedies held over comedies, which a Quin anecdote confirms. While a theatre manager, Quin received many scripts from playwrights who hoped to get them produced. Quin held onto the manuscript of one tragedy so long that its angry author came calling. Quin told him to rummage through all the manuscripts in the nearby bureau to find his. After a lengthy search, the playwright had still not found the manuscript of his tragedy. 'Well', Quin told him, 'be content. Take two comedies and a farce for it.'[32]

Franklin would continue to follow the theatre on subsequent visits to London. In 1757 he went to England in an effort to settle the grievances the Pennsylvania Assembly had with the colonial proprietors, Thomas and Richard Penn. Franklin's son William, now in his mid-twenties, accompanied him. They reached London in July. The new theatrical season would begin that September. The first week of December William Franklin wrote to a Philadelphia friend, informing her that he had been 'now and then partaking of the publick diversions and entertainments of this bewitching country'.[33]

One particular entertainment stood above the rest, giving William Franklin an almost unlimited subject for discussion. He could hardly say enough about David Garrick, the foremost Shakespearean actor of the era. He observed, 'The high entertainment which that inimitable imitator of Nature, Garrick, has afforded me, is a topick unbounded and inexhaustible!' That season the Franklins had the opportunity to see Garrick star with Hannah Pritchard in *Romeo and Juliet*. They could also have seen Garrick play the titles roles in *Hamlet*, *King Lear* and *Richard III*. Garrick's roles that season were not limited to tragedies and histories. The Franklins could also have seen him play Benedick in *Much Ado about Nothing*, with Hannah Pritchard as Beatrice.[34]

King Lear is considered Garrick's greatest role. Since the late seventeenth century, Tate's version of *King Lear* had dominated the London stage, but in 1756 Garrick had begun revising Tate's text and reintroducing passages from Shakespeare's original. Garrick would continue to reintroduce more and more of Shakespeare's lines as he continued performing Lear. In short, the version the Franklins could have seen in 1757 was a *King Lear* in transition, one beholden to the conventions of the Restoration stage but one that looked forward to the Romantic revival of Shakespeare's original text in the early nineteenth century.[35]

Benjamin Franklin, who was afflicted with intermittent fever and headaches that autumn, may not have attended the theatre as often as his son, but years later he did meet Garrick socially. Franklin's friend Joshua Steele devised a system for recording speech in the manner of musical notation, which he set forth in *An Essay towards Establishing the Melody and Measure of Speech to Be Expressed and Perpetuated by Peculiar Symbols*. As part of his book, Steele printed a letter he had received congratulating him on a successful experiment. Steele had transcribed one of Garrick's Shakespearean performances using the system of notation he had invented. His correspondent observed, 'Actors are the only artists that cannot eternize themselves by their works; but you have fallen upon a way to make Garrick live as long as his Shakespear.'[36]

Steele presented a copy of his book to Franklin. In the margin of the page on which Steele's correspondent describes the experiment,

Franklin recorded his memory of the event. After recording Garrick's performance at the theatre, Steele demonstrated his system in a social gathering, which included David Garrick, his wife Eva and Benjamin Franklin. Steele took the opportunity to read aloud the Shakespearean text he had transcribed from Garrick's performance. David and Eva were astonished. So was Franklin. Steele had recorded the subtle nuances of Garrick's performance so accurately that he could practically replicate it.[37]

Having left Samuel Palmer in 1725 to take a position with John Watts, Franklin continued to keep an eye on the latest developments in the world of books. There is no saying for sure whether he read Pope's Shakespeare, which Jacob Tonson published that year. Tonson and Watts often collaborated. When Franklin worked for him, Watts and Tonson issued several joint publications. Franklin did read Pope's *Odyssey*, the early volumes of which appeared that same year. Quoting lines from Pope's *Odyssey* in his journal on his return trip to Philadelphia in 1726, Franklin revealed his efforts to follow the latest literary developments. Most likely he read Pope's Shakespeare as well.[38]

* * *

Eager to continue his intellectual pursuits once he returned to America, Franklin joined some like-minded Philadelphia friends to form the Junto, a club designed for mutual self-improvement. Franklin and other members of the Junto became convinced that a communal library made good economic and educational sense. Under his leadership, they formed the Library Company of Philadelphia in 1731. Shareholders had the privilege of borrowing books and selecting which books the library would add to its holdings. The Library Company was a great success and inspired many early American subscription libraries, which would be instrumental in disseminating Shakespeare's writings throughout the North American colonies.[39]

The Library Company did not obtain an edition of Shakespeare as part of its original collection, but Philadelphia was gradually becoming more interested in his plays in print, if not on the stage. Franklin's friend James Logan had a copy of *King Lear* in his library, but this particular edition suggests that perhaps Logan was not as dedicated a Shakespearean as formerly assumed. He owned Tate's *King Lear*.[40]

Though a scrupulous bookman, Logan, like many of his fellow Quakers, took little interest in the stage. Unlike other leading American intellectuals of the era, he did not own the works of Ben Jonson or Beaumont and Fletcher, either. The greatest classical scholar in colonial America, Logan did have one book in his library with a Ben Jonson connection. He owned Jonson's personal copy of Manilius's *Astronomicon*, a lengthy astrological poem written in Latin hexameters.[41]

In late 1729 Franklin took over the *Pennsylvania Gazette* from Samuel Keimer and turned it into the most dynamic newspaper in the colonies. Through a growing network of printing partners, Franklin exerted a significant influence on the press throughout British North America. After employing Thomas Whitmarsh as a journeyman in Philadelphia, Franklin formed a partnership with him. Whitmarsh would go to Charleston, South Carolina to open a printshop and establish a newspaper of his own, the *South Carolina Gazette*.

During the 1730s, scattered references to Shakespeare appeared in the *South Carolina Gazette*. In June 1732 Whitmarsh published a letter from an angry contributor known solely as 'F. C.' Complaining about Whitmarsh's corrections to his previous newspaper contributions, F. C. compared himself to Shakespeare. F. C. said Whitmarsh was like those modern dramatists who imagined they could improve upon Shakespeare. In typically long-winded fashion F. C. said that Whitmarsh resembled the 'poetaster who pittying the lot of humanity in the condition of the antiquated bard Shakespear declared with a countenance replete with indications of compassion that it sensibly touched him when he beheld the fortunes of one who in his day was possessed of a great share of reputation; that it would be an act of filial piety in one of the laureat tribe to bestow on the old patriarch a more becoming dress, nor suffer him to mourn perpetually under the inquiries of time'.[42]

Whitmarsh apparently published this angry contributor's latest letter without editing it, thus proving to his subscribers how badly F. C. stood in need of editing. The excessive verbiage practically obscures the point F. C. was trying to make. To the credit of fellow Carolina readers F. C. did assume they possessed a basic knowledge of the history of Shakespearean stage adaptation.

Though F. C. did not appreciate it, Whitmarsh's editorial scrutiny demonstrates the care he brought to the *South Carolina Gazette*. Sadly, Whitmarsh died in September 1733. Franklin found a replacement in Lewis Timothy, another Philadelphia journeymen. Timothy relocated to Charleston, took over Whitmarsh's operation and continued to edit and publish the *South Carolina Gazette*.

Timothy reached South Carolina in time to witness the birth of the Charleston stage. Several plays were performed in the courthouse in 1735. Early the next year the city got a proper venue when the Queen Street Theatre opened with a performance of a George Farquhar comedy, *The Recruiting Officer*. Dr Thomas Dale, a Leyden-trained physician and an accomplished poet, commemorated the opening performance with 'Epilogue to *The Recruiting Officer*', which he published in the London *Gentleman's Magazine*. Dale's tribute to Farquhar may owe a debt to Shakespeare. Dale's epilogue to *The Recruiting Officer* resembles Rosalind's epilogue in *As You Like It*. Both playfully celebrate cross-dressing, which allowed a level of sexual freedom otherwise difficult to achieve.[43]

Shakespeare references appeared in the *South Carolina Gazette* during Timothy's tenure. The first week of September 1735 the newspaper published 'A Duel of Dunghill Soldiery', a poem containing a Shakespearean allusion. Presenting a tale filled with braggadocio, buffoonery, racist innuendo and scatological humour, 'A Duel of Dunghill Soldiery' is an early example of Southern humour. It anticipates many of the themes and motifs of the humour of the Old Southwest, which would flourish during the middle third of the nineteenth century.[44]

According to the headnote introducing the poem, a sea captain and a Charleston barber – 'a young Tonsor of this town' – threatened each other with sword and pistol as they argued over 'the favours of a certain sable beauty'. The poem itself begins:

> Two Hotspurs unnoted for martial adventures,
> To give the world proof they were right bully ranters,
> Talk'd big to each other of prowess and fighting,
> Tho' some say, their breeches more savour'd of sh——ng.[45]

As 'A Duel of Dunghill Soldiery' turns out, both Hotspurs shy away from the fight and shake hands before they ever cross swords. Though this Carolina poet's use of the name does not necessarily indicate a reading knowledge of *Henry IV, Part I* – the play that introduced the original Hotspur – it does suggest that the character was so well known in colonial America that the name had become a *blason populaire* for any hot-headed man itching for a fight.

Another indication that Shakespeare was being read in South Carolina occurs in Timothy's *Gazette* a couple years later, when a local man named John Dart advertised that a volume from his multi-volume edition of Shakespeare had been stolen. The last week of June 1738 Dart placed an advertisement in the newspaper offering a reward for its return. Whoever had stolen his Shakespeare hesitated to return it. Dart would run the advertisement for the next three weeks.[46] Besides reflecting the value books held in the colonies, Dart's advertisements reinforce Shakespeare's growing importance to American readers. Stolen books signal that the demand for a literary work has outstripped the supply. That South Carolinians were stealing copies of his works suggests that Shakespeare had taken on a cult status among readers in eighteenth-century Charleston.

Franklin established partnerships with other printers throughout colonial America. As Lemay observes, his purpose for the partnerships was twofold. He sought to profit from these business arrangements, of course, but he genuinely wished to help young printers establish themselves.[47] Franklin would supply the capital; his partners supplied the labour. They appreciated his support, but Franklin could be a hard taskmaster. He expected much from his partners.

James Parker, who had served his apprenticeship in New York, boarded with Franklin while living in Philadelphia. Parker was a great reader, which was enough for him and Franklin to become friends. Though he enjoyed Parker's company in Philadelphia, Franklin sent him back to New York to form another partnership. Franklin hoped Parker would secure the lucrative position as printer to the New York legislature. He did. Parker also started his own newspaper, the *New York Gazette*. Even after they dissolved their original partnership, Franklin continued to help Parker. He sent printing jobs Parker's way and, as postmaster general, appointed Parker comptroller of the post office.[48]

Parker was grateful for Franklin's help and worked hard to fulfil his responsibilities to him, as their correspondence verifies. In one letter Parker details his recent business activities. Given their shared love of literature, Parker summarises his hard work on Franklin's behalf with an allusion to *Henry VIII*, in which Cardinal Wolsey laments:

> Had I but served my God with half the zeal
> I served my King, he would not in mine age
> Have left me naked to mine enemies.

Concluding his letter to Franklin, Parker wrote: 'I think I cannot say quite tho' very near as Cardinal Woolsey did: tho' I have not served my God so faithfully as I have you, yet I am of opinion, he will not cast me off, in my old age.'[49]

Wolsey's words in *Henry VIII* echo the Book of Psalms: 'Cast me not away in time of age.' Parker's clever allusion conflates Shakespeare and the psalms. Wolsey contrasts his service to God with his service to the king, though, given the belief that the king was God's divinely ordained representative on earth, the two forms of service should not have been at odds.[50] Parker presents a secular version of the same idea, contrasting God with Franklin, already a symbol of the modern entrepreneurial spirit.

Franklin incorporated references to Shakespeare in the *Pennsylvania Gazette*, though they often came second-hand. In other words, Franklin's Shakespearean references in his newspaper occur in articles he republished from the British press. In July 1733 he reprinted 'Of Anger, Envy, and Malice', an essay he found in a London magazine. Following his mentor, Lewis Timothy reprinted the essay in the *South Carolina Gazette* the following month.[51]

Suggesting the possibility of escaping anger by letting it run its course, the London essayist quotes from Shakespeare: 'Anger is like / A full hot horse; allow him but his way, / Self-mettle tries him.'[52] The essay ascribes the quotation to Shakespeare without naming the specific play. It, too, comes from *Henry VIII*. After Cardinal Wolsey provokes the ire of the Duke of Buckingham in the play's opening scene, Norfolk counsels Buckingham to control his emotions, to let reason temper his anger.[53]

In early 1736 Franklin encountered a poem in the London *Gentleman's Magazine* titled 'A Tale of the Travellers', which he liked well enough to reprint. Published anonymously and previously assumed to be of American origin, the poem is by the Rev. Walter Chamberlaine, the uncle of Richard Brinsley Sheridan.[54] Structured as a dialogue, it presents an exchange between three allegorical travellers: Water, Fire and Reputation. As they travel together, the three discuss what to do should one get lost. Water says it will be easy to find him by listening for his loud gurgling sound. Fire says it will be easy to find him by looking for his light:

> In Miltons page I glow, by art,
> One flame intense and even;
> In Shakespears blaze a sudden start,
> Like lightning flash'd from heaven.

Reputation cannot respond similarly: 'If I be lost, tis ten to one, / You never more will find me.' Though 'A Tale of the Travellers' belongs to British literature, Franklin's reprint of it in the *Pennsylvania Gazette* reflects his assumption that Philadelphia readers would get its literary references and appreciate what Fire means when he says that Shakespeare's words flash like lightning.

In the coming years Franklin would advertise editions of Shakespeare for sale in the *Pennsylvania Gazette*. In 1744 he advertised a neatly bound, eight-volume set of Shakespeare's plays for sale, presumably the latest edition, that is, the duodecimo edition of Theobald's *Works of Shakespeare*, which had appeared in 1740. After the octavo edition of Hanmer's Shakespeare appeared in 1745 the Library Company of Philadelphia acquired a copy for its collection.[55]

Hanmer's Shakespeare was republished in a smaller format – a humbler band of duodecimos – in 1750-51, which Franklin would add to his personal library. His ownership of this edition has hitherto escaped attention, but four volumes from the edition that Franklin owned survive at the University of Pennsylvania. The title pages of two of the volumes – four and seven – contain the autograph of his grandson William Temple Franklin. Raised by Benjamin Franklin, Temple grew up in his grandfather's library and, upon his death, received the bulk of his collection by bequest. Sadly, Temple did not inherit his grandfather's passion for books. After receiving the bequest, he saw the library solely as capital and tried to convert it to cash. Temple added few books to the library on his own. Nearly all the books that survive with Temple's autograph come from his grandfather's library.[56]

As tensions escalated between America and Britain in the coming decades, Benjamin Franklin would find cause to quote Shakespeare himself. In one newspaper article, 'On the Candidacy of Barlow Trecothick', he signs himself 'New England', a pen name identifying him with the land of his birth. After quoting some remarks from London writers who characterised Bostonians as evil, malicious, inhuman creatures, 'New England' says he will 'recriminate a little': 'I shall do it gently. I will not bring railing accusations of my own making against you Englishmen. And it must be supposed that you touch your own failings tenderly, "Nought is aggravated, nought set down in anger."'[57]

The quoted phrase stems from the last act of *Othello*. In the speech Othello delivers just before stabbing himself, he tells Lodovico how he wants him to relate the murder of Desdemona in the official correspondence:

> I pray you, in your letters
> When you shall these unlucky deeds relate,
> Speak of me as I am; nothing extenuate,
> Nor set down aught in malice.[58]

That Franklin's quotation varies from the original does not show an ignorance of Shakespeare: quite the contrary. Franklin was quoting from memory. He knew *Othello* well enough that he had internalised the play and could recall favourite lines.

Franklin's use of Othello's speech shows how Shakespearean quotations could be modified for any situation. They occur elsewhere in early American literature. The naval officer who wrote an account of the English West Indian Expedition during the Seven Years' War would use Othello's words as his title page motto to validate the truthfulness of his narrative: 'Nothing extenuate'.[59]

Abigail Adams would use the same quotation from *Othello* in her correspondence, altering it to suit. After John Adams sent her a political pamphlet, she offered her husband some thoughts on the mean-spirited pamphleteer: 'The writer appears to have ransakd Pandimonium, and collected into a small compass the iniquity and abuses of several generations, "sitting down all in malice and naught extenuating"'.[60] Whereas Othello cautions against using negative language, Abigail Adams cleverly revised Shakespeare's phrase to capture the pamphleteer's malicious tone. Among Revolutionary American leaders, Shakespeare's words would become so well known that even the slightest allusion could be recognised and would provide a sense of shared intimacy. Clever reworkings of Shakespearean phrases became one way for men and women in Revolutionary America to demonstrate their wit.

After 'On the Candidacy of Barlow Trecothick' Franklin contributed additional essays to the London press defending the rights of the American colonists. The eighth number of 'The Colonist's Advocate', an anonymous essay series he published in the London *Public Advertiser*, appeared shortly after Lord North came to power. Disliking the new prime minister, Franklin hearkened back to a more even-tempered and open-minded one, William Pitt, the first earl of Chatham. Franklin remembered Pitt as a 'great man, of whom, with all his faults, we may well say, "We ne'er shall look upon his like again"'. Franklin adapted these words from something Hamlet says about his father. He 'was a man, take him for all in all, / I shall not look upon his like again.'[61]

Hamlet has no higher compliment than to call his father a man. To be a man, that is, to represent an ideal of manhood would become a great compliment in the Augustan age. When French portraitist Joseph Duplessis painted Franklin's portrait during the Revolutionary War, he placed it within an elaborate gold frame with a single word under the portrait: *vir*, the Latin word for man.

Though the references in Franklin's writings demonstrate that his knowledge of Shakespeare was much greater than formerly recognised, his interest in Shakespeare should not be overestimated. Other contemporary American readers expressed their passion for Shakespeare in more striking terms and quoted lines from his plays more readily. A comparison with the Rev. Samuel Johnson provides a useful counterbalance.

Among the references to Shakespeare in Johnson's writings, one specifically concerns Franklin. In 1750 the trustees of the Philadelphia Academy (later, the University of Pennsylvania) asked Franklin to sketch out an English curriculum. The result was *The Idea of the English School*, a pamphlet he would publish the following year. Before publication, Franklin sent a draft of the work to Johnson for his advice. In *An Introduction to the Study of Philosophy*, a textbook he had written years earlier, Johnson recommends that students read Shakespeare among other great English poets. He repeated the advice to Franklin, telling him: 'You might do well to mention Milton and Telemachus and the Travells of Cyrus with the works of Shakespear, Addison and Pope and Swift ... as the best English classics.'[62]

For the most part Franklin took Johnson's advice. In *The Idea of the English School* he recommends François Fénelon's *Adventures of Telemachus*, Andrew Ramsay's *Travels of Cyrus* and every other English author Johnson recommended – except Shakespeare.[63] Franklin's omission does not reveal a dislike. After all, he would add Hanmer's Shakespeare to his personal library after receiving Johnson's letter. Instead, Franklin's omission of Shakespeare from *The Idea of the English School* suggests that he questioned Shakespeare's usefulness as a pedagogical tool. Students could read the other authors and use them as models to improve their writing by imitating their style, much as he had polished his own writing style by imitating essays in thc *Spectator*.

Franklin apparently felt that the complexities of Shakespeare's style made his writings inappropriate for students learning to write English composition. MacLaurin has observed that Shakespeare's style was more ornate than the other authors Franklin recommended as models of writing. In his analysis of *The Idea of the English School* Lemay puts the matter more concisely. Franklin omitted Shakespeare from his list of writers for students to imitate for one simple reason: Shakespeare was inimitable.[64]

4

William Parks and the *Virginia Gazette*

As editor and publisher of the *Maryland Gazette*, which he founded in 1727, William Parks befriended several men of letters in colonial Maryland who contributed essays and poetry to the newspaper. He also published books that helped develop the local literary culture. In 1728 he issued *The Mouse-Trap: or, The Battle of the Cambrians and Mice*, Richard Lewis's English translation of Edward Holdsworth's mock-heroic Latin poem, *Muscipula*. *The Mouse-Trap* is the first book of *belles lettres* published in the South.

Now recognised as the finest Augustan poet of colonial America, Lewis displays both his poetic ability and his learning in *The Mouse-Trap*. The lengthy explanatory notes he appended to his translation reflect his wide reading. Glossing a reference to Plinlimmon, the highest point of the Cambrian Mountains in Wales, Lewis explains: 'Plinlimmon rises to a great height, and on that side where it limits Montgomeryshire, sends out the River Severn; next to Thames the most noted river of Britain: It takes its name, according to the monkish writers, from Sabra, who was thrown into it by Guendoler, daughter of Corineus Duke of Cornwal; – Her story may be found in a wretched play, called *Locrine*; falsely attributed to Shakespeare.'[1]

Brief as it is, Lewis's reference indicates his extensive knowledge of Shakespeare. *Locrine* was a spurious play first included with Shakespeare's collected works in the 1664 reissue of the Third Folio. The Fourth Folio of 1685 also included *Locrine*, as did Rowe's Shakespeare. Not until Pope's edition was *Locrine* tossed from the canon of Shakespeare's work. In his preface Pope calls it one of those 'wretched plays' that could not be admitted as Shakespeare's.[2] Lewis's note suggests not only that he had read an earlier collected edition of Shakespeare that included *Locrine*, but also that he knew Pope's introduction well enough to recall the words he used to describe *Locrine*.

Works like *The Mouse-Trap* let William Parks establish a reputation as a publisher who encouraged the development of American literature. The most important colonial printer besides Benjamin Franklin, Parks replicated his Maryland success in Virginia. By the summer of 1730 he had relocated to Williamsburg, where he established his press on the Duke of Gloucester Street. Though founded in 1607, Virginia did not have a printing press until William Parks came to Williamsburg.

In 1736, six years after establishing his press, Parks founded the colony's first newspaper, the *Virginia Gazette*. The newspaper would change hands several times during the colonial period, but its name stayed the same. Complicating matters further, two competing colonial Williamsburg newspapers would also be titled the *Virginia Gazette*. The papers are typically differentiated by their editors or proprietors. In short, many colonial Virginia journalists, male and female, would improve upon Parks's pioneering efforts, but none could better his title.

By the time Parks established his *Virginia Gazette*, he had placed himself at the centre of Williamsburg's literary life. He encouraged many local writers to contribute to the paper. Parks gave them an outlet to vent their spleen, exercise their wit and demonstrate their knowledge. Their contributions to his newspaper during its first few years kept its contents lively. The columns of Parks's *Virginia Gazette* also reflect the widespread knowledge of Shakespeare in early eighteenth-century Virginia.

Parks published the first issue of his *Virginia Gazette* on 6 August 1736. No copies survive, but a copy of the declaration of principles that Parks published in his first issue does. Someone had the forethought to recognise that Parks's introductory essay might turn out to be something important and saved it. Here's how Parks encouraged his readers to contribute articles to the newspaper:

> If any ingenious, public-spirited gentlemen, who have time to spare, will employ their leisure hours in the service of the publick, by writing any speculative letters, poems, essays, translations, etc. which may tend to the improvement of mankind in general or the innocent diversion or entertainment of either sex, without offence to any in particular, they may depend on a place in this paper; and their names concealed if desir'd.[3]

Parks had privately given the same message to his writerly Virginia friends even before the first issue of his *Gazette*, which published

'Monitor, No. 1', the initial instalment of what would become a major contribution to colonial newspaper literature. Patterned on the *Spectator* and similar essays in the English periodicals, these were narrated in the persona of a self-appointed monitor, who assumed the responsibility of observing the behaviour of his Virginia neighbours and giving them advice. The twenty-two-part series would continue off and on from August 1736 to February 1737.

The 'Monitor' essays remain among the most memorable features of the early years of Parks's *Virginia Gazette*. They also contain the newspaper's first known reference to Shakespeare. (So many issues of the *Virginia Gazette* do not survive that modifiers like 'first known' must always be used when discussing its contents.) Richard Beale Davis calls the 'Monitor' series 'the most original group of essays in the first thirty years of the *Virginia Gazette*'s history'.[4]

In addition to his newspaper Parks published much miscellaneous writing. The 15 October 1736 issue of the *Gazette*, the same one containing 'Monitor, No. 9', announced the release of *Poems on Several Occasions ... By a Gentleman of Virginia*. A handsome volume printed in what Lawrence Wroth describes as Parks's 'serene and stately typographical style', *Poems on Several Occasions* almost disappeared from history.[5] It survives in a unique copy at the Boston Athenaeum among other books from George Washington's library. In other words, if Washington had not added this volume of poems to his Mount Vernon library, its contents would be lost to posterity.

Poems on Several Occasions appeared anonymously. Its authorship went unnoticed until the twentieth century when the Rev. William Dawson was identified as its author.[6] Born in England, Dawson studied at Queen's College, Oxford University, where William Stith, a Virginian who would establish his literary reputation as the author of *A History of the First Discovery and Settlement of Virginia*, was studying. The two men became friends, and Stith helped Dawson emigrate to Virginia once they completed their university work. Dawson took his bachelor's degree in 1725, his master's in 1728.

In addition to his formal course of study at Oxford, Dawson immersed himself in English literature. After Jacob Tonson published his lavish quarto edition of Pope's Shakespeare, Dublin publishers released it in a less expensive octavo edition. The Dublin edition appeared in 1726. The 'William Dawson' named in its list of subscribers is likely the same William Dawson who was a graduate student at Oxford during the time of its publication. As *Poems on Several Occasions* demonstrates, Dawson was a great Shakespeare enthusiast.

Upon taking holy orders in 1729, Dawson emigrated to Virginia, presumably through Stith's influence. He would remain close to the family. After settling in Williamsburg, Dawson married his friend's sister, Mary Randolph Stith. He served as a tutor before becoming professor of moral philosophy at the College of William and Mary. Dawson also befriended Parks and joined his literary circle. Parks encouraged him to write for publication. When Dawson mentioned a set of poems he had written at Oxford, Parks asked to see the manuscript. He liked the poems well enough that he agreed to publish the collection. The result was *Poems on Several Occasions*, the first collection of poetry published in Virginia.[7]

Dawson's verse shows his mastery of the metrical patterns, literary allusions and figures of speech that were fashionable in Augustan England.[8] He used a variety of forms – epigrams, epistles, hymns, songs – which together reveal a deep knowledge of English literature. He wrote 'To Sylvia, on Approach of Winter', for example, in the carpe diem tradition. Some hear the sound of Cavalier poets Robert Herrick and Edmund Waller in this poem, but to Jay Hubbell's ear it echoes the songs of Shakespeare's romantic comedies.[9]

Swem has argued that the respect *Poems on Several Occasions* pays Shakespeare represents its defining feature. Not only does Dawson show his familiarity with Shakespeare's plays, he also recognises their excellence.[10] Two poems in the volume mention Shakespeare by name. 'An Epistle to ——— Esq.' addresses an anonymous Cornish friend. The speaker of the poem imagines his friend gazing toward the ocean from the coast of Cornwall:

> Of what new labour boast?
> High on a clift, which e'en transcends the flight
> Of Shakespear's boldest muse, dost thou delight
> The studious mind?[11]

Shakespeare represents a pinnacle of literary achievement for Dawson. The best way to express the lofty thought of his school chum, he decided, would be to elevate him above Shakespeare. Dawson is not suggesting that his friend really soared above Shakespeare. Rather, he is using hyperbole, a commonplace device of Augustan verse, that let him convey his respect for his friend's intellect.

The concluding work in *Poems on Several Occasions* treats Shakespeare more extensively and also pays homage to Rowe. Dawson's association between the two reflects how closely Rowe had become linked with Shakespeare after his edition appeared and how the edition enhanced Rowe's standing as a dramatist. 'On the Corruptions of the Stage' begins with the following stanza:

Long did the stage with nervous sense delight,
Exalt the ravish'd soul, and charm the sight;
Whilst Shakespear, Row and all those sons of fame,
(Our greatest glory, and our greatest shame)
With lofty buskin, or facetious lay,
Held o'er the captive mind despotic sway.
With noble ardor then they trod the scene,
We came, we saw, we gaz'd ourselves to men.[12]

The line 'With lofty buskin, or facetious lay' reveals the extent of Dawson's appreciation. Not only did he enjoy the tragedies – the buskin is a traditional symbol of tragedy – he also liked Shakespeare's comedies. Both could capture the thoughts and feelings of real men and women, letting audiences witness Shakespeare's profound insight into the human condition.

The last line of the opening stanza achieves its power through the use of allusion and double entendre. Echoing Caesar's famous saying – 'I came, I saw, I conquered' – Dawson turns the act of attending a Shakespeare play into a kind of conquest, a way to understand true manhood. The last part of the line has a double meaning. When Dawson says that 'we gaz'd ourselves to men', he is suggesting that he and his fellow enthusiasts could see Shakespeare's characters in action on stage, watch how true men behave and, in so doing, find models to follow. They gazed themselves toward men and into men. Like Hamlet's tribute to his father, Dawson's poem celebrates becoming an exemplar of true manhood as an ideal achievement.

The speaker of 'On the Corruptions of the Stage' brings the story of English drama to the present, which, as its title suggests, is a story of decay. The stage has now been reduced to little more than a vehicle for superficial sensationalism. He continues:

In vain Mercutio jests, poor Juliet mourns in vain.
Phogh! who can bear th'intolerable strain!
Where strong and manly sense disturbs our ease,
And passions, too affecting e'er to please.[13]

After expressing regret that Shakespeare's finely wrought characters in *Romeo and Juliet* are lost on modern audiences, Dawson's exclamation – Phogh! – marks a vocal shift and adds considerable sophistication to the poem. The following three lines speak in the voice of a modern theatre-goer, someone who abhors the kind of theatre Shakespeare represents, who scorns the strain of highly wrought emotions brought alive on stage, who dislikes anything that disturbs a free-and-easy attitude toward life, who does not think strong passions make good entertainment. Continuing in the voice of this superficial theatre-goer, he looks down on Shakespeare enthusiasts, calling them 'fools of sense' who 'doat of Shakespear's scene'.[14]

Like *Poems on Several Occasions*, the articles in the *Virginia Gazette* that mention Shakespeare during the mid-1730s appeared anonymously or pseudonymously. After Parks had promised in the first issue of his *Gazette* to keep contributors' names concealed if desired, he kept his promise. He kept it so well, in fact, that the authors of the original Shakespeare-related items in the *Gazette* remain unidentified. Regardless of their anonymity, their contributions to the newspaper show a fairly extensive knowledge of Shakespeare's work. The *Gazette* articles also demonstrate how Shakespeare could be put to use. They reflect the power his words hold, their value for instruction as well as entertainment and their ongoing relevance.

'Monitor, No. 17', the lead article of the 31 December 1736 issue, contains the earliest known reference to Shakespeare in the *Virginia Gazette*. Like the *Spectator* essays on which they were modelled, the 'Monitor' essays were not all written by the same author. The stylistic similarities among some of the essays let them be grouped together in terms of authorship. Robert Arner, who has written the fullest critical treatment of the 'Monitor' essays, identifies the author of No. 17 as the same person who wrote Nos. 6 and 7. All three share a similar ribaldry but also have much else in common: a sharp wit, a keen sense of satire, an imaginative prose style and a subtle allusiveness that reflects an extensive knowledge of Latin verse and English drama.[15]

No. 17 offers readers a detailed account of Monitor's origins and career. (Placed in inverted commas, the word 'Monitor' refers to the title of the essay series; without the inverted commas it refers to the persona.) Parodying the traditional concept of transmigration, Monitor takes himself through a series of rebirths from man to dog, ape, bear and back to man. Arner finds that Monitor's origin story recalls Nano's version of how Pythagoras's soul becomes transformed into Androgyno from Jonson's *Volpone*, a work No. 6 had referenced.[16]

During his bear phase, Monitor is captured and dragged to the stake, that is, put into a bear-baiting arena. The dogs prove too many and too much, mortally wounding the bear. Dr Faustus, who happens to be in the crowd of onlookers, wafts his magic wand and recites a spell drawn, as he says, from Shakespeare:

> By my rough magic, I have oft bedim'd
> The noon-tide sun —
> — Graves at my command
> Have wak'd their sleepers, op'd and let them forth.

With these words, Monitor instantly assumes his original human form to the surprise and delight of the onlookers. Impressed with Dr Faustus's words and actions, Monitor indentures himself to him. Upon completing his seven-year indenture, Monitor sails for Virginia, where he establishes himself as a fortune teller, boasting that he could interpret dreams, predict the first ship of the season to enter the York river and determine who would die a maid.[17]

Arner admires Monitor's use of both Shakespeare and Christopher Marlowe in No. 17, but, in this instance, he overstates the author's learning. Privileging literary history over folk culture, modern readers often assume that references to Dr Faustus are references to Marlowe's *Dr Faustus*. Not necessarily. Early American readers typically encountered the character the same way Marlowe had, that is, via *The Remarkable Life of Dr Faustus*, a popular folkbook that circulated throughout the English-speaking world for centuries. Monitor's reference to Dr Faustus is not a reference to Marlowe but a reference to the folkbook character.

Monitor's Shakespeare quotation does not come directly from Shakespeare, either. Instead, it comes from *Thesaurus Dramaticus*, a collection of memorable excerpts from English drama. Though weighted more toward the leading dramatists of the Restoration stage – Congreve, Dryden, Otway, Rowe – the *Thesaurus Dramaticus* did contain a good sampling from such Renaissance dramatists as Beaumont, Fletcher, Jonson and Shakespeare. Approximately a quarter of the entries, in fact, come from Shakespeare. The author of 'Monitor, No. 17' was not the only colonial Virginia reader to make use of *Thesaurus Dramaticus*. As a young man, Thomas Jefferson would transcribe excerpts from this anthology in his commonplace book.[18]

Organised by subject, *Thesaurus Dramaticus* functions the same way as other anthologies of familiar quotations. It provides a ready reference for any occasion. Monitor's Shakespeare quotation falls under the subject entry 'Necromancer', which is attributed to *The Tempest*.[19] The quotation does share some words with Prospero, but the compiler of *Thesaurus Dramaticus* played fast and loose with *The Tempest*, moulding Shakespeare's words to suit.

Though Monitor did not take the words of the spell directly from *The Tempest*, Dr Faustus's use of Shakespeare reveals much. Putting Shakespeare's words in the form of a magic spell, Monitor acknowledges their power. Identifying Shakespeare as the author of those words, Monitor suggests that saying his name aloud in itself could function as a magic spell. With Shakespeare's words and Dr Faustus's actions, Monitor blends folklore and book culture, using the oral tradition to bolster the impact of his periodical essay.

While using Shakespeare's words to raise the dead, Monitor applies them in a playful and light-hearted manner. They seem more intended to delight than instruct. A few months after No. 17 another contributor to the *Virginia Gazette* would use Shakespeare in a more didactic way. The essay is untitled, but a few keywords in its opening paragraph can be pressed into service to form its title. Let's call it 'Grieving Immoderately'.

'Grieving Immoderately' suits a prevalent social tradition in colonial America, where people commonly gave each other books about mourning as gifts upon the death of a loved one. In the colonial South William Sherlock's *Practical Discourse Concerning Death* was the most popular mourning book. In New England John Flavel's *Token for Mourners* performed a similar function.[20] 'Grieving Immoderately' fits into the same didactic tradition as Sherlock and Flavel, though the essay is secular, not religious. To illustrate their works, Sherlock and Flavel quote Scripture; the *Gazette* contributor quotes Shakespeare. 'Grieving Immoderately' warns readers against excessive displays of emotion and gives them advice regarding how to restrain their grief.

Admitting that grief is expected in times of loss, the *Gazette* contributor recalls an episode from *Macbeth*:

> This brings to my mind a passage, exquisitely well copied from Nature, in the character of Shakespear's Macduff. When Lenox brings him word, that the tyrant Macbeth, had inhumanly butcher'd his wife, and both his children, and Macduff is in all the storm of grief and passion, upon so shocking an incident, the young king bids him dispute it like a man; to which the grieved Macduff finely replies,
>
> – I shall do so;
> But I must also feel it like a man:
> I cannot but remember such things were,
> That were most precious to me!

> While the flood and torrent of grief is upon us, reason and consolation, as above hinted, will not be able to stem the tide; but we must endeavour, by every reflection of prudence and religion, to fortify against the assaults of passion.[21]

The *Gazette* contributor apparently quotes the lines from memory, making one mistake in recounting the scene. It is not Lennox but Ross who gives Macduff the news that his whole family has been slain. Alternatively, the *Gazette* contributor could be recalling Davenant's *Macbeth*, not Shakespeare's. As Davenant rewrote the play, Lennox, not Ross, gives Macduff the sad news.

Though recommending against an excessive display of grief, the *Gazette* contributor still admires Macduff, who, while aware he should control his emotions, realises that conduct advice sometimes fails in the face of profound loss. Despite its author's admiration for Macduff, 'Grieving Immoderately' stresses that mourners must control their passions.

The essay subsequently draws upon an episode from the first act of *Hamlet*. While Hamlet grieves for the loss of his father, Uncle Claudius warns his nephew against an excessive display of grief. Upholding Claudius's speech to Hamlet, the *Gazette* contributor says that Shakespeare 'has declaimed as finely upon this subject in his *Hamlet*, as, perhaps, any of our divines have ever from the pulpit: his way of thinking is so just, and his expressions so strong and pathetick, that no long discourse upon this topick, can have half the weight and efficacy'.[22]

When Shakespeare wrote *Hamlet* the kind of message Claudius delivers had already become part of Protestant religious discourse. Funeral sermons often cautioned mourners against displaying their grief, reminding them that the person they were mourning was already in a better place. Ironically, the speech that the arch-villain Claudius delivers has the quality of a sermon.[23]

After identifying Shakespeare as a source of advice for mourners, the *Gazette* contributor quotes a twenty-line excerpt from Claudius's speech. Claudius warns Hamlet that an 'unmanly grief' shows 'a will most incorrect to heav'n, / A heart unfortified, a mind impatient, / An understanding simple, and unschool'd'.[24] Claudius's words present advice by negation: he tells Hamlet what to do only by telling him what not to do. He says how to be manly by identifying what is unmanly, how to be patient by defining impatience. Regardless, the *Gazette* contributor still found Claudius's words effective.

Excerpted in the *Virginia Gazette*, Claudius's speech shows how easily a Shakespearean text could be shifted from one context to another. In this instance self-serving words on the part of the speaker become conduct advice when taken out of context. Such reuse of Shakespearean texts is not unusual. The words that Polonius speaks to his son Laertes in the third scene of *Hamlet* – 'Neither a borrower nor a lender be'; 'This above all: to thine own self be true' – have frequently been extracted as conduct advice. When Polonius, a thick-headed dolt, speaks them in *Hamlet* they sound facile. Only when they are separated from the play do they sound like good advice.

Similarly, Claudius's words sound like advice from a seventeenth-century conduct book – once they are extracted from *Hamlet*, that is. Read in context, they have a dark and decidedly ironic tone. Claudius knows that such noisy expressions of grief could reveal his murderous perfidy. To save himself Claudius must stifle his nephew's grief, so he shapes his words to Hamlet as a piece of sound counsel. What resembles sage advice is not advice at all: these are the words of a murderer and a tyrant who is trying to silence the one person who can take him down.

According to the use of his works in the *Virginia Gazette*, Shakespeare could be made to suit different genres of periodical literature. Whereas 'Monitor, No. 17' shows how a Shakespeare quotation could enhance a newspaper essay, 'Grieving Immoderately' demonstrates how Shakespeare could be shaped to suit a newspaper advice column. An item from the *Virginia Gazette* a few months after 'Grieving Immoderately' shows how Shakespeare could be updated to suit the emerging genre of newspaper verse.

In June 1737 a Virginia poet using the pen name 'Musaephilus' contributed a forty-line narrative poem to the *Gazette* titled 'A Tale Extracted from Shakespeare'. This pseudonymous contributor introduced the poem with the following headnote addressed to William Parks: 'I desire you to insert the following poem in your next *Gazette*; and if trifles of this nature shall be thought to contribute any thing to the entertainment of the publick, or the support and encouragement of your press, I shall, perhaps, from time to time, transmit you some other small pieces.'[25]

The episode that Musaephilus extracted from Shakespeare comes from the second act of *Henry VI, Part I*. The scene has received short shrift in modern times, often being omitted from recent productions.[26] Musaephilus's use of the episode emphasises its importance. The scene features Sir John Talbot, the most charismatic figure in the play. After his success against the French on the battlefield, he faces an enemy of a different sort. The Countess of Auvergne invites Talbot to her castle ostensibly to congratulate him on his victory but really to take him prisoner. This is the story that 'A Tale Extracted from Shakespear' retells. The poem begins:

> When Talbot ravag'd all the plains of France,
> And e'en to Paris made his bold advance;
> Griev'd at her country's woes, a patriot dame,
> Wily and beautiful, Auvergne her name,
> With courteous speech and message, sends a page
> To bid the foremost hero of the age.

With these opening lines, Musaephilus summarises the preceding action but also give away much of the ensuing story. Mentioning Auvergne's wiles, Musaephilus conveys her underhanded reason for inviting Talbot to her castle. In *Henry VI, Part I* Auvergne's ulterior motive does not become apparent until after Talbot has accepted the invitation and entered her castle.

The next six lines of the poem appear in quotation marks, designating them as the invitation spoken by Auvergne's page. They correspond with the following six lines, which Auvergne's messenger speaks in *Henry VI, Part I*:

> The virtuous lady, Countess of Auvergne,
> With modesty admiring thy renown,
> By me entreats, great lord, thou wouldst vouchsafe
> To visit her poor castle where she lies,
> That she may boast she hath beheld the man
> Whose glory fills the world with loud report.[27]

Alternatively, Auvergne's page in 'A Tale Extracted from Shakespear' delivers the following message:

> Too fierce the war for her to stir; nor can
> She in the field behold the godlike man.
> She therefore humbly begs him to accept,
> Within her castle-walls, a homely treat:
> That there she might with safety feast her sight;
> And boast, that she had seen the glorious knight.

The most obvious change Musaephilus made while adapting the episode from Shakespeare's play is the verse form. The messenger in *Henry VI, Part I* speaks in blank verse; the page in 'A Tale Extracted from Shakespear' speaks in heroic couplets. (That Musaephilus rhymes 'accept' with 'treat' provides a clue to English pronunciation in early eighteenth-century Virginia.) Musaephilus also punctuates the poem to make it suit the conventions of Augustan verse. Whereas Shakespeare's run-on lines give the messenger's speech a more natural feel suitable for dramatic performance, Musaephilus's heavily end-stopped lines emphasise the artificiality of the rhyme.

Musaephilus was doing with *Henry VI, Part I* what Davenant had done with *Macbeth*, what Dryden had done with *Troilus and Cressida*, what Cibber had done with *Richard III*, what so many other playwrights did as they adapted Shakespeare for the Restoration stage. They changed his blank verse into heroic couplets. While the whole idea of rewriting Shakespeare into rhyme may make modern readers cringe, it suited the Augustan aesthetic. Rewriting Shakespeare was elevating Nature.

'A Tale Extracted from Shakespear' does something else the Restoration playwrights did. Just as Dryden used one aspect of *Antony and Cleopatra* to create *All for Love* and Rowe borrowed a theme from *Richard III* for *Jane Shore*, Musaephilus takes an episode from *Henry VI, Part I* and develops it into a stand-alone narrative poem. Like Dryden and Rowe, Musaephilus recognised Shakespeare's work as a rich source of brief dramatic episodes that could stand independently from the original plays.

Though showing some similarities with the dramatists of the London stage, Musaephilus was doing something different from the dramatists in terms of genre and medium. Whereas they were rewriting Shakespeare to suit current fashions in drama, Musaephilus applied Shakespeare to suit a new genre and a new medium, turning a dramatic episode into a newspaper poem.

Musaephilus anticipates a specific genre of popular poetry in eighteenth-century America that would grow with importance during the Revolutionary era: the versification, a type of poetry-writing that involves transposing a serious work of prose into a satirical poem.[28] 'A Tale Extracted from Shakespeare' shows that blank verse could be re-versified to rhyme. Unlike most early American versifications, 'A Tale Extracted from Shakespear' does not parody but pays homage.

Besides altering the verse form, Musaephilus simplified Shakespeare's diction while rewriting the story of Talbot and Auvergne. As Davenant had done with *Macbeth*, Musaephilus omitted obsolete words. Gone is 'thou wouldst vouchsafe'. Musaephilus would have no vouchsafing going on in his poem. A Shakespearean circumlocution also disappears. In *Henry VI, Part I* Talbot's 'glory fills the world with loud report'. In 'A Tale Extracted from Shakespear' Talbot is a 'glorious knight'.

Though Musaephilus retains Talbot's glory, his revision oversimplifies the original, omitting Shakespeare's comment on the relationship between war and warrior, minimising how Talbot's martial success has enhanced the significance of the battle in which he has fought.[29]

Keeping the poem within the physical limits of a newspaper column, Musaephilus quickened the pace of the episode. As soon as Auvergne enters, she springs her trap. A fast pace may not have been the sole reason for abbreviating the scene. In *Henry VI, Part I* the meeting with Auvergne diminishes Talbot's heroic qualities. Upon seeing Talbot, she registers her shock: 'It cannot be, this weak and writhled shrimp / Should strike such terror to his enemies.'[30]

Auvernge's words in *Henry VI, Part I* reduce the superhuman military hero to human proportions. They anticipate a similar example from early American literature, Thomas Morton's typename for Miles Standish in *New English Canaan*. The trouble-making Morton calls the military hero of the Plymouth Colony 'Captaine Shrimp'.[31] Alternatively, the phrase Auvergne uses in *Henry VI, Part I* could be a sexual innuendo, a way of impugning Talbot's virility. Omitting the phrase 'writhled shrimp', Musaephilus sustains Talbot's heroic dimensions and eliminates a vulgarism that may have seemed unworthy of Shakespeare.

Musaephilus altered Shakespeare's imagery as well. When Auvergne orders her men to seize Talbot, he is unfazed in both *Henry VI, Part I* and 'A Tale Extracted from Shakespear', but the figures of speech he uses in each differ. In both works Talbot explains that he himself is merely a part of something far greater. Shakespeare has Talbot ask Auvergne: 'Are you now persuaded, / That Talbot is but shadow of himself?'[32] Musaephilus, on the other hand, has Talbot say to Auvergne: 'You see / Only a part, a little part of me. / This here is only warlike Talbot's head, / That orders and disposes all'.

Whereas Shakespeare's Talbot likens himself to a shadow, Musaephilus's Talbot uses 'head' as a comparable figure of speech. Having Talbot call himself a shadow, Shakespeare follows Castiglione's *Book of the Courtier*, which insists that the courtier be bold on the battlefield but modest everywhere else.[33] Making Talbot more headstrong, so to speak, Musaephilus diminishes his modesty. The head metaphor suits the Augustan mindset. Musaephilus creates an image of a well-ordered world, one where the commander is a microcosm of his army. As an individual's head controls the body, the commander controls his army. Besides what it contributes to Talbot's personality, the shadow image in *Henry VI, Part I* is evocative in itself, suggesting that the leader of an army is an image, a projection, a faint and evanescent semblance of the whole. Recall what the Fool calls King Lear once he has given away his kingdom: 'Lear's shadow'.

After Musaephilus ends the episode, he tacks on two more lines that introduce another military hero to the poem, updating it with an eighteenth-century example of success on the battlefield: 'Without his troops, e'en Marlborough's self was man; / With them, the hero glitt'ring o'er the plain.' This second example lets Musaephilus generalise from Talbot's behaviour, turning 'A Tale Extracted from Shakespear' into what one modern reader calls 'a glowing tribute to the British fighting man'.[34]

Musaephilus, of course, is referring to John Churchill, the first Duke of Marlborough, whose success at Blenheim during the War of the Spanish Succession proved to be one of the great victories of the British army in the eighteenth century. Shortly after the battle, English poets paid tribute to Marlborough. In 'The Campaign' Joseph Addison compares Marlborough to the avenging angel who directed the Great Storm of 1703: 'Calm and serene he drives the furious blast; / And pleas'd th' Almighty's orders to perform, / Rides in the whirlwind, and directs the storm.'[35]

With 'A Tale Extracted from Shakespear' Musaephilus continues the tradition of paying homage to Marlborough that Addison had started. Through much of the eighteenth century, Marlborough would remain among the most greatly respected military men in colonial America. While redecorating Mount Vernon, George Washington special-ordered a bust of Marlborough and several other military heroes to adorn his home. His London agent, who could not locate busts of Marlborough or any of the other figures in the sizes Washington requested, informed him that he could get busts of other prominent men, including Addison, Aristotle, Dryden, Jonson, Milton and Seneca. Poets and philosophers? No, Washington replied, he was uninterested in any of these figures. To decorate his home he wanted men of action, not men of letters. Washington would reconsider his reply: years later he would purchase a bust of Shakespeare to adorn Mount Vernon. In a list of purchases Washington calls it 'a bust of the immortal Shakespear'.[36]

Surviving books with colonial Virginia provenance supply further evidence to supplement the enthusiasm for Shakespeare expressed by contributors to the *Virginia Gazette*. For example, James Power, a prominent attorney and a representative in the House of Burgesses for King William County, owned a copy of the eight-volume duodecimo edition of Pope's Shakespeare. Adorned with Power's engraved armorial bookplate, the edition survives among the rare books at the College of William and Mary.[37]

Given the interest in Shakespeare that Virginia readers and newspaper contributors evinced, Parks kept his eyes peeled for other Shakespeare-related items he could reprint in the *Gazette*. He found one burlesque poem in the London papers. Parks does not say which paper but the *Whitehall Evening-Post*, his source for other items reprinted in the *Gazette*, had printed it on 12 February 1736. Parks also borrowed the headnote to the poem from his source: 'We hear the following prologue is to be spoken at the theatre in Drury-lane, upon the revival of *King John*, alter'd from Shakespeare, by the reviver, and author of the alterations.'[38]

Parks does not supply any further context, so it is unclear how well his Virginia readers would have understood the article's background. It pertains to another Shakespeare play altered for the Augustan stage. When word got out that Colley Cibber was rewriting *King John*, he was soundly attacked in the press. When Cibber's *Papal Tyranny in the Reign of King John* was in rehearsal, a rumour went around London that some law students planned to demolish it in the press. Cibber wrote the students at the Inns of Court asking them to be kind: about the worst thing he could have done. Predictably, they attacked with renewed fervour.[39]

The verse epistle Parks reprinted is a burlesque of Cibber's letter to the law students. It begins with a salutation – 'To you, most learned youngsters of the law' – and ends with a plea: 'Then for the sake of Shakespeare, and King John, / O! save me for this time, or I'm undone.'[40] Though Virginia readers may not have fully appreciated the background to this poem, Parks's inclusion of it in the *Virginia Gazette* let them feel privy to London's latest dramatic intrigues.

After Parks came across 'A Fit of Spleen, in Imitation of Shakespeare' in the *Whitehall Evening-Post*, he reprinted it in the 22 July 1737 issue of the *Virginia Gazette*. The poem appeared anonymously, but it was written by the Rev. Dr Benjamin Ibbot, an Anglican divine.[41] The misogyny expressed in its opening lines hardly befits a man of the cloth: 'Farewell, vain world! and thou its vainest part, / O lovely woman! fram'd for man's destruction!'

Initially it seems unclear what makes Ibbot's poem an imitation of Shakespeare. Departing from typical early eighteenth-century poetry, he wrote 'A Fit of Spleen' in blank verse instead of heroic couplets. His verse form could be a nod to Shakespeare, but it could equally be an imitation of *Paradise Lost*. Ibbot's diction, not his verse form, is what makes 'A Fit of Spleen' imitate Shakespeare, but his words are problematic. After using the exclamation – 'Farewell, vain world!' – to begin the poem, he repeats it at the start of the second and third verse paragraphs, as well.

'A Fit of Spleen' demonstrates Shakespeare's growing importance as a cultural marker even as it reflects an uncertain knowledge of Shakespeare's work. The last words the eponymous hero of *Macbeth* speaks are, 'Farewell vain world, and what's most vain in it, ambition.' Here's the problem: these are not the last words of Shakespeare's Macbeth; they are the last words of Davenant's Macbeth.[42] Unwittingly, the Rev. Dr Ibbot was writing an imitation of Davenant, not Shakespeare.

The Shakespeare references in the *Virginia Gazette* during its first few years demonstrate how powerful his words had become in colonial America since the start of the eighteenth century. The name 'Shakespeare' was now something that literate people recognised and revered. The variety of uses to which his words were put demonstrate their flexibility. They could cast spells that bring the dead back to life; supply examples for authors of a newspaper advice column; provide narratives for the author of newspaper verse; and give an editor material to enhance the quality of his newspaper, to lend it a level of prestige that showed current and would-be readers that colonial America had a newspaper that exuded class and intelligence.

5

Dr Alexander Hamilton and the Ancient and Honourable Tuesday Club of Annapolis

Dr Alexander Hamilton loved to read. Not to be confused with Alexander Hamilton, the first treasury secretary of the United States, Dr Hamilton was an Edinburgh-trained MD who had emigrated to Annapolis, Maryland, where he established a reputation as a physician and a wit. In 1744 Hamilton took a months-long journey from Maryland to Maine for his health, which he documented in the *Itinerarium*, a book-length manuscript he enjoyed sharing with friends. Best known as a chronicle of the quaint and quirky social life of mid-eighteenth-century America, the *Itinerarium* also reveals Hamilton's charm. Reading formed a frequent activity during the calmer moments of his journey. While in Philadelphia that September he had the chance to read some Shakespeare. On Friday, the fourteenth, he 'read one of Shakespeare's plays'.[1] For the mid-1740s Hamilton's reading selection was not unusual. People throughout British North America that decade were reading more Shakespeare than ever before.

* * *

Correspondence, diaries, historical writings, library catalogues, newspaper advertisements, periodical essays, personal narratives: all attest to the growing interest in Shakespeare among colonial American readers. In the January 1741 issue of the *American Magazine*, the first issue of the first magazine published in British North America, Andrew Bradford reprinted an article from the *London Magazine* presenting a set of character sketches of English worthies. The article says that

Shakespeare's 'excellent genius open'd to him the whole heart of man, all the mines of fancy, all the stores of nature, and gave him power beyond all other writers to move, astonish, and delight mankind'.[2]

Curiosity about Shakespeare in New England accelerated during the 1740s. In 1743 Boston bookseller, bookbinder and stationer Samuel Eliot sold what he called a 'collection of the most valuable authors'. His advertisement lists several of the authors, starting with a name that attests to the collection's quality: Shakespeare. That same year in New Haven, Connecticut the Yale College library was catalogued for the first time. The last page of the catalogue lists a nine-volume set of Shakespeare.[3]

Whereas Franklin's friend and Yale alumnus Samuel Johnson had recommended Shakespeare as part of the English curriculum for the Philadelphia Academy, the Yale library catalogue placed its copy of Shakespeare under the heading 'Plays and Books of Diversion'. Since Jeremiah Dummer's bequest in 1714, Yale had continued to acquire works of English literature its students could read for pleasure, giving them a break from their studies and helping them become more well-rounded. Other books of diversion at Yale included Pope's *Dunciad* and Rowe's *Tragedies*.

Toward the decade's end the *Independent Advertiser*, the Boston newspaper founded by Samuel Adams, reprinted an article from the British press, 'A Character of the Spaniards, Hollanders, Italians and French'. Reflecting English prejudice toward Europeans, this essay ends with a twenty-line passage adapted from the third act of *Henry V*, which, the essayist claims, exposes the 'vanity of the French with the justest humour and spirit'. Written to parallel King George II's leadership at the Battle of Dettingen during the War of the Austrian Succession with King Henry V's leadership at the Battle of Agincourt in the Hundred Years' War, the essay was six years old by the time it reached Boston, but it reflects how Shakespeare's history plays could be applied to interpret more recent events.[4]

Another kind of evidence reinforces New England's attention to Shakespeare during the late 1740s, when John Smibert, the first professional portrait painter in British North America, received a sculpture from Peter Scheemakers, an old friend in London. Earlier that decade Scheemakers had created the most renowned sculpture of his career, a memorial to Shakespeare for Poets' Corner in Westminster Abbey. He sent Smibert a cast of the model of his Shakespeare monument. Scheemakers's *Shakespeare* pleased Smibert very much.[5]

While studying art in Europe, Smibert had carefully copied many of the old masters, and he displayed his copies in Boston. He also brought an impressive collection of other drawings, paintings, prints and sculpture when he emigrated to New England. Wayne Craven calls Smibert's Boston studio 'America's first public art gallery'. It became an essential destination for early American artists and art lovers passing through Boston.[6]

Hamilton visited Smibert's studio twice during the summer of 1744, once when he was heading north to Maine and again on his way back to Maryland. He especially enjoyed Smibert's copy of Nicolas Poussin's *Continence of Scipio*, which he describes at length in the *Itinerarium*. Hamilton also liked the statuary. He mentions both the *Venus de Medici* and a head of Homer. Smibert had a small version of the *Laocoön*, as well. Hamilton arrived five years too earlier to see Scheemaker's *Shakespeare*, but his behaviour resembles that of other colonial American art lovers who visited Smibert's Boston studio once he installed the *Shakespeare*. After Smibert's death in 1751 his studio remained open and continued to welcome people curious about the history of art.[7]

Quotations from Shakespeare surface throughout colonial American writings of the 1740s. James Parker made creative use of *Hamlet* in an editorial for the *New York Gazette*. In February 1748 Parker had published two letters critical of Philadelphia Quakers, which riled some of his readers. Responding to those who attacked the *Gazette*, Parker celebrated the press as 'the grand bulwark of liberty, light, truth and religion'. He recognised an aspect of newspapers that persists to the present: those who grumble most about the press are the ones whose faults the papers expose. Parker continued:

> If I have openly injur'd any, I am willing as openly to vindicate them, or to give them all the satisfaction that reason requires without being sway'd with either their high words or low promises.
>
> But let the stricken deer go weep, the hart
>
> Ungall'd go play. Shakespear.[8]

Other eighteenth-century authors quoted Shakespeare to confirm and illustrate the point they wished to make. Parker did something different: he quoted *Hamlet* as a counterpoint to his argument.

Hamlet says these words to Horatio directly after Claudius has interrupted the *Mousetrap* and stormed away. Once Claudius has escaped the trap set for him, Hamlet switches metaphors, turning Claudius from a mouse into a deer. Shakespeare's careful diction clarifies that he was describing a deer during a bow and stable hunt. Harts, that is, mature deer with significant antler development, were reserved for the chase, a more elite form of hunting, and thus left unmolested. During bow and stable hunts, stricken deer were tracked down by hunting dogs.[9]

Parker's *Hamlet* quotation implicitly compares the critics of the press with the tyrannical Claudius. Whereas Parker expresses a willingness to vindicate anyone his newspaper has injured, his quotation implies that he will leave them to their fate. In short, Parker uses the quotation to castigate the enemies of a free press, essentially telling them to go off and die by themselves.

Many Philadelphians were reading Shakespeare during the 1740s. In 1743 John Wallace and Company, a local importer, advertised a set of Shakespeare along with 'a large collection of the best English plays'. A sale catalogue Franklin published in 1744 lists three volumes from a multi-volume edition of Shakespeare. Philadelphia bookbinder Joseph Goodwin auctioned a 600-volume library piecemeal in early 1745. The auction catalogue lists an eight-volume edition of Shakespeare's plays.[10]

William Black, who visited Philadelphia the same year as Hamilton, met a Shakespeare enthusiast there, though his account of her is not exactly positive. Also a native of Scotland, Black had emigrated to America and settled in Virginia. He came to Philadelphia in 1744 as secretary to the commissioners appointed by the Virginia governor to meet with their counterparts from Maryland and Pennsylvania and negotiate a treaty with the Iroquois. Black's personal diary of the trip shows that in addition to their Scottish heritage he and Hamilton also shared a vivacious wit and a pungent literary style.

On Wednesday evening, 13 June, Black and a Philadelphia friend attended a party held at a large home in town. Black met a company of five young women and two men. One woman dominated the conversation. Black does not supply her real name but does coin a typename for her, Mrs Talkative. She 'began a discourse on love, wherein she pull'd all the other sex to pieces. Setting forth the constancy of their sex, and the unstability of ours, every one of the young ladies put in an oar and helpt her out.'[11]

Having exhausted that subject, Mrs Talkative turned her attention to dramatic literature, criticising plays and playwrights at length. Black recorded some details of the conversation: 'Addison, Prior, Otway, Congreve, Dryden, Pope, Shakespeare, etc. etc. etc. were names often in question; the words genius – and no genius – invention, poetry, fine thing, bad language, no style, charming writing, imaginary and diction ... with many more expressions, which swim on the surface of criticism, seem'd to have been caught by these female fishers for the reputation of wit.'[12]

Though Black's diary serves as evidence reinforcing the knowledge of Shakespeare in colonial America, it does so begrudgingly. Black's clever literary style cannot mask the animosity he felt toward Mrs Talkative and her ilk. Though Mrs Talkative had obviously read much dramatic literature and criticism, Black found her knowledge superficial. The source of his animosity remains unclear. Did he find literary criticism an inappropriate topic for party conversation? Or did he consider it a subject inappropriate for women to discuss? Either way, Mrs Talkative clearly got under his skin. Black's diary entry for that evening continues at considerable length. Once he and his Philadelphia friend returned home, Black could hardly stop talking about Mrs Talkative.

Copies of Shakespeare's collected works in Virginia reinforce his growing importance to American literary culture. Augustine Washington owned a six-volume edition of Shakespeare at the time of his death in 1743. His library inventory is insufficiently detailed to identify the precise edition, Pope's most likely. Pope was a favourite with Augustine Washington, whose library contained Pope's translation of Homer's *Iliad*. George Washington – Augustine's son – had turned eleven the year his father died, so he was about the right age to start enjoying Shakespeare. Some may think eleven too young, but another future president was even younger when he started reading Shakespeare. With the encouragement of his parents John and Abigail Adams, John Quincy Adams read Shakespeare when he was ten.[13]

William Stith contributed a revealing reference to Shakespeare during the 1740s. *The History of the First Discovery and Settlement of Virginia* is a big history about a small chunk of time. Devoting three hundred pages to the story of Virginia without getting past 1624, Stith has much to say about the colony during Shakespeare's time, a little too much perhaps. Thomas Jefferson found Stith's details 'often too minute to be tolerable, even to a native of the country, whose history he writes.'[14] Stith explains that in 1620, the Virginia Company, then in need of a new treasurer, hoped to hire Henry Wriothesley, the third earl of Southampton, to fill the position.

While active with the Virginia Company, Southampton was also a patron of the theatre. Shakespeare, who enjoyed his support and friendship, dedicated both *Venus and Adonis* and *The Rape of Lucrece* to him. Stith characterises Southampton as follows: 'He was, in truth, an early, constant, and great encourager of this settlement of Virginia, as well as of all other noble works and enterprises; and is particularly memorable, for his generous patronage, and single munificence, to Shakespear, the glory and prodigy of the English stage. For he is said to have given him, at one time, a thousand pounds, to enable him to go through with a purchase, which he understood, he had an inclination to make.'[15]

Stith's word choice verifies that his source was Rowe's life of Shakespeare. Here's what Rowe says: 'Lord Southampton, at one time, gave him a thousand pounds, to enable him to go through with a purchase which he heard he had a mind to. A bounty very great, and very rare at any time, and almost equal to that profuse generosity the present age has shewn to French dancers and Italian eunuchs.'[16] Rowe contrasts the support great playwrights received in Shakespeare's day with the inability of modern theatre-goers to recognise good writing when they heard it. Stith saw no need to perpetuate Rowe's facetious remark, but otherwise he borrowed what Rowe said about Southampton.

Calling Shakespeare 'the glory and prodigy of the English stage', Stith revealed his profound respect for him, something he shared with his brother-in-law William Dawson, now president of the College of William and Mary. Stith's Shakespeare discussion also contributes to his history of Virginia. The presence of Southampton in both Virginia history and Shakespeare biography let Stith create a parallel. Captain John Smith founded Virginia – the first permanent English settlement in North America – in 1607, the same year Shakespeare published *The Rape of Lucrece*. In other words, the era that nurtured Shakespeare also gave rise to British North America. Both represent the enduring legacy of the English Renaissance.

* * *

Dr Hamilton enjoyed the Shakespeare play he read on 14 September 1744 so well that he read more Shakespeare a few days later. He recorded in the *Itinerarium*: 'This forenoon I spent in reading of Shakespear's *Timon of Athens, or Manhater*, a play which, tho not written according to Aristotle's rules, yet abounding with inimitable beauties peculiar to this excellent author.' Other colonial Americans read *Timon of Athens* as well. Captain Henry Lee, a prominent landholder in Westmoreland County, Virginia, owned a copy of *Timon of Athens, A Tragedy* at the time of his death in 1747.[17]

Though Hamilton says he read Shakespeare's *Timon*, the precise title he uses in the *Itinerarium* says different. Shakespeare titled his play *Timon of Athens, A Tragedy*. *Timon of Athens, or Man-Hater* was the title of Thomas Shadwell's altered version of Shakespeare's play, which quickens the drama's pace and adds a love plot. Hamilton's title for the play suggests that he read Shadwell's version. John Adams's diary presents the same problem. He called the play *Timon of Athens, The Man hater*.[18]

Most likely both Hamilton and Adams read Shakespeare's *Timon*, not Shadwell's. The specific titles they use in their writings suggest that the phrase 'Man-hater' had become a commonplace subtitle for Shakespeare's tragedy once Shadwell's version appeared. Much as text from Davenant's *Macbeth* was quoted as Shakespeare's, aspects of Shadwell's *Timon* bled into Shakespeare's in the popular imagination. Regardless which version Hamilton read, his dual impulse – to evoke yet repudiate Aristotle's rules of tragedy – jibes with Augustan critical discourse, which sought to balance the positive and negative elements of Shakespeare's writings.[19]

Discussing the propriety of judging Shakespeare by Aristotle's rules, Hamilton participated in a frequent conversation among contemporary critics. Rowe had broached the issue in his life of Shakespeare. Brief as it is, Hamilton's critical discussion in the *Itinerarium* not only indicates his familiarity with Shakespeare's works, it also shows his knowledge of drama criticism. The *Itinerarium* reflects Hamilton's general knowledge of dramatic literature, as well. Discussing the oddball characters who people the *Itinerarium*, Lawrence Wroth finds them akin to 'the *dramatis personae* of an old play'. Yet Hamilton's detailed personal descriptions are also quite forward-looking. Wroth continues, 'His eye for the characteristics of his fellow man was as sharp as the lens of the candid camera.'[20]

Upon returning to Maryland after his travels, Hamilton resumed his medical practice. He enjoyed life in Annapolis but still felt something was missing. Since he had been active in Edinburgh club life, he assembled several professional men in Annapolis to organise a social club. He foresaw a club that would meet once a week, when members could get together, enjoy a simple meal and pleasant conversation, telling stories and cracking jokes.

Consequently, Hamilton and several like-minded Annapolis friends formed the Tuesday Club, which met for the first time on 14 May 1745. The club proved successful, largely due to Hamilton's winning personality. Years later fellow club member Upton Scott called him 'a man of strict honor and integrity, of a friendly, benevolent disposition and a most cheerful, facetious companion amongst his friends, whom he never failed to delight with the effusions of his wit, humor and drollery, in which acquirement he had no equal'.[21]

Serving as club secretary, Hamilton took responsibility for keeping its minutes. Throughout its existence, he would chronicle the club's activities. He revised the minutes into the *Records of the Tuesday Club*, which he used to draft a club history. After completing the first two volumes, he abandoned his draft history and then wrote a new draft, which became the final three-volume version, *The History of the Antient and Honorable Tuesday Club*. By the time he was finished, Hamilton had created the riproaringest, knee-slappingest hoot-and-a-half in the history of colonial American literature.

The longstanding members formed the core of the Tuesday Club, and Hamilton treated them with loving care as he revised his text. He assigned all of them humorous names. Club president Charles Cole, an Annapolis merchant, became Nasifer Jole. In the manner of Restoration drama many are typenames. John Bullen, a fairly wealthy landowner, became Bully Blunt, though he started going by Sir John once the club knighted him. Hamilton himself became Loquacious Scribble. And Jonas Green became Jonathan Grog, P.P.P.P.P. – Purveyor, Punster, Punchmaster General, Printer and Poet. Some visitors to the club also received typenames. The eminently clubbable Benjamin Franklin attended a meeting when he was visiting Annapolis after his electrical experiments had earned him international scientific fame. Hamilton dubbed him 'Mr Electro Vitrifice'.

Besides assigning names as he revised, Hamilton added much else while expanding the contents of his club history. His additions take many different forms: humorous episodes, mock-historical disquisitions, pseudo-philosophical reflections and quasi-erudite allusions. Hamilton also added many references to Shakespeare as he revised.

The phrase 'longstanding' provided an almost endless source of fun during club meetings, as Hamilton's *History* reveals. Sir John, 'a person of a very happy turn to the burlesque, which made him an exceeding good clubs man', delivered the anniversary address one year, defining what it meant to be a longstanding member of the Tuesday Club. Addressing the club in general and President Jole in particular, Sir John says:

> Now, as for their standing, they are standing as they yet stand and exist. They are standing, as they stand cordially together. They are standing as they prop up your honor's chair, and are mutual buttresses to each other, they are standing as they stand, when they address your honor, they are standing, as they are people of good understanding, they are standing as they live in mutual good understanding one with another, and lastly, they are standing, being the cause (as it is said) of many a standing joke, so that what Sir John

> Falstaffe said of himself (here Sir John looked very stern, and clap'd his hand on his sword) may properly be said of your honor, and your longstanding members, vizt: That they not only have much wit themselves, but are the cause of much wit in other men.[22]

Depicting Sir John's physical gestures and facial expressions as he speaks in the manner of Falstaff, Hamilton brilliantly captures the moment. After Sir John's reference to a speech Falstaff makes in the second scene of *Henry IV, Part II*, Loquacious Scribble offers him a bottle of sack, which Sir John refuses. The offer reflects Hamilton's knowledge of *Henry IV, Part I*: 'Sir John would not take him up upon sack, not affecting that liquor so much as his namesake, the renown'd Sir Jno: Falstafe.'[23]

Hamilton continued to tinker with the *History of the Tuesday Club* the rest of his life. He never published it, but, then again, he never intended to publish it. It was a history written for the amusement of himself and his circle of friends. It would not appear in print until 1990. The published version of the history fills over 1300 pages. Hamilton obviously had so much fun writing it he could hardly stop, as the typename he assigned himself – Loquacious Scribble – affirms. Yet there is another reason he let the book swell to epic proportions. Hamilton understood that a history of a local club could be much more than a history of a local club.

Essentially the story of the Tuesday Club is a history of the world. Hamilton's club history is premised on the microcosm / macrocosm analogy. In other words, the history of a club in Annapolis, Maryland – the microcosm – parallels the history of larger systems of social organisation. To verify the analogy Loquacious Scribble asks a rhetorical question: 'Will you have the impudence to say, that Julius Caesar was a greater man than Nasifer Jole Esqr, because the first was emperor over great territories, and the latter only president of a little paltry club; surely no.'[24]

Reinforcing his argument, Hamilton draws upon the graveyard scene from *Hamlet*. When the Gravedigger unearths Yorick's skull Hamlet seems melancholy at first, but as he reflects upon death, especially the death of great men, his mood becomes almost gleeful. Reducing great men to objects of satire, Hamlet shows little admiration or even compassion for them.[25] In the *History of the Tuesday Club* Hamilton recalls what Shakespeare, speaking through Hamlet, says about Alexander the Great and Julius Caesar:

> Our famous dramatic poet also observes of Alexander the Great, 'that he died, was buried, returned to dust, dust is earth, of earth

is made Lome, with lome we stop a beer barrell'. Pray can any president be reduced lower than this mighty Alexander; and then that inimitable bard subjoins

Imperial Caesar, dead and turn'd to clay,
Might stop a hole to keep the wind away,
Oh! that that earth, which kept the world in awe,
Should patch a wall, t'expell the winter's flaw![26]

Hamilton introduces his *Hamlet* quotation by placing it within the macrocosm / microcosm analogy he is developing. He follows it with another example, comparing the anatomy of a mite with that of an elephant. He clearly intends the *Hamlet* quotation to strengthen his analogy, but it does not really apply. Reducing Alexander to dust and Caesar to clay, Shakespeare offers examples showing the mutability of all things. The *Hamlet* quotation verifies that Alexander the Great and Nasifer Jole parallel one another because both will perish. Otherwise, it does little to validate the microcosm / macrocosm analogy.

Despite its irrelevance to his point, Hamilton's use of *Hamlet* shows that by the mid-eighteenth century, Shakespeare had achieved an all-purpose applicability. A Shakespeare quotation could bolster whatever argument an author wished to make. His words had achieved such a level of respect they could lend authority to any line of thought. The epithet – 'our famous dramatic poet' – reinforces Hamilton's fond respect for Shakespeare. He names numerous other English playwrights in the *History of the Tuesday Club* – Beaumont, Cibber, Congreve, Fletcher, Jonson, Massinger – but there is no question he means Shakespeare when he mentions 'our famous dramatic poet'.

Shakespeare reappears throughout the *History of the Tuesday Club*. Sometimes Hamilton makes direct reference to him or his works; other times he makes more subtle allusions. At one point Hamilton relates a favourite anecdote about King James I and his court jester, Archie Armstrong. Archie puts his fool's cap on the king's head for allowing Prince Charles to go to Spain to woo the Infanta Maria. The king asks Archie what he would do if the prince returned from Spain safely. Hamilton relates Archie's response in direct discourse: '"Then nunkle," said Archie, "I'll send mine nown cap to the king of Spain, and he shall wear it."' To recreate the story. Hamilton has borrowed from *King Lear*, reusing a word that the Fool uses to address King Lear: 'How now, nuncle?' In short, Hamilton used the story of King Lear and his Fool to interpret and embellish the story of King James and his jester.[27]

Hamilton divided the *History of the Tuesday Club* into books and the books into chapters. The opening chapters of the books mostly follow the same pattern. Loquacious Scribble chooses a subject and then provides its history, tracing it through classical times; the Dark Ages, an era he finds especially dark; the later Middle Ages or, to use Hamilton's term, the 'Gothic times', a much brighter and more creative period of history; the Renaissance; the Enlightenment; and the American experience. Inevitably the history of each subject culminates with the founding of the 'ancient and honorable Tuesday Club of Annapolis in Maryland, now the club of clubs, and the only true ancient club upon earth'.[28]

Putting the Tuesday Club on such a pinnacle, Hamilton mocks the notion that modern civilisation can recapture ancient greatness. Though his attitude is tongue-in-cheek, it nevertheless reiterates a prevalent colonial American literary theme: in the New World it is possible to begin civilisation afresh and achieve classical excellence.

The first chapter of Book VII, 'General History of Conundrums, Puns, Riddles, Rebuses, Anagrams, Chronograms, Posies and Acrostics', follows the same pattern. Loquacious Scribble starts his history of wit and humour in the Garden of Eden, identifying Satan as a punster and drawing examples from *Paradise Lost* to prove his point. He then traces the history through ancient Greece and Rome. Wit and humour fell into darkness until the Gothic times, when the literature that had escaped 'the fury of war, fire and desolation' was rediscovered, and 'wit began again to raise her disconsolate head'.[29]

The use of rhyme in the late Middle Ages manifests a renewed interest in wit and humour: 'Poetry too, at this time, began to raise her mortified head, from among the rubbish of ignorance and barbarism, and was so overjoyed, that she began at once to carrol it, in pleasant jingle, and delectable rhime.' Hamilton provides examples from Chaucer to Pope of authors who have used rhyme and thus verifies its ongoing worth. He cannot finish his discussion without considering two major exceptions: 'Tho some old fashioned fellows, such as Milton and Shakespear among the English, have dizened her up, in her ancient plain stole of the blank rithmos, yet she still most affects the company and conversation of our jingle jangle men.'[30]

Hamilton's discussion of blank verse represents a flash forward in his history of wit and humour, which then returns to the late Middle Ages. He presents a brief discussion of occult practices during these 'glorious and enlightened times'. Despite his facetiousness, Hamilton or, at least, his mouthpiece Loquacious Scribble admires the ingenuity and creativity of occult practitioners.[31]

The unsystematic and superstition-filled quality of intellectual work in the Gothic times encouraged artists and inventors: 'In the middle of this hurly burly, and stumbling over one another in the dark, they light upon several chance discoveries, which they never thought of or looked after, some of which turned out for use, others for no use, and others for nothing but mischief.' The history of wit and humour follows suit. This same period gave rise to numerous conundrums and many other forms of humour.[32]

For Loquacious Scribble, who simultaneously combines playful facetiousness and deadpan seriousness, the Renaissance and the Enlightenment blighted the Gothic era's seedbed of creativity. Instead of letting the hit-or-miss process of intellectual discovery continue, a 'parcel of wrong headed fellows' squelched this hurly burly creativity. In the field of poetry, he takes to task Dryden, Milton, Pope and Shakespeare, 'meddling coxcombs' who 'would not let this glorious model of literature stand, but pulling it to pieces, in order to scrutinize and examin every part, like a parcel of inquisitive pragmatical puppies, as they were, it exceeded their skill to set the novel gothic fabric up again in its pristine form, and so, in its place, they erected a foolish and simple structure of their own in the false taste.'[33]

Though the great superstructure of wit and humour erected during the Gothic times had been destroyed, it survives in pieces, like the ruins of a Gothic cathedral. Occasionally it reappears, as in the playful sermons of Shakespeare's contemporary Lancelot Andrewes. It could also be found outside literary history in conversations that occurred in ale houses, bawdy houses, chop houses and nuthouses and among such people as porters, watermen and blackguard boys. Furthermore, it could be heard in certain parts of London, especially Wapping.[34] Located adjacent to the Thames, Wapping was peopled by bargemen, sailors, shipbuilders, victuallers and others who supported the seafaring trade. Hamilton's reference to Wapping confirms his idea that watermen helped preserve and perpetuate the colourful language of centuries past.

Lamenting the loss of so much wit and humour, Hamilton asks a series of rhetorical questions, including, 'When again shall our theatrical performances overflow with that quaint punning, with which they teemed in the days of Shakespear and Ben Johnson?'[35] Hamilton clearly appreciated the humour Shakespeare put into his plays, something that other eighteenth-century authors – Pope, most notably – did not.

Hamilton's specific mention of porters, whose speech helped preserve English wit and humour, calls to mind the Porter in *Macbeth*. In his editorial efforts to align Shakespeare with Augustan tastes, Pope represents what Hamilton calls a 'meddling coxcomb'. Relegating the Porter's bawdy speech to a footnote, Pope sought to elevate Shakespeare's text, ignoring what the speech contributes to the play's linguistic texture.

Recognising the value such playful humour has for literature, Hamilton included the Tuesday Club's witty repartee in his *History*: a rare glimpse inside the eighteenth-century club. One particular verbal exchange echoes what Shakespeare's Porter says about how drink can make the lecher 'stand to, and not stand to'. The deputy president of the Tuesday Club quips, 'Ha, ha, ha, the longstanding members methinks are waggish.' Not to be outdone, Mr Electro Vitrifice extends the joke: 'Longstanding members, I think gentlemen, with submission, are not so properly waggish, because if they stand they cannot wag.'[36]

In the opening chapter of Book VIII Hamilton returns to an idea he had touched upon in the *Itinerarium*, namely, the relationship between Shakespeare's plays and Aristotle's rules. The opening chapter of Book VIII takes a different approach from other opening chapters in the *History of the Tuesday Club*. Instead of being structured as a history of the subject, the chapter comes in the form of a proposal, as its title clearly indicates: 'A Modest Proposal, for the New Modelling and Improvement of Our Modern Theatre'.

Like Jonathan Swift, Hamilton based his modest proposal on the structure of a classical oration. Like Swift's, Hamilton's sardonic proposal identifies a problem in need of a solution. Hamilton's problem is the uncertain legitimacy of tragicomedy as a dramatic genre. While constituting a critical burlesque, his chapter nonetheless contributes to drama criticism.[37]

Drama was becoming increasingly important in Hamilton's Annapolis. In early 1748 some local gentlemen staged an amateur dramatic performance, about which nothing else is known. Professional theatre in Annapolis began during the summer of 1752, and the city's first recorded performance of a Shakespeare play occurred on 11 December 1752, when a local acting troupe, the Annapolis Company, performed *Richard III*.[38]

Other members of the Tuesday Club enjoyed reading plays. Robert Morris, for one, had a great sense of humour, as Hamilton's typename for him verifies: Merry Makefun. Given Morris's love of comedy, it is unsurprising to see a copy of Congreve's *Works* in his library. Merry Makefun was not averse to tragedy. He also owned a copy of William Whitehead's *Roman Father*, an adaptation of Corneille's *Horace*. If Morris owned any Shakespeare, his library inventory does not show it. Besides Congreve and Whitehead, it lists two dozen additional plays, which are not inventoried separately.[39]

Hamilton's proposal does contain some history. Describing the flaws in the present system, he offers a historical perspective on the origins of tragicomedy, tracing it back to Plautus's *Amphitryon* but rapidly bringing the story to Gothic times, 'when some bold geniuses, either contemning, or altogether ignorant of the rules of Aristotle, wrote for the stage, and from their exuberant fancies, hammered out, most surprizing theatrical pieces, taken chiefly from Scripture history, where the tragic and comic humor were most ingeniously interwoven'.[40]

As he had in his history of wit and humour, Hamilton celebrates the Gothic times, which brought together many disparate elements to create new combinations blending literature, performance and the oral tradition. Speaking of the authors of tragicomedy during the Gothic times, he says:

> They betook themselves to legends, prophane historians and romance writers, to supply matter for their scenes, and the heroes of both history and romance, vizt: kings, princes, dukes, generals, great captains, and knight errant saints were introduced into their solemn tragical scene, and clowns, fools, shepherds, porters, taylors and coblers, made up the comic list, and these being blended together in one piece, compleated and perfected, that excellent moderen high relished *olla podrida* [literally, putrid pot; figuratively, a mixture of odds and ends] called tragicomedy, in which some of our English dramatic writers, particularly Shakespear, and Beaumont and Fletcher, have shown their great skill.[41]

Once again Hamilton upholds Shakespeare, who recognised what had been created among his predecessors in the Gothic times and perpetuated their dramatic traditions.

Modern tragicomedy, Hamilton suggests, has gone awry by intermingling the tragic and the comic too much: 'Nothing is more common, in our tragicomic performances, than to see a king and a cobler, or any other base mechanic, talk together in blank verse, and even sometimes change characters, the cobler rising to the tip top of the sublime, and his majesty sinking apace to the dialect of Wapping.'[42] He compares modern tragicomedy to a whipped syllabub. The froth at the top of the drink corresponds to the sublime aspect of tragicomedy, which should not mix with the bottom part of the drink.

The two parts do get mixed together in the stomach of the drinker: 'With tragicomedy, our metaphorical syllabub ... has no visible effect on the judgement or intellectual stomachs of common readers and spectators.' But 'critics and connoisseurs' have a more difficult time digesting tragicomedy. The whipped syllabub 'being mishmashed, mingled and swallowed, a strong stomach never feels it, but in the stomachs of the weak and sickly, it is transformed into expanded air, which passes off with noisy eructations above, and often below'.[43] Hamilton understood a truism of scatalogical humour: nothing enhances a fart joke more than highfalutin Latinate diction.

Modern playwrights have gone wrong because their overreliance on Aristotle's rules has led them into error. Clearly, Hamilton had read more on the subject since the *Itinerarium*. Aristotle intended his rules as a set of directions to aid the playwright. Though they could guide a genius, they could not make one. Hamilton compares Aristotle's rules with a kitchen recipe: 'The ingredients of a genius, were necessarily to be furnished by nature, and the rules in this case, were no more, but as a receipt in cookery to teach how to compound these ingredients, so as to make them palatable.'[44]

Indiscriminately applying Aristotle's rules, modern playwrights observe the unities of time, place and action, but their plays are 'so destitute of all other embelishments, or rather strokes of nature, that the representation of them has proved an effectual hypnotic to the audience, and called down the drowsy deity to lull their flagging senses'. Shakespeare, a great genius who paid little regard to the rules of art, followed nature to create enduring works. Shakespeare's plays, Hamilton continues, 'have outlived those of his nicer contemporaries, those also, of the century following, and will surely outlive our finest theatrical performances, that were wrote but yesterday, and probably may be dead and damned tomorrow'.[45]

Later in the *History of the Tuesday Club* Hamilton presents a poem by the club's poet laureate Jonas Green, which incorporates the characteristic humour of its members. After transcribing the poem, Hamilton discusses how some critics had suggested that Green should revise this and other poems further. Hamilton expresses pleasure that Green did not succumb to the critics. Had he taken their suggestions, his poems 'would thereby have suffered, as much in their clubical turn, and humor, as the works of the celebrated Shakespear, suffered in their natural sublime elegance, and beautiful simplicity, by being too much thumbed and beslubbered by the critics in the age next to him'.[46]

Taken together, Hamilton's numerous Shakespeare references in the *History of the Tuesday Club* present a complex and sometimes contradictory picture. Hamilton recognised the rhetorical power a Shakespeare reference could have, but he did not always agree with his poetics. Calling Shakespeare an 'old fashioned fellow' for using blank verse instead of rhyme, Hamilton expresses an opinion he shared with the Restoration playwrights who rewrote Shakespeare to make him rhyme. Whereas Hamilton lists Shakespeare with other figures from the Renaissance and the Enlightenment who sought to impose order, regularity and a sense of decorum on the earthy and exuberant literature of Gothic times, he also recognises that Shakespeare did incorporate jokes and puns and bawdy innuendo characteristic of the earlier age, aspects of Shakespeare's work Pope had sought to expunge. For Hamilton, it is no surprise that Shakespeare excelled at tragicomedy. His natural talent allowed him to combine different styles – high and low – to create great drama.

6

The Colonial American Stage

The second week of June 1752 the *Virginia Gazette*, now edited by William Hunter, announced the arrival of the London Company of Comedians. According to the announcement, one 'Mr Hallam', a London actor-manager, would soon arrive with his acting troupe, bringing both scenery and costumes, 'entirely new, extremely rich, and finished in the highest taste'. Painted in London, the scenery was unexcelled for beauty and elegance. The announcement assured Williamsburg theatre-goers that they would enjoy much the same experience as London theatre-goers enjoyed in terms of the quality of the performances and the timeliness of the productions.[1]

The 'Mr Hallam' mentioned in the announcement was Lewis Hallam, an actor whose roles on the London stage had included Francis in *Henry IV, Part I*, Roderigo in *Othello* and Stanley in *Richard III*. While Lewis led his actors across the Atlantic, his older brother William, the proprietor of a minor London theatre who had organised and financed the acting troupe, would remain in London. William Hallam's role makes him the first backer in the history of the American stage.[2] The word 'first' occurs frequently in the colonial history of American theatre, a story of superlatives.

The London Company of Comedians consisted of twelve actors, not counting the three Hallam children who could be pressed into service in small parts as necessary. Besides managing the theatre, Lewis Hallam would play comic roles and serious old men. Patrick Malone and William Rigby would take turns playing the male leads. On the London stage Lewis's wife Sarah had played Desdemona in *Othello*, Mrs Page in *The Merry Wives of Windsor* and Lady Percy in *Henry IV, Part I*. On the colonial American stage Sarah Hallam would play the female leads, earning herself a lasting reputation as the 'Queen Mother of the American Stage'.[3]

Lewis Hallam's acting troupe left London for Virginia on the *Charming Sally*. After rehearsing aboard the sloop during the voyage, they had several plays ready for performance upon disembarking at Yorktown on 2 June 1752. They proceeded overland to Williamsburg to secure a licence from Governor Robert Dinwiddie and to find a suitable venue. According to Williamsburg resident Dr George Gilmer, an Edinburgh-trained physician who had established a medical practice in town and who also served as apothecary, the governor, following a prevalent stereotype, disliked actors on account of their supposedly loose behaviour. Williamsburg residents were so excited about having a London-quality acting troupe in town that the governor relented and granted the company permission to perform.[4]

With licence in hand, Lewis Hallam purchased a playhouse from Williamsburg tavern keeper Alexander Finnie, which had been built for an earlier touring company. Hallam remodelled the theatre, giving it a pit, boxes, a gallery and a balcony. Trying to make it closely resemble the London theatres, he added a characteristic, but quite hazardous feature: sets of iron spikes to separate the different seating areas. Confident that both the Williamsburg Theatre and the company's first production would be ready soon, he placed an advertisement in the *Virginia Gazette* the third week of August, announcing the title of the first play. On this auspicious occasion – the premiere performance of the London Company of Comedians – they would perform Lord Lansdowne's *Jew of Venice*. To enhance the prestige of the performance, Hallam promoted it as Shakespeare's *Merchant of Venice*.

The 28 August 1752 issue of Hunter's *Virginia Gazette*, which reprints the advertisement for Hallam's production of *The Merchant of Venice*, leads with a contemplative essay, 'A Morning Walk'. Hunter did not name his source, but he extracted 'A Morning Walk' from *Dialogues Concerning Education* by Scottish philosopher David Fordyce. Like many erudite writers of his day, Fordyce dramatised his scholarly material to make it more palatable for general readers. He further enhanced *Dialogues Concerning Education* with reference to Shakespeare. Walking through his fields at the break of day, Fordyce saw the dawn 'imbrown the face of nature, and, as Shakespear has it, dapple the drowsy east with spots of grey'. Fordyce borrowed Shakespeare's words from Don Pedro's cheery good morning speech in the last act of *Much Ado about Nothing*:

> Good morrow, masters. Put your torches out.
> The wolves have preyed, and look, the gentle day,

> Before the wheels of Phoebus, round about
> Dapples the drowsy east with spots of grey.[5]

Though he excerpted the text from Fordyce, Hunter coined an original title for the piece. 'A Morning Walk' applies to a walk through rural Virginia as well as across the Scottish countryside. In *Much Ado about Nothing* Don Pedro's speech appeals to audiences on two levels. One line of the speech provides an erudite classical reference; the next provides a down-to-earth visual description of the dawn landscape. Fordyce omitted the classical allusion to stress the description, emphasising the pastoral over the mythological. Published in the *Virginia Gazette* as Williamsburg was gearing up for the first major Shakespearean performance on the American stage, 'A Morning Walk' reinforces the power of Shakespeare's words as a filter for viewing the world.

* * *

By no means was the Williamsburg production of *The Merchant of Venice* the first time Shakespeare was staged in America. That distinction goes to an amateur production of *Romeo and Juliet* that took place in New York two decades earlier. The sole information about this performance occurs in an announcement in the 23 March 1730 issue of the *New-York Gazette*. Far more than an announcement, the article fills two columns of the newspaper. It is signed 'Joachimus Bertrand', the driving force behind the production. Within the article Bertrand identifies himself as a physician. Mentioning the role he would play in *Romeo and Juliet*, he says, 'The part of the apothecary [will] be perform'd by my self in *propria persona*, which I hope will be kindly taken and look'd upon as a great condescention in a physician.'[6]

Using his name as a clue, one commentator has identified Bertrand as a French settler: slight evidence on which to build an identification. European names were liable to change in America. A Bertrand in New York could have been a Bertram in Berlin. If Bertrand earned a medical degree, he must have left a paper trail. Candidates for medical degrees then were generally required to write dissertations. In 1709 one Samuel Joachimus Bertram earned a medical degree at the University of Jena, writing his dissertation on artesia, that is, the occlusion or closure of a natural channel of the body. A German physician emigrating to British North America would not have been unusual. Thomas Dale, George Gilmer and Alexander Hamilton were not the only graduates from prestigious medical schools in

Europe who emigrated to colonial America, which offered plenty of opportunities for practising physicians.[7]

In those less regulated days, a man did not necessarily need a medical degree to call himself a physician or a surgeon. The surgeon's trade, in the words of Lemuel Gulliver, was simply 'to cure wounds, and hurts in the body got by accident or violence'.[8] If any of Bertrand's patients wrote testimonials to his medical skill, none survived. No testimonials have survived, that is. Joachimus Bertrand is known to history solely because he staged a production of *Romeo and Juliet* in New York in 1730.

Everything that has been written about Bertrand stems from this one article in the *New-York Gazette*. Within it Bertrand tells a two-part anecdote, which he attributes to Dryden, who had supposedly heard it from Shakespeare's grandnephew Charles Hart. There appears little truth to the anecdote. Its pertinence to the practice of medicine explains Bertrand's interest. The anecdote's appearance in his *New-York Gazette* article marks its first known appearance in print.[9]

In the story both the apothecary of the parish and the curate treat Shakespeare cruelly during his boyhood. The apothecary gives young Shakespeare a clyster, as an enema was called back then. Like bloodletting and induced vomiting, this procedure was typically performed as a way to balance the four humours of the body. In the anecdote the apothecary applies the clyster-pipe with such force he almost kills young Shakespeare. Though this story may be apocryphal, it would explain a revolting moment in *Othello*, the time when Cassio lifts his fingers to his lips and Iago compares them to clyster-pipes.[10]

While the apothecary's treatment of young Shakespeare seems incompetent, the curate's treatment of the boy seems downright sadistic. In the second part of Bertrand's anecdote the curate prescribes an opiate for him every Sunday. The results are predictable. Under the medicine's influence Shakespeare falls asleep during the sermon, after which the curate whips him for falling asleep. Despite these weekly whippings, Shakespeare never does break his habit of falling asleep during sermons, which continues into adulthood.

Besides being a theatrical announcement, Bertrand's article also constitutes a critical appreciation. Trying to make his production as appealing as possible, he aligns *Romeo and Juliet* with Augustan tastes, calling Shakespeare a 'judicious author' and stressing the tragedy's moral basis.[11] Bertrand quotes two lengthy passages from *Romeo and Juliet*. The second passage, a twenty-three-line extract from one of Romeo's speeches in the last act, begins: 'O mischief thou art swift / To enter in the thought of desperate men.' After the extract Bertrand observes: 'This scene is one of the most beautiful in all Shakespear's works, it is the *pictura loquens*, which forever preserves both features and colouring, and will last as long as the shop of an apothecary is to be found upon the face of the earth, I hope much longer.'[12]

Bertrand's *Gazette* article is quite skimpy when it comes to production details. Its only concrete details about the production concern the venue: 'But as this tragedy will be the first to be acted at the Revenge Meeting-house, which is fitting up for that purpose, I hereby invite the ladies to be present the first night.'[13] The Revenge Meeting House was an abandoned building in search of new life. When the Rev. John Millington, rector of St Mary's Church at Stoke Newington, died in 1728, he bequeathed his library to the SPG, stipulating that the collection be kept together and sent to the British plantations in America. The SPG decided to send the Millington bequest to New York and asked Governor Montgomerie to have the New York assembly pass an act for the library's preservation.[14]

James Alexander thought the Revenge Meeting House would make a perfect location for the library. He discussed his idea with several of New York's political leaders, all of whom were familiar with the Revenge Meeting House. They agreed the assembly should purchase the building.[15] But the city of New York, not the colony of New York, took responsibility for the Millington bequest and housed the library in City Hall. The Revenge Meeting House remained unoccupied until Joachimus Bertrand turned it into a playhouse. Once the curtain closed on his production of *Romeo and Juliet*, both the Revenge Meeting House and Joachimus Bertrand disappear from history.

Twenty years would pass before another Shakespeare play would be produced on the American stage. The last week of February 1750 a touring company reached New York and advertised its forthcoming performance of *Richard III*. The preceding year actor-manager Walter Murray and actor-playwright Thomas Kean had brought their company from the West Indies to Philadelphia, where it performed for a season. The Murray-Kean Company likely performed some Shakespeare during its time in Philadelphia, but the scanty records do not say so. The only play the company performed in Philadelphia for sure was Addison's *Cato*. Eventually the Quaker-dominated Pennsylvania government blocked the theatre and ran the Murray-Kean Company of Comedians out of town.

The acting troupe reached New York the third week of February 1750. In Nassau Street Murray found a suitable venue he could use as a theatre, and he and his players got to work. Typically acting companies coming to a new town in colonial America had to find a suitable building to turn into a theatre before they could stage a performance. The company announced that it would open the theatre on 5 March 1750 with *Richard III*. As Hallam's company would do in Williamsburg two years later, Murray and Kean used a Shakespeare play to open the theatre. Their production represents the first time *Richard III* would be performed on the American stage.[16]

Their advertisement for the production appealed to New Yorkers on many levels. People who appreciated the Shakespearean tradition would enjoy the Murray-Kean *Richard III*. Those who preferred more modern theatre would also enjoy the production, which was based on Cibber's *Richard III*. History buffs would enjoy watching the play's historical characters come alive on stage, and those who took pleasure in seeing battles and bloodshed depicted would enjoy the play as well. The New York production of *Richard III* would have something for everyone.

Murray and Kean remained in New York into the summer of 1751, when they planned to relocate to Virginia. They enlisted the help of Alexander Finnie, who placed an advertisement in the *Virginia Gazette* notifying its readers that an acting company would soon arrive from New York. Since Williamsburg did not have a proper theatre, Finnie sought subscribers to fund construction. Anyone with a pistole to spare could subscribe. (A pistole was a Spanish coin current in colonial America, which was worth sixteen shillings, ten pence.) Subscribers were entitled to a box seat for the opening night performance.[17]

Like 'A Morning Walk', another article in the *Virginia Gazette*, 'Observations on the Late Performance of *Othello*', reflects the local interest in Shakespeare. A reprint from the London press, 'Observations' shows that Virginia readers remained curious about the London stage and wanted to keep pace with the latest theatrical news. When a special performance of *Othello* appeared at Drury Lane, Virginians were curious to know how it went. They seemed ready for a professional theatre all their own.[18]

Finnie generated enough interest among potential Williamsburg theatre-goers that construction of the new theatre soon began. The last week of September Murray and Kean advertised that they would open the theatre on Monday, 21 October 1751. Finnie's original subscription scheme did not generate enough capital to fund both the theatre's construction and the production of its first play, so Murray and Kean sought more subscribers. The advertisement they placed in the *Virginia Gazette* says they needed funds partly 'to procure proper scenes and dresses'.[19]

This new subscription scheme was successful enough to let the Murray-Kean Company open in Williamsburg on 21 October 1751.

Shakespeare again provided class and cachet. Murray and Kean reprised their production of *Richard III* from New York. Even with Shakespeare's help, the Murray-Kean Company had little success in Williamsburg. A month after opening the theatre, the troupe left town to perform in nearby Norfolk. The following month the players went to Petersburg, Virginia, to perform, after which the company disappeared for several months. By the end of August 1752, it resurfaced as the Annapolis Company and was performing at various locations around the Chesapeake Bay.[20]

Robert Upton, the next important figure in American stage history, came to the colonies at the behest of William Hallam, who sent him in advance to prepare for the arrival of the London Company of Comedians. The first advance man in the history of the American stage, Upton had many responsibilities before the Hallams arrived. He had to obtain permission for the company to perform, erect a suitable building and settle details regarding promotion and publicity. Though the first, Upton hardly deserves any other superlatives as an advance man. Upon his arrival in America, he encountered a splinter group from the Murray-Kean Company or, as Lewis Hallam called them, a 'sett of pretenders'. Upton joined up with them and, again according to Lewis Hallam, 'quite neglected the business he was sent about from England; for we never heard from him after'.[21]

On Saturday night, 26 October 1751, at the First Nassau Street Theatre in New York the Upton Company performed *Othello*. Starring in the title role himself, Upton became the first Othello of the American stage. As an afterpiece the Upton Company performed David Garrick's *Lethe*, marking the American premiere of this farce. Though Shakespeare's greatest eighteenth-century defender, Garrick himself was not a great writer. *Lethe* achieved modest popularity as an afterpiece, but not because of its writing. The London comedian Samuel Foote criticised Garrick's inadequate learning as well as his lack of literary ability. When a friend handed Foote an anonymous French play and suggested that Garrick must have written it, Foote disagreed. He replied, 'First, I am sure it's not Garrick's, because there is Greek in it; secondly, I am sure it is not Garrick's, because there is Latin in it; and thirdly, I am sure it is not Garrick's, because there is English in it.'[22]

Though a slight work, *Lethe* represents another vehicle Garrick used to assert Shakespeare's greatness. Here's its premise: for one day and one day only Aesop would let Charon ferry people across the Styx to Elysium, where they could enjoy the waters of Lethe and forget their troubles. The play presents a series of humorous characters who make the journey. Upon disembarking, Mrs Riot, the play's most memorable character, complains to Aesop that the watermen on the Styx are as rude as those on the Thames. Why, they had seated her, a lady of fashion, with the wives of tradesmen and mechanics!

Grumbling to Aesop, Mrs Riot next wonders about the theatre in Elysium but doubts its taste: 'Your taste here, I suppose, rises no higher than your Shakespears and your Johnsons; oh you goats and vandils! In the name of barbarity take 'em to yourselves, we are tir'd of 'em upon Earth – one goes indeed to a playhouse sometimes, because one does not know how else one can kill one's time – every body goes, because – because – all the world's there.'[23]

The Upton Company repeated its performance of *Othello* and *Lethe* four nights later and again in January 1752. That same month the troupe performed *Richard III*, with Upton in the starring role.[24] Upton's acting abilities have gone unrecorded, but his managerial skills left much to be desired. His troupe lasted less than two months longer. On Wednesday, 4 March 1752, the Upton Company gave its last performance. Upton wrote an epilogue for the occasion to bid farewell to America. He boarded a ship back to England at the end of the week and slipped into oblivion.

* * *

By all accounts the 15 September 1752 Williamsburg performance of *The Merchant of Venice* went well. Patrick Malone played Shylock. Lately the London stage had made the title character more sympathetic, but Malone's performance was reactionary: he played Shylock for laughs. Sarah Hallam was the only woman in the troupe with the *gravitas* to play Portia. Lewis Hallam took the role of Launcelot Gobbo, and their twelve-year-old son Lewis, in his first appearance on any stage, played Portia's servant. Young Lewis made the only notable gaff that evening, a mistake he remembered the rest of his life. While researching the history of the American stage, William Dunlap interviewed him decades later: 'He had one line to speak, apparently an easy task, but when he found himself in presence of the audience he was panic-struck. He stood motionless and speechless, until, bursting into tears, he walked off the stage, making a most inglorious exit.'[25]

The *Virginia Gazette* reported that the play was 'perform'd, before a numerous and polite audience, with great applause'. The *Gazette* also printed the prologue, which John Singleton, the actor who played Gratiano, had written for the occasion. William Rigby, who played Bassanio that night, recited the prologue, letting people know that it would 'celebrate the laurel'd poet's fame'. In terms of content, the prologue is not dissimilar to the history of the stage Hamilton had written as part of his modest proposal in *The History of the Tuesday Club*. Structured as an eighteenth-century progress piece, the prologue retells the history of the stage from ancient Greece to Great Britain and then across the Atlantic to the New World:

> The muse still labour'd to encrease her fame;
> Summon'd her agents quickly to appear,
> Haste, to Virginia's plains, my sons, repair,
> The goddess said. Go confident to find
> An audience sensible, polite and kind.[26]

On Thursday, 9 November 1752, the Hallam Company staged *Othello*, a performance whose significance stems more from the audience than the players that evening. The leaders of the Cherokee nation, their warriors and their wives had recently reached Williamsburg. Governor Dinwiddie welcomed them to town and invited them to attend the theatre. The accounts in the colonial newspapers assert that the Cherokee assumed the stage violence was real.[27] In retrospect the contemporary accounts sound more like racial stereotypes than actual occurrences. Like other Native Americans, the Cherokee had a rich performance culture. It seems unlikely they would confuse acting with reality.

The experience of the Hallam Company in Williamsburg demonstrates that being an actor could be quite dangerous. About 11:00 Friday night, 1 December 1752, three robbers broke into the playhouse and attacked Patrick Malone, who was living there and apparently serving as night watchman. They knocked him down and threw him onto the iron spikes, one of which penetrated his leg. Malone lost a lot of blood and remained dangerously ill long after the attack. The robbers escaped into the night.[28]

According to another eighteenth-century stereotype, actors were always in debt. There's an old chestnut about an actor who asks his manager how to fill up the house for his benefit performance. The manager replies, 'Invite your creditors.' When it came to members of the Hallam Company, there may be some truth behind the stereotype. Dr Gilmer said that the company's Williamsburg run was quite lucrative for Lewis Hallam and his actors, but their extravagant spending put them deep in debt: 'Notwithstanding [that] they take in so much money never were debts worse paid.'[29] Gilmer is not the only source verifying the extravagance of Hallam's players. Some members of the London Company of Comedians became so indebted to Williamsburg bookbinder and shopkeeper John Stretch that Lewis Hallam deeded the playhouse to Stretch and his business partner to cover the actors' debts, using the property as collateral to secure their debts and thus keeping them out of jail and on stage.[30]

In 1753 the London Company of Comedians left Virginia for New York. Lewis Hallam came away with many fond memories. After their departure Hallam grew nostalgic for Williamsburg, where he and his players 'perform'd with universal applause, and met with the greatest encouragement; for which we are bound by the strongest obligations, to acknowledge the many and repeated instances of their spirit and generosity.'[31]

Hallam petitioned New York authorities for a licence to perform, but the city hesitated to grant him one. To help his case he published his petition in the *New York Mercury*. Hallam said that he hardly imagined that in New York, 'a city, to all appearance so polite as this, the muses would be banish'd, the works of the immortal Shakespear, and others the greatest geniuses England ever produc'd, deny'd admittance among them, and the instructive and elegant entertainment of the stage utterly protested against'.[32]

The plea worked, and Hallam obtained the necessary licence. Before he and his players could perform they had to rebuild the Nassau Street Theatre. The company began its New York run in September, but the first recorded Shakespeare performance of the season did not occur until 12 November 1753, when the company staged *Richard III*, with Rigby in the title role, Sarah Hallam as Elizabeth and Lewis Hallam the younger as Prince Edward.[33]

Two months later, in January 1754, the Hallam Company performed *King Lear*, the first known performance of that play in America. Like the contemporary London productions, the Hallams followed Tate's version of the play. Patrick Malone took the title role. Lewis Hallam played Kent, with Sarah Hallam as Cordelia. Their son received more stage experience playing an attendant. Later that month the company staged *Romeo and Juliet*, with Rigby as Romeo to Sarah Hallam's Juliet. Lewis Hallam the younger played Romeo's servant Balthasar.

In February 1755 Lewis Hallam took the London Company of Comedians to Jamaica. Earlier John Moody had enjoyed success on the Kingston stage playing Lear, Hamlet and Romeo. Moody left Jamaica to return to London, but the traditional story that he worked his passage home as a sailor before the mast is apocryphal. Moody joined Garrick's company at Drury Lane, where he would create his first great Irish character, Sir Callaghan O'Brallaghan, in Charles Macklin's

Love à-la-Mode. The core of Moody's troupe remained intact and in Jamaica, now led by David Douglass, an actor whom Moody had recruited from England. Douglass had been planning to return to England to recruit more actors, but with the Hallams' arrival, the two acting companies joined forces. Sadly, Lewis Hallam contracted yellow fever and died in 1756. After a respectful period of mourning, Sarah Hallam, a practical woman, married David Douglass. Their acting troupe, still known as the London Company of Comedians but often simply called the Douglass Company, left Jamaica to return to the mainland colonies in 1758.[34]

By mid-October the troupe had reached New York, where its leader made a crucial error: Douglass invested what little capital the company had to construct a new theatre at Cruger's Wharf before securing a permit to perform. He never imagined that New York authorities would deny him permission. When they did, Douglass found himself in a tough spot. Without permission to perform, he lacked the ability to raise sufficient capital to let him relocate to another town. He applied to the authorities again, hoping they would grant him permission to perform long enough to generate the necessary capital. Barring that, he considered opening a school for acting, a 'histrionic academy' that would let him raise the money.[35]

Some New Yorkers misunderstood Douglass's plan for a histrionic academy, seeing the school as a sneaky way to perform plays in the guise of education. The second week of December he humbly wrote the *New York Mercury* to clarify the misconception: 'All that I proposed to do was, to deliver dissertations on subjects, moral, instructive and entertaining, and to endeavour to qualify such as would favour me with their attendance, to speak in publick with propriety.'[36] Douglass's humble explanation worked: he received permission to perform through the first week of February.

The Douglass Company opened on 28 December at Cruger's Wharf Theatre with a performance of Rowe's *Jane Shore*. Sarah Hallam took the title role, which she had previously played in London. For the first performance of *Jane Shore* at Cruger's Wharf she recited a prologue to counter the local animosity toward the theatre:

Much has been said at this unlucky time
To prove the treading of the stage a crime.
Mistaken zeal, in terms oft not so civil,
Consigns both play and players to the devil.
Yet wise men own, a play well chose may teach
Such useful morals as the parsons preach;

May teach the heart another's grief to know,
And melt the soul in tears of generous woe.[37]

The second week of January the Douglass Company performed *Othello* at Cruger's Wharf. And on 7 February 1759, the day their licence to perform would expire, the players said goodbye to New York with *Richard III*.

That June the company went to Philadelphia and performed *Richard III* at Society Hill Theatre. Owen Morris, who had been with Douglass since Jamaica, was becoming more important to their acting company. For this performance he played Stanley. By now the new Hallam generation was coming into its own. Though boys had played female roles in Shakespeare's day, the roles, at least some of them, became reversed in colonial America. Given the surfeit of male roles in *Richard III*, Nancy Hallam played the Duke of York: the kind of opportunity that would be denied her once she established a reputation as the greatest beauty on the American stage.

Lewis Hallam the younger emerged as the leading actor of the Douglass Company. He had matured considerably since the night he ran off the Williamsburg stage in tears during *The Merchant of Venice*. Alexander Graydon, who often saw him at Philadelphia's Southwark Theatre, said that Hallam was 'a pleasing performer' and 'a thorough master of all the tricks and finesse of his trade' with a manner that was 'both graceful and impressive'. Hallam was 'as much the soul of the Southwark theatre, as ever Garrick was of Drury Lane'.[38]

Douglass brought *Hamlet* to Philadelphia's Society Hill Theatre. When the production opened on 27 July 1759, it marked the first time that play was performed on the American stage. Lewis Hallam the younger played the eponymous hero of Shakespeare's most renowned play, with Douglass in the coveted role of the Ghost. Sarah Hallam Douglass played Gertrude, and Morris took the part of Horatio. The company reprised *Hamlet* in September and, later that month, staged *King Lear*, with John Harman in the title role, Morris as Albany and Hallam as Edgar to his mother's Cordelia.

Since the play titled *King Lear* still meant Tate's *King Lear*, Edgar was Cordelia's love interest. *King Lear* thus represents the first in a series of somewhat creepy performances of two lovers played by mother and son. In October 1759 the Douglass Company staged *Macbeth*: another first for the American stage. Hallam played the title role, with his mother as Lady Macbeth. Nancy Hallam took another male role, playing the part of Fleance, and Morris played Lennox. In

November the Douglass Company staged *Romeo and Juliet*. Lewis Hallam played Romeo to his mother's Juliet.

Poised to become the leading actor on the American stage, Lewis Hallam the younger received a brief challenge to his burgeoning status in late 1759 when John Palmer arrived from London. A decade earlier Garrick had given Palmer his start at Drury Lane. Palmer's roles on the London stage had included Gratiano in *The Merchant of Venice* and Cassio in *Othello*, but he established his overall acting reputation by playing young gallants, dashing military officers and fops that few could top. The roles at which he excelled earned him the sobriquet 'Gentleman John'. Though he was quite personable, some found Gentleman John's acting a little stiff. One contemporary wag said Palmer looked like he had 'swallowed a curtain rod'.[39]

Once Palmer arrived in Philadelphia, he took over the title role for a repeat performance of *Macbeth* at Society Hill Theatre on 1 December 1759. On 21 December the Douglass Company staged *Romeo and Juliet*. Once again Palmer took over the male lead, relegating Hallam to the role of Mercutio. Palmer remained with the Douglass Company when it went to Maryland the following year. At a performance of *Othello* at the New Theatre in Annapolis Douglass took the title role himself. Palmer played Iago, and Hallam was relegated to the role of Cassio. By the end of April Palmer had left the colonies to return to London, much to Hallam's relief.[40]

The Douglass Company continued performing throughout colonial America for another decade, but the pattern of Shakespearean performance this company and earlier ones had established during the 1750s held fast. Colonial American theatre-goers experienced the stage differently from the English. According to one traditional story, an English country gentleman became so emotionally affected by a performance of *King Lear* that he complained to the manager, asking him to stage a comedy instead. Colonial American theatre-goers preferred Shakespeare's tragedies over his comedies. Occasionally Douglass would add a new Shakespearean work to his company's repertoire, but the tragedies continued to dominate. The reputation of Douglass's company improved so much that his players were welcomed in many cities throughout colonial America.

Douglass still felt more comfortable travelling from one city to the next with some insurance, specifically, a letter of recommendation from a prominent colonial authority. John Bernard, a leading comedian on the American stage at the end of the century, befriended both Lewis Hallam the younger and Owen Morris. Bernard's autobiographical writings provide vital information about eighteenth-century

American life. When Philadelphia was the nation's temporary capital, Bernard befriended George Washington, Thomas Jefferson and other national leaders and recorded some of their entertaining and instructive anecdotes for posterity.[41]

Bernard's writings also contain information about the Douglass Company not recorded elsewhere. He wrote that Douglass travelled with a 'character', that is, a letter of recommendation from a colonial governor, much like acting companies in Elizabethan times would carry a passport from a nobleman to avoid being pounced upon as vagrants.[42] In 1761 Douglass had a 'character' from the governor and council of Virginia:

> The company of comedians under the direction of David Douglass has performed in this colony for near a twelvemonth; during which time they have made it their constant practice to behave with prudence and discretion in their private character, and to use their utmost endeavours to give general satisfaction in their public capacity. We have therefore thought proper to recommend them as a company whose behaviour merits the favour of the public and who are capable of entertaining a sensible and polite audience.[43]

Even with such a glowing recommendation, the Douglass Company met resistance in New England, where prejudice against the stage lasted much longer than anywhere else in colonial America. In the 1760s the troupe introduced the theatre to Newport, Rhode Island. The players performed *Othello* at the King's Arms Tavern with Douglass in the title role. The performance was not promoted as *Othello*, however. Instead, it was billed as *Moral Dialogues in Five Parts*, the five parts being the tragedy's five acts. Douglass minimised the dramatic nature of his material to make it more acceptable for a conservative New England audience.

All the information about this performance stems from a copy of a now-lost playbill. Morris saved the playbill long enough to share it with Bernard, who transcribed it for his autobiography. The date of the performance presents the biggest evidentiary problem. In his transcription Bernard records 'Monday, June 10th' as its date without providing a specific year. The text of the playbill has often been reprinted, but it is usually dated either 1761 or 1762. Assuming Bernard's day and date are correct, then *Moral Dialogues* must have been performed in 1765.[44]

The playbill's text makes it easy to see why it has been reprinted so often. It is fascinating. The full title is *Moral Dialogues in Five Parts*

Depicting the Evil Effects of Jealousy, and Other Bad Passions, and Proving that Happiness Can Only Spring from the Portrait of Virtue. The text itself is divided into different entries for each major role. After naming the actor, the playbill provides a brief description of the role and what it taught. Each entry ends with a clever couplet reinforcing the moral lesson. The entry for Morris, who played Brabantio, may be the most revealing:

> *Mr Morris* – will represent an old gentleman, the father of Desdemona, who is not cruel or covetous, but is foolish enough to dislike the sable Moor, his son-in-law, because his face is not white, forgetting that we all spring from one root. Such prejudices are very numerous, and very wrong.
>
> Fathers beware what sense and love ye lack,
>
> 'Tis crime, not colour, makes the being black.

This plea for racial tolerance is astonishing for colonial America. The last section of the playbill announces that the performance will begin at seven that evening and end at 10:30, early enough to let each spectator 'go home at a sober hour, and reflect upon what he has seen before he retires to rest'.[45]

Perhaps nothing better illustrates Douglass's place in early American cultural life than something he did in 1763. That year he renamed his acting troupe the American Company of Comedians. Douglass and his players had become such an important part of American cultural life that the name change was absolutely appropriate. As the American Company of Comedians, Douglass's acting troupe looked forward to the arrival of American independence.

7

John Mercer, Governor Dinwiddie and the *Dinwiddianae*

'John Mercer, Esq; of Virginia': this entry occurs in the list of subscribers appended to the first volume of *The Works of Shakespear*, that is, the eight-volume Dublin edition of the text prepared by William Warburton and based on Pope's edition.[1] Though this detail has previously escaped the attention of those who study colonial book culture, it contributes much to the story of books and reading in early America. It marks the start of what would become one of the most creative uses of Shakespeare in the history of American literature.

Born in Dublin in 1705, John Mercer maintained close ties with his native Ireland after emigrating to Virginia in his teens. He took advantage of opportunities in the New World unavailable in the Old. Mercer acquired a sloop and established a successful import / export business between Virginia and Dublin. He created a comfortable life for himself in Virginia. The year he turned twenty he married Katherine Mason, the sister of his friend and business associate George Mason, who shared his new brother-in-law's passion for Shakespeare. The Mercers settled at Marlborough on the Potomac, where they would build a grand house on a large estate. John taught himself law, established his own practice and became a prominent legal scholar.[2]

Pursuing his professional and scholarly interests, Mercer assembled the greatest law library in colonial Virginia. His legal scholarship culminated in two major works, *A Compleat Collection of the Laws of Maryland* and *An Exact Abridgement of the Laws of Virginia*. As his acquisition of Warburton's Shakespeare reveals, Mercer's bookish interests went far beyond the law. His library excelled in many fields of knowledge. Mercer assembled the greatest library in colonial Virginia after William Byrd.

Mercer was well read in several branches of polite literature. His collection of *belles lettres* included essays, poems, plays and English translations of classical verse. He owned books by nearly all the leading authors of English literature. Shakespeare remained a desideratum until 1747, when Mercer learned that Warburton's Shakespeare would be published in Dublin by subscription. He wrote to his mother back in Ireland to have her place the order.[3]

Warburton's Shakespeare could be found elsewhere in colonial America. In 1754 New York bookseller Garrat Noel advertised the eight-volume edition for sale in the *New York Mercury*. Simultaneously, Noel advertised two other pertinent books: William Dodd's *Beauties of Shakespeare* and Charlotte Lennox's *Shakespeare Illustrated*.[4]

From its initial publication in 1752 through the colonial period, Dodd's *Beauties* would remain among the most popular items of Shakespeareana in early America. Though William Byrd III inherited his father's Shakespeare folio, he added a copy of *Beauties* to the Westover library. This statement is not intended as a criticism. Many early American readers who owned Shakespeare's collected works added Dodd's *Beauties* to their libraries. Robert Carter, to take another Virginian for example, had an eight-volume edition of Shakespeare in his library at Nomini Hall, but he, too, obtained a copy of Dodd's *Beauties*.[5] Whereas Pope had denoted memorable passages within his edition of Shakespeare, Dodd essentially separated the functions of locating memorable passages from reading Shakespeare's plays.

A pioneering effort to identify Shakespeare's sources, Lennox's critical study denigrates Shakespeare by emphasising his reliance on source material for his plots and downplaying his artistry, use of language and psychological insight. Many contemporary readers were offended by *Shakespeare Illustrated*. Garrick, Lennox's most vocal critic, thought she took more delight in exposing Shakespeare's errors than illustrating his beauties. One of Garrick's friends joked that *Shakespeare Illustrated* should be titled *Shakespeare Ill-Treated*.[6] Regardless of contemporary opinion, the presence of Lennox's study in New York indicates that early American readers were getting more curious about Shakespeare's work, so curious that they were going beyond the primary texts to read the secondary literature.

Dr James Napier, the director of the field hospital that Major-General Edward Braddock would establish at the start of the French and Indian War, owned a copy of Warburton's Shakespeare. Not only did Napier enjoy Shakespeare himself, he shared Warburton's edition with others. In fact, Napier loaned so many books from his library that he sometimes forgot who borrowed what. He was disappointed that the person who borrowed the first volume of Warburton's Shakespeare – the volume containing *The Tempest*, *A Midsummer-Night's Dream* and *The Merry Wives of Windsor* – never returned it. Advertising for its return in the *New-York Gazette, or The Weekly Post-Boy*, Napier conveyed his disappointment with the borrower: 'The loss of the volume of Shakespear wou'd spoil the whole sett.'[7]

Napier was not the only doctor in colonial America reading Shakespeare in the 1750s. Dr Bayley Green, a physician in Yorktown, Virginia who owned an excellent medical library, also had a shelf of English literature, which included a multivolume set of Shakespeare's dramatic works. Like Napier, Green apparently lent individual volumes to friends, who hesitated to return them. 'A man lost ten percent on the value, by lending his books,' Benjamin Franklin quipped. Franklin knew one man 'who never returned a borrowed book, because no one ever returned books borrowed from him'. Dr Green's loss percentage was much greater than Franklin's facetious estimate. When Green's estate was inventoried after his death in 1755, it contained only four volumes of an eight-volume set of Shakespeare. Green's inventory shows that the presence of a book title in a colonial inventory represents much more than what one reader read. Friends, neighbours and family members all read favourite books from a person's library. Their reluctance to return borrowed volumes of Shakespeare to Dr Green testifies to the level of enjoyment the plays gave them.[8]

Mercer's passion for books and reading motivated his purchase of Warburton's Shakespeare. In the field of dramatic literature, he owned the collected works of Ben Jonson, Thomas Killigrew and William Wycherley. Warburton's edition was not the only item of Shakespeareana Mercer added to his library. He also acquired the Duke of Buckingham's *Works*, which contains two plays derived from Shakespeare, *The Tragedy of Julius Caesar, Altered* and *The Death of Marcus Brutus*.[9]

Shakespeare became much more to Mercer than simply a source for pleasure reading. Warburton's edition took on the quality of a law book, providing Mercer with precedents to gauge contemporary behaviour. When he ordered the edition in 1747, he scarcely realised he would have cause to put Shakespeare to satirical use, but that is exactly what happened the following decade as he lampooned Governor Robert Dinwiddie for his greed, mismanagement of the French and Indian War and challenge to the local, democratically elected legislature. Mercer's *Dinwiddianae* turns Shakespeare's words, themes and characters into touchstones to interpret the actions and policies of the Virginia governor.

Dinwiddie came to the governorship with considerable administrative experience. Born and educated in Scotland, he attended the University of Glasgow, where he received an excellent education. He subsequently followed the path of many fellow Scots and entered the transatlantic mercantile trade. The British colonies intrigued him so much that he settled in Bermuda, where he became one of the island's leading citizens. Appointed surveyor general of royal customs for the southern district of North America in 1738, Dinwiddie oversaw the Bahamas, Jamaica and the mainland colonies from Pennsylvania southwards.[10]

The position of surveyor general entitled Dinwiddie to join the council of a colony of his choice. He chose Virginia, settling there in 1741. The following decade he became lieutenant governor, taking his oath of office on 21 November 1751. Traditionally, the lieutenant governor or 'deputy viceroy', as Mercer styles him in the *Dinwiddianae*, served as the working governor of Virginia. He was the one who lived in the colony and assumed the day-to-day administrative tasks while the royal governor remained in England collecting a hefty sinecure.

Dinwiddie stirred up controversy during the first six months of his administration. In April 1752 he requested and received approval from the Virginia council to charge a fee of one pistole for each land patent he signed. The fee promised a substantial revenue for the crown but placed a burden on the Virginia colonists, many of whom were busy acquiring lands to the west. The Pistole Fee Controversy, as it became known, sparked a bitter dispute with the House of Burgesses. More than half a century had passed since any Virginia governor had dared to impose a tax on the colonists without securing approval from the colonial legislature. The House of Burgesses declared the pistole fee unlawful and sent Attorney General Peyton Randolph to London to persuade the Board of Trade to strike it down. The Lords of Trade ultimately reached a compromise, upholding the governor's authority to charge the fee but limiting its applicability.[11]

In the *History of Virginia*, a work written in the first third of the nineteenth century but left unpublished until the final third of the twentieth, Edmund Randolph observes, 'It has been stated that Mr John Mercer was the first in Virginia who distinctly elucidated upon paper the principles which justified the opposition to the Stamp Act. He showed them in manuscript to his friends. They spread rapidly so as to produce a groundwork for and uniformity of popular sentiment.'[12]

Though Edmund Randolph confuses the Stamp Act with the Pistole Fee Controversy, his discussion nonetheless forms a crucial piece of evidence verifying Mercer's authorship of the anonymous *Dinwiddianae*.[13] Furthermore, Randolph's confusion reinforces the similarities of the two schemes to generate revenue for the crown. Both concern an issue central to the American Revolution: no taxation without representation. The Virginians objected to the pistole fee because it was imposed by the royal governor, not by their elected representatives in the House of Burgesses. The Pistole Fee Controversy is one of many political issues underlying the *Dinwiddianae*. Like all works of topical humour, the *Dinwiddianae* requires a fair knowledge of contemporary events, so some additional background will help put Mercer's Shakespearean allusions into their political context.

In the mid-eighteenth century the French longed to make the Ohio River – 'La Belle Rivière' – and its rich, fertile land part of French North America. William Smith, the historian of New York, characterised the situation as he pondered the beginnings of the Seven Years' War in *Review of the Military Operations in North America*: 'The French, jealous of the growth of the English colonies, were now meditating all possible arts to distress them, and extend the limits of their own frontier.'[14] In 1754 reports of French incursions into the Ohio valley filtered back to Williamsburg, prompting Dinwiddie to recruit troops to send west to defend British territory against the French and their Native American allies. George Washington, at twenty-two, took command of the Virginia regiment and led the campaign. He and his men left in late March 1754, reaching Will's Creek, Maryland, the following month.

From Will's Creek Washington wrote to Maryland governor Horatio Sharpe to inform him of the situation. The letter, according to biographer Stephen Brumwell, 'includes a dramatic rallying cry worthy of Shakespeare's warrior-king Henry V'. Brumwell had in mind the Once-more-unto-the-breach oration in the third act of *Henry V*. Washington wrote: 'I know you are solicitous for the public weal and warm in this interesting cause – that should rouse from the lethargy we have fallen into, the heroick spirit of every free-born Englishman to assert the rights and privileges of our king (if we don't consult the benefit of ourselves) and rescue from the invasions of a usurping enemy, our majesty's property, his dignity, and lands.'[15]

On 28 May 1754 Washington's forces engaged a French and Indian party led by Joseph Coulon de Villiers, sieur de Jumonville. The British and French exchanged gunfire. Fifteen minutes later Jumonville was dead. Afterwards the French claimed their troops had been on a mission to deliver a peaceful warning. From the British perspective Washington's actions against the French threat were justified. Jumonville's death would have profound implications. Essentially, it sparked the Seven Years' War.

Washington did not let the skirmish with Jumonville stop his campaign. At Great Meadows his men built Fort Necessity. Soon a much larger party of French and Indians under the command of Louis Coulon de Villiers – Jumonville's brother – headed toward the fort hell bent on revenge. Around twelve hundred men strong, the French and Indian party sought dark justice for Jumonville's death.

The Battle of Great Meadows began as the French attacked Fort Necessity on 3 July 1754. The French pinned Washington and his men inside the poorly designed fort. Fierce fighting continued all day to little avail. By nightfall Washington could tell the French had the Anglo-American forces greatly outmanned, outgunned and outmanoeuvred. He prudently surrendered. Though the Battle of Great Meadows was a disappointing loss for Washington, his men were remembered with pride, as the *Dinwiddianae* shows.

The *Dinwiddianae* remained unpublished until Richard Beale Davis prepared a scholarly edition in the twentieth century, but it circulated in manuscript throughout the Chesapeake region during the mid-eighteenth century. A combination of prose and poetry, it mixes humorous dialect letters with satirical verse. As it circulated in manuscript, the collection became known as the *Little Book*. The letters, which begin and end the collection, are dated 1756-1757, so they postdate most of the poems they frame.

The personae of the letters writers – Thomas Browncoat, Titus O'Grewell, Timothy McOates – are variations on the Southern poor white, a character type strongly associated with the literature of the American South from Augustus Baldwin Longstreet to William Faulkner. The *Dinwiddianae* shows that this character type already formed a part of Southern literature in colonial times. A century before Mark Twain, Mercer experimented with the use of mock-illiterate dialect. An example: Titus O'Grewell sent the *Dinwiddianae* to a correspondent with the message: 'I have shent you the littell BOOK maade all of white paper and black ink and tread ... I duzzent know vat is in de book but I supposes dem to be plaaguy mischeefush.'[16]

'The Remonstrance', the second poem in the *Dinwiddianae*, is undated, but topical references place it around the same time as the first poem, which is dated 4 November 1754, that is, during the bleak months after the Battle of Great Meadows. Addressed to Governor Dinwiddie and written in thirty-seven ballad stanzas, 'The Remonstrance' takes the governor to task for his mismanagement of the early days of the French and Indian War, as the American theatre of the Seven Years' War became known. The speaker of the poem critiques Dinwiddie's self-centred administrative decisions and the use of his office to line his pockets. 'The Remonstrance' begins with an indictment of Dinwiddie's inability to recruit competent soldiers to fight the war:

In times to come, you may be blam'd,
For some, by past endeavours,
As when your fighting list you cramm'd,
With shop keepers and shavers.[17]

Virginia had plenty of men ready and willing to fight, Mercer suggests. Instead of recruiting the competent and courageous, Dinwiddie had been recruiting men unsuited to the battlefield, such as shopkeepers and shavers. The term 'shaver' could mean a sharper, a pillager or any other underhanded double-dealer who used unscrupulous methods to get money. Thomas Jefferson typically used the term in a conjoined pair: 'swindlers and shavers'. Another conjoined pair combining the word 'shavers' with a reference to *The Merchant of Venice* formed a proverbial phrase that circulated in early America: 'Shylocks and shavers'.[18]

In the eleventh stanza the speaker of 'The Remonstrance' turns around Dinwiddie's Scotch dialect to accost the governor and castigate him for his ignorance:

You don n'o ken? What, not know them!
Whose valour stands unshaken,
Who on the beauteous rivers stream
Too lately were mistaken.

In his notes to 'The Remonstrance' Mercer explains that the beauteous river is the Ohio and that the men of unshakeable valour are those 'Virginia troops lately defeated at the Meadows'.[19]

These notes are just a few of many that fill the blank spaces of the *Dinwiddianae*. The use of explanatory notes in satirical verse was not unusual for the eighteenth century. Richard Lewis's *Mouse-Trap* provides a good example of an annotated satirical poem from American literature. The best example from British literature is Pope's heavily annotated version of *The Dunciad*, which Mercer knew from the collected edition of Pope's writings at Marlborough.[20] Mercer's legal expertise gave him another model for his explanatory notes. In his edition of the *Dinwiddianae*, Davis converts Mercer's lengthy notes to footnotes, but in the surviving manuscript they appear as marginal glosses. Physically Mercer's notes to the *Dinwiddianae* resemble Edward Coke's notes in *Coke upon Littleton*, a standard law text in which the annotations practically usurp the work they explain.

The eighteenth stanza marks a shift in 'The Remonstrance' in terms of both subject and tone. Whereas the first seventeen stanzas keep the satire moderate and forgiving, a bitter edge surfaces once the speaker of the poem informs the governor that 'The Remonstrance' will not end until 'your noble deeds are shown'.[21] Characterising Dinwiddie's actions as 'noble deeds', the speaker of the poem is being facetious.

The sarcasm continues in the nineteenth stanza:

> Of toils and dangers on the way
> Of hair breadth scapes to sing,
> Themes out of reach of my low lay
> No tribute will I bring.[22]

The phrase 'hair breadth scapes' comes from *Othello*, of course, but its occurrence in the *Dinwiddianae* presents an interpretive problem. Is Mercer's use of this phrase a Shakespearean allusion, or does it simply repeat a phrase that had already entered the vernacular? Similar questions must be asked with every familiar phrase from Shakespeare that occurs in early American literature. To be sure, more people say, 'Something is rotten in Denmark' than know the line comes from *Hamlet*. Since Mercer obtained Warburton's Shakespeare the previous decade and since the *Dinwiddianae* makes several other Shakespearean references, including a direct reference to *Othello*, his use of the phrase 'hair breadth scapes' deserves recognition as a deliberate literary allusion.

Recalling Othello's words, the phrase contrasts the character's life-threatening dangers with Governor Dinwiddie's luxurious travel, which Mercer describes at length in a note:

> From Williamsburg to Winchester is about 220 miles of good road, on which his Honour travelled in his chariot, by short and

> easy stages – thro'out the journey he was gallantly attended, and commodiously, if not luxuriously accomodated – having with him a great variety of liquors, and all kinds of necessarys stowed in a close carriage, drawn by six strong horses – and it's well known to be the universal practise of the Virginians, not only to lodge and entertain travellers, but to show out in the best manner they are able, and according to the quality of their guest.[23]

A reference Mercer makes later in 'The Remonstrance' identifies some consistency between Dinwiddie and another Shakespearean character, Sir John Falstaff. Mercer's use of Falstaff differs greatly from Dr Alexander Hamilton's. Whereas *The History of the Tuesday Club* demonstrates a bemused respect for Falstaff, Mercer selects the character's most loathsome act to comment on an aspect of Governor Dinwiddie's administration. In the thirty-second stanza the speaker of 'The Remonstrance' returns to the theme of recruiting soldiers:

> Whilst public funds, and the Kings press,
> Are wofully misused,
> The roial ear with falsehoods base,
> Is shamefully abused.

In other words, Dinwiddie was misusing public funds and lying to the king and privy council about his activities. Mercer's annotations gloss the reference to *Henry IV, Part I*: 'Sir John Falstaff says, "I have misused the kings press – d[amna]bly" by which I presume is meant the Kings treasure intrusted to the care of that renowned knight for en-listing men for the service.'[24]

In *Henry IV, Part I* Falstaff accepts a bribe from every able-bodied man who can afford one and then fills the ranks of his regiment with men too poor and decrepit to buy their way out. By the time he has finished recruiting soldiers, his regiment looks like he has 'unloaded all the gibbets and pressed the dead bodies'.[25] Mercer's parallel suggests that the English recruitment practices Shakespeare satirised a century and a half earlier persisted in colonial America. As Falstaff breached Hal's trust and embezzled the funds in his care, Dinwiddie has breached the public trust. Mercer's comparison with Falstaff implies that the governor took funds intended for the army and put them to personal use.

After Washington's defeat at the Battle of Great Meadows, the British command dispatched Governor Horatio Sharpe. Having formerly served as lieutenant colonel of foot in the West Indies, Sharpe made a good choice to assume command of Fort Cumberland in western Maryland. Though Washington respected Governor Sharpe, other Virginians questioned his abilities. In one of the preliminary letters to the *Dinwiddianae*, Thomas Browncoat comments, 'I hears Sha[r]p is to rule the roast, over the soljers in these parts, whereof I am very much disgruntled in behalf of the publick; for how shud he know how to mannige matters for us, that has no experience of our countree affairs.'[26] Such complaints would multiply as the American Revolution approached: how could British officers and officials lead the colony without local knowledge?

In February 1755 General Edward Braddock reached America as commander-in-chief of the British forces. Sharpe continued to serve the military, providing Braddock with logistical support. Braddock recognised Washington's military capabilities and asked him to be his aide. Washington accepted the position. Disgruntled by the British reluctance to give colonial officers either the leadership positions or the salaries they deserved, Washington arranged to serve as a volunteer with neither rank nor pay.

In the spring of 1755 Braddock led an expedition to gain control of the forks of the Ohio River. As Braddock and his men neared Fort Duquesne in early July, Washington warned the general that the French fought differently in America than they did in Europe and urged him to attack Indian-style. Though he had recruited Washington as his aide, Braddock ignored his advice, planning to fight in rigid formation, the way the British had fought, and won, in the past. His outspoken aide offered to lead the provincial troops separately, so they could, in Washington's words, 'engage the enemy in their own way'.[27] Braddock met the offer with scorn and, on 9 July 1755, promptly led the British and colonial troops to slaughter.

During the Battle of the Monongahela, as the conflict became known, the French and Indians ambushed the British, killing hundreds of men, including many officers. The casualties overwhelmed Dr Napier and his crack medical staff. Braddock himself was mortally wounded. On 17 July Washington, Napier and the other survivors reached Fort Cumberland. Sharpe returned to the fort to oversee the construction of defences.

Like Mercer, though without his sarcasm, other contemporary writers quoted Shakespeare to interpret the French and Indian War. In *A Review of the Military Operations in North-America*, for example, William Smith uses Shakespeare to relate General Phinneas Lyman's victory against the enemy forces at Lake George. A Connecticut native, Yale graduate and practising lawyer, Lyman had been appointed major-general of the Connecticut forces. He built Fort Edward on the upper waters of the

Hudson river, where he assembled thousands of troops before the arrival of General William Johnson. The British victory was largely due to Lyman's leadership, but, as Smith tells the story, a group of conspirators maliciously accused Lyman of cowardice. Smith explains:

> A notable instance of the amazing latitude to which an invidious spirit is capable of proceeding: so true is the poet's observation,
> Men that make
> Envy and crooked malice nourishment,
> Dare bite the best.
> Shakesp.

Smith does not name the precise source for his quotation, but these words come from a speech Archbishop Cranmer makes in the last act of *Henry VIII* as he defends himself against the malice of Gardiner, Bishop of Winchester.[28]

'Dialogue', the next poem in the *Dinwiddianae*, resumes the story of Dinwiddie's tenure as governor of Virginia during the French and Indian War. The poem's full title is: 'Dialogue between the Deputy Viceroy of Xxxx and His First Minister, upon the 8th Day of November, 1755, It Being the Memorable Day of the Dissolution of the General Assembly: To which Are Added the Notes and Observations of Benjamin Browncoat AM.'

This lengthy title practically requires its own set of notes. A kinsman to Thomas Browncoat, one of the barely literate letter writers in the *Dinwiddianae*, Benjamin Browncoat is another fictional persona. With a graduate degree, Benjamin can lay claim to a better education than Thomas, but Mercer's reference to Benjamin's master's degree reinforces the facetious nature of his notes. The self-taught Mercer turned formal university studies into another satirical target. Dated 8 November 1755, the day Governor Dinwiddie prorogued the assembly, the poem itself contains information after that date, most importantly the appointment of John Campbell, the fourth Earl of Loudon, who accepted the position of commander-in-chief of the British and colonial forces in North America to replace General Braddock in January 1756.

The cowardly 'Robin', as Mercer calls Robert Dinwiddie in 'Dialogue', is happy to let others fight the war, especially since he is unwilling to put his head near enough to battle 'to have it scrap'd, or taken off'. He says:

> Let Louden with his fighting pack,
> Whose souls delight in thwack and thwack;

Dispute the cause with gun and blade.
Their trade is war – I'm for sheer trade.[29]

Loudon did not reach America until July. In *North America: A Descriptive Poem*, a book written to celebrate his arrival, William Donaldson pays homage to the new commander. Donaldson's twenty-sixth stanza ends with the line, 'The current serves, – and Campbell's at the helm.'[30] Like Mercer, Donaldson supplies explanatory notes to gloss otherwise cryptic lines of verse. The line 'The current serves' is shorthand for a famous passage from Shakespeare that depicts the affairs of men using the tide as a metaphor. Donaldson quotes the passage in his notes. Given the numerous times they occur in early American literature, these lines are worth quoting here:

There is a tide in the affairs of men,
Which taken at the flood, leads on to fortune;
Omitted all the voyage of their life
Is bound in shallows and in miseries,
On such a full sea are we now afloat,
And we must take the current when it serves,
Or lose our ventures.

Donaldson ascribes this passage to Shakespeare but otherwise says nothing about their precise source. They come from something Brutus tells Cassius in the fourth act of *Julius Caesar*, which embodies the traditional belief that opportunities missed are opportunities lost.[31]

Sanders, the 'first minister' mentioned in the long title of 'Dialogue', questions Robin's policy of commissioning justices, which differs from the way previous Virginia governors had appointed them. Benjamin Browncoat explains that the government formerly sought able gentlemen to serve king and country, commissioning them as justices of the peace and allowing them the freedom to serve as long as they wished. This course of action gave them 'a security which reflected honour upon their stations and which embolden'd them to behave with proper resolution, in their office, which is attended with a certain expense and trouble without the least prospect of gain'.[32]

Under Governor Dinwiddie, Browncoat continues, the commissions for justices of the peace were purged. Each justice was asked to qualify for the commission or refuse: an ultimatum that damaged the body politic. Developing his metaphor, Browncoat applies the traditional medical concept of the four humours. Dinwiddie's actions hurt the body politic because they 'discharged many of its salubrious juices, and retain[ed] a vast load of peccant humors, which cannot regularly pass unless either by stool or vomit'.[33]

Providence has not entirely deserted Virginia, Browncoat says. Many men continued to fill the position of justice of the peace 'with the highest honour – notwithstanding those foibles (to borrow the phrase of a matchless writer) are unshunable like death, and even fated to us, as we do quicken – Shakespeare confines his observations to a particular misfortune – here it's applyed to human infirmitys'.[34]

Browncoat alludes to something Othello says. The phrase 'particular misfortune' refers to Desdemona's supposed betrayal. In the third act Othello tells Iago:

> Yet, 'tis the plague of great ones;
> Prerogatived are they less than the base;
> 'Tis destiny unshunnable, like death:
> Even then this forked plague is fated to us
> When we do quicken.[35]

Othello pities himself, believing his greatness condemns him to dire misfortune, which those who fall short of greatness can avoid. Browncoat democratises what Othello says. It is not only the great who must face unshunnable destiny: all humanity must confront misfortune.

Other colonial Virginia poets found *Othello* a useful touchstone. Robert Bolling, the finest poet in the colony, quotes something Lodovico says as he bids Iago to look upon the murdered Desdemona:

> O Spartan dog,
> More fell than hunger, anguish, or the sea:
> Look:
> This is thy work, the object poisons sight.

This quotation from *Othello* forms an epithet to 'A Prayer', a poem of personal vituperation in which Bolling attacks James Johnson, a confidant and advisor of the father of the young woman Bolling was wooing but not winning.[36] Whereas Mercer creates an ironic contrast between Othello and the target of his satire, Bolling quotes *Othello* to reinforce the similarity between Iago and the target of his poetical attack.

Justifying his actions to Sanders in 'Dialogue', Robin compares himself to Governor Sharp, who spent his time 'with danger and fatigue' seeking 'unprofitable glory'. Horatio Sharp, Robin observes, resembles 'his namesake in the play'.[37] The play Robin means is *Hamlet*. Browncoat supplies the following gloss: 'The intelligent reader will be at no loss in applying this to the present governor of Maryland – nor in discovering that the sentiment refers to those beautiful remarks of Hamlet upon Horatio in the first scene of [the] third act – Horatio, thou art e'en as just a man etc.'[38]

The quoted line signals Hamlet's ensuing monologue, represented by Browncoat's *et cetera*. In the monologue Hamlet praises the type of person Horatio represents, someone who is 'not a pipe for Fortune's finger'. Before finishing his encomium, Hamlet exclaims: 'Give me that man / That is not passion's slave and I will wear him / In my heart's core – ay, in my heart of heart – / As I do thee.'[39] Recalling these 'beautiful remarks' in his annotation, Browncoat gives Robin too much credit. Hamlet admires Horatio's refusal to let fate and passion guide his behaviour; Robin thinks Sharp a fool for risking his life when he could stay safe and make money instead.

'Address to the Colony' is the short title for another poem in the *Dinwiddianae*. Its long title is 'The Little Booke Addressed to the Colony 1756 by the Author of the *Dinwiddianae* with Notes by the Publisher'. Ascribing the notes to a separate identity, Mercer builds two different voices into 'Address to the Colony'. Like Benjamin Browncoat, the 'Publisher' is another persona Mercer assumes.

Describing the present state of Virginia, the speaker of the poem asks a rhetorical question in one line: 'Are citys, traffick, science wanting?' He answers the question in the next: 'Fate of wretches doomed to planting!'[40] This answer does not necessarily capture the speaker's view. Rather, it encapsulates an opinion that some narrow-minded Virginians held. They believed that the demands of their plantations prevented them from developing great cities or pursuing the arts and sciences.

The word 'planting' calls forth a lengthy note from 'Publisher'. Though Mercer never intended the *Dinwiddianae* for publication, by attributing his notes to the publisher he could write them as if they were directed to a London readership that knew little about life in Virginia. The lengthy note establishes a contrast between 'He' and 'You', 'He' being a generalised planter and 'You' being a collective identity for those who, like the speaker of the poem, wish to improve and advance the colony. Thinking Virginia is already too crowded, 'He' rejoices upon seeing 'ev'ry cruel method of depopulating succeed'. Alternatively, 'You' argues 'that the riches and strength of all places, rise in proportion to the well regulated numbers of free people'. 'He' remains unconvinced, asserting that an increase in the population of Virginia would be

> ...detrimental to the breeding of swine, which he wisely prefers to ev'ry other consideration. Like honest Launcelot in the play, whose passions are perfectly at rest, but in one instance, the conversion of a Jew – at which Launcelot seems much disturbed, terrifying himself with dreadful apprehension, 'that this makeing of Christians will raise the price of hogs, and that we shall not have shortly, a rasher on the coals for money'.[41]

In *The Merchant of Venice* Launcelot Gobbo says these words to Shylock's daughter Jessica when she mentions her plans to convert to Christianity. Once again Mercer takes precedent from Shakespeare, underscoring the absurdity of the planter's argument by comparing it with something the buffoonish character says in *The Merchant of Venice.*

Bringing 'Address to the Colony' to a close, the speaker of the poem shifts from comedy to tragedy, borrowing words of advice Polonius gives Laertes in *Hamlet*: 'Untread the path you've been pursuing / In whatso'ere you mean to do, / 'Bove all – to thine own self be true.'[42] 'Address to the Colony' demonstrates how Polonius's advice had taken on the quality of conduct literature in eighteenth-century America. It is not the only example. Around this same time William Smith, not the historian of New York but the educator of Philadelphia, quoted Polonius's speech at length. In a commencement address to the graduating students of the College of Philadelphia, Provost Smith quotes Polonius as he brings his address to a close, modifying the speech to suit the graduating students. Smith interrupts the quotation to interject two paragraphs of his own advice and then dismisses his audience by quoting Polonius's next line: 'Farewel! my blessing season these things in you.'[43]

Whereas Provost Smith uses Polonius's words to end his commencement address with calm and equanimity, the speaker of Mercer's 'Address to the Colony' reaches such a high level of pique he must cut himself short. Smith identifies with Polonius; Mercer's speaker identifies with Hamlet. Though the preceding notes to the poem are ascribed to 'Publisher', the final note occurs in the speaker's voice. He draws a parallel between himself and Shakespeare's hero: 'I must leave off or grow mad, or which is much the same poetical and exclaim with Hamlet "The time is out of joint, O cursed spight / That I was ever born, to set it right."'[44]

After 'Advice to the Colony' the *Dinwiddianae* contains only one more poem, 'Ad Virginia Dolentum', which is dated 30 April 1757. Two weeks earlier, Governor Dinwiddie had informed the House of Burgesses that he would be returning to Britain for health reasons. With the object of his satire gone, Mercer had neither the need nor the desire to continue writing witty satirical verse.

Shakespeare pervades the *Dinwiddianae*. Though Mercer drew upon his reading of Warburton's Shakespeare for his references, the plays he cites are consistent with those being performed on the colonial American stage. The tragedies are foremost, with the histories and comedies represented by one play each. But Mercer's use of Shakespeare is complex and varied. The greatness of Othello provides an ironic contrast to Dinwiddie. The character of Falstaff, on the other hand, provides another parallel with Dinwiddie, at least in terms of Falstaff's least attractive aspect, the embezzlement of funds intended for recruiting armed forces. Horatio Sharp in the *Dinwiddianae* recalls his namesake in *Hamlet* in terms of courage, stoicism and equanimity. Throughout the *Dinwiddianae* the strongest identification with a Shakespearean character occurs between the author of the *Little Book* and Hamlet. Both see themselves as men alone in the world faced with the responsibility of righting wrongs no matter the personal consequences.

But Mercer himself was not alone, at least not in terms of his use of Shakespeare to illustrate the conflicts that colonial Americans faced during the French and Indian War. Other authors similarly quoted Shakespeare. Though the conflict effectively began with Jumonville's death in 1754, Great Britain did not declare war on France until 1756. When news of the declaration reached America, it inspired Samuel Davies to write a new instalment of his anonymous essay series, the 'Virginia Centinel'. Leo Lemay, who first identified Davies as the author of the 'Virginia Centinel', has observed that the essays reflect many of the same themes as Mercer's *Dinwiddianae*.[45]

Davies had previously criticised the degeneracy of modern tastes, complaining that 'plays and romances [are] more read than the history of the blessed Jesus.'[46] But the 'Virginia Centinel' shows that Davies read plays himself and knew Shakespeare's work quite well. Announcing the declaration of war in 'Virginia Centinel, No. 9', Davies encouraged readers to do what they could for the war effort. The essay concludes with a ten-line passage from King Henry V's Once-more-unto-the-breach oration. Davies presents a carefully edited version of the speech, omitting the first two lines, quoting lines 3-9 and then skipping to lines 15-17:

In peace, there's nothing so becomes a man
As modest stillness and humility:
But when the blast of war blows in our ears,
Then imitate the action of the tyger;
Stiffen the sinews, summon up the blood,
Disguise fair nature with hard-favour'd rage;
Now lend the eye a terrible aspect —
Now set the teeth, and stretch the nostrils wide;
Hold hard the breath, and bend up every spirit
To his full height. Now on, you noblest English etc.[47]

Davies's use of *et cetera* to end his quotation would become a fairly common practice among early American writers quoting Shakespeare. Using *et cetera*, authors essentially told their readers, 'You all know the rest of this quotation. I don't need to repeat any more.'

Davies quotes Shakespeare again in his next number. 'Virginia Centinel, No. 10' is best known for its scathing denunciation of the Virginia regiment and, implicitly, its young leader, Colonel George Washington. Davies punctuates his denunciation with a couplet from something the Duke of York says to the Duke of Somerset in *Henry VI, Part II*: 'Shew me one scar character'd on their skin, / Men's flesh preserv'd so whole but seldom win.'[48]

After this quotation Davies presents some historical examples to show how luxury has deprived armies of their courage and manly strength. Once this essay appeared in the 3 September 1756 issue of Hunter's *Virginia Gazette*, the officers of the Virginia regiment, then stationed at Fort Cumberland, wrote to their commanding officer to demand satisfaction for these baseless aspersions or else they would resign en masse. The officers assumed that Dinwiddie had sanctioned the essay: sensitive comments in the *Gazette* generally required the governor's approval.[49] As Robin says in 'Dialogue':

I hae the press, under my thumb,
To spak my pleasure, or be dumb,
So that nathing can be printed,
Until it hath by me been minted.[50]

Robin, like any tyrant, celebrates his ability to control the press and give the public whatever information he wishes regardless of its truth.

The real-life Dinwiddie was never so reckless. He reassured the troops of his confidence and arranged for Richard Bland, a well respected Virginia legislator, to write an essay for the *Gazette* complimenting the regiment.[51]

Though the *Dinwiddianae* and the 'Virginia Centinel' are topical works, reference to Shakespeare let both Mercer and Davies generalise from local experience to show that what was happening in colonial Virginia reflected universal human experiences, experiences Shakespeare had dramatised a century and a half earlier. The particular plays that each author used reveal how their application of Shakespeare differed.

Mercer had a collected edition of Shakespeare to draw from, but he stuck to some of the most well known Shakespearean plays in colonial America: the tragedies plus *The Merchant of Venice* and *Henry IV, Part I*. Davies, alternatively, cited Shakespeare's texts almost as historical works. He draws upon two particular history plays, *Henry V* and *Henry VI, Part II*, which gave him pertinent examples to support his arguments. Regardless which plays they quoted, both Mercer and Davies demonstrated the power and relevance of Shakespeare's words to interpret and understand what was happening in colonial America during the French and Indian War.

8

The Labyrinth of Mental Nature: Reading Shakespeare, Becoming John Adams

When Louis-Joseph de Montcalm, the commander-in-chief of the French forces in North America, laid siege to Fort William Henry, a British fort at the southern tip of Lake George, in August 1757, the British commander and his officers began dispatching urgent messages to colonial governors imploring them to send more troops and armament. Colonel John Chandler sent so many express dispatches he was having trouble finding men to carry more. Learning about his friend's plight, John Adams, then reading law in Worcester, Massachusetts, told Chandler that he had been leading the sedentary life of a law student for so long his health had begun to suffer. Speaking in an offhand manner, Adams said he wouldn't mind getting back in the saddle for a few days. Though Adams did not realise it at the moment, Chandler understood that he was volunteering to deliver some military dispatches.

At daybreak the morning after their discussion Chandler showed up at Adams's chamber door with dispatches for Rhode Island governor William Greene and a horse saddled and ready to ride. Though Adams had seldom ridden recently, he accepted his role as messenger, packed a bag and hopped on the saddle, trusting himself to the horse. John Adams was off on the road to Rhode Island.

Providence frequently puts a large potato in a little pig's way, according to an eighteenth-century saying, but Providence – the one in Rhode Island – had nothing to offer John Adams. Upon reaching the city, he learned that Governor Greene was not there. He was with the general assembly at Newport. Adams put Providence behind him and headed toward Newport. The road took him through Narragansett Woods, where he met two gentlemen riding the opposite way. He asked if they knew whether Greene was still in Newport. One gentleman told him the governor had left Newport, which he could say with certainty because the gentleman next to him was the governor. Adams presented the dispatches to Greene, who opened them on the spot. The governor asked Adams many questions but had no reply for Chandler. Their business concluded, they soon parted ways.

Adams proceeded to Newport before continuing to Bristol. His overall route gave him an excellent view of the colony, which let him break free from the stereotypes associated with Rhode Island. Passing through Bristol, he could tell that, contrary to popular belief, the city was remarkable for much more than its women and its geese. Riding through Rhode Island on a Sunday, Adams was surprised to see so many people out and about. Baptists dominated the colony, and Adams discovered that their Sabbath Day customs differed from those in Puritan Massachusetts. He found a Rhode Island Sunday 'much more gay and social than our Sundays in Massachusetts'. Adams stopped at several roadside inns during this four-day ride. In his autobiography he recalls, 'At the inns as usual there were scenes and characters, for the amusement of Swift or even Shakespeare.'[1]

Recognising similarities between the settings and characters of Shakespeare's plays and the scenes and people within the taprooms of Rhode Island, Adams revealed his knowledge of Shakespearean drama, which differed from that of many contemporaries, who mainly knew the tragedies. Adams obviously enjoyed Shakespeare's ability to recreate the loud and rowdy denizens of roadside taverns: an indication that he appreciated Shakespeare's comedies as well as the histories and tragedies. Despite its breadth, Adams's knowledge of Shakespeare still remained spotty before his mission to Rhode Island.

John Adams was born in Braintree (now Quincy) Massachusetts, on 19 October 1735. Both his parents loved books, and they taught John to read at an early age. Reading became a lifelong passion for him. He entered Harvard in 1751 when he was fifteen. The college library still had its set of Rowe's Shakespeare, which Adams could have read, but there is no proof he did. He kept a commonplace book at Harvard to record memorable passages from his reading, but nowhere does the surviving manuscript volume cite Rowe's Shakespeare. It does contain one undated Shakespearean quotation, which Adams may have transcribed at Harvard or shortly after he graduated in 1755. But that quotation does not come directly from Shakespeare. It comes from Cibber's altered version of *Richard III*.[2]

Upon completing his legal studies with Putnam in 1758, Adams, now twenty-three, moved back to Braintree. That November Jeremiah Gridley and Oxenbridge Thacher presented him to the Boston bar, and Adams was sworn in as an attorney. He continued deepening his legal study even after he opened his practice. Adams understood that the proper study of the law involved far more than legal theory and case reports. It encompassed practically every field of knowledge. He sought to make himself a well-rounded scholar. Adams was quite unlike the lawyer who brought a copy of *Coke upon Littleton* to the theatre to read during a performance of *Macbeth*. The play only caught the lawyer's attention when Macbeth asked the witches what they were going to do, and they answered, 'A deed without a name'. Hearing these words, the lawyer looked up from his book and exclaimed, 'A deed without a name! Why, 'tis void.'

At the start of what Adams correctly foresaw as a distinguished legal career, he thought much about the meaning of fame. Into a miscellaneous notebook he wrote, 'Contemptu famae, contemni virtutem'. He followed this Latin tag with a translation of his own: 'A contempt of fame generally begets or accompanies a contempt of virtue.' Neither Adams nor his modern editors identify his source, but these words come from an episode in Tacitus's *Annals*, an ancient Roman classic that significantly influenced Revolutionary American thinkers, setting down many of the basic principles of political liberty. Criticised for his plan to erect a temple to honour his mother and himself, the emperor Tiberius bows to public pressure and repudiates the temple. In his speech Tiberius courts the people's favour by professing his contempt for fame. His behaviour prompts Tacitus to remark that holding fame in contempt also means condemning merit.[3]

Recalling further literary expressions of fame and ambition, Adams mentioned an episode from *Othello*. As Cassio fears he has ruined his reputation by drinking too much, Iago tells him: 'Reputation is an idle and most false imposition, oft got without merit and lost without deserving. You have lost no reputation at all, unless you repute yourself such a loser.' The cynical attitude toward reputation suits Iago. Adams observed, 'I believe persons of his character, are most inclined to feel and express such an indifference about fame.'[4] Adams eschewed Iago's cynicism, believing that fame could be something positive when coupled with virtue.

After passing judgment on Iago, Adams recalled another Shakespearean character, Richard III. He observed, 'Crooked Richard says all men alike to some loved vice incline, Great men choose greater sins – Ambitions mine!'[5] Richard's words gave Adams another negative aspect of ambition, as if it must always be coupled with sin. In this instance, Adams was recalling Cibber, not Shakespeare. Having read his version of *Richard III* earlier, Adams remembered it well. His conflation of Shakespeare and Cibber provides another example of how original texts and altered versions bled into one another during the eighteenth century.

Adams did not leave his Cibber quotation hanging. Instead, he interpreted what Richard III says and linked him with Iago and Tiberius. Though Adams saw nothing wrong with people following their ambitions and achieving fame, he did find fault when ambition was used to justify morally reprehensible behaviour. After quoting 'Crooked Richard', Adams observed, 'Some such reflections and excuses, I suppose, the worst men always make to justify, or palliate to them selves and others, their own worst actions. Making such a reflection is throwing conscience a bone to pick.'[6]

The letters Adams drafted upon returning to Braintree reveal much about his attention to the law once his formal studies had ended. In October and November 1758 he wrote 'Letters to Three Friends on Studying Law'. He told the first friend that he had left the schoolroom for 'the cell of a hermit', where 'old Roman lawyers and Dutch commentators are my constant companions'. Casting legal commentators as companions, Adams revealed his personal tendency to see favourite writers as close friends. He would treat Shakespeare similarly. Ending the letter to the first friend, Adams acknowledged that legal study should go far beyond law books. It should encompass 'the whole circle of science and literature, the history, wisdom, and virtue of all ages'.[7]

Adams told the second friend that the old cliché about the boring nature of the law was nonsense: 'The common place cant of the present day that the study of law is the most dry, unentertaining study in the world ... I take to be full as wise as Lady [Riot]'s contempt of Shakespears tragedies in the *Lethe* of Mr Garrick.'[8] Adams's awareness of Garrick's farce reveals his extensive knowledge of modern English drama. Professional theatre had yet to reach Massachusetts when he wrote these words. His knowledge of Garrick's *Lethe* suggests that Adams read in his study what he could not see on stage. That he remembered Mrs Riot's contempt shows that Adams kept an ear out for Shakespearean references, no matter how obscure. He would follow this impulse throughout his life.

To the third friend Adams made another Shakespearean reference. He expressed regret that they had both ignored their mutual promise to stay in touch and compared their neglect to 'the vows of perpetual constancy made by a young fellow, when in the most violent hurry'. Adams recalled the advice Polonius gives Ophelia after Hamlet has sworn his love to her. Ophelia says that Hamlet's intentions were honourable, but her cynical father disabuses her of that notion. He cautions her against the promises that any young man makes in the heat of passion:

> I do know
> When the blood burns, how prodigal the soul
> Lends the tongue vows. These blazes oh my daughter
> Giving more light than heat, extinct in both,
> You must not take for fire.[9]

Within the context of the play Polonius's advice to his daughter functions similarly to Claudius's advice to Hamlet. Though seemingly well intended, both promote selfish ends in the guise of conduct advice.

Quoting Polonius, Adams appears less interested in understanding how the speech functions in *Hamlet* than using it as a clever comparison. But Adams's use of the speech does more: it goes to the heart of what stirs our passions, which is not limited to the love of another. Adams parallels emotional and physical love with intellectual endeavour. His words form an endearing testament to the passion that scholarship can create for the true lover of learning:

> The soul is no less prodigal in lending the tongue vows, when the blood glows with ambition of getting learning or virtue, than when it burns with a very different passion, the passion alluded to in these lines. And perhaps the protestations of the lover, are as sincere as the resolutions of the scholar. And as the generous lover, who by such vows, has deceived and deflowered an innocent, virtuous lady, would think him self bound in honour, and in conscience, to fulfil his promises, so should the generous schollar esteem it a violation of his conscience, a base, ungenerous, debauching and ruining of himself, to forget his vows of industry.[10]

These words demonstrate in miniature how far Adams could go, rhetorically speaking, when he started from Shakespeare. Polonius's speech fired his imagination, letting him apply a dramatic plot about a shameful rake who seduces a young woman to bring alive the scholar's promise to work hard in the pursuit of knowledge. Written to amuse his third friend, Adams's words appeal to any and all scholars dedicated to learning.

Polonius's lines also let Adams resume his reflection on an idea that runs throughout Shakespeare's tragedies: ambition. Though 'Letters to Three Friends' mainly discusses the love of learning, Adams did sneak virtue into the discussion. An ambitious drive toward learning or virtue works like love. It gets the blood boiling and motivates people to pursue their passion for knowledge or virtue or, ideally, both.

The cumbersome title modern editors have assigned the next section of Adams's manuscript notebook reflects its miscellaneous quality: 'A Letter to Richard Cranch about Orlinda, A Letter on Employing One's Mind, and Reflections on Procrastination, Genius, Moving the Passions, Cicero as Orator, Milton's Style, etc.' Written in late 1758, these notes begin with a set of questions that seek to define wisdom: 'What is wisdom? Is it, to write dramatic poetry, like Milton or Shakespear? Is it to write on astronomy and physicks like Newton, or is it to know the human mind like Lock? Does it consist in genius and learning?' After asking these yes-or-no questions as he grapples with the meaning of wisdom, Adams answered them in the negative: 'No[.] Genius and learning have been oftener mad than wise. It is not to act or think beyond man kind.'[11]

Adams's questions divide knowledge into three categories: poetry, science and philosophy. Grouping Shakespeare and Milton together as examples of great poets, he took a conventional attitude. Eighteenth-century American readers generally considered Shakespeare and Milton the two finest poets in the history of English literature. Adams borrowed from a more recent poet to craft his definition of wisdom. He yoinked a line from Pope's *Essay on Man*: 'The bliss of man (could pride that blessing find) / Is not to act or think beyond mankind.'[12]

Though Pope had the answer to his questions, Adams was not done pondering the subject of poetical genius. In the letter to an unidentified correspondent that forms part of this set of miscellaneous notes, he returns to the subject. A poetical genius, Adams wrote, is someone with 'a faculty of feigning and combining into one regular, correct, consistent plan or story, a great number and variety of characters, actions, events etc.' The greatest poets are those with the greatest variety, consistency and number of characters, actions and events. A great poet also connects the various aspects of a work into a whole. Emphasising character and plot in his definition of poetical genius, Adams excluded lyric poets. His definition makes epic poets and dramatists the greatest poets. Once again, Shakespeare and Milton suit Adams's poetic ideal.[13]

When he reached the subject of moving the passions, Adams contrasted orators with dramatists. Whereas orators articulate their own passions to inflame their listeners, dramatists use their characters to elevate the passions of their audience. To prove his point he quoted an eleven-line excerpt from Othello's eloquent farewell to the life he had known. Aware that Desdemona's love is inextricably linked to his life as a soldier, the apparent loss of her love represents the end of his occupation as a warrior-hero. Othello's elegy to lost love takes the form of a valediction to the soldier's life.[14] Adams begins his quotation partway into the third line of Othello's speech:

> Oh now forever
> Farewell the tranquil mind! farewell content;
> Farewell the ploomed troops and the big war
> That make ambition virtue! Oh! farewell!

Othello's speech supports Adams's argument that Shakespeare could use 'the utmost grandeur of sounds' to convey 'deep grief, misery, and despair'.[15]

Besides demonstrating the sonorous manner with which Shakespeare let his great characters express grief, Othello's speech extends the twin theme of ambition and virtue. Whereas Richard III uses his ambition to justify all sorts of horrific behaviour, ambition itself, Adams reflected, does not have to be negative. According to Othello, war could turn ambition into a virtue. Ventidius, one of Antony's leading officers, says much the same in *Antony and Cleopatra* when he calls ambition the 'soldier's virtue'. Once Othello says farewell to war, however, he loses his psychological release. No longer can he vent his jealousy-fuelled ambition. Adams, who suffered from jealousy-fuelled ambition himself, would channel his to the public good.

To fulfil his own ambitions Adams first had to deepen his knowledge of many fields of study. His miscellaneous notebook shows him trying to stay focused. As he pursued diverse areas of intellectual interest, he sometimes had trouble encompassing them all. He admitted to an unknown correspondent: 'I have so many irons in the fire, that every one burns. – I have common, civil, natural law, poetry, oratory, in Greek, Latin, French, English to study, so that when I set down to read or think, so many subjects rush into my mind that I know not which to chuse.' He never would quench his thirst for knowledge. Decades later Adams would observe, 'The more one reads the more one sees we have to read.'[16]

The references in Adams's earliest diary reveal how he used Shakespeare to understand the world around him. He spent one evening in December 1758 with a drink-addled Braintree neighbour named Ben Veasey, who railed against lightning rods all night. Veasey's complaints were not unusual in themselves. Lightning was God's messenger, people believed. Thunder and lightning were both traditional signs of God's anger. Given this belief, some thought that the Franklinian lightning rod sought to subvert divine justice. The Rev. Thomas Prince facetiously called the inventor of lightning rods 'the sagacious Mr Franklin', cautioning people that they could not, should not, would not save themselves from divine wrath simply by fixing pointy metal rods to their homes. Prince exclaimed, 'Oh! there is no getting out of the mighty hand of God!' This exclamation caught on, becoming a popular saying in Massachusetts, as a bemused Adams noted.[17]

To capture his neighbour's behaviour Adams compared Veasey with Shakespeare's greatest tragic hero: 'His brains were in a ferment with strong liquor and he railed, and foamed against those points and the presumption that erected them, in language taken partly from Scripture and partly from the drunken disputes of tavern philosophy, in as wild mad a manner as King Lear raves, against his daughters disobedience and ingratitude, and against the meanness of the storm in joining with his daughter against him in Shakespears *Lear*.'[18]

Upon finding a local Lear in his Braintree neighbourhood, Adams thought more about how Shakespeare could have invented his characters. By understanding Shakespeare's psychological insights, Adams felt sure he could better understand how the mind worked. He exclaimed, 'Let me search for the cluc, which led great Shakespeare into the labyrinth of mental nature! Let me examine how men think.' Naturally, Shakespeare had never met real people who exhibited all the attributes of his greatest characters, but he had encountered people demonstrating similar attributes in a lesser degree. Applying his imagination to what he observed, Shakespeare envisioned how his tragic protagonists would behave in the extreme situations they faced. If Adams could discern how Shakespeare threaded his way through the labyrinth of mental nature, then perhaps he could follow his trail.

The comparison with King Lear specifically recalls the second scene of the third act, in which Lear apostrophises the storm: 'You sulphurous and thought-executing fires, / Vaunt-couriers of oak-cleaving thunderbolts, / Singe my white head!' Lear continues for several more lines, calling on the storm not only to destroy him but also to exterminate all life on the planet and destroy the possibility of life beginning anew. The Fool briefly interrupts him, but Lear resumes his apostrophe to the storm, imploring, 'Rumble thy bellyfull! Spit fire; spout rain!' After these exclamations, Lear softens his tone, realising the thunder and lightning are not his ungrateful daughters, no matter how much they may resemble them.

Precisely which edition of Shakespeare that Adams knew in the late 1750s remains uncertain. Scattered volumes from different editions containing evidence of his ownership survive at the Boston Public Library. The only surviving volume from which he could have read *King Lear* before the night with Ben Veasey is the fourth volume of the London reprint of Hanmer's Shakespeare. Besides *King Lear*, the volume contains *King John*, *Richard II* and *The Winter's Tale*. Whether Adams owned other volumes in this nine-volume set is unknown.[19]

The following decade Adams would return to this same scene from *King Lear*. During the winter of 1766-67, his friend Jonathan Sewall published a series of essays in the *Boston Gazette* defending the actions of Massachusetts royal governor Francis Bernard. Though their political views increasingly diverged, Adams and Sewall remained good friends. Speaking of Sewall years later, Adams would say, 'He possessed a lively wit, a pleasing humour, a brilliant imagination, great subtlety of reasoning and an insinuating eloquence.'[20]

To defend Governor Bernard, Sewall used the pen name 'Philanthrop'; to refute Sewall, Adams used the pen name 'Misanthrop'. After excerpting Philanthrop's most outrageous statements, Misanthrop asks a series of yes-or-no questions: 'Is this fellow mad, or drunk? Is this decent freedom? Is this piety, Christian piety, the true spirit of Christianity[?]' Asking all these questions about Philanthrop's wild statements, Misanthrop evokes the image of *King Lear*: 'Upon reading this choice collection of rhetorick, I cant help, recollecting King Lear in the cold storm, calling out to the howling winds, the flashing lightning, and hoarse, tremendous thunder, "Rumble thy fill – etc."'[21]

That Adams used the same speech from *King Lear* to characterise both Veasey's boisterous critique of lightning rods and Jonathan Sewall's misguided defence of an autocratic royal governor demonstrates how mad raving, drunken railing and political reasoning could resemble one another. As Adams recognised, Lear's storm speech provides a touchstone for irrational attacks on man, nature and the universe.

With 'Misanthrop, No. 2' Adams returned to Shakespeare. Misanthrop boasts about his ability to navigate 'the winding labyrinths of hypocrisy, chicanery and dissimulation, the real springs, and original movements in the minds of men'. To aid his pursuit Misanthrop applies his occult powers and summons a magical sprite:

> A little familiar spirit attends me, whom, in imitation of Shakespeare I have called Ariel. This little spright, who hops about upon the

> clouds and rainbows, rides upon the sun beams, dives down to the center of the earth, 'thro the springs and subterranean canals; and indeed can circulate 'thro the mass of a mans blood upon a globule of mercury, or dart 'thro the pore of the nerves in the cerebrum or cerebellum, upon a particle of nervouse juice or animal spirit; is of great service to me, and never fails to unriddle the most mysterious phaenomena, in politicks or ethicks.[22]

After reading Philanthrop's latest essay in the *Boston Evening Post* Misanthrop summons Ariel and requests his help to understand it. Ariel flies away to the newspaper office, where he peeps into its account books, totals the number of subscribers and summons the exact same number of companion sprites. Opening a parenthesis, Adams explains how this supernatural process works: 'Such is the association of these ethereal inhabitants that any one of them, can at a call have any number he wants to attend him in any enterprise.' A sprite attends each newspaper, so when one is delivered its accompanying sprite can enter the reader's brain. A sprite enters Philanthrop's brain, allowing him to report his thoughts to Ariel, who, in turn, informs Misanthrop, thus letting him reconstruct Philanthrop's thought process.[23]

'Misanthrop, No. 2' further illustrates how Shakespeare sparked Adams's imagination. Reading *The Tempest*, he became intrigued with the character of Ariel, so much so that it inspired him to create a delightful fantasy of his own. In terms of its imagery 'Misanthrop, No. 2' is unlike anything Adams had written before, but idea-wise it suits other works Shakespeare stimulated him to write. Adams is still concerned with the labyrinth of mental nature. Fantasy, as a literary style, gave him another way to penetrate the brain and explore its 'much ruffled regions'.[24]

Adams published neither 'Misanthrop, No. 1' nor 'Misanthrop, No. 2'. He did publish a response to Philanthrop, for which he used a different persona, a plain-speaking farmer named Humphrey Ploughjogger. Adams had assumed this identity to respond to an earlier set of essays Sewall had written. Aware that sophisticated literary allusion and elaborate fantasy were inappropriate for this earthy and uneducated farmer-persona, Adams omitted the Shakespeare references from his published reply.

Increasingly curious about Shakespeare's ability to turn psychological insight into drama, Adams drafted a critical essay on the subject, 'Shakespeare's Characters and Figurative Language'. In this, his first stab at literary criticism, he had trouble starting and never really finished the essay, but what Adams did write reveals much about his devotion to Shakespeare and the importance of *belles lettres* for recording thought.

The essay begins with some observations on Shakespeare's female characters – Lady Macbeth, Hamlet's mother Gertrude and Lady Anne from *Richard III* – but abandons the subject before its second paragraph, which discusses how Macbeth and Lady Macbeth together represent 'the horror of both divine and human vengeance, that attends guilty minds'.[25]

Shakespeare exaggerates his vicious characters far beyond the bounds of reality: 'He draws ingratitude, treason, hypocrisy, murder, in the strongest colours of horror. – In thinking of any thing, every image that can resemble it, rises at once in strong colours in Shakespears mind.'[26] Struck by how news of the death of Lady Macbeth leads her husband to ponder the meaning of life, Adams quoted Macbeth's famous lines:

> Out out brief candle!
> Lifes but a walking shadow, a poor player
> That struts and frets his hour upon the stage
> And then is heard no more! It is a tale
> Told by an ideot, full of sound and fury
> Signifying nothing.[27]

Adams enjoyed how the metaphors in this passage hang together, the way each builds upon the preceding one. He also liked how Shakespeare integrated biblical references within Macbeth's speech. Adams did not name any specific verses, but the Bible often uses the image of a shadow to express life's insubstantiality. Though a distinctive character, Macbeth, like Lear, also represents a certain character type. Adams generalised from Macbeth's behaviour, suggesting that people in similar situations would behave similarly: 'After having committed every vice and folly, in order to attain the goods of this life, they find that these goods are all trifles, light vain, idle toys, and then they compair life to such things with great wisdom. Oh the horror and despair, the distress and anguish of a guilty mind.'[28]

Though 'Shakespeare's Characters' mentions *Hamlet*, *Othello* and *Richard III*, Adams keeps returning to *Macbeth*. He devotes the fullest attention to the title character, naturally, but other roles come in for criticism. Adams disparages Malcolm and Donaldbain. After Macbeth has murdered their father, they run away to escape his enmity. Adams finds their behaviour cowardly. Instead of staying put and confronting the ruthless tyrant, they flee the land until they can return safely.

'Shakespeare's Characters' does not develop Adams's argument any further, but even in its embryonic state it has historical ramifications. Within two decades Adams and his fellow American patriots would stand their ground against the tyrannical British government.

Adams also discussed the symbolism in *Macbeth*. Quoting the Old Man's recollection of what he saw before Duncan's murder – 'A faulcon towering in her pride of place, was by a mousing owl haukt at and killed' – Adams recognises that these two birds of prey offer an omen of Macbeth's murder of Duncan. Once the Old Man recalls this omen, Ross interjects another, which Adams quoted: 'Duncans Horses, beauteous and swift, the minions of their race, turned wild in nature, broke their stalls, flung out, contending gainst obedience, as they would make war with man.' Adams omitted a crucial part of the conversation. As Ross and the Old Man discuss these omens, Macduff enters the scene to inform them that Macbeth had killed the two suspected assassins, whom Malcolm and Donaldbain had supposedly hired. Ross says that the behaviour of the victim's sons went against nature, like the behaviour of Duncan's horses.

Unsurprisingly, Adams's discussion circles back to the theme of ambition. The next phrase in 'Shakespear's Characters' – 'Thriftless ambition that will raven up thy own lifes means' – comes from what Ross says about sons who murder their father.[29] Quoting all these related passages from Shakespeare in his notebook during the late 1750s, Adams essentially created an anatomy of ambition. He explored the subject from many different angles. Characterising ambition as thriftless, Ross presents the subject from a new perspective. He gives ambition a self-devouring quality. A son who murders his father destroys one of the two people who gave him life in the first place.

'Shakespeare's Characters' ends as Adams considers the theme of sleep in *Macbeth*. He seems most interested in Shakespeare's use of personification. Sleep is kind: it 'knits up the ravelled sleeve of care'. Once personified, sleep becomes vulnerable. Like a person, it, too, can be murdered, as Macbeth discovers once guilt prevents him from falling asleep. The sleep paragraph ends 'Shakespeare's Characters'. In other words, the essay ends but never concludes. Though filled with provocative ideas, 'Shakespeare's Characters' lacks the purpose and organisation of a coherent literary essay.

The brief discussion of female roles in 'Shakespeare's Characters' verifies that Adams, a twenty-three-year-old bachelor, had a limited understanding of women. At this point in his life, he understood women largely through stereotype and cliché. Shakespeare's female characters, he says, represent 'the weakness of woman's reason, and strength of their passions'.[30] His understanding of women would deepen considerably after he met Abigail Smith in the summer of 1759.

Abigail was the teenaged daughter of William Smith, not the historian of New York or the educator of Philadelphia but the Congregational minister of Weymouth, Massachusetts. Bright, well-read, perceptive and compassionate, Abigail was like no woman John had ever met. Shakespeare was one of many authors she and her sisters read growing up in the Weymouth parsonage. In a letter to her sister Elizabeth, Abigail recalls that they read *Macbeth*, a play 'full of horrour'.[31] Abigail Smith and John Adams struck up a correspondence that would endure throughout their courtship. They would marry in 1764 but continued corresponding whenever they were apart. Their letters to each other form the single best husband-and-wife correspondence in American literature.

John and Abigail shared similar literary tastes. They liked many of the same authors, none more than Shakespeare. Quotations, references and allusions to Shakespeare fill their letters to each other. In one letter Abigail wrote to John during their courtship she paints a daring picture, portraying herself in bed at night as she longs for him. Abigail feels tortured because she has not seen John for nearly a fortnight. She expresses her feelings with reference to Shakespeare, but not to, say, *Romeo and Juliet*, as a more conventional woman might, but to the darker and more disturbing tragedies. Abigail imagines herself beset by 'half a dozen ugly sprights. One will catch me and leep into the sea, another will carry me up a precipice (like that which Edgar describes to Lear), then toss me down, and were I not then light as gosemore I should shiver into atoms – another will be pouring down my throat stuff worse than the witches broth in *Macbeth*.'[32]

Abigail made a mistake as she recalled *King Lear*: Edgar describes the cliff to Gloucester, not Lear, but the purpose underlying her use of Shakespeare is clear. Her references demonstrate the love of literature she shared with John, but they also form an intellectual sleight-of-hand. In a letter that gets increasingly intimate, Abigail's literary references partly deflect from her physical and emotional longing for the man she loves.

References to Shakespeare would remain an enduring feature in the letters of Abigail Adams. Like John, she came to know the comedies as well as the tragedies and histories. Rarely did she miss the chance to quote apt lines to support whatever point she wished to make. She enjoyed Shakespeare's language and insight. Abigail understood that quotations from his plays could lend authority to her writings, no matter whether she was heaping praise or casting aspersions.[33]

John Adams's growing maturity deepened his understanding of women and their relationships with men, something his attention to Shakespeare reinforced. Much as he compared Ben Veasey to King Lear after an evening with him, he compared another acquaintance, Dr Bela Lincoln, to Petruchio in *The Taming of the Shrew*. Adams was not the only early American author to use this comedy for comparison. Two decades later Daniel Smith, a Virginia native who would become one of the founders of Tennessee, stayed at a frontier tavern while on a surveying trip through the Cumberland Gap. In his journal Smith observes, 'If paper was plenty I would attempt a description of our uncomfortable situation – with a Xantippe of a landlady, something like a Petruchio of Shakespeare or Nabal for a landlord their dirty children leaky boat drunkenness etc. but I am by no means equal to the task.'[34]

Since Petruchio mentions Xantippe (Socrates's wife) in the first act of *The Taming of the Shrew*, Smith's reference to her may reflect his knowledge of the play – or not. In eighteenth-century America the name 'Xantippe' was a *blason populaire* used to characterise any peevish and ill-humoured woman. Upon being asked hypothetically what he would do if his wife interrupted him in his study when he was deep in thought, Adams mentioned Xantippe, pairing her with a character from Shakespeare, Richard III: 'No man, but a crooked Richard, would blame his wife, for such an accidental interruption. And no woman, but a Xantippe, would insist upon her husbands company, after he had given her his reasons for desiring to be alone.'[35]

Whereas Smith's limited supplies on the frontier deprived him of the paper necessary to develop his story, Adams, with paper aplenty, developed his comparison between Bela Lincoln and Shakespeare's overbearing and underhanded husband, recording how this American Petruchio treated his wife Hannah one evening at the home of her father, Col. Josiah Quincy, and her stepmother.[36]

Describing the arrival of Dr and Mrs Lincoln, Adams observes: 'The doctor gave us an ample confirmation of our opinion of his brutality and rusticity. He treated his wife, as no drunken cobler, or clothier would have done, before company.' Adams did not stop there. He called Dr Lincoln 'a hoggish, ill bred, uncivil, haughty, coxcomb, as ever I saw.' To prove his point Adams recorded the conversation that took place that evening. This diary entry reflects Adams's growing ability to dramatise his experiences. Shakespeare not only influenced the content of Adams's writings, he also influenced their style.

In Adams's version of events, Elizabeth Quincy asks the doctor a question. Seeing that her husband was speaking with Adams, Hannah answers her stepmother's question. Dissatisfied with Hannah's answer, Elizabeth Quincy addresses Bela again, saying, 'Doctor, you did not hear my question.'

'Yes I did,' he replies, 'and the answer to it. My wife is so pert, she must put in her oar, or she must blabb, before I could speak.'

Shocked by the doctor's treatment of his wife, Adams kept a careful eye on her, concerned how she would react. She shrugged her shoulders and laughed off what her husband said, but Adams could see the sadness behind her laughter. She 'sunk into silence and shame and grief'.

'Oh my dear, do let my father see that letter we read on the road,' Hannah says, daring to address her husband again.

'He shant,' Bela replies, speaking 'like the great Mogul, like Nero or Caligula', to use Adams's three-part simile.

'Why, Doctor, do let me have it! Do!'

'I wont,' he replies with a face 'as stern as the Devil, sour as vinegar'.

'Why sir,' she asks, 'what makes you answer me so sternly, shant and wont?'

'Because I wont,' he says.

'I wish I had it,' she laughs, covering the contempt she felt for her husband.

After capturing their conversation in his diary, Adams concluded that Dr Lincoln 'really acts the part of the tamer of the shrew in Shakespear. Thus a kind look, an obliging air, a civil answer, is a boon that she cant obtain from her husband. Farmers, tradesmen, soldiers, sailors, people of no fortune, figure, education, are really more civil, obliging, kind, to their wives than he is.'

Though Adams's scorn for Bela and sympathy for Hannah Lincoln are appealing, his comments should not pass without criticism. Petruchio in *The Taming of the Shrew* is not the only figure Adams used to criticise Bela Lincoln. He also criticised Lincoln by comparing him with members of the working class, implying that such boorish, insensitive behaviour may be associated with farmers or tradesmen, but not with doctors and lawyers. Given that Adams would emerge as a defender of American liberty, his elitism is unsettling.

Adams would call Shakespeare 'that great master of every affection of the heart and every sentiment of the mind as well as the powers of expression'.[37] His words reflect the way he read Shakespeare as a young man. He read Shakespeare for social, literary and psychological reasons. In terms of their social function, Shakespeare's plays provided a body of knowledge Adams shared. He could quote from one play or another and know his friends would understand and enjoy what he meant. In the case of one particular person, Abigail Smith, Shakespeare's words brought them closer together and solidified their growing love.

Enjoying Shakespeare's plays as he enjoyed other great works of literature, Adams appreciated their 'powers of expression', the way they used language to create art. Besides enjoying the plays in and of themselves, he drew inspiration from Shakespeare. Adams deserves recognition as a great writer in his own right. His creative use of dialogue shows how he incorporated dramatic elements in his writings. Adams would also use dramatic characters and situations to enhance his political rhetoric. Shakespeare's work encouraged Adams to take chances with his own writing, to experiment with imagery to see how he could bring his ideas alive.

Shakespeare's body of work was also a psychological tool to help Adams better understand how the mind worked. Shakespeare threaded his way through the 'labyrinth of mental nature'; Adams was determined to follow. This intricate path toward understanding worked in a general way, but it also worked when applied to specific aspects of human behaviour. Like many of Shakespeare's most memorable characters, Adams himself was afflicted with great personal ambition, which he sometimes found uncomfortable. Shakespeare's characters helped Adams understand and come to terms with his ambition and channel it to improve the lot of his countrymen.

9

The 1760s

When William Tudor was researching his biography of Revolutionary patriot James Otis in the early nineteenth century, he approached Otis's surviving friends for information. James Perkins, a Boston merchant, was one person whom Tudor contacted. As a young man, Perkins had been on intimate terms with the Otis family. He responded to Tudor's request with an anecdote that captures Otis's personality and literary tastes.[1]

When Perkins was a young man, the story goes, many of his contemporaries were reading and discussing the latest poets. Their behaviour seemed like a fashionable affectation to Otis. 'These lads are very fond of talking about poetry, and repeating passages of it; the poets they quote I know nothing of,' Otis told young Perkins. 'Take care, James, that you don't give into this folly. If you want to read poetry, read Shakespeare, Milton, Dryden and Pope, and throw all the rest in the fire, these are all that are worth reading.'

James Otis, one of many Revolutionary American leaders with discriminating literary tastes, first established his political reputation as a defender of American rights during the Writs of Assistance Case in 1761. To understand Otis's role in this case Tudor approached another acquaintance, John Adams, who had witnessed the court proceedings when it went to trial.

In 1760 Charles Paxton, the Massachusetts customs commissioner, cracked down on illegal trade and sought help from law enforcement to uncover evidence to secure convictions. Writs of assistance were general, not specific. Unlike search warrants, which require probable cause, writs gave customs officers the authority to enlist the aid of sheriffs and constables to pursue smuggled goods. As Adams put it, the writs gave customs officers the authority to break open 'houses, stores, shops, cellars, ships, bales, trunks, chests, casks, [and] packages of all sorts, to search for goods, wares, and merchandises, which had been imported against the prohibitions or without paying the taxes imposed by certain acts of Parliament, called the acts of trade'.[2] Understandably, the local merchants were furious. They brought suit to have the procedure declared illegal. The merchants hired Oxenbridge Thacher and James Otis to defend them. The case would come before the court in the February 1761 term in the Council Chamber in Boston. Adams took careful notes, which form the primary evidence to document what happened. He retold the story several times. From a literary standpoint his finest account occurs in his reply to Tudor's request for more information. In his letter Adams initially describes what the scene would look like were it a painting but then switches to the language of the theatre. Before introducing the main actors, he says, 'I have given you a sketch of the stage, and the scenery, and the brief of the cause, or, if you like the phrase better, the tragedy, comedy, or farce.'[3]

Adams places himself in the scene with a self-effacing caricature. Writing in the third person, he explains: 'Samuel Quincy and John Adams had been admitted barristers at that term. John was the youngest; he should be painted looking like a short thick archbishop of Canterbury, seated at the table with a pen in his hand, lost in admiration.'[4] Adams's simile recalls a moment from the last act of *Henry VIII* when the archbishop of Canterbury sits in admiration of the king. Adams sits in admiration of Otis, the leading actor of the drama. Otis's courtroom behaviour left him awestruck.

It was not just the theatricality of the scene that impressed Adams. He was stunned by Otis's argument. Otis opposed the writs on constitutional grounds, arguing that all general writs violated the English Constitution and consequently threatened American liberty. Otis dared to argue a radical legal theory, that the courts were obliged to void any legislation deemed unconstitutional.[5] Adams portrays Otis as a classical orator-hero, using words that reveal Adams's ongoing tendency to see the world in dramatic terms:

> Otis was a flame of fire! – with a promptitude of classical allusions, a depth of research, a rapid summary of historical events and dates, a profusion of legal authorities, a prophetic glance of his eye into futurity, and a torrent of impetuous eloquence, he hurried away every thing before him. American Independence was then and there born; the seeds of patriots and heroes were then and there sown ... Every man of a crowded audience appeared to me to go away, as

> I did, ready to take arms against writs of assistance. Then and there was the first scene of the first act of opposition to the arbitrary claims of Great Britain. Then and there the child Independence was born. In fifteen years, namely, in 1776, he grew up to manhood, and declared himself free.[6]

Precisely where and when the American Revolution began remains a historical controversy. The Stamp Act of 1765 is the watershed event, but several earlier controversies anticipated it. According to what Adams says about Otis, the Revolution began in Massachusetts in 1761 with the Writs of Assistance Case. Other authorities place it in Virginia the previous decade with the Pistole Fee Controversy. Yet others identify the 1763 Parson's Cause in Virginia as the formative event in the development of Revolutionary ideology. In all these episodes the American colonists were responding to efforts of the British government to impose its power and limit their rights as subjects of the crown.

The colonists who defended their rights in these cases often brought Shakespeare's words to bear. Their passion for Shakespeare reflects a difficulty Americans faced. Rebelling against England, they were rebelling against much they held dear. The colonists did not want to jettison British culture; they merely wanted to participate in the governmental decisions that affected their welfare. In the coming years excerpts from Shakespeare's tragedies and history plays – dramas of tyranny – would prove increasingly useful as the colonists sought ways to articulate the rights they deserved.

* * *

Attention to Shakespeare in colonial America flourished during the 1760s. More and more people owned personal copies of his works, as estate inventories and surviving books indicate. From the South through the Middle Colonies to New England, Americans were buying and reading multi-volume editions of Shakespeare, making him an important part of their libraries and their lives.

Professional men in colonial America often had Shakespeare on their shelves. Dr John Jackson of Queen Anne's County, Maryland, had five volumes of Shakespeare's works in his library when he died in 1768. A kindly soul, Jackson was known for attending the county's poor people. The odd number of Shakespeare volumes listed in his estate inventory suggests that his generosity extended to his library. There were no five-volume eighteenth-century editions of Shakespeare.

Jackson had apparently loaned out at least one volume from a multi-volume edition, which the borrower had not returned. Charles Carroll of Annapolis, the son of Charles Carroll the Settler, had three volumes of Shakespeare's *Works* at Dooheragen Manor, his 12,000-acre plantation at Elk Ridge, about thirty miles west of Annapolis. His son and heir, who is known as Charles Carroll of Carrollton and who would sign the Declaration of Independence, vividly remembered the prominent place his father's Shakespeare held in their home.[7]

Dr John Eustace, a physician in Wilmington, North Carolina, had an excellent collection of English literature, which included Theobald's Shakespeare. Eustace left no comments about Shakespeare, but his letters affirm his literary interests. Eustace enjoyed Laurence Sterne's *Tristram Shandy* so much he initiated a correspondence with him and presented Sterne with a fancy walking stick.[8]

James Grindlay, a lawyer who practised before the South Carolina Court of Common Pleas, had one of the finest libraries in the colony. In 1765 the library in Grindlay's Charleston home held over five hundred volumes. Walter B. Edgar, who has surveyed all known library inventories from colonial South Carolina, determined that Grindlay's was the largest library in the colony for which a detailed inventory survives. Law books dominated Grindlay's library, but he had a fine collection of *belles lettres*, including several volumes of plays. Grindlay owned an eight-volume Shakespeare, a two-volume edition of Congreve's *Works* and a four-volume French edition of Molière's *Oeuvres*.[9]

Besides identifying the best libraries in colonial South Carolina, Edgar analysed their contents. He compiled lists of authors whose works appear most frequently in the inventories. Edgar arranged his results according to subject. Shakespeare was the single most popular belletristic author in the colony, ranking above Milton, Pope and Swift. Extrapolating from Edgar's data, Richard Beale Davis has applied his conclusions about literary tastes in South Carolina throughout the colonial South: Shakespeare ranked above all other classic English poets from Maryland to Georgia.[10]

Even with the numerous copies of Shakespeare in the colony, South Carolinians still kept stealing individual volumes from multi-volume sets. Samuel Carne was a generous man with an excellent library: a risky combination. He was happy to loan books to friends, happy, that is, until he catalogued his library in 1763 and discovered dozens of volumes missing. The friends who borrowed books from Carne's library apparently found it easier to retain the books than the information within them. Carne advertised in the *South Carolina*

Gazette asking borrowers to return his books. The advertisement names the missing volumes by author. His list of books loaned but not returned includes the first two volumes of a Shakespeare and the first two tomes of *Gargantua and Pantagruel*.[11]

In Virginia John Herbert of Chesterfield County, whose estate was inventoried after his death in 1760, owned 'Shakespeare's Plays', the first item in his list of books. This short title does not list the number of volumes in the edition, but the appraisers assigned it the same value as an eight-volume edition of the *Spectator*. Most likely, Herbert owned an eight-volume Shakespeare. Around the same time fellow Virginian John Baylor had a seven-volume edition of Shakespeare in his personal library at Newmarket, his luxurious home in Caroline County.[12]

Besides the evidence estate inventories provide, surviving volumes reinforce the burgeoning popularity of Shakespeare during the 1760s. William Browne of Four-Mile Tree in Surry County, Virginia owned the eight-volume duodecimo edition of Shakespeare prepared by Hugh Blair and published at Edinburgh. The copy of the sixth volume of Blair's Shakespeare that survives at Colonial Williamsburg contains Browne's bookplate and an autograph dated 1768.[13]

Browne could have purchased his copy of Blair's Shakespeare in Williamsburg. Alexander Purdie and John Dixon, the current proprietors of the *Virginia Gazette*, had a huge stock of books at the *Gazette* office in the late 1760s and early 1770s, according to one undated sales catalogue. In 1772, its approximate date, the catalogue listed three different multi-volume editions: Capell's Shakespeare, Theobald's Shakespeare and 'Shakespeare's Works a Scotch Edition'.[14]

Capell's Shakespeare, which appeared in 1767 and 1768, was the newest edition to appear that decade, but it was not the only one. In 1765 Samuel Johnson published his long-awaited edition. Though based on Warburton's text, Dr Johnson's Shakespeare does restore some passages from the original quarto texts. It is not Johnson's editing but his prefacing that elevates his edition above the others. Johnson's preface is the single finest critical essay on Shakespeare to appear in the eighteenth century. Capell's edition, on the other hand, represents a major contribution to textual editing. Whereas Shakespeare's previous editors copied from whatever edition came before theirs, Capell reverted to the original quarto and folio texts to prepare his edition from scratch.[15]

Copies of Johnson's Shakespeare could be found throughout colonial America. Wilson-Miles Cary, a justice in Elizabeth City County, Virginia, acquired a copy of the edition in 1767, which survived with his armorial bookplate through the nineteenth century. In New Jersey

William Peartree Smith obtained a copy of Johnson's Shakespeare, which currently survives at Princeton University adorned with his engraved bookplate.[16]

The list goes on. A North Carolina man named Samuel Johnston, whose family had emigrated from Scotland when he was a toddler, attended Yale College but returned to North Carolina to read law. After establishing his legal career and entering politics, Johnston purchased a plantation on the outskirts of Edenton in 1765. Plantation owners typically named their estates. Johnston was no exception. He gave his plantation a short but elegant name: Hayes. Befitting a proper Southern gentleman, Johnston assembled an excellent personal library at Hayes, including a copy of Dr Johnson's Shakespeare.[17]

James Milner, another native of Scotland who had emigrated to North Carolina, also practised law. He had an excellent library at his home in Halifax, which included a collection of Shakespeare's works. In addition, Milner owned a copy of Richard Farmer's *Essay on the Learning of Shakespeare*, which Dr Johnson considered the definitive treatment of the subject.[18]

Boston bookseller John Mein imported what he advertised as 'the celebrated Mr Samuel Johnson's Edition of Shakespeare'. He also had for sale a book listed in his catalogue as 'Pieces Written before 1600, by Shakespeare, etc.' This short title represents John Bowie's eighteenth-century collection of sixteenth-century drama, *Miscellaneous Pieces of Antient English Poetry*, which includes 'The Troublesome Raigne of King John', a work falsely attributed to Shakespeare on the title page. The attribution shows how Shakespeare's name was being used as a marketing device.[19]

The finest bookstore in colonial Boston, Mein's was one of John Adams's regular haunts during the 1760s, when he was assembling a great library of his own. Adams's reference to Mein's Bookstore occurs in his diary entry for 30 January 1768, a soul-searching entry in which he wonders about all his recent travel. As a lawyer he had to travel the circuit, arguing cases before courts as far away as Maine, which was then part of Massachusetts. His intinerant lifestyle deprived him of the benefits of a more sedentary existence, and he was having trouble developing the legal, political and philosophical ideas he wished to develop. He found himself living 'a life of here and everywhere, to use the expression, that is applyed to Othello, by Desdemona's father. Here and there and everywhere, a rambling, roving, vagrant, vagabond life.'[20]

Adams misremembered *Othello*. It is Roderigo, not Desdemona's father, who calls Othello 'an extravagant and wheeling stranger / Of here and everywhere'.[21] The comparison nevertheless applies. To describe the roving life of an itinerant circuit lawyer Adams compared himself to Othello. The comparison may be a little extravagant, but it is typical of the grandiose image of himself Adams created. The reference to Mein, which comes toward the end of the entry, makes his bookshop an oasis. It represents an alternative to Adams's restless and wandering life. Stocked with great books, it contained the raw materials Adams needed to create a library that would give him the information, and the stability, to see his ideas to fruition.

Booksellers from Georgia to New Hampshire advertised Shakespeare for sale during the 1760s. Some advertisements do not name the precise edition, simply listing the title as 'Shakespeare's Works' or 'Shakespeare's Plays'. In Portsmouth, New Hampshire Robert Fowle, for example, advertised for sale 'Shakespear's Works 10 vol.' Other booksellers did name specific editions. Charles Crouch, a bookseller in Charleston, South Carolina, advertised Johnson's Shakespeare for sale. Rivington and Brown, who had bookshops in New York and Philadelphia, advertised the 1762 printing of Theobald's Shakespeare. Garrett Noel, a New York competitor, also has Theobald's Shakespeare for sale. William Rind, an Annapolis bookseller, advertised Hanmer's Shakespear in the 1760s.[22]

The sale catalogue of William Dunlap, a Philadelphia printer and bookseller, may be the most revealing of any to survive from the decade. The imprint is undated, but an autograph on the title page of the unique copy at the Library of Congress is dated 1761. Besides an eight-volume edition of Theobald's Shakespeare, Dunlap advertised many individual plays for sale. He subdivided them into two categories, tragedies and comedies. Since Dunlap lists many of the best-loved plays of the Restoration stage and since they are listed by title, not author, it is impossible to tell whether the Shakespeare titles listed are his original plays or the altered versions by Restoration dramatists. Regardless, Shakespeare is well represented. Since Dunlap did not make a separate category for histories, Shakespeare's history plays are listed among the tragedies. The list includes *Cymbeline*, *Hamlet*, *Henry IV*, *Henry V*, *Julius Caesar*, *King Lear*, *Macbeth*, *Othello*, *Richard III* and *Romeo and Juliet*. Though Dunlap lists a total of twenty-four comedies for sale, only one Shakespeare play is among them: *The Merry Wives of Windsor*. Shakespeare was still not widely recognised for his comedic talent. *The Merry Wives of Windsor* was popular because it brought back the best-loved character from the history plays, Sir John Falstaff.[23]

Dunlap's sale catalogue suggests a parallel between reading tastes and the theatre. On the colonial American stage Shakespeare's tragedies and histories remained popular, but his comedies received little attention. In November 1761 the Douglass Company performed *Hamlet* in New York. The following month the company debuted the first American production of *Henry IV, Part I*, with Douglass as Falstaff. *The Merchant of Venice* remained the sole Shakespeare comedy performed on the American stage.[24]

Shakespeare's comedies did find some early American enthusiasts. Every year through the 1760s Philadelphia publisher Andrew Steuart issued the *Universal American Almanack*. Its compiler called himself 'Andrew Aguecheek', taking his pen name from a character in *Twelfth Night*. In the first *Universal American Almanack*, the author makes the Shakespeare connection explicit. In a postscript to the preface Andrew Aguecheek says:

> It has been customary for almanack-makers to publish their works under a fictitious title; such as, Poor Richard, etc. But in this I differ for my real name is Aguecheek. I have not room, in this page, to say anything of my family. Those who have a desire to know who I am, I refer them to Shakespear, who has introduced my grandfather's great grandfather, Sir Andrew Aguecheek, in his *Twelfth Night*, as a very great astronomer or star-gazer.[25]

Ghosts haunt the story of Shakespeare in colonial America. Don't be scared. The word 'ghost' is a bibliographical term. This explanation may not help: many people find bibliography scarier than ghosts. A ghost is an entry in a standard bibliography for which no copies of a book survive. The ghost entry is based on other types of evidence, such as newspaper advertisements announcing publication. In *American Bibliography* Charles Evans lists two Shakespeare ghosts for 1761. According to Evans, New York printer Hugh Gaine issued editions of *King Lear* and *The Tempest* that year. Both entries are based on an advertisement in Gaine's newspaper, the *New York Mercury*.[26]

The advertisement, which appeared on 20 July 1761, announced that on 'this day is published by ... Hugh Gaine, the following plays'. This announcement introduces a list of twenty-five plays: thirteen comedies, including *The Tempest*, and twelve tragedies, including *King Lear*. Alden Vaughan takes Gaine at his word, arguing that he printed these plays because he could sell enough copies to turn a profit.[27]

Ghosts deserve more credit than they usually get, but in this case Vaughan may give the ghosts too much credit. Since many early American books survive in unique copies, it would not be too unusual for no copies of an entire printing to survive. But being 'published', as Gaine used the term in his advertisement, did not necessarily mean that he had printed them locally. Inexpensive, small format editions of both *King Lear* and *The Tempest* appeared in London around the same time.[28] Gaine could have 'published' the plays by importing them and making them available to the reading public, which is what he would do in 1765, when he advertised many more individual plays for sale, including *Coriolanus*, *Julius Caesar*, *King Lear*, *Macbeth* and *Othello*.[29]

When Franklin and his friends created the Library Company of Philadelphia in 1731, it was the first of its kind. As Franklin himself says in his autobiography, the Library Company of Philadelphia was the 'mother of all the North American subscription libraries'. The others were a little slow in coming, but by the end of the 1760s, practically every major American city and several minor ones had subscription libraries of their own.[30]

The Redwood Library Company in Newport, Rhode Island had an eight-volume set of Warburton's Shakespeare in its holdings. It also had a volume of criticism, John Upton's *Critical Observations on Shakespeare*, a work that could be found elsewhere in colonial America. In Virginia Robert Carter had a copy of Upton's *Critical Observations* in his library at Nomini Hall. The presence of Upton's work at the Redwood Library suggests that its members not only wanted to read Shakespeare, they also wanted to understand what they were reading more fully and sought help from literary criticism. It is questionable how much Upton helped. His amateurish view of the editing process clouded his judgment and nudged him toward literary theory, already a nasty term. Dr Johnson found Upton afflicted with the 'rage of emendation', observing, 'Every cold empirick, when his heart is expanded by a successful experiment, swells into a theorist, and the laborious collator at some unlucky moment frolicks in conjecture.'[31]

Subscription libraries caught on in Pennsylvania more than any other colony. Besides the original Library Company, Philadelphia had the Union Library Company and the Association Library Company. All had copies of Shakespeare in their collections. The catalogues of both the Union Library and the Association Library list eight-volume editions of Shakespeare, most likely Theobald's. We know the Association Library's Shakespeare was being used in the 1760s because the librarian had to place an advertisement in the *Pennsylvania Journal* to request the return of the third volume.[32]

The Juliana Library Company in Lancaster, Pennsylvania had Theobald's Shakespeare in its holdings. Like the Redwood Library, the Juliana also had a volume of Shakespeare criticism, Elizabeth Montagu's *Essay on the Writings and Genius of Shakespeare*.[33] Montagu met a mixed reception with contemporary readers. Thomas Morris generally liked her book but quibbled with her assertion that Shakespeare wrote and Garrick acted with the same inspiration. Contrary to Montagu, Morris found their forms of inspiration antithetical: 'Shakespeare wrote from his heart; Garrick played from his head.' Dr Johnson judged the book more harshly. When Montagu's *Essay* came up in conversation with James Boswell, Johnson observed, 'There is not one sentence of true criticism in her book.'[34]

Another Pennsylvania subscription library, the Union Library of Hatboro, also had an eight-volume set of Theobald's Shakespeare.[35] Its surviving records from the mid-1760s show that shareholders frequently borrowed individual volumes from the set. Women were not generally allowed to hold shares in eighteenth-century library companies – with one exception. They could inherit shares. After David Rees, one of the Hatboro library's original shareholders, died in 1762, his wife Margaret inherited his share and held it until her death five years later. As a shareholder, she regularly borrowed books from the library. Her literary tastes included essays, history, novels, poetry and plays. On 21 October 1765 she borrowed the seventh volume of Theobald's Shakespeare, which contained *Julius Caesar* and *Antony and Cleopatra*.[36]

James Young was another Hatboro shareholder who withdrew Theobald's Shakespeare. On Friday, 14 February 1766, Young borrowed the second and third volumes. Since both were devoted to Shakespeare's comedies, Young's interest in them suggests that American curiosity about Shakespeare's comedic work was growing, albeit slowly. Young would read more Shakespeare, but not right away. On 25 February, the day he returned the two Shakespeare volumes he had borrowed, Young checked out two volumes of Addison's collected works. He apparently wished to read some literary criticism before he read any more Shakespeare. The following year he would work his way through the entire eight-volume set.[37]

When Young returned the second volume of Shakespeare in February 1766, it did not stay on the library shelf for long. Less than two weeks later Amos Watson borrowed it, along with the eighth, giving himself a mix of comedies and tragedies. The plays in these two volumes offered Watson some continuity. Reading *The Merchant of Venice*, *The Taming of the Shrew*, *Othello* and *Romeo and Juliet*, he could imagine himself in Italy. Watson must have liked what he read. Upon returning these two volumes from Theobald's Shakespeare a week later, he borrowed two more, the first and fifth volumes, which gave him another set of related comedies and histories. With the two parts of *Henry IV* and *The Merry Wives of Windsor* he could read the complete adventures of Sir John Falstaff.[38]

Watson took a break from Shakespeare, but not for long. A few weeks later he borrowed the fifth and sixth volumes, letting him read the rest of the history plays and some of the greatest tragedies, *King Lear* and *Macbeth*. He returned these two volumes after keeping them for a month, but Watson was not done with Shakespeare. In January 1767 he checked out the seventh volume, creating the opportunity to read *Cymbeline* and *Troilus and Cressida*, among other plays.[39]

The material culture offers a different sort of evidence to verify American interest in Shakespeare during the 1760s. In Providence, Rhode Island printer Sarah Goddard located her shop at the Sign of Shakespeare's Head. John Carter, who had apprenticed in the shop of Benjamin Franklin and David Hall, began working for her in 1767. The following year he took over her printshop and her newspaper, the *Providence Gazette*. He liked the sign so well he kept it. Carter actively encouraged the independence movement in both the columns of his newspaper and the books he printed. In short, books advocating the principles of political liberty during the American Revolution could be found in Providence at the Sign of Shakespeare's Head.[40]

George Washington was not the only one to adorn his home with a bust of Shakespeare. In a 1762 advertisement in the *New-York Gazette* a local merchant advertised busts of Shakespeare 'finely executed in plaster of paris'. Later that decade a Boston merchant advertised busts of Shakespeare in marble. Shakespeare's head became so recognisable among New Yorkers that it inspired a 'Lecture on Heads', a 1767 phrenological lecture, which used Shakespeare as an example.[41]

After Scheemakers's *Shakespeare* at Smibert's Boston studio, the most handsome image of Shakespeare in colonial America may have been the one Samuel Chase had installed in his stately Annapolis home, *Shakespeare Visited by the Muse*. Chase, the 'Maryland Demosthenes' who would sign the Declaration of Independence, began constructing the house in 1769. *Shakespeare Visited by the Muse* is a bas-relief in Italian marble that formed part of the mantel in his drawing room.[42]

Shakespeare penetrated deep into the wilderness, as the adventures of Thomas Morris demonstrate. After the Seven Years' War ended, the British needed to appease the Native Americans who had supported the French and dissuade them from further hostilities. A body of twelve hundred troops under the command of General John Bradstreet assembled at Albany, New York. Morris, now a captain of the 17th Regiment of Foot, joined Bradstreet. Crossing Lake Erie, the expedition reached Cedar Point in August 1764. Bradstreet detached Morris to lead a small group of men to head up the Maumee River to reconcile the Indians to their recent change of allegiance from the French to the British.[43]

On 27 August Captain Morris and his men reached the Swifts (present-day Grand Rapids, Ohio). Three days later Morris recorded in his journal: 'The little chief made me a present of some melons and offered to sell me a volume of Shakespears which I bought for a very little powder.'[44] How Shakespeare ended up in Native American hands on the banks of the Maumee River may seem like an unfathomable mystery. The book, it seems, was part of the spoils of Braddock's defeat at the Battle of the Monongahela. Apparently one of Braddocks's men had a copy of Shakespeare in his haversack. The Indian who obtained the volume may not have been able to read it, but he held onto it nonetheless. Its years-long survival demonstrates the symbolism books could hold. Even for those who cannot read them, books have value. They are talismans, symbols of power and mystery.[45]

A week later Morris reached a native village further up the Maumee. He dispatched his men to reconnoitre while he remained on the river. In his published journal Morris says, 'I had the good fortune to stay in the canoe, reading the tragedy of *Anthony and Cleopatra*, in the volume of Shakespear which the little chief had given me.' Years later Morris would remember reading *Antony and Cleopatra* in a canoe on the Maumee River as one of the greatest pleasures of his life.[46]

* * *

Nothing that happened during the 1760s affected the American colonies more than the Stamp Act, which King George III signed into law on 22 March 1765. The act required Americans to pay taxes on official papers – contracts, deeds, wills – by purchasing stamped papers on which those documents had to be written. Other paper goods were taxed as well, including newspapers and playing cards. Furthermore, the act stipulated that violations would be tried by the Admiralty courts, in which royally appointed judges would render verdicts without juries. In short, the Stamp Act denied Americans two fundamental rights: the right to be taxed solely by elected representatives and the right to trial by jury. It would take effect on 1 November 1765. Benjamin Franklin, who was in London when the act passed, was asked how the Stamp Act could be revised to make it more palatable to his countrymen. Franklin joked that he could fix it by changing a single character in the document: remove the numeral one from '1765', the year it would take effect, and replace it with a two.[47]

News of the Stamp Act reached America in May. Protests were fast in coming. The most eloquent defence of colonial rights that year occurs as part of a four-part series John Adams published in the *Boston Gazette*, 'Dissertation on the Canon and the Feudal Law'. This essay series stemmed from weekly readings between Adams and Jeremiah Gridley that had taken place the winter before the Stamp Act became law. In other words, though Adams did not publish his 'Dissertation' until after the Stamp Act protests, he had largely written it beforehand. Adams built a protest against the Stamp Act into the last and best number of the series, which appeared on 21 October 1765.[48]

'Dissertation, No. 4' questions the metaphor of England as the 'Mother Country', wondering how a parent could treat its child so cruelly. Adams asks a series of rhetorical questions reminiscent of Shylock's If-you-prick-us-do-we-not-bleed speech from *The Merchant of Venice*: 'Is there not something extremely fallacious, in the common-place images of mother country and children colonies? Are we the children of Great-Britain, any more than the cities of London, Exeter and Bath? Are we not brethren and fellow subjects, with those in Britain, only under a somewhat different method of legislation, and a totally different method of taxation?'[49]

Adams soon makes his debt to Shakespeare explicit, suggesting that if England resembles any mother, it resembles Lady Macbeth. Recalling her words with horror, Adams describes Lady Macbeth as a woman 'who "had given suck, and knew / How tender 'twas to love the babe that milk'd her". But yet, who could "Even while 'twas smiling in her face, / Have pluck'd her nipple from the boneless gums, / And dash'd the brains out".' Adams would return to Lady Macbeth's words when he disparaged the idea of England as the Mother Country. After quoting the same speech in a letter to a friend, Adams exclaims, 'Stop Mother! You may pluck away the nipple, if you please but the boy is too big for the rest – have a care, Mamma!'[50]

To Adams the Stamp Act seemed designed to undermine the search for knowledge, suppressing the written word by taxing the paper on which it is printed. Adams, who could talk a blue streak, applied his conversational skills to his writing. In 'Dissertation, No. 4' he celebrates the spirit of liberty that had led to some of the greatest moments in British history. He argues that the spirit itself is insufficient without proper understanding. Before No. 4 ends it becomes an impassioned plea for the pursuit of knowledge:

> This spirit however without knowledge, would be little better than a brutal rage. Let us tenderly and kindly cherish, therefore the means of knowledge. Let us dare to read, think, speak and write. Let every order and degree among the people rouse their attention and animate their resolution. Let them all become attentive to the grounds and principles of government, ecclesiastical and civil. Let us study the law of nature; search into the spirit of the British constitution; read the histories of ancient ages; contemplate the great examples of Greece and Rome; set before us, the conduct of our own British ancestors, who have defended for us, the inherent rights of mankind, against foreign and domestic tyrants and usurpers, against arbitrary kings and cruel priests, in short against the gates of earth and hell.[51]

Adams's writings about the Stamp Act did not end with 'Dissertation, No. 4'. In December he resumed his diary, something he had neglected for almost a year. In the 18 December 1765 entry he discusses how the Stamp Act was affecting the American mind. He calls it an 'enormous engine, fabricated by the British Parliament, for battering down all the rights and liberties of America'. Adams also notes the innumerable 'monuments of wit, humour, sense, learning, spirit, patriotism, and heroism erected in the several colonies and provinces, in the course of this year'.[52] On Christmas day Adams began drafting 'Clarendon to Pym', an essay that fits with other American monuments to wit, learning and patriotism written in the aftermath of the Stamp Act.

Though virtually no one defended the Stamp Act in the American press, the *Boston Evening Post* did reprint an essay from the English press defending it. The essay was signed 'William Pym', and it inspired responses from both Otis and Adams. Ever since the Writs of Assistance Case, Otis had been defending American rights in person and in the press. Adams called Otis a 'wedge to split the knotty lignum vitae block of parliamentary usurpation over the colonies'. Adams's metaphor repeats a traditional saying, which he could have found in *Troilus and Cressida*, a work that anticipates several aspects of Adams's thought. As Ulysses says, 'Blunt wedges rive hard knots'.[53]

Whereas Otis replied to Pym using the pen name 'Hampden', Adams used the pen name 'Clarendon' in his replies. 'Clarendon to Pym', which Adams drafted as part of his Christmas diary entry, recalls a scene from *Henry VIII*, 'which may be very properly recommended to modern monarks, queens, and favourites'.[54] The draft mentions the volume and page number in which the scene occurs. The specific citation reveals that Adams had obtained a new edition of Shakespeare since making his earliest known Shakespearean references during the late 1750s. The new edition was a small octavo edition of Blair's Shakespeare published in Edinburgh in 1761. Four volumes from the edition bearing Adams's autograph on their title pages survive today at the Boston Public Library.[55]

The scene Adams had in mind was the second scene of the first act, in which Queen Katharine successfully persuades King Henry to remove the burdensome taxes on his subjects. Henry decrees that the tax be removed and the protesters pardoned. Five days after drafting 'Clarendon to Pym' Adams reread *Henry VIII*. The scene he remembered from it apparently inspired him to reread the play as he revised 'Clarendon to Pym' for publication.[56]

On 4 January 1766 Adams received the latest issue of the *Boston Gazette*, which contained Otis's new essay, 'Hampden to Pym'. Adams encapsulated Otis's essay in his diary: 'Hampden writes to Pym on the failure of justice in America, on the shutting up of the courts of justice, since October. He has given the public Mr Otis's arguments before the governor and council, from Magna Charta, Ld. Coke, the judges oaths etc. – and promises to give more.'[57]

Another item in the same issue of the *Gazette* astonished Adams. A contributor known solely as 'A. B.' submitted the exact same scene from *Henry VIII* that Adams had mentioned in his first draft of 'Clarendon to Pym'. A. B. introduced the scene with the following headnote:

> Looking over Shakespear['s] *Henry VIII*, I felt a singular pleasure in reading one of the scenes, which I thought peculiarly adapted to the present circumstances of our most gracious sovereign's American subjects – As it is a part of the English history, and shows the success of the people's application for relief from a burthensome tax, or 'trembling contribution' to a monarch in all respects much inferior to him, who now fills the British throne, it may be agreeable to your readers to have it inserted in your *Gazette*.[58]

Adams wrote in his diary: 'I find that somebody has published the very scene in Shakespears H[enry] 8, which I have put into Ld. Clarendons letter to Pym.' Others recognised the relevance of the scene from *Henry VIII*. Coming across the 30 December issue of the *Boston Gazette*, a Southern newspaper editor reprinted both the scene and A. B.'s headnote as the lead article to the 26 February 1766 issue of the *North Carolina Gazette*.[59]

Wanting to make his argument as original as possible, Adams dropped his reference to *Henry VIII* as he revised 'Clarendon to Pym', but the idea that another American patriot was thinking about the same scene from Shakespeare at the same time reminded Adams of Francis Bacon's 'doctrine of secret, invisible connections and communications, and unknown undiscovered laws of nature'.[60]

Aware of the colonists' growing resentment, the British colonial government tightened its grip over Massachusetts. Adorned in their characteristic red coats, additional regiments of British soldiers reached Boston in October 1768 to enforce the law. On 5 March 1770 a group of British redcoats fired into a crowd of Bostonians, killing five townspeople. The incident became known as the Boston Massacre.

The soldiers were brought to trial. Strange to say, Adams agreed to represent them. Though an ardent American patriot, he understood that it was crucial to uphold the law no matter who had violated it. Unwilling to let mob rule and vigilante justice take over, Adams wanted to prove that Massachusetts was governed by the rule of law. The accused would be treated fairly before the bar of justice. Other patriots agreed. Josiah Quincy, Jr, for one, joined the defence team.

Born in Boston, Quincy had attended Harvard, where he read well beyond the college curriculum. Upon encountering a copy of Dodd's *Beauties of Shakespeare*, Quincy was struck by the power and elegance of Shakespeare's words. He transcribed many excerpts from Dodd's compilation, filling seventy manuscript pages before he was finished. Shakespeare seems more important to Quincy for these selected extracts than for the plays themselves. According to his library inventory, Quincy did not own a separate edition of Shakespeare. Besides Dodd's *Beauties*, the only other volume of Shakespeare in his library was a copy of *Coriolanus*.[61]

Quincy's writings demonstrate his use of Shakespeare. On a journey from Boston to South Carolina Quincy encountered rough seas, which compelled him to quote *The Tempest* in his journal: 'The sky it seems would pour down livid flames, / But that the sea, mounting to th' welkin's cheek, / Dashes the fire out.' The differences between the quoted lines and Shakespeare's original not only verify that Quincy was quoting from memory, they also show him conflating Shakespeare and Milton. In Shakespeare's original, the sky pours down 'stinking pitch', but in Quincy's quote, the sky pours down 'livid flames'. Quincy's flames come from the first book of *Paradise Lost*. Upon being tossed from heaven, Satan falls toward 'The seat of Desolation, void of light, / Save what the glimmering of these livid flames / Casts pale and dreadful'.[62]

None of Quincy's Shakespeare quotes are more significant than the one that occurs in his closing arguments for the Boston Massacre trial. In his second to last paragraph Quincy quoted a 'learned judge'. The judge's identity has hitherto escaped identity, but it was Michael Foster, whom William Blackstone called 'a very great master of the crown law'. Foster's essay 'Of Homicide', which sought to reconcile and clarify the inconsistencies in the case law, was a crucial source for Quincy.[63]

Quoting the word 'mercy' from the coronation oath, Foster's essay reminded Quincy of Portia's famous speech from *The Merchant of Venice*:

> 'Ministers' (says a learned judge) 'appointed for the ends of public justice, should have written on their hearts the solemn engagements of his Majesty, (at his coronation) to cause law and justice IN MERCY to be executed in all his judgments'.
>
> The quality of mercy is not strained;
>
> It droppeth like the gentle rain from heaven —
>
> It is twice blessed;
>
> It blesses him that gives, and him that takes.[64]

Quoting Shakespeare alongside Judge Foster, Quincy combined literature and legal precedent. The defence that he and Adams mounted was largely successful. The jury acquitted six soldiers but convicted two of manslaughter. The two were branded on the thumbs and then released.

Though many American Revolutionaries were reading the same Whig histories and French philosophical treatises to formulate their theories of natural law and natural rights, Shakespeare provided a different kind of discourse. As a whole, Shakespeare's works reflect the political philosophy of the Elizabethan and Jacobean eras, emphasising most importantly the divine right of kings. But individual passages in many different plays, mainly the tragedies and histories but occasionally the comedies, emphasised natural rights. Shakespeare's words became so well known in America that by the start of the 1770s they let Revolutionary thinkers communicate their ideas in familiar, but dramatic terms.

10

Thomas Jefferson and His Williamsburg Circle

After Thomas Jefferson left Shadwell – his family home in the Virginia Piedmont – one early February afternoon in 1770 to conduct some business in nearby Charlottesville, the house caught fire. The blaze spread quickly, and Shadwell was soon engulfed. Both the house and its contents were almost completely consumed. The *Virginia Gazette* reported that Jefferson's home 'burnt to the ground with all his furniture, books, papers, etc.' He was less concerned with the furniture or the et cetera: the loss of his books and papers pained him much more.[1]

A letter to his friend John Page describes the damage in greater detail. Jefferson laments: 'My late loss may perhaps have reached you by this time, I mean the loss of my mother's house by fire, and in it, of every paper I had in the world, and almost every book. On a reasonable estimate I calculate the cost of the books burned to have been £200. sterling. Would to god it had been the money; then it had never cost me a sigh!'[2]

The papers he lost included the legal notes he had compiled for the forthcoming session of the general court. With their loss he was unsure how he would defend his clients, but he could do little now but accept what had happened. In his letter to Page, he says how he coped with the loss of the legal papers: 'I troubled my head no more with them. These are gone, and "like the baseless fabric of a vision, Leave not a trace behind".'[3] Jefferson quotes Prospero's evocative words to capture the sense of loss he felt with the destruction of his library. Prospero's simile works as a farewell to lost things. It has a wistful quality, yet one that reflects acceptance. Jefferson's quotation from *The Tempest* reflects his literary knowledge and suggests that a copy of Shakespeare's works perished in the fire as well.

Jefferson did not lose all his books and papers. At least one crucial document – his literary commonplace book – survived the blaze. Its contents can help reconstruct the Shadwell library. The commonplace book reveals that the library contained several Shakespeare-related items. Jefferson had a copy of *Thesaurus Dramaticus*, from which he excerpted passages from *Henry VI, Part II*; Dryden's altered version of *Troilus and Cressida*; and Lansdowne's *Jew of Venice*. He also selected excerpts from the two plays Buckingham had based on *Julius Caesar*: *The Tragedy of Julius Caesar, Altered* and *The Death of Marcus Brutus*. These excerpts suggest that Jefferson also owned a copy of Buckingham's *Works*. The lion's share of the Shakespeare quotations in his commonplace book come from a collected edition of the plays. Jefferson does not name the specific edition, but his precise wording and punctuation verify that he read Hanmer's Shakespeare.[4]

The first Shakespeare quotation in the commonplace book comes from something Caesar says to Calpurnia in the second act of *Julius Caesar*. Having dreamt about awful events in the Senate chamber and having heard about bad omens confirming her fears, Calpurnia urges Caesar to stay home, whereupon he replies:

> Cowards die many times before their deaths;
> The valiant never taste of death but once.
> Of all the wonders that I yet have heard,
> It seems to me most strange that men should fear
> Seeing that death, a necessary end,
> Will come when it will come.[5]

Beyond what these lines say about facing up to death Jefferson also appreciated them as poetry. He would quote them again in 'Thoughts on English Poetry' to demonstrate the intricate system of scansion he invented. He used these lines from *Julius Caesar* to illustrate his method of denoting four different levels of metrical stress. In the opening line of this passage the first syllable of the word 'Cowards' earns a triple stress, whereas the word 'times' only receives a double stress. Jefferson's system of scansion seems unnecessarily complicated, but it reflects an impulse of his era, to standardise English pronunciation.[6]

The remaining quotations from *Julius Caesar* in his literary commonplace book reveal how Jefferson read the play. His next two excerpts, which both come from the fourth act, are followed by two from the first act and one from the third. Their order suggests that Jefferson read *Julius Caesar* twice. Passages that had not caught his attention the first time around he noticed the second time through the play.

His last quotation from *Julius Caesar* has some continuity with his first. Both treat the theme of death. He transcribed five lines from a conversation between Brutus and Casca. Brutus speaks the first two lines, Casca the next two and Brutus the fifth. Jefferson presents the excerpt as one continuous utterance without designating the individual speakers:

> That we shall die, we know; 'tis but the time,
> And drawing days out, that men stand upon,
> And he that cuts off twenty years of life,
> Cutts off so many years of fearing death.
> Grant that and then is death a benefit.[7]

Brutus and Casca speak these words in an effort to rationalise their forthcoming assassination of Caesar. Excerpted from their context, the lines form a stand-alone comment on the advantage of dying young.

Directly after this passage, Jefferson added a quotation from *Henry V*. In terms of both theme and diction, his first excerpt from *Henry V* is so similar to the final one from *Julius Caesar* that it reveals another dimension to Jefferson's reading process. The last *Julius Caesar* quotation apparently reminded him of something he had read in a different Shakespeare play. Remembering the play, he picked up the volume of Hanmer's Shakespeare containing *Henry V*, paged through it to find the familiar quotation and then transcribed it.

Faced with the prospect of battling a vast French army at Agincourt, the Earl of Westmorland wishes the English had more troops. In response King Henry asserts that their numbers do not matter. Applying a bit of traditional wisdom – the more danger the more honour – he says:

> If we are mark'd to die, we are enow
> To do our country loss, and if to live,
> The fewer men, the greater share of honour.
> God's will! I pray thee wish not one man more.[8]

These lines form part of King Henry's St Crispin's Day speech, in which he musters all the rhetorical skill at his command to inspire his men. As Jefferson reread Henry's speech, he transcribed an additional passage from it: 'But if it be a sin to covet honour, / I am the most offending soul alive.'[9] According to Christian belief, it is a sin to covet honour, but Henry knows he must play upon his soldiers' sense of honour to motivate them to fight the French. In his St Crispin's Day speech, the word 'honour' is more rhetorical device than an expression of its true meaning.[10]

Henry's speech got Jefferson thinking about the idea of honour, reminding him of something else he had read in Shakespeare: Falstaff's memorable denunciation of the heroic code of honour in *Henry IV, Part I*. Jefferson then reread Falstaff's speech and transcribed practically the whole thing. Taken together, Jefferson's excerpts from *Henry V* and *Henry IV, Part I* show that thoughts of death got him thinking about the meaning of honour, looking at it from various angles and points of view. He would continue to contemplate what honour meant. When he ended the Declaration of Independence with the signers' mutual pledge of honour, it came as a result of much thought, thought partly inspired by what he had read in Shakespeare.

Falstaff's denunciation let Jefferson stop thinking about honour for the time being and turn his attention to *Coriolanus*. He excerpted four passages as he read the play. Whereas Jefferson dipped into *Henry V* and *Henry IV, Part I* to contemplate the idea of honour, he read *Coriolanus* more thoroughly. Perhaps he was reading the play for the first time. His initial quotation comes from the opening speech of the fourth act:

> Extremity was the trier of spirits,
> That common chances common men could bear;
> That when the sea was calm, all boats alike,
> Shew'd mastership in floating; Fortune's blows
> When most struck home, being greatly warded, crave
> A noble cunning.[11]

Coriolanus speaks these words to his mother Volumnia, stringing together several proverbs she had taught him. As he did with his excerpts from *Julius Caesar*, Jefferson extracted the nuggets of traditional wisdom while omitting the dramatic context.

Some of Jefferson's entries in his literary commonplace book date from his student days at William and Mary. Once he finished college, he started reading law and began keeping a legal commonplace book. Like John Adams, Jefferson kept reading literature even after he started reading law, though his approach differed somewhat. Whereas Adams found that literature complemented law, Jefferson saw literature as a temporary refuge from the law. Years later he recalled his legal education to John Bernard.

'I was bred', Jefferson told Bernard, 'to the law; that gave me a view of the dark side of humanity. Then I read poetry to qualify it with a gaze upon its bright side; and between the two extremes I have contrived through life to draw the due medium.' As their conversation continued, Bernard asked him to name his favourite poets. He recorded Jefferson's answer indirectly: 'Shakespeare and Pope, he said, gave him the perfection of imagination and judgment, both displaying more knowledge of the human heart – the true province of poetry – than he could elsewhere find.'[12]

Other copies of Hanmer's Shakespeare could be found in Jefferson's Virginia. At Enniscorthy, a mansion atop Green Mountain, Jefferson's neighbour Colonel John Coles had a copy of the nine-volume 1748 edition of Hanmer's Shakspeare, every volume of which he adorned with his bookplate. And the library inside the Governor's Palace in Williamsburg held a copy of Hanmer's Shakespeare, as well.[13]

Norborne Berkeley, Baron de Botetourt, the governor of Virginia, may have brought his Shakespeare with him when he came there in October 1768. It formed part of a fine personal library of over three hundred volumes. By the time Botetourt reached Virginia, a set of Shakespeare was practically *de rigeur* for the proper English gentleman's library, but other books in his library reveal Botetourt's dedication to the history of drama. He also owned an eight-volume set of Molière's *Oeuvres* and ten volumes of Robert Dodsley's *Select Collection of Old Plays*, a set that contains numerous works from the history of English drama, including *Gorboduc*, one of the earliest English tragedies; John Ford's *'Tis Pity She's a Whore*; and John Webster's revenge tragedy, *The White Devil*.[14]

Botetourt continued expanding his library in Williamsburg. He also remained interested in Shakespeare. The year after he came to Virginia, devotees back in England celebrated the Shakespeare Jubilee, which was widely reported in the American press. Garrick organised the festivities at Stratford-upon-Avon and served as master of ceremonies for the Jubilee. He also wrote an ode for the occasion, which he delivered with musical accompaniment. Garrick capitalised on the event and published the poem as *An Ode upon Dedicating a Building, and Erecting a Statue, to Shakespeare, at Stratford upon Avon*. In addition, he wrote *The Jubilee*, a popular stage play that would run on the London stage for years to come. Governor Botetourt kept up with literary events in England: he obtained a copy of Garrick's *Ode* soon after its publication and added it to his colonial governor's bookshelf.[15]

Unlike previous Virginia governors, who remained in England and sent their lieutenants to America to do the work of governing, Botetourt came to Virginia himself. His commitment to the governorship endeared Botetourt to the Virginians, who found him charming and gregarious. As governor, he became a patron of Virginia education. He founded the Botetourt Medal at the College of William and Mary to reward scholastic excellence. Sadly, Botetourt's governorship did not last long. Only two years after his arrival he died of erysipelas, a bacterial infection also known as St Anthony's fire.[16]

John Murray, the fourth Earl of Dunmore, had been appointed governor of New York in 1770, but he came to Williamsburg the following year to fill the vacancy left by Botetourt's death. Dunmore was no Botetourt, but he did share his predecessor's passion for books. The library Dunmore brought to Virginia contained over 1300 volumes. No complete inventory survives but stray volumes with evidence of his ownership partly reveal its contents. Dunmore owned a set of Pope's Shakespeare, which survives at Colonial Williamsburg. Like George Washington, Governor Dunmore was a devotee of the theatre. When Washington was in Williamsburg, the two attended the theatre together – until politics separated them.[17]

Colonial Virginia welcomed its greatest Shakespearean to its shores in 1770, when the Rev. Samuel Henley arrived to fill the position of Professor of Moral Philosophy at William and Mary. An accomplished Orientalist, Henley is best known to literary history as the translator and annotator of William Beckford's *Vathek*, which he published in 1815. Between his tenure as a professor at William and Mary and his publication of *Vathek*, Henley devoted his greatest intellectual effort toward annotating Shakespeare. He contributed annotations to several different editions of Shakespeare that appeared during the 1780s and 1790s.[18] Though written after his time in Virginia, Henley's annotations attest to the level of erudition and intellectual enthusiasm he brought to Williamsburg.

A year younger than Jefferson, Henley was born in Abbots Kerswell, Devonshire in 1744. Personal experience affected his scholarship; his Devonshire boyhood surfaces in several annotations. In *The Merry Wives of Windsor* Mrs Page describes Ford's madness to his wife, relating how he 'buffets himself on the head, crying, peer out, peer out'. Glossing this passage, Henley recalled a childhood nursery rhyme: 'Shakespeare here refers to the practice of children, when they call on a snail to push forth his horns: "Peer out, peer out, peer out of your hole, / Or else I beat you black as a coal."'[19]

As a Dissenter, Henley was forbidden from attending Oxford or Cambridge. Instead, he went to Caleb Ashworth's Dissenting Academy, completing four years of academic studies – the equivalent of a bachelor's degree – in 1766. Two years later he entered the ministry and obtained a position with a congregation of Protestant Dissenters near Cambridge. He eventually became affiliated with the Church of England, being admitted sizar at Queen's College, Cambridge, where he ingratiated himself with the Cambridge intelligentsia.[20]

Once the professorship at William and Mary became vacant, Governor Botetourt, as a patron of education, appealed to Edward Montagu, Virginia's agent in London, for a man of ability and integrity for the college. After consulting with the Bishop of London, Montagu recommended Henley. On 8 January 1770 Henley received the King's bounty. He reached Virginia that April to assume his professorship at William and Mary. One can sense Henley's excitement in an annotation he would write for *The Tempest*: 'It is by no means surprising that the novelties of the new world should have greatly excited general curiosity.'[21]

Coming to Virginia, Henley brought with him an excellent library. His collection of books reveals a wide range of intellectual interests. He described his library as 'a collection of books, consisting of scarce and valuable editions (many on large paper, and in the best bindings) of the Greek and Roman classics, and the principal writers in the Italian, French, and English languages. Together with a large collection of engravings, etchings, and mezzotints, by the greatest masters; many of which were proofs, and the rest choice impressions'.[22]

Beyond this general description, the contents of Henley's Virginia library are known by a partial inventory and a handful of surviving volumes. His collection of English literature shows he was both a scholar and a collector. He had a copy of the rare ten-book first edition of *Paradise Lost* and a sixteenth-century edition of William Langland's *Vision of Pierce Plowman*. He owned books treating such subjects as aesthetics, antiquities, botany and literary criticism. Henley's knowledge of botany complemented his study of literature: several of his annotations gloss Shakespeare's botanical references. Other works in Henley's library show his interest in modern literary trends. His collection of criticism included Montagu's *Essay on Shakespeare*.[23]

The partial catalogue does not list any Shakespeare editions, but Henley was familiar with several. Five years after he left Virginia he published his first extensive set of Shakespeare notes as part of Edmond Malone's *Supplement* to the Johnson-Steevens Shakespeare. His notes in Malone's *Supplement* cite the First Folio as well as Hanmer's, Johnson's and Warburton's Shakespeare. Henley possessed a deep knowledge of English Renaissance drama. Other plays he cites in Malone's *Supplement* include John Fletcher's first drama, *The Faithful Shepherdess*, a pastoral tragicomedy; *The Maid's Tragedy*, a Beaumont and Fletcher collaboration best known for the touching apostrophe, 'Upon my buried body lie / Lightly, gentle earth'; and *Bussy d'Ambois*, a George Chapman tragedy that found new life on the Restoration stage regardless of Dryden's disdain.[24]

Henley and Jefferson became good friends, and they kept in contact after Henley returned to England. Their correspondence testifies to the friendship they developed in Williamsburg. In a letter to Jefferson years later Henley would reflect, 'Different as our situations are from what they once were, I shall ever look back with sincere pleasure on the friendship with which you honoured me.' Another time he articulated his pleasure with Jefferson's friendship and stated that 'neither length of time, change of situation, nor the convulsions which have torn asunder the bands that once held our united countries' had in the least altered his feelings of friendship.[25]

Jefferson left no details about their personal interaction, but statements made by British friends attest to Henley's pleasant company and lovable bookishness. As a young man, the botanist and antiquarian Dawson Turner had breakfast with Henley one morning. Turner fondly remembered his agreeable conversation: 'It was impossible for any man to be more amusing and instructive in conversation, or of greater amenity of manner, than Dr Henley.'[26] Jefferson talked books with Henley, too. He became familiar with the professor's fine collection while rebuilding his own after the Shadwell fire. Occasionally Jefferson convinced Henley to sell him some books from his library.[27]

Though Jefferson and Henley became good friends, precisely when their friendship began remains a mystery. The references to Shakespeare in the writings of both men reveal possible points of contact. Together with Washington's diaries, Jefferson's memorandum books contain the fullest information about the Williamsburg stage in the late 1760s and early 1770s, though the memoranda of both men can be quite frustrating. Washington and Jefferson regularly recorded when they attended the theatre, but almost never did they record the titles of the plays they saw.

On Tuesday, 23 October 1770 Jefferson attended a performance of the American Company at the Old Theatre in Williamsburg. Though he did not record what play he saw, it may have been *Cymbeline*, the greatest hit in the American Company's current repertoire. Two months earlier the company had performed *Cymbeline* at the New Theatre in Annapolis with Nancy Hallam as Innogen or Imogen, as the character's name was styled in the eighteenth century. The reviewer for the *Maryland Gazette* offered a clever reference to *Hamlet* before devoting the rest of the review to the star of

Cymbeline. The rapturous review verifies that Nancy Hallam was now the greatest sex symbol on the American stage:

> The actors are, indubitably, intitled to a very considerable portion of praise. But, by your leave, gentlemen (to speak the language of Hamlet), here's a metal more attractive. On finding that the part of Imogen was to be played by Miss Hallam, I instantly formed to myself, from my predilection for her, that most sanguine hope of entertainment. But how was I ravished on experiment! She exceeded my utmost idea. Such delicacy of manner! Such classical strictness of expression! The musick of her tongue! The Vox Liquida, how melting! ... How true and thorough her knowledge of the character she personated! Her whole form and dimensions how happily convertible, and universally adapted to the variety of her part![28]

Maryland minister and schoolteacher Jonathan Boucher, who attended the performance with the *Gazette* reviewer, conveyed his appreciation in verse. 'To Miss Hallam' begins:

> Hail, wondrous maid! I grateful hail
>   Thy strange dramatic power;
> To thee I owe that Shakspere's tale
>   Has charmed my ears once more.[29]

Suggesting that the Annapolis performance of *Cymbeline* had given him the chance to enjoy Shakespeare again, Boucher reveals his familiarity with Shakespeare's works, which the catalogue of his library verifies. Boucher had a substantial collection of Shakespeareana. Since his library was not catalogued until 1806, it is difficult to say which books he owned by the time he saw *Cymbeline*, but those published before 1770 include Monatgu's *Essay on Shakespeare*, Upton's *Critical Observations on Shakespeare* and an edition of *Henry VIII* annotated by Joseph Grove, the author of *The History of the Life and Times of Cardinal Wolsey*.[30]

Boucher's correspondence verifies his passion for Shakespeare. Pompous and pedantic, the Rev. Boucher is the Doctor Blimper of colonial Maryland. His letters are peppered with references to his reading. In one letter Boucher tells George Washington about his painful toothache: 'Like Macbeth, it has murder'd sleep beyond the power of laudanum to recall.' In a letter to William Smith – the Philadelphia educator – Boucher uses a phrase from *Henry IV, Part I* to demean himself as 'a fellow of no mark nor livelihood'.[31]

The second stanza of 'To Miss Hallam' reveals that Rowe's longstanding critical attitude toward Shakespeare held firm:

> 'Twas his to paint, with touch refined,
> Beyond the rules of art,
> Each varying passion of the mind,
> And probe the human heart.[32]

The same day the American Company performed *Cymbeline* in Annapolis, 30 August 1770, Douglass placed the following announcement in the *Maryland Gazette*: 'The company's engagement in Virginia will prevent them from performing here any longer than the end of next month.'[33] The 23 October performance Jefferson saw was the first performance of the American Company after it had left Annapolis for Williamsburg that autumn.

Henley's annotations reveal his in-depth knowledge of *Cymbeline*, but they also show that his time in Virginia helped him understand the play more fully. His most important annotation glosses the sixth scene of the third act. As it begins, Imogen enters alone after she has run away from her father. In this scene she first appears disguised as a boy named Fidele. Wearing, say, a doublet and hose, Nancy Hallam was dressed more provocatively in men's clothes than in the flowing princess garments she had worn earlier in the play.

As Fidele, she stands before a cave wondering if anyone is inside. She calls out to possible inhabitants, 'If any thing that's civil, speak; if savage, / Take or lend. Ho! No answer? Then I'll enter.'[34] In other words Imogen says to the unknown cave dwellers, if you are civilised, speak to me. If you are not, please accept my money or give me some food. Once Imogen enters the cave, Belarius, Guiderius and Arviragus arrive on the scene. After a day in the field, Guiderius has proven himself the 'best woodman'. Though the word 'woodman' meant hunter, it also had a bawdy meaning in Shakespeare's day not unrelated to the modern slang term, 'wood'. In *Measure for Measure* Lucio says of Vincentio that he is 'a better woodman than thou takest him for'.[35]

Henley's annotation glosses both what Imogen yells into the cave and the term 'woodman':

> May not, *if any thing that's civil*, intimate the chance of this cave's being the abode of *one amenable to the laws of society*, in opposition to the greater probability of its belonging to an *out-law*? – Robin Hood, Adam Bell, and Clym of the Clough, were all of them

> *woodmen* of the latter kind; and it may be observed, that persons of a similar character, who still range the woods beyond the precincts of Virginia and the reach of laws, subsist entirely on the deer they can shoot; are not only famed for being the best marksmen, but are called *woodmen*, to the present hour.[36]

Henley's annotation shows he was a keen listener. Much as he brought to bear his knowledge of Devonshire folk speech in other annotations, this one shows he listened to how people talked in Virginia. Henley identified words from Shakespeare's English that were obsolete in Augustan England but had survived in Virginia. First settled in Shakespeare's time, Virginia preserved many words from Shakespeare's English.

The American term typically contained an 's' in the middle – woodsman – and the meaning varied slightly. Woodmen were good hunters; colonial woodsmen were also good hunters, but their name had an 's' in it because it referred to where they lived: the woods. A variant gave the term a negative connotation: backwoodsman, which was current by 1755, when Dr Alexander Hamilton used the word in a letter to a kinsman. In Henley's Virginia Governor Dunmore spoke derogatorily of 'those who are called the back-woods-men, who are hunters like the Indians and equally ungovernable'.[37]

Henley's time in Virginia brought him to the Eastern Shore, where he heard even more words that survived from Shakespeare's day. Glossing something the King of France says in the last act of *All's Well that Ends Well* – 'I am not a day of season' – Henley explains, 'That is, of *uninterrupted rain*: one of those *wet days* that usually happen about the vernal equinox.' After his explanation, he observes, 'The word is still used in the same sense in Virginia, in which government, and especially on the eastern shore of it, where the descendants of the first settlers have been less mixed with later emigrants, many expressions of Shakspere's time are still current.'[38] For a linguist with Henley's expertise, Virginia was a living laboratory for researching the history of the English language.

Henley was also intrigued with the African slaves he encountered. To his credit he was unafraid to challenge the day's racial stereotypes. Henley wondered whether people from Europe and Africa differed at heart. Living in Virginia, he had the chance to test the acuity of some African slaves. He asked one 'how it happened that, as Adam and Eve were white, he, their descendant should be black'.

'I don't know', the man replied, 'but, prick your hand and prick mine, my blood is as red as yours'.

Henley was delighted with this response. It reminded him of a scene from *The Merchant of Venice*, so he built the personal episode into his annotations for the play and thus recorded it for posterity. The Prince of Morocco, one of Portia's suitors, pleads with her to consider his suit, arguing that she should not be prejudiced against him solely because of the colour of his skin. 'Bring me the fairest creature northward born,' he implores, 'And let us make incision for your love, / To prove whose blood is reddest, his or mine.'[39] Backed by Shakespeare, the perceptive reply from the Virginia slave prompted Henley to reconsider the essence of European and African, colonist and slave.

The folk heroes Henley mentions by name in his annotation to *Cymbeline* – Adam Bell and Clym of the Clough – represent one point of contact between Jefferson and Henley. As Jefferson recreated his personal library on a grander scale after the Shadwell fire, he replaced books he had lost. Though his copy of Hanmer's Shakespeare was apparently destroyed in the fire, Jefferson replaced it with a more recent and more scholarly edition, Capell's Shakespeare. Jefferson's copy survives at the University of Virginia, complete with his marginalia. The notes he wrote in the margins of Capell's Shakespeare mainly consist of references to Thomas Percy's *Reliques of Ancient Poetry*. Jefferson was clearly reading Shakespeare with a copy of Percy at hand and making cross-references in the margins.

Jefferson's writings show no interest in Percy before Henley's arrival, but they show considerable interest in Percy afterwards. Henley was friends with Percy and maintained a correspondence with him from Virginia. One of Jefferson's Percy references occurs in the margins of *Much Ado about Nothing*. Don Pedro predicts that Benedick will abandon the life of a bachelor and get married. Benedick replies, 'If I do, hang me in a bottle [a kind of basket], like a cat, and shoot at me; and he that hits me, let him be clapped on the shoulder and called *Adam*.'[40]

Preceding the name 'Adam' Jefferson placed an asterisk, which corresponds to a note he wrote in the margin referencing a ballad in Percy's *Reliques*, 'Adam Bell, Clym of the Clough, and William of Cloudsley'. In his headnote to the ballad Percy recalls *Much Ado about Nothing* and acknowledges that Benedick's 'Adam' alludes to the folk hero Adam Bell.[41] It seems unlikely that Henley and Jefferson both discovered references to Adam Bell in Shakespeare without discussing them with one another.

Jefferson similarly annotated other plays in Capell's Shakespeare, including *All's Well that Ends Well*, *Love's Labours Lost*, *Measure for Measure* and *The Merry Wives of Windsor*. Jefferson's marginal notes reveal that, like John Adams, he did not limit himself to Shakespeare's histories and tragedies. He also read the comedies – and read them with the eye of an aficionado and a scholar.

Like Henley, Jefferson developed a fascination for the English language. Henley heard the language of Shakespeare as he listened to Virginians speak; Jefferson suspected that Shakespeare's vocabulary survived in rural England. Toward the end of his life he wrote to John Evelyn Denison, speaker of the House of Commons, to encourage him to support the research and publication of English county glossaries: 'When these local vocabularies are published and digested together into a single one it is probable we shall find that there is not a word in Shakespear which is not now in use in some of the counties of England, from whence we may obtain its true sense.'[42]

Beyond his friendship with Henley, Jefferson's social life was branching out in other ways during the early 1770s. In October 1770 he paid his first visit to The Forest, the plantation of John Wayles. After the death of her husband Bathurst Skelton, Wayles's daughter Martha had moved back to The Forest. Jefferson greatly enjoyed her father's company. He called Wayles 'a most agreeable companion, full of pleasantry and good humor, and welcomed in every society'.[43] The friendship Jefferson developed with the father facilitated his courtship with the daughter.

Martha was an accomplished woman. She was well read, and she could play the harpsichord and the pianoforte. Jefferson, who shared her love of music, played the violin. Their courtship progressed quickly. They got together often, and they exchanged letters when apart. They were married at The Forest on 1 January 1772. After her death Jefferson destroyed their personal correspondence, preferring to keep secret what they wrote to each other when they were apart. His desire for privacy is understandable, but his destruction of their correspondence represents a great loss to American literature. In terms of literary quality, their letters may have rivalled the correspondence of John and Abigail Adams.[44]

Two Shakespeare-related pieces of sheet music from The Forest survive at the University of Virginia with Jefferson's collection of songs, ballads and cantatas. They provide tantalising clues about the literary and cultural life he enjoyed during his courtship. The two pieces are part of the incidental music from *The Merchant of Venice* composed by Thomas Augustine Arne, who is best known as the composer of 'Rule, Britannia'. 'To Keep My Gentle Jessy', one piece from *The Merchant of Venice* Jefferson obtained from Wayles, Arne scored for high voice and keyboard, with figured bass and a separate part for flute. Arne also composed 'The Serenade', the other piece from *The Merchant of Venice* in the Wayles / Jefferson collection. Better known by the first line, 'My Bliss Too Long My Bride Denies', 'The Serenade' is scored for high voice and harpsichord with figured bass and also contains a separate part for flute or guitar. Imagine the fun Thomas and Martha had performing these songs from *The Merchant of Venice* at The Forest.[45]

Jefferson's marriage also connected him to the Skipwith family. Martha's half-sister Tabitha had married a young Virginia gentleman named Robert Skipwith. One day at The Forest during the summer of 1771 he and Jefferson spoke at length about literature and learning. Jefferson promised to help him assemble a library of his own. Skipwith wrote a follow-up letter to remind him of his promise.

Skipwith's letter provides a hint of their conversation. Apparently Jefferson got so carried away with erudite scholarly books that Skipwith found it necessary to temper his enthusiasm. Describing the kinds of books he wanted, Skipwith wrote: 'I would have them suited to the capacity of a common reader who understands but little of the classicks and who has not leisure for any intricate or tedious study. Let them be improving as well as amusing and among the rest let there be Hume's history of England, the new edition of Shakespear and the short Roman history you mentioned and all Sterne's works.'[46] By the 'new edition of Shakespear' Skipwith meant Capell's Shakespeare. Clearly, Jefferson told Skipwith about the new edition and convinced him to acquire a copy. Sure enough, when Skipwith received the library catalogue Jefferson compiled for him, it listed Capell's Shakespeare.[47]

The cover letter to the catalogue reinforces the importance Jefferson placed on Shakespeare. He justifies reading fiction at length, subsuming plays and narrative verse within the larger category of fiction. Ideally, a work of literature should be judged by the effect it has on the reader. A good book should draw its readers into the world it creates and keep them there in an almost dreamlike state of suspension.[48] To illustrate the power of literature, Jefferson offers the following example: 'I appeal to every reader of feeling and sentiment whether the fictitious murther of Duncan by Macbeth in Shakespeare does not excite in him as great horror of villainy, as the real one of Henry IV by Ravillac as related by Davila?'[49] Jefferson was not suggesting that Skipwith read *Macbeth* in lieu of Davila's *History of the Civil Wars of France*. The well-read gentleman need not choose between the two. He should read both.

Fiction, Jefferson observes, could fulfil the purpose of inculcating moral virtue more efficiently than fact. History was too uneven. Few episodes in history could excite the 'sympathetic emotion of virtue' at its highest level. Fiction, alternatively, could evoke a reader's sympathy because imaginary characters can be fashioned in a way real personages cannot. Fictional characters can illustrate and exemplify '...every moral rule of life. Thus a lively and lasting sense of filial duty,' he says, 'is more effectually impressed on the mind of a son or daughter by reading *King Lear*, than by all the dry volumes of ethics and divinity that ever were written.'[50]

The literary criticism Jefferson read reinforced his theory about the moral value of reading Shakespeare. In the coming years he added to his library a copy of William Richardson's *Philosophical Analysis and Illustration of Some of Shakespeare's Remarkable Characters*.[51] First published in 1774, Richardson's is the first book devoted to an examination of Shakespeare's characters. He analyses Macbeth, Hamlet, Jaques and Imogen. Richardson's *Analysis* deserves recognition as a pioneering work in the study of character psychology. His ideas closely coincide with what Jefferson had written in his letter to Skipwith three years earlier.

Dabney Carr was another member of Jefferson's family who became a Shakespeare enthusiast. Carr had attended school with Jefferson and later married his sister Martha. Jefferson praised Carr's 'spotless integrity, sound judgment, handsome imagination, enriched by education and reading'. Carr had a ten-volume edition of Shakespeare in his library. Reinforcing his interest, he also owned Montagu's *Essay on Shakespeare*.[52]

Elected to the House of Burgesses in 1771 and again in 1772, Carr was another Shakespeare enthusiast poised to be a young leader of the American Revolution. On 12 March 1773 he introduced a resolution to the House of Burgesses to create intercolonial committees of correspondence. After the resolution passed, Governor Dunmore dissolved the legislature, but the Virginians independently resolved to correspond with the other colonies. These committees of correspondence essentially became shadow governments that superseded the colonial legislatures and royal governments. They would lead to the Continental Congress in 1774. Sadly, Carr would not live to witness American independence. He died on 16 May 1773. He was twenty-nine.

After Carr's death his library went up for sale. Jefferson agreed to extend credit to Bernard Moore, a young local man who was embarking on the study of law, so that he could purchase books from Carr's library. In addition to law books Moore may have acquired Carr's copy of Shakespeare. In an undated letter to Moore written around this time,

Jefferson supplied a day-in-the-life schedule of reading. Read law in the morning and history in the afternoon. Save *belles lettres* for the evening: 'Read the best of the poets, epic, didactic, dramatic, pastoral, lyric etc but among these Shakespear must be singled out by one who wishes to learn the full powers of the English language.'[53]

Two decades earlier Franklin had hesitated to recommend Shakespeare as a model of English writing for students. Now Jefferson elevated Shakespeare above all other English poets and dramatists as a model. Continuing his advice to Moore about reading Shakespeare, Jefferson applied the advice Horace gave Roman poets: 'Turn over the Greek models by night, and turn them over again by day.'[54]

George Wythe, another member of Jefferson's Williamsburg circle, was also a Shakespeare enthusiast. The two met while Jefferson was a student at William and Mary. Wythe would subsequently direct Jefferson's legal studies. His library is known mainly because he willed it to Jefferson, who received the collection after Wythe's murder in 1806. Wythe had a significant Shakespeare collection, which contained three odd volumes of plays, the first six volumes of the duodecimo edition of Theobald's Shakespeare and the Johnson-Steevens Shakespeare, complete with Malone's *Supplement*, which means that Wythe had in his collection Henley's first set of published Shakespeare annotations.[55]

Henley developed a reputation as a troublemaker in Williamsburg, mainly because many people he encountered did not understand him. Henley was a wag and an instigator. He would poke and prod people, challenging their ideas to shake them up and move their thought in new directions. Those unaware of this impulse took everything Henley said literally and, in so doing, took offense. Henley was on firmer ground when he set religion and politics aside and stuck to literature and science.

He worked hard to bring Virginians together to pursue both literature and science. The first week of January 1772 Henley placed an advertisement in the *Virginia Gazette* announcing a course of lectures about the 'elementary ideas of poetry, including the general principles of composition'. In other words, he would be teaching a poetry-writing workshop to the general public. The course makes him a pioneer in what would become known as continuing education. According to Henley's announcement, the first lecture would start at four o'clock on Monday, 10 February. Tuition was a little steep: three pistoles. Nothing else is known about Henley's poetry-writing course. It may have never happened. Four days before the first scheduled lecture he was still scrambling to recruit students.[56]

The following year Henley turned toward the sciences to bring Virginia intellectuals together. He befriended such local figures as Theodorick Bland and James MacClurg, two Edinburgh-trained physicians who enjoyed writing poetry. Together they formed the Virginia Society for the Promotion of Useful Knowledge. According to its initial articles of organisation, the Society encompassed several subjects within its purview: agriculture, American history, commerce, geography, natural history, natural philosophy, physic and practical mathematics.

At its first meeting in May 1773, John Clayton was elected president, John Page vice president and Henley secretary. St George Tucker, then a student at William and Mary, was chosen assistant secretary. Many other prominent Virginians joined the organisation at its first general meeting, including Thomas Jefferson.[57]

Washington was also interested in joining, but at the time he was busy preparing to take his stepson Jack Custis to college. On Jonathan Boucher's recommendation, Washington had decided to send Jack to King's College (later, Columbia University). While in New York, Washington attended the American Company's production of *Hamlet* at the John Street Theatre. Lewis Hallam the younger took the title role, with David Douglass as Claudius, Sarah Douglass as Gertrude, Nancy Hallam as Ophelia and Owen Morris as the Gravedigger. After he returned home Washington did join the Virginia Society for the Promotion of Useful Knowledge. His simultaneous interest in Shakespeare and science indicates how well rounded Washington was.[58]

In June 1774 the Society held its second annual meeting, which was well attended. Jefferson was there, and so was Washington. Both renewed their memberships. Page was elected president, Wythe vice president. Henley attended as well. Washington's precise contact with Henley is unknown, but the same day as the meeting he purchased a copy of a recent pamphlet Henley had written, suggesting that Washington did know the colony's finest Shakespeare scholar.[59]

All this talk about a scientific society may seem to take the story of Shakespeare in early America far afield. Not really. The eighteenth century was the era of the virtuoso, a time when an accomplished gentleman read Shakespeare, wrote poetry, played a musical instrument, and kept current with the latest scientific developments. Sometimes science and literature overlapped. Henley, for instance, expanded his knowledge of agricultural science in Virginia, which he used to enhance his understanding of Shakespeare, as his annotations reveal.

Watching Diomedes pitch woo to Cressida in the last act of *Troilus and Cressida*, Thersites exclaims, 'How the devil Luxury, with his fat rump and potato-finger, tickles these two together!' George Steevens wrote a lengthy annotation for this passage using the name 'Collins', an identity he assumed to annotate Shakespeare's bawdy passages. Glossing the phrase 'potato-finger', Collins avoids the obvious interpretation, though the finger / phallus comparison had already entered early American literature. Who can forget Ebenezer Cook's Hudibrastic description of a native tobacco pipe in 'The Sot-Weed Factor': "In length, scarce longer than one's finger / Or that for which the ladies linger'.[60] Avoiding the phallic association, Collins talks around Shakespeare's salacious meaning as he glosses 'potato-finger': 'This root, which was in our author's time but newly imported from America, was considered as a rare exotic, and esteemed a very strong provocative.'[61]

Since potatoes had become such a large staple crop in the British Isles after Shakespeare's time, Collins adds further context from the history of agriculture, excerpting a lengthy passage from John Gerard's *Herball* to give an idea of what the potato symbolised for Shakespeare. Cribbing from John Campbell's *Political Survey of Britain*, Collins distinguishes the Virginia potato from another kind. One is called 'potato', the other 'battata'.[62]

Henley's annotation concentrates on the potato as it extends Collins's line of thinking. He recognises that Collins had not adequately distinguished the different potatoes. Those cultivated in Virginia belong to a different category altogether. Henley notes: 'The potatoes of Virginia are, however, very different in appearance, flavour, and growth, from the English; so different, as to constitute them a distinct species.'[63] Taken together, the annotations by Collins and Henley form a dialogue on potato cultivation that shows two Shakespeare scholars working hard to avoid saying the word 'penis'.

Henley's note may not contribute much to the critical interpretation of *Troilus and Cressida*. Considered in the totality of Shakespeare scholarship, this annotation is small potatoes. Considered biographically, it reveals much about Henley's intellectual life in Virginia and his attitude toward annotating. Henley befriended some of the greatest men and minds in Virginia. Besides being scientists and litterateurs, they were also farmers, who, in the case of Jefferson and Washington, devoted much thought and effort to agricultural experimentation. Henley took in everything he saw in Virginia, which he applied to understand and explain Shakespeare.

11

The Blast of War

The political arena offered far greater drama than the colonial stage during the run up to the Revolutionary War. On 16 December 1773, as David Douglass and his American Company of Comedians were preparing to open their new season in Charleston, South Carolina, patriots to the north staged a dramatic protest in Boston, Massachusetts. Led by Samuel Adams, they protested the Tea Act, which allowed the East India Company to ship thousands of pounds of tea to North America. The Tea Act benefitted both the company and the crown to the disadvantage of the American colonists, who had to pay steep duties on the tea. When the heavily laden ships reached Boston, Governor Thomas Hutchinson insisted the tea be landed and the duties paid. In a meticulously planned and carefully choreographed effort patriots adorned in Native American dress boarded the ships and dumped the tea into Boston harbour.

The protest dramatised the differences between Britain and America. Tea, a drink Colley Cibber called a 'sober, sage, and venerable liquid', symbolised the British.[1] The Native American costumes symbolised the colonists' increasingly close identification with the land where they lived over their mother country. Beyond its significance to the American Revolution the Boston Tea Party, as the iconic event became known, deserves recognition as the year's most memorable piece of political theatre.

Parliament reacted swiftly to punish Massachusetts for the destructive protest, passing the Coercive Acts, retaliatory legislation that included the Boston Port Bill, which banned the loading or unloading of any ships in the harbour. After the Port Bill passed it would take effect on 1 June and remain in force until peace and obedience was restored to the city. News of the punitive legislation spread quickly, outraging colonists throughout British North America.

The American Company of Comedians wound up its lengthy season in Charleston that May. On Thursday the nineteenth it punctuated the season with *King John*. Though neither the players nor the audience knew it, *King John* would be the last play produced on the colonial American stage.[2] As the final play performed during the colonial era, *King John* is oddly appropriate. In the role of Philip the Bastard – the strongest character in the play – Lewis Hallam the younger castigates those who wish to rebel against King John:

> Know the gallant monarch is in arms
> And like an eagle o'er his eyrie towers,
> To souse annoyance that comes near his nest.
> And you degenerate, you ingrate revolts,
> You bloody Neroes, ripping up the womb
> Of your dear mother England, blush for shame![3]

King John gets poisoned in Shakespeare's play, but otherwise his son succeeds him in an orderly fashion. Philip the Bastard gets the last word: 'Nought shall make us sure / If England to itself do rest but true.'[4] Needless to say, England's conflict with its American colonies would turn out very differently. As the Revolutionary polemicists argued, England did not remain true to itself, at least, not to the principles of natural rights the English constitution embodies.

While the Douglass Company was ending its season in Charleston, colonial legislatures were conveying their solidarity with Boston. Many passed legislation protesting the Coercive Acts. In Williamsburg, for example, the House of Burgesses passed a resolution making 1 June 1774 a day of prayer and fasting to protest the Coercive Acts and to show Virginia's solidarity with Massachusetts. Learning about the resolution the Virginia legislators passed, Governor Dunmore promptly dissolved the House of Burgesses.

Dunmore's actions did not prevent the burgesses from reconvening unofficially. They left the capitol and walked down the street to Raleigh Tavern to debate what to do next. The erstwhile burgesses agreed to a general congress of delegates from throughout colonial America. Other colonies – New York, Pennsylvania, Rhode Island – similarly called for an intercolonial congress to adapt common measures to resist the crown. The colonies used different methods to select their congressional delegates. Representatives from throughout Virginia, to continue the example, convened in August. Besides electing delegates to the intercolonial congress, the Virginia Convention provided a forum for airing grievances. This general congress, which would assemble in September, would become known to history as the First Continental Congress.

Articulating their anger and frustration with the British government, the colonists quoted Shakespeare for support. A contributor to the *Pennsylvania Packet* using the pen name 'A British American' recalled lines from Shakespeare to celebrate the principles underlying the English constitution but lamented the British government's refusal to apply them to their colonial subjects. Unless all Americans united in protest, their rights and freedoms would be destroyed.

'A British American' – B. A. for short – quotes the most famous speech in *Richard II*, the lyrical paean to England that John of Gaunt delivers from his deathbed. B. A. does not quote the speech's most famous lines – 'This royal throne of kings, this sceptred isle ... This blessèd plot, this earth, this realm, this England'. Instead, B. A. quotes from its conclusion. After celebrating what England has traditionally symbolised, John of Gaunt describes what it has become under the weak and ineffectual rule of Richard II. B. A. briefly introduces the quotation, which he casts into prose:

> When I think of England, that once renowned seat of freedom and justice, I cannot, in the agony of my mind, help exclaiming in the prophetic language of John of Gaunt, as given by the inimitable Shakespeare – 'England bound in with the triumphant sea, whose rocky shore beats back the enemies of watry Neptune, is bound in with shame, with inky blots and rotten parchment bonds, that England that was wont to conquer others, hath made a shameful conquest of itself, Ah!'[5]

The keyword in B. A.'s introduction is 'prophetic'. Relating the past, *Richard II* predicts the future. What happened under Richard II has happened again under the rule of a greedy, selfish, incompetent ruler. A land that had symbolised freedom and justice has become filled with shame. John of Gaunt's speech caught the attention of readers throughout Revolutionary America. B. A.'s article was widely reprinted. Williamsburg printer and publisher Clementina Rind, for example, reprinted it in her *Virginia Gazette*, and other newspapers in New York and New England reprinted it as well.[6]

On 5 September 1774 the First Continental Congress convened at Carpenters' Hall in Philadelphia. The list of delegates verifies an enduring truism: great leaders are great readers. The passion for Shakespeare among some delegates – John Adams, Samuel Chase, George Washington – has been discussed. Others deserve mention. John Dickinson, for one, had quoted at least two different Shakespeare plays in his previous writings, *Othello* and *Henry IV, Part II.*[7]

Many members of the First Continental Congress had collections of Shakespeare in their home libraries. Charles Thomson, the congressional secretary, had an excellent personal library, which included a nine-volume edition of Shakespeare. Thomas Lynch, Jr, a delegate from South Carolina, had an eight-volume edition of Shakespeare in his library. So did Robert Treat Paine, a delegate from Massachusetts. Abraham Clark, a delegate from New Jersey, owned a recent London edition of Shakespeare. And Richard Henry Lee, another delegate from Virginia, also merits recognition as a Shakespeare enthusiast.[8]

According to a traditional story, Lee, who had been serving in the Virginia House of Burgesses, walked out of the capitol in Williamsburg one day with two fellow burgesses. Standing on its porch shortly before the Revolutionary War began, they were unsure when they would see each other again. Lee took out his pencil and inscribed the opening lines from *Macbeth* onto one of the columns of the capitol:

> When shall we three meet again?
> In thunder, lightning, and in rain;
> When the hurly-burly's done,
> When the battle's lost and won.[9]

The story seems too good to be true. Though it may be apocryphal, it does reflect Lee's very real passion for Shakespeare's writings. He owned a twelve-volume edition of Theobald's Shakespeare and a nine-volume duodecimo edition. Lee's interest would continue for years to come. After the war he obtained a copy of Thomas Davies's three-volume *Dramatic Miscellanies*, which contains numerous observations about Shakespearean drama. Both actor and bookseller, Davies drew upon a lifetime of professional experience to compile his entertaining collection of anecdotes and critical interpretations.

By the time the First Continental Congress adjourned in late October, it had passed a series of resolutions, which were collected together as an association, to which the delegates affixed their names. The eighth resolution is what officially ended the history of the colonial American stage. To encourage economy, industry and frugality Congress discouraged 'every species of extravagance and dissipation, especially all horse racing, and all kinds of gaming, cock fighting, exhibitions of shews, plays, and other expensive diversions and entertainments'. Satirising the association under the pen name 'Bob Jingle', one waggish Loyalist complained about the ban on plays and other entertainments. Bob Jingle found the ban wasn't quite right: it left little to do but 'eat, sleep and sh-te'.[10]

Patrick Henry, who had represented Virginia at the First Continental Congress, faced a political challenge the following March at the second Virginia Convention. That month delegates from all parts of the colony gathered at St John's Church in Richmond, which had been chosen for the convention because Williamsburg, the colonial capital, was becoming too hot for local citizens challenging the British administration. Elected by voters across the colony, this group of over a hundred delegates included nearly all of Virginia's foremost leaders.

The convention began on Monday, 20 March, when the delegates started to debate the dire situation the American colonies faced. By Thursday the debate reached fever pitch. When it came to a resolution stipulating that the Virginia colonists arm themselves in their own defence, one voice rose above the rest, that of Patrick Henry. Many Virginians recognised the necessity of war, but some still needed convincing. To that end, Henry delivered the most memorable speech of his life, which culminates:

> Gentlemen may cry, peace, peace – but there is no peace. The war is actually begun! The next gale that sweeps from the north will bring to our ears the clash of resounding arms! Our brethren are already in the field! Why stand we here idle? What is it that gentlemen wish? What would they have? Is life so dear, or peace so sweet, as to be purchased at the price of chains and slavery? Forbid it, Almighty God! – I know not what course others may take; but as for me, give me liberty, or give me death!

When William Wirt was researching *Sketches of the Life and Character of Patrick Henry* in the early nineteenth century, he contacted many people who had known him. Strongly influenced by what Jefferson said, Wirt depicts Henry as a natural genius akin to Shakespeare: 'He was, indeed, a mere child of nature, and nature seems to have been too proud and too jealous of her work, to permit it to be touched by the hand of art. She gave him Shakspeare's genius, and bade him, like Shakspeare, to depend on that alone.' John Randolph of Roanoke – another person Wirt contacted for information – found the comparison with Shakespeare imprecise; it did not adequately capture Henry's ability to perform before an audience. Instead, Randolph called Henry 'Shakspeare and Garrick combined'.[11]

Recent discoveries have revealed that Henry was more widely read than the natural genius of Wirt's *Sketches*. A schoolbook in his library suggests that he read some of Shakespeare's speeches in his youth. *The Preceptor: Containing a General Course of Education, Wherein the First Principles of Polite Learning Are Laid Down*, a popular textbook Robert Dodsley first published in London in 1748, exposed its readers to Shakespeare.[12]

In a section titled 'On Speaking' Dodsley included a set of speeches from Shakespeare for students to memorise and recite, explaining that the speeches would acquaint students 'with the higher and more poetical stile of their own language'. The first lesson presents 'The Progress of Life', as Dodsley titled Jaques's All-the-world's-a-stage speech from *As You Like It*. Overall, the lessons are weighted more heavily toward the history plays. Dodsley took two lessons from *Henry IV, Part II* and three from *Henry V*, including the Once-more-into-the-breach oration. Another lesson presents Cardinal Wolsey's Farewell-to-greatness soliloquy from *Henry VIII*. In short, Dodsley's *Preceptor* let Henry develop his oratorical skills by reading and memorising famous speeches from Shakespeare.

Henry's Liberty-or-death speech sounds like Shakespeare because it echoes a speech Cassius makes in the first act of *Julius Caesar*. To convince Brutus to rise up against Caesar, who presumably wishes to emasculate the Roman senate and declare himself king, Cassius argues:

> I cannot tell what you and other men
> Think of this life; but for my single self,
> I had as lief not be as live to be
> In awe of such a thing as I myself.[13]

Henry's speech shares many similarities with Cassius's. Both Cassius and Henry claim to be unaware of other men's views. In addition, each claims to speak solely for himself. And, finally, each expresses a preference for death over life under a tyrannical ruler. The close parallels between his speech at the Virginia Convention and Cassius's speech in *Julius Caesar* suggest that Henry had read and internalised *Julius Caesar* by the time he gave his most famous speech.[14]

Most likely, Henry had read *Julius Caesar* by 1765, when he presented the Virginia Resolutions in the House of Burgesses to protest the Stamp Act. Introducing those resolutions, he had said that 'in former times Tarquin and Julius had their Brutus, Charles had his Cromwell, and he did not doubt but some good American would stand up in favour of his country.'[15] Henry's Caesar-had-his-Brutus speech, as it is known, suggests that Brutus, more than Cassius, was the Shakespearean character the American Revolutionaries took as their model.

Unlike Cassius and the other conspirators, Brutus was motivated not by jealousy but by altruistic principles. After Brutus has killed himself in the final scene of *Julius Caesar*, Mark Antony pays tribute to him:

> This was the noblest Roman of them all.
> All the conspirators save only he
> Did that they did in envy of great Caesar.
> He only, in a general honest thought
> And common good to all, made one of them.
> His life was gentle, and the elements
> So mixed in him that Nature might stand up
> And say to all the world 'This was a man!'[16]

Julius Caesar influenced other early American writers. Like her brother James Otis and her husband James Warren, Mercy Otis Warren was also a Shakespeare enthusiast. Having never seen any plays performed on stage, she learned about the theatre by reading Shakespeare. The closet dramas she wrote reflect Shakespeare's impact. *The Adulateur*, her first play, is an allegory of Revolutionary Boston, dramatising a story about a rapacious governor who tramples the peoples' rights. The governor is challenged by two patriots with familiar names. Brutus, the first patriot, represents James Otis, and Cassius represents Samuel Adams.[17]

Josiah Quincy, Jr also saw a parallel between the action Brutus takes against Caesar and the American cause. In *Observations on the Boston Port Bill*, the most detailed and erudite protest against Parliament's punitive legislation, Quincy alludes to *Julius Caesar*. He famously asks the following rhetorical question: 'Is not Britain to America, what Caesar was to Rome?'[18]

Once the second Virginia Convention drew to a close in late March, it did not take long before the colonists' decision to arm themselves proved to be the right one. Massachusetts had made a similar decision, and members of their militia – the Minutemen – went into action the following month. Early Wednesday morning, 19 April, under orders from General Thomas Gage, the royal governor of Massachusetts, eight hundred redcoats marched on Concord, where the colonists had a large cache of guns and ammunition. Having been warned by Paul Revere and others, the Minutemen were ready. They assembled at Lexington prepared to clash with the British troops. When the British commander ordered the Americans to disperse, they refused. The redcoats fired upon the Minutemen, killing eight and forcing the remainder to retreat toward Concord.

The Minutemen, altogether about one-quarter the size of the British force, established a new position on the farther side of the Old North Bridge over the Concord River. This time they successfully resisted the advancing troops and humiliated the British, forcing them to retreat to Boston and harassing them as they went. The Massachusetts militia adapted to the terrain; the redcoats did not. The British army had learned little since Braddock's disastrous defeat at the Battle of the Monongahela two decades earlier. Their inability to adjust their fighting techniques to local conditions Franklin found absurd. An acquaintance told him that the British troops complained about the ill usage they received from the Minutemen, who got behind stone walls and fired at them. Franklin wondered 'whether there were not two sides to the wall'.[19]

The gale from the north Patrick Henry had predicted was not long in coming. News of the Battle of Lexington and Concord reached the other colonies before the month was out. Jefferson called the mood of Revolutionary America after Lexington and Concord both a 'state of excitement' and a 'state of exasperation'. Upon learning of the battle, he informed a correspondent: 'Within this week we have received the unhappy news of an action of considerable magnitude between the king's troops and our brethren of Boston ... This accident has cut off our last hopes of reconciliation, and a phrenzy of revenge seems to have seized all ranks of people.'[20]

The individual colonies had their own militias, which had provided their only form of defence throughout the colonial period, but none had ever confronted as formidable a foe as the British army. Washington would initially form the Continental army from the militia companies around Boston, but otherwise he kept his army and the local militias separate. Militias would remain an important part of the American fighting force throughout the Revolutionary War. They would provide local defence, allowing

Washington to turn the Continental army into a concentrated fighting force, which could engage the enemy in major conflicts.[21]

After the Battle of Lexington and Concord militia companies throughout Revolutionary America stepped up their training. In June 1775 the Scottish traveller Janet Schaw witnessed an assembly of the militia in Wilmington, North Carolina. While chuckling at the sight, she painted a vivid picture: '2000 men in their shirts and trousers, preceded by a very ill-beat drum and a fiddler, who was also in his shirt with a long sword and a cue at his hair, who played with all his might. They made indeed a most unmartial appearance.' Schaw followed this humorous depiction of the militia with a sobering sentence for any British soldier who dared encounter the poorly caparisoned North Carolina militia: 'But the worst figure there can shoot from behind a bush and kill even a General Wolfe.'[22]

Later that day Schaw met Robert Howe, a colonel in the North Carolina militia, when she dined with several other militia officers. Josiah Quincy, Jr, who had met Howe when he passed through North Carolina two years earlier, found him 'a most happy compound of the man of sense, sentiment and dignity, with the man of the world, the sword, the senate and the bucks'.[23] Schaw's impression differed considerably. Before dinner she had been reading a volume of Shakespeare containing *Henry IV, Part I*. After Colonel Howe arrived, he brashly entered her apartment and picked up the book, which he brought open in his hand into the company. Piqued at the freedom he took with her personal belongings, Schaw reproved him with a remark about his manners and breeding. Howe admitted his mistake and accepted whatever punishment Schaw wished to exact.

'You shall', she said, 'read aloud a few pages which I will point out, and I am sure you will do Shakespear justice.'

He took the book from her and quickly noticed that she had chosen the passage in which Falstaff describes the sorry regiment he has assembled: 'I had a hundred and fifty tattered prodigals lately come from swine-keeping, from eating draff and husks. A mad fellow met me on the way and told me I had unloaded all the gibbets and pressed the dead bodies.' Schaw could see that Colonel Howe recognised her parallel because his face 'coloured like scarlet'. Still, he accepted his punishment and read the whole passage, though without his characteristic vivacity.[24]

Once the British troops retreated to Boston after the clash at Lexington and Concord, the Massachusetts militia posted sentinels across the Charles River on Prospect Hill to oversee the city, thus beginning the siege of Boston. In June the tension between Massachusetts and the British forces would snap, resulting in the Battle of Bunker Hill. General Gage ordered Major-General William Howe to attack the hill, but the redcoats met ferocious resistance from the Massachusetts militia. The British won the battle, but only at a big and bloody cost, suffering over a thousand casualties in an attacking force of 2500. The dynamic would soon change. On 2 July 1775 General George Washington, having been unanimously appointed commander in chief of the Continental army, reached Cambridge, Massachusetts to take control.

Washington found the Massachusetts troops eager to fight. Joseph Ward, aide-de-camp and secretary to General Artemas Ward, conveyed his personal enthusiasm to John Adams. He was confident the Continental army would triumph over the British. Ward exclaimed: 'That the united efforts of the free the brave and the hardy millions of independent Americans whose minds are enlightened and animated with the divine spirit of freedom, should ever be enslaved by British tyrants is incredible among men!'[25]

Ward shrewdly foresaw that the American struggle had world-wide ramifications: 'If America should be enslaved it is probable freedom will expire thro the world. It is a great and a glorious prize which the Americans contend for, the happiness of all future ages, and the freedom of the world as the liberties of all nations may in some degree be connected with ours.' He ended his letter with a somewhat modified and abbreviated quotation from King Henry's St Crispin's Day speech in *Henry V*: 'I am not the most covetous of gold, and care not who my garments wear; but if to covet honour, be a crime, I am the most offending soul alive!'[26]

Philip Freneau – the Poet of the Revolution – imagined what Boston was like during the British occupation in *A Voyage to Boston*, the latest in a series of poems he wrote to parody General Gage. The speaker of this poem meets the 'Genius of America', who gives him a magic vest that makes him invisible and tells him to enter the 'dome of state / Where Gage resides our Western potentate'. The poet's portrayal of Gage and his minions resembles the famous scene from *Paradise Lost* as Satan gathers the other fallen angels around him. Gage, 'chief of all the Pandemonium crew', asks the others to explain the British humiliation at Lexington and Concord.[27]

Gage's minions offer a few fatuous excuses but cannot explain how the Americans fought so well: 'They fought like those who press for death's embrace / And laugh the grizly monarch in the face'. Gage ultimately concludes that he and his men should attack an enemy more suited to their abilities, so they resolve to steal a sheep. As Gage and his 'black guard crew' fall asleep, the poet leaves the statehouse, returning the magic vest to the Genius of America before celebrating the bravery of the American troops and their dedication to liberty.[28]

Though *A Voyage to Boston* borrows its imagery from Milton, Freneau used Shakespeare to promote the poem. It was not the only time he made creative use of Shakespeare. In another poem he wrote during the Revolutionary War, Freneau characterises Shakespeare as someone

Who looked the world of nature through,
Who soaring high, where others failed,
Invention's brightest heaven assailed,
And saw beyond the dark disguise
What lay too deep for vulgar eyes![29]

Published in November 1775, *A Voyage to Boston* appeared with the following lines from King Henry's Once-more-unto-the breach oration on the title page:

In peace there's nothing so becomes a man,
As modest stillness and humility;
But when the blast of war blows in your ears,
Then imitate the action of the tyger,
Stiffen the sinews, summon up the blood.[30]

Typically, a title-page motto serves as a *mise en abyme*, a brief text encapsulating the greater work in which it appears. The title-page motto of *A Voyage to Boston* works differently. It serves as a countertext to the larger poem. In Freneau's epic parody Gage and his minions behave like buffoons. The lines from Shakespeare inform American readers how to behave in response. Even as they laugh at *A Voyage to Boston*, they should get angry that their lives are governed by incompetence and insensitivity. From the title page of Freneau's poem Shakespeare's words tell American readers how to behave in the face of inept leaders: they should ready themselves for battle. Philadelphia publisher William Woodhouse enjoyed the Shakespearean title-page motto so much he used it as advertising copy to promote *A Voyage to Boston*.[31]

The Second Continental Congress reconvened in September. Bringing together strong-willed leaders from throughout the colonies, the Continental Congress sometimes led to personality conflicts. Benjamin Harrison, a delegate from Virginia, assumed an increasingly important role as independence approached, often serving as chair when Congress went into a committee of the whole. John Adams disliked Harrison. He called him 'another Sir John Falstaff', finding his 'conversation disgusting to every man of delicacy or decorum, obscene, profane, impious'. Furthermore, Adams said that Harrison was 'perpetually ridiculing the Bible, calling it the worst book in the world'. Regardless, Adams tried to be polite to Harrison for the sake of the important work they had to accomplish.[32]

Some delegates felt a sense of helplessness that autumn. British troops continued to occupy Boston, and there seemed little the Continental army could do to alter the situation. These uneasy delegates feared the British government would force the colonies to concede on humiliating terms. The first week of October Silas Deane, a delegate from Connecticut, expressed feelings of frustration in a letter to his wife: 'I often say to myself, *Blessed are the Dead*, if as Hamlet says, in that same sleep of theirs, there were no dream. You will think me melancholy, and you are not much out of the way. The soul distressing uncertainty in which we are respecting our northern friends, with the weight, and fatigue of business is almost too much.'[33]

Deane's letter presents a weird conglomeration of references. His italicised phrase comes from the Book of Revelations: 'And I heard a voice from heaven saying unto me, Write, Blessed are the dead which die in the Lord from henceforth: Yea, saith the Spirit, that they may rest from their labours; and their works do follow them.'[34] Deane's *Hamlet* reference comes from the To-be-or-not-to-be soliloquy, but he somewhat misrepresents what Hamlet says. While seeing death as the surcease of pain, Hamlet expresses fear and trepidation regarding whether people dream after death:

> To sleep, perchance to dream – ay, there's the rub,
> For in that sleep of death what dreams may come
> When we have shuffled off this mortal coil
> Must give us pause.[35]

Deane interprets Hamlet to mean that no dreams will come in the sleep of death, but what gives Hamlet pause is the uncertainty regarding what happens after death. Regardless of his interpretation, Deane portrays himself in the letter to his wife as a Hamlet-like figure, a melancholy man who has been wronged, who has been plagued by a tyrant, who feels the need to do something to ameliorate his predicament but who also feels helpless so to do.

The American Revolutionary as Hamlet: Deane was not the first to manifest the idea. In the *Dinwiddianae* Mercer had assumed a Hamlet-like persona, one who tries to remedy the behaviour of Virginia's royal governor. Other Revolutionary American references to *Hamlet* similarly cast the patriot as a protector. American authors who identified with Hamlet saw themselves as obliged to set right the wrongs perpetrated by the British colonial government.[36]

Released in January 1776, Thomas Paine's *Common Sense* triggered a new version of Shakespeare's most famous soliloquy. With *Common Sense* Paine made the case for American independence more forcefully than anyone before him. Paine convinced many Americans that declaring independence was the right thing to so. He did not convince everyone. William Smith, the Philadelphia educator, was not necessarily against independence, but he did think his fellow Americans should proceed more cautiously.

Writing under the pen name 'Cato', Provost Smith published a series of letters in the *Pennsylvania Ledger* appealing for caution in turbulent times. 'Cato, No. 4' is prefaced by 'Alas Poor Cato!', a poem written under the pseudonym 'Hamlet'. Smith uses the soliloquy as a rhetorical template for structuring his political ideas:

> To write or not to write, that is the question —
> Whether 'tis nobler in the mind to bear
> Th' unlicens'd wrongs of furious party-zeal,
> Or dip the pen into a nest of hornets
> And still, by teazing, wake them?[37]

This playful poem serves a useful rhetorical purpose. Owen Aldridge explains: 'The lines wittily defend Smith for taking up an unpopular cause and suggest that he is exposing himself to public obloquy for patriotic reasons.' Cato says that this soliloquy 'was really put into my hand by a friend', but Paine did not buy it. He could tell that both Hamlet and Cato were Smith's personae. Paine joked, 'Cato's title to soliloquies is indisputable; because no man cares for his company.'[38] Paine may judge Smith too harshly. Two decades earlier Smith had identified with Polonius when he quoted Shakespeare. Now he identified with Hamlet.

As a delegate to the Continental Congress, Deane was the one who initiated the plan to capture Fort Ticonderoga and allotted funds for the expedition, which proved to be a brilliant success. Ethan Allen and his Green Mountain Boys captured Fort Ticonderoga from the British, seizing possession of both the fort and its valuable weaponry. Colonel Henry Knox assumed the arduous task of transporting all the cannons and ammunition from Fort Ticonderoga to Cambridge, Massachusetts.

Knox had trained himself in the art of artillery. As the proprietor of the London Bookstore in Boston, he imported a large quantity of military books, which he had read in his spare time. Knox first met Washington in Cambridge after he and his wife Lucy escaped through enemy lines during the siege of Boston. They became good friends, and Knox joined the Continental army as a civilian consultant. He was later commissioned as a colonel and subsequently became chief of artillery. Knox brought the heavy Ticonderoga artillery on a 300-mile trek through forest and field, across frozen streams and up and down the Berkshire hills in western Massachusetts. When he reached Cambridge, no one, with the possible exception of Lucy Knox, was happier to see him than General Washington, who now had sufficient firepower to threaten the British.[39]

Washington decided to take possession of Dorchester Heights, which had a commanding view of the British positions in Boston. By pointing the Ticonderoga artillery down toward the British troops, he would force them to make a decision of their own: fight or flee. The biggest challenge Washington faced beforehand was taking Dorchester Heights undetected. To that end, he ordered his troops to bombard Boston for three nights running to divert British attention from their true objective. Under the cloak of darkness on Monday, 4 March 1776, Washington and his troops took full possession of Dorchester Heights.

The next morning the British officers discovered what had happened and made preparations to assault Washington's position. Before they could get their troops ready, a sudden storm arose, forcing them to call off their attack. Though the adverse weather conditions forestalled the redcoats, Washington prepared for the worst and kept his men working throughout the storm. In other words, the cold rain that stopped the British assault did nothing to prevent American troops from working to strengthen their defences.

On the evening of 16 March the American troops moved their heavy artillery forward to Nook's Hill, menacingly close to Boston. Daybreak revealed the sight of American cannons pointed down on them. The British commanders saw that Boston was untenable. They ordered an evacuation and left the city to the Continental army. Boston celebrated the victory and hailed General Washington. Harvard College awarded him an honorary doctorate of laws. Washington appreciated the honour but knew that any celebrations were premature. With Boston under American control, he made preparations to defend the colonies south of New England.

Actually, Washington had already taken steps to strengthen other ports south of Boston. In December 1775 he had sent General Charles Lee to Newport, Rhode Island, where Lee stayed until March 1776, when he went to New York to bolster its defences. By the end of that month Lee assumed command of the southern department, taking up residence in the Governor's Palace in Williamsburg.

Virginia's coastal geography presented so many complications Lee scarcely knew where to start establishing his defences. On 5 April he informed Washington: 'I am like a dog in a dancing school – I know not where to turn myself, where to fix myself – the circumstance of the country intersected by navigable rivers the uncertainty of the enemy's designs and motion who can fly in an instant to any spot they chuse with their canvass wings!'[40] Possessing two qualities essential for any good letter writer, Lee was well read, and he had a keen wit. The vivid simile demonstrates Lee's desire to make his letter to Washington both informative and entertaining. It comes from William Congreve's *Way of the World*. In the final scene of this renowned comedy the slow-witted Tony Witwould has trouble comprehending what is happening as the plot reaches its denouement: 'I understand nothing of the matter, – I'm in a maze yet, like a dog in a dancing school.'[41]

Before he finishes describing his dilemma, Lee switches from Congreve to Shakespeare: 'I may possibly be in the north, when as Richard says, I shou'd serve my sovereign in the west.' These words come from *Richard III*. When King Richard asks Stanley if his followers are on Britain's western shore, Stanley informs him that they are in the north. Richard replies, 'Cold friends to me. What do they in the north / When they should serve their sovereign in the west?'[42]

Swapping a Congreve comedy for a Shakespeare history, Lee reflects the seriousness of his situation, but he cannot mask his delight with the Shakespearean allusion. Lee wrote two additional letters that same day, one to Robert Howe in North Carolina and another to Richard Henry Lee, then in Philadelphia serving in the Continental Congress. Charles Lee omitted Congreve but reused Shakespeare in both letters.[43]

Once Boston was secure, Washington left the city to take measures for New York's security, reaching Manhattan on 13 April 1776.

Above: 1. William Byrd's Westover, shown here as it appears from the James River, housed the finest library in colonial Virginia, which included one of the few Shakespeare folios in British North America.

Right: 2. The Rev. Samuel Johnson, President of King's College (later, Columbia University), recommended Shakespeare to friends, students and fellow educators.

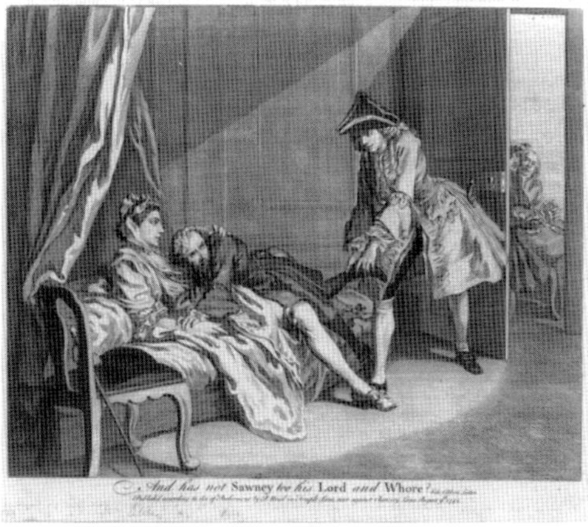

Below right: 3. After James Ralph published *Sawney* the name stuck. For the rest of Alexander Pope's life, 'Sawney' was used in satirical attacks against him, as in this engraving, *And Has Not Sawney Too His Lord and Whore* (1742), which depicts Colley Cibber seizing Pope by the leg and pulling him off a woman.

Left: 4. David Garrick, shown here in his role as Hamlet, was not only the greatest Shakespearean actor of his era, he was also Shakespeare's greatest eighteenth-century advocate.

Below left: 5. In this ink and wash drawing Dr Alexander Hamilton portrays himself as Loquacious Scribble, the persona he assumes in the *History of the Tuesday Club*.

Below: 6. Based on a painting by Henry Fuseli, this engraving depicts Shylock approaching Bassanio seeking his pound of flesh in *The Merchant of Venice*, the most popular Shakespeare comedy on the colonial American stage.

Above: 7. William Smith, Provost of the Academy of Philadelphia (later, University of Pennsylvania), put *Hamlet* to use for both educational and political purposes.

Right: 8. Based on a painting by John Singleton Copley, this engraving depicts John Adams as a man of learning and a man of the world.

Below right: 9. Though typically portrayed in old age, Abigail Adams appears as a young woman in this engraving. From her teenage years until the end of her life, she remained an ardent admirer of Shakespeare and quoted his works numerous times in her correspondence.

Left: 10. James Otis was one of many Revolutionary American patriots who read Shakespeare and recommended his works to others.

Below: 11. In this drawing Pierre du Simitiere captures the contemporary Redwood Library, one of many subscription libraries that helped circulate Shakespeare's writings in colonial America.

12. In this early nineteenth-century rendition, the artist emphasises the histrionic nature of the Stamp Act protests.

Above: 13. Lady Macbeth, depicted here in a mezzotint based on a painting by Henry Fuseli, became a symbol of Mother England in Revolutionary America.

Above right: 14. John Adams and Josiah Quincy, Jr stepped up to defend the British soldiers accused of murder during the Boston Massacre, portrayed in this famous engraving by Paul Revere.

Right: 15. Thomas Jefferson read Shakespeare, studied Shakespeare scholarship, discussed Shakespeare's plays with others and recommended Shakespeare as essential reading.

16. The Boston Tea Party, depicted here in a nineteenth-century lithograph, is arguably the greatest piece of political theatre of the American Revolutionary era.

17. Carpenters' Hall, where the First Continental Congress met in 1774, also housed the Library Company of Philadelphia. Congressional delegates were granted access to its holdings, essentially making it the first library of Congress.

18. Delivering the Liberty-or-death speech, the most famous speech of his life, Patrick Henry was, in the words of John Randolph of Roanoke, Shakespeare and Garrick combined.

19. After Washington's success at Princeton in January 1777, depicted here in a nineteenth-century lithograph, he went into winter quarters at Morristown, New Jersey, where, as the correspondence of his officers and men indicates, Shakespeare was among their reading material.

20. When Washington resigned his commission before Congress on 23 December 1783, he impressed almost everyone, except John Adams, who found his resignation had the quality of a theatrical performance.

Above left: 21. Mrs. Siddons, depicted here in a painting by Thomas Gainsborough, was the most famous Shakespearean performer in late eighteenth-century London. Seeing her in performance became a desiderata of Americans visiting London once the Revolutionary War ended.

Above right: 22. John Jay was one of many defenders who quoted Shakespeare to support the Constitution.

General Horatio Gates, who had served under Washington during the siege of Boston, accompanied him to New York. Once they entered the city, Gates got a bad feeling about the place. He informed John Adams, 'Here we are surrounded by crowds of Tories, and I wish our army may be free of those vermine. I hold a cautious eye, and as Shakespear says will try, to delve a yard below their mines, and blow them at the moon.'[44]

Gates is yet another Revolutionary who identifies with Hamlet. His words come from the speech Hamlet delivers at the end of the third act:

> For 'tis the sport to have the enginer
> Hoist with his own petard, and't shall go hard
> But I will delve one yard below their mines
> And blow them at the moon.[45]

Whereas Deane had quoted the maudlin and melancholy Hamlet, Gates quotes Hamlet in a different mood, a Hamlet ready to attack those plotting against him. Gates's quotation is a show of bravado. His military experience, which went back to the Battle of the Monongahela, when he was badly wounded, told him that New York would be nearly impossible to defend.

Other Revolutionary leaders were working toward American independence elsewhere. While some Virginians continued serving in the Continental Congress in Philadelphia, others remained in Williamsburg to attend the next Virginia Convention, which would draft the state constitution. As a delegate to the Continental Congress, Richard Henry Lee could not be present for the start of the Virginia Convention, but he corresponded with Patrick Henry, who played a crucial role in it. Lee sent Henry a copy of John Adams's *Thoughts on Government*, a pamphlet offering instructions about the form the state governments should take.

Wythe, a fellow Congressional delegate, had asked Adams to write him a letter, which he could forward to the Virginia Convention as its participants drafted the state constitution. Adams complied. When Lee read the letter, he recognised its significance and took it to Philadelphia printer John Dunlap to have him set it in type. *Thoughts on Government* would influence several state constitutions. In his detailed survey of Adams's political theory, Richard Alan Ryerson calls *Thoughts on Government* 'the most elegant, succinct, and effective pamphlet of his long career, and the finest statement of America's new republican orthodoxy as it separated from the British Empire.'[46]

Beyond its political theory *Thoughts on Government* also reflects Adams's attitude toward poetry as a medium of expression. The opening paragraph quotes Pope's *Essay on Man*: 'For forms of government let fools contest, / That which is best administered is best.' Adams quotes Pope only to refute him:

> Nothing can be more fallacious than this: But poets read history to collect flowers not fruits – they attend to fanciful images, not the effects of social institutions. Nothing is more certain from the history of nations, and the nature of man, than that some forms of government are better fitted for being well administered than others.[47]

Poetry complements history and political science: it does not supplant them. Though Adams read Shakespeare for psychological insight, Shakespeare's plays were no substitute for treatises of political theory. *Thoughts on Government* draws upon more pertinent works, including James Harrington's *Oceana*, from which Adams derived his definition of a republic: 'an empire of laws, and not of men'.[48]

In the cover letter to the copy of *Thoughts on Government* he sent Patrick Henry, Lee takes pride in Virginia's contribution to the fight for American rights but says that it is time for Virginians to assume a leadership role once more:

> This I take to be the time and thing meant by Shakespeare when he says 'There is a tide in the affairs of men which taken at the flood leads on to fortune – That omitted, we are ever after bound in shallows' etc. Let us therefore, quitting every other consideration heartily unite in leading our countrymen to embrace the present flowing tide, which promises fair to waft us into the harbor of safety, happiness, liberty and virtue.[49]

Sure enough, the Virginians caught the tide Shakespeare foretold. On 15 May the Virginia Convention instructed its Congressional delegates to propose a declaration of independence and form a confederation. On Friday, 7 June 1776, Lee, voicing these instructions on the floor of the Continental Congress, moved to declare that 'these united colonies are, and of right ought to be, free and independent states.'[50] The motion absolved Americans from allegiance to the crown, severed any and all political connections between the American states and Great Britain, provided measures for obtaining assistance from foreign powers and proposed a confederation uniting the states.

Within a week the Continental Congress formed a committee to draft articles of confederation. The committee was composed of one delegate from each colony, with John Dickinson of Pennsylvania as chair. On 15 November 1777 Congress would approve the final version of the Articles of Confederation, which it would send to the states for ratification. Maryland, the last state to ratify the document, would not do so until 1 March 1781.

Lee's call for independence generated considerable debate. Robert R. Livingston, a delegate from New York, argued that it was too rash and urged that American independence should be postponed for the time being. Livingston was not alone. Delegates from other middle colonies hesitated to break with Britain completely. Foreseeing a time when they might be willing to join the independence movement, they argued that unless and until all the American colonies could come together as a whole, the fight for independence would be doomed.

Led by John Adams and the Virginians, those in favour of independence attempted to persuade reluctant delegates from the other colonies, arguing that officially declaring independence would confirm a pre-existing fact. The outbreak of hostilities on the part of the British at Lexington and Concord had effectively cut the last remaining ties with the colonies. The American people deserved independence, and they looked to the Continental Congress to lead the way. Adams and others effectively refuted the arguments of hesitant Congressional delegates but did not convince everyone.

The decision was forestalled until the beginning of July. Should Congress declare independence at that time, it would want to proceed as quickly as possible. To that end, it would be convenient to have a written declaration in place. Congress appointed another committee to draft this document. Besides Adams, Franklin and Jefferson, the Committee of Five, as it became known, also included Livingston and Roger Sherman, a delegate from Connecticut. Congress may have appointed Livingston to the Committee of Five to help solidify New York's commitment to independence. The committee assigned Jefferson the task of drafting the formal document that would declare independence from Great Britain.

As Jefferson understood it, his purpose in drafting the Declaration of Independence was not to advance new ideas but to codify the main ideas toward liberty and freedom that his fellow Americans had already accepted. The Declaration was intended as a purposeful political document, not a philosophical or legal treatise on natural law. Decades later Jefferson would recall its composition: 'Neither aiming at originality of principle or sentiment, nor yet copied from any particular and previous writing, it was intended to be an expression of the American mind, and to give to that expression the proper tone and spirit called for by the occasion. All its authority rests then on the harmonising sentiments of the day, whether expressed, in conversations, in letters, printed essays, or in the elementary books of public right, as Aristotle, Cicero, Locke, Sidney, etc.'[51] Livingston contributed little to the text of the Declaration of Independence. He tired of all the political theory the delegates discussed. Later that year Livingston would say that he would not 'give one scene in Shakespeare for 1000 Harringtons, Lockes and Adams'.[52]

Livingston's words reflect a similar attitude toward Shakespeare as Jefferson's. Shakespeare could synthesise moral, political and philosophical ideas, embody them within a single character or dramatise them in a memorable speech. One soliloquy could encapsulate what took a political scientist an entire book to say.

In another late reminiscence Jefferson elaborated the relationship between his extensive reading and the composition of the Declaration: 'Whether I had gathered my ideas from reading or reflection I do not know. I know only that I turned to neither book or pamphlet while writing it. I did not consider it as any part of my charge to invent new ideas altogether and to offer no sentiment which had ever been expressed before.'[53] The comment rings true. Though parts of the Declaration echo passages in such works as John Locke's *Two Treatises of Government* and Algernon Sidney's *Discourses Concerning Government*, Jefferson had already read and synthesised these and many similar works before he wrote the Declaration.

In addition to Locke and Sidney, the name 'Shakespeare' could be added to those authors whom Jefferson had read beforehand and who affected the Declaration of Independence, which is largely comprised of a series of statements using the subject pronoun 'he' to mean King George III. The king himself becomes the primary target of Jefferson's verbal attack in this part of the Declaration, which Samuel Adams called the 'Catalogue of Crimes'.[54]

Consider the following item: 'He is at this time transporting large armies of foreign mercenaries to compleat the works of death, desolation and tyranny, already begun with circumstances of cruelty and perfidy scarcely paralleled in the most barbarous ages, and totally unworthy the head of a civilized nation.'[55] This item from the Declaration of Independence echoes a passage from *Richard III*. In the fourth act, as Richard tries to convince his brother's wife Elizabeth to let her daughter marry him, he says:

> In her consists my happiness and thine;
> Without her follows to myself and thee,
> Herself, the land and many a Christian soul,
> Death, desolation, ruin and decay.[56]

Jefferson's phrase, 'death, desolation and tyranny' clearly echoes Shakespeare's 'Death, desolation, ruin and decay'. In addition, the emphasis King George puts on military might over what is right resembles King Richard's statement in the last act: 'Our strong arms be our conscience, swords our law.'[57]

Despite the parallels between King Richard in Shakespeare's play and King George in the Declaration of Independence, it is difficult to say how much Jefferson intended the parallel. The Founding Fathers read Shakespeare so often and so thoroughly that his words became part of the lingua franca of the era. Writing an indictment of tyranny in Revolutionary America, who wouldn't think of *Richard III*?

12

Band of Brothers

After the Continental Congress declared independence and officially created the United States of America its president John Hancock informed Washington of the fact, sending him copies of the Declaration of Independence with instructions to have them read to the troops. On Tuesday, 9 July 1776, Washington ordered that the document be read before the entire army. At six o'clock that evening all the brigades in New York City formed themselves into hollow squares. A man placed in the centre of each square read the Declaration for everyone to hear. Washington positioned himself inside one square while an aide read the Declaration in a loud, clear voice. Once he finished the brigade gave three hearty cheers: another great piece of Revolutionary theatre.[1]

By dint of hard work and determination Washington expanded his army to 19,000 troops, but most were either raw recruits or poorly trained militiamen: hardly a match for the British, whose fleet was anchored off New York in late June. The redcoats began landing on Staten Island on 3 July. General William Howe commanded 32,000 regular troops, at that time the largest expeditionary force in British history. Though inspired by the Declaration of Independence, the American troops could only go so far on inspiration. The superior British forces defeated the Americans at one battle after another, seizing Long Island, landing on Manhattan, and forcing Washington's army first to Harlem Heights and then to White Plains. Fort Washington, the remaining stronghold on Manhattan, fell on 16 November, with the British taking nearly three thousand prisoners of war.

And still the British persisted. From Fort Washington, they crossed the Hudson River into New Jersey and forced the evacuation of Fort Lee. They pursued the Americans across New Jersey to the Delaware River. Washington crossed the river and found temporary refuge in Pennsylvania the second week of December. As he had the previous December, Washington feared the Continental army would simply disappear once the volunteer enlistments expired at the year's end. With winter fast approaching General Howe decided against continuing into Pennsylvania and attacking Philadelphia. Instead, he dispersed his army into garrisons throughout New Jersey. The Hessian troops, a mercenary force enlisted to aid the British, were garrisoned in Trenton.

Washington planned a daring counterattack. He would cross the Delaware River from Pennsylvania into New Jersey and surprise the Hessians. The third week of December General John Sullivan arrived with reinforcements. Sullivan had served in the Continental army throughout the siege of Boston. Some questioned his military capabilities, but Washington never lost confidence in Sullivan, who would play an important role in the coming days. So would Henry Knox. Washington ordered Knox to take charge of the dangerous river crossing.

After Washington's army crossed the Delaware Knox reported the incident to his wife Lucy: 'Floating ice in the river made the labour almost incredible, however perseverance accomplished what at first seem'd impossible.' Knox downplayed his personal role, but, in the words of General James Wilkinson, another officer who crossed the Delaware that cold and blustery Christmas night, the treacherous crossing would have failed 'but for the stentorian lungs and extraordinary exertions of Colonel Knox'.[2]

It was almost light by the time Washington's army had finished crossing the river. He split the men into two columns, commanding one column himself and ordering Sullivan to take command of the other. Sure enough, they surprised the Hessians, capturing over nine hundred prisoners while losing only three men. Defeating the Hessian garrison at Trenton greatly boosted the morale of the American troops, but Washington did not stop his winter offensive there. Learning the British and Hessian forces had withdrawn to Princeton, he ordered another surprise attack.

Washington and his men crossed the Delaware River again and returned to New Jersey. Knox's next letter to Lucy vividly tells the story. 'Our troops march'd with great silence and order and arriv'd near Princeton a little after day break,' he wrote. 'I believe they were as much astonish'd as if our army had dropp'd perpendicularly upon them.' Conveying his hope for continued success, Knox told Lucy, 'There is a tide in the affairs of men such if taken at the flood lead on to victr'y. For my part my Lucy I look up to Heaven and most devoutly thank the great Governor of the Universe for producing this turn in our affairs of America.'[3]

Brutus says that the tide 'leads on to fortune', not victory, in *Julius Caesar*, but Knox's version suits the situation the Continental army faced in light of the successful battles at Trenton and Princeton. Brutus's words would become the most frequently quoted lines from Shakespeare during the Revolutionary War. As victory seemed within their grasp American leaders would echo Brutus over and over.

In the face of Washington's aggressive tactics Howe consolidated the garrisons in New Jersey and established winter quarters in New York City. Washington's army, in turn, went into winter quarters at Morristown, New Jersey. Though Howe's consolidation gave the British troops greater security, they still faced the problem of obtaining sufficient forage for their horses. Whenever British regiments went into the field that winter, it seemed, Continental troops attacked them. The New Jersey militia was largely responsible for initiating this forage war, but Washington actively encouraged his men to keep attacking small parties of British troops. The size of the Continental army dwindled that winter, but it remained large enough to pursue an active *petite guerre* campaign.[4]

The intellectual level of the Continental army spiked with the arrival of Henry Lee. A native of Virginia and a graduate of the College of New Jersey (later, Princeton University), Lee was an excellent classicist. With the outbreak of the Revolutionary War he had decided to devote himself to the battlefield. He became captain of the cavalry in Colonel Theodorick Bland's Virginia regiment in 1776. Summoned by Washington, Bland's regiment reached Morristown that winter, when it was reorganised as the First Continental Light Dragoons. Washington detached Lee's company to join the forage war. Lee performed his duties so well Washington would give him command of an independent partisan corps, which became known as Lee's Legion. Lee himself earned the sobriquet 'Light Horse Harry' Lee. Despite his success on the battlefield, Lee continued to cultivate his intellect. He enjoyed Shakespeare but considered Sophocles a better tragedian.[5]

At Quibbletown, New Jersey the fourth week of January another Virginia regiment successfully attacked a considerably larger British force. The Americans suffered four wounded; the British suffered many more casualties, though the precise number remains unknown. The most detailed modern account simply describes the British losses as 'heavy'. From Morristown one of Washington's officers wrote to the press to convey some uncertainty regarding a contemporary report about British losses: 'The 300 British troops killed by us in the

Quibbleton affair, came to life shortly after; having only, in imitation of Shakespear's fat knight, counterfeited death, in order to avoid the fury of our brave militia.'[6]

This Morristown officer refers to the battle scene in the last act of *Henry IV, Part I*, in which Falstaff feigns death to save himself. When the danger has passed, Falstaff rises up and famously says, 'The better part of valour is discretion, in the which better part I have saved my life.'[7] Falstaff's words occur earlier in American literature. The previous decade Agricola, the pseudonymous author of *The Squabble: A Pastoral Eclogue*, used the character of Corin to depict the non-violence of the Pennsylvania Quakers: 'Here Corin adopts the opinion of Old Falstaff, thinking "the better part of valour is discretion".'[8]

Ostensibly, the Morriston officer's purpose in writing to the newspaper was to correct some misinformation that had been circulating about the extent of enemy losses at Quibbletown. Instead, he used a literary allusion to make a joke. Showing off his knowledge of Shakespeare to entertain readers seems more important to him than supplying basic factual information. Ending his article, this Morristown officer set his humour aside to provide some facts, which are not nearly as interesting as his fiction.

General Sullivan, who was stationed at Chatham, New Jersey, wrote Washington in February to caution him against proceeding any further east. Making his argument, Sullivan quotes from *Julius Caesar*:

> I recollect once to have read that on the fatal Ides of March, when Cesar was going to the capitol Artemidorus presented him with a paper containing those words 'Cesar beware of Brutus Take heed of Cassius Come not near Casca Have an eye to Cinna; trust not Trebonius; Brutus loves thee not These men have all but one mind and that is bent ag[ains]t Cesar If thou art not immortal look about thee: security gives way to conspiracy.'[9]

After this quotation, just slightly abbreviated from the original, General Sullivan relates what happens once Caesar receives the paper from Artemidorus, who urges him to read it instantly. Caesar never does read it and dies with the paper in his pocket. Sullivan admits that he put little stock in dreams or superstitions, but in this instance, his feelings of foreboding compelled him to write. Assuming the role of Artemidorus in the letter, Sullivan cautions his leader against venturing from a place of safety. Eastern New Jersey was filled with Tories who could lay a trap for Washington. Sullivan says that his warning is not based on 'those dreams and prodigies which even staggered Cesars resolution', but on the 'unanimous voice and opinion of all the people'.[10]

Though many eighteenth-century readers knew their Shakespeare well enough to recall his most poignant passages from memory, General Sullivan's quotation seems less like something he had memorised and more like something he was cribbing from a copy of *Julius Caesar*. It suggests that he had a volume of Shakespeare with him when he wrote the letter to Washington. Perhaps rereading *Julius Caesar* in his winter quarters sparked Sullivan's imagination, prompting him to see a parallel between Washington and Caesar and recognise a similar danger.

Books were not unusual among combat soldiers during the Revolutionary War. Captain Johann Ewald, a Hessian officer fighting for the British, was amazed by how many military handbooks the American troops carried in their knapsacks. The British troops, on the other hand, carried, 'bags of hair-powder, boxes of sweet-smelling pomatum, cards (instead of maps), and then often, on top of all, some novels or stage plays'.[11] Though Ewald does not mention any plays among the belongings of the American troops he encountered, Sullivan's letter hints that copies of Shakespeare did find their way to the front lines.

The outbreak of the Revolutionary War largely stopped the flow of imported books from England, but enough copies of Shakespeare were in circulation that they were not too difficult to find. Some booksellers kept Shakespeare in stock after the war began. Robert Bell – the most aggressive bookseller in Revolutionary Philadelphia – sold many books that appealed to the delegates in town for the Continental Congress, including the works of prominent Whig historians and essayists John Trenchard and Thomas Gordon. Alongside *Cato's Letters*, the *Independent Whig* and Gordon's *Tacitus*, Bell also had Shakespeare for sale.[12]

Oliver Wolcott, a signer of the Declaration of Independence from Connecticut, found a multi-volume edition of Shakespeare at a local bookshop when he was in Philadelphia. He bought it as a present for his precocious eleven-year-old daughter, who had already expressed an interest in Shakespeare. Loyalist property was often seized by the Americans and sold to generate capital for the war effort, providing another way many fine books entered the marketplace during the Revolutionary War. In Philadelphia the government seized the property of Hugh Fergusson, a Loyalist with an excellent collection of *belles lettres*. Fergusson's three volumes of Shakespeare were sold with the rest of his confiscated property.[13]

Sometimes copies of Shakespeare showed up in the oddest places. Thomas Walker Jr, Jefferson's friend and neighbour, accidentally carried off someone else's dilapidated black leather trunk from Fredericksburg in late 1776. Strangely, he did not open the trunk until the following year. When he finally did, Walker could tell by the contents it was not his. Besides a pair of pistols, some ivory sword handles, a bayonet and sundry other articles, it contained five books: the third volume of Charles Johnstone's novel *Chrysal: or, Adventures of a Guinea*; a miscellaneous volume of plays; and the fourth, fifth and sixth volumes of Shakespeare's *Works*.[14]

After Dunmore fled the Governor's Palace in Williamsburg, the Virginia Convention decided to raise funds by auctioning his personal belongings, including his books. The auction put over a thousand books on the market, which ended up in the libraries of Patrick Henry, Thomas Jefferson and other prominent Virginians.[15] John Scarsbrook Wills, who had represented Isle of Wight County in the Virginia Conventions of 1775 and 1776 and who would rise to the rank of brigadier general during the war, obtained Dunmore's six-volume set of Pope's Shakespeare, which he presented to his daughter Barsheba. The set, which survives at Colonial Williamsburg, contains the autographs of both Barsheba Wills and her husband Thomas Darden, whom she would marry in 1792.[16]

Samuel Henley fled Virginia after the war broke out in 1775. Hoping to return, he left his library behind. He boxed up his books in two huge containers and put them in care of James Madison, not the future US president but the current president of William and Mary. A few years after Henley's departure, Madison had the containers moved to the president's house for safekeeping. During the move, one container burst open, revealing that the Virginia humidity had severely damaged the books, which were all stuck together.

To determine their fate Madison consulted Jefferson. The two agreed it would be in Henley's best interest to sell the books. As the property of a British subject, his library was subject to confiscation by the Americans, who could seize his books, sell them, and refuse to pay him anything. Madison wrote to Henley, who authorised him to sell the books. Even before receiving Henley's authorisation, Madison set a price for each title, and Jefferson selected some for himself. Most importantly, Jefferson acquired Henley's first edition of *Paradise Lost*. Henley's library also contributed to his friend's Shakespeare collection. Jefferson obtained his copy of Montagu's *Essay on Shakespeare*.[17]

North Carolina provides further examples. In Edgecombe County William McLellan, a Tory, sold his library before fleeing the Carolinas.

James Hill, who bought McLellan's books, thereby acquired a seven-volume edition of Shakespeare. The property of royal governor Josiah Martin was seized and sold at public auction. Martin's library contained a nine-volume edition of Shakespeare. Revolutionary patriot Colonel Thomas Eaton was the winning bidder.[18]

Washington had an excellent field library, which contained numerous books of military theory and practice. It might have also contained some Shakespeare. After having the opportunity to read his father's Shakespeare in his youth and after having one volume of Shakespeare from the Custis collection at Mount Vernon for many years, Washington added another Shakespeare volume to his library, the first volume of John Bell's 1774 edition. The volume, which survives at the Folger Library, contains *Macbeth*, *As You Like It*, *Othello* and *All's Well that Ends Well.*[19]

Given its date Washington most likely bought the book in Philadelphia while attending the Second Continental Congress in 1775. He acquired several military books at the time. After Congress commissioned him Commander in Chief of the Continental army, he did not have the chance to return to Mount Vernon. He went directly from Philadelphia to Cambridge, Massachusetts, bringing his new books with him. They would form the core of his camp library.[20]

The presence of this particular Shakespeare volume in Washington's library shows an interest in the comedies as well as the tragedies. One comedy had a special resonance for Washington. The Latin motto that adorned his coat of arms – *Exitus acta probat* – can be translated, 'All's well that ends well.' Washington's writings reveal his knowledge of another comedy, *Twelfth Night*.

Like any good letter writer, Washington shaped his letters to suit individual correspondents, so perhaps it is unsurprising to discover a Shakespeare allusion in a letter to Francis Hopkinson, poet, songwriter and signer of the Declaration of Independence. After seeing Hopkinson's home in Bordentown, New Jersey, Captain Ewald wrote, 'This man was one of the greatest rebels, nevertheless, if we dare to conclude from the library, and mechanical and mathematical instruments, he must have been a very learned man.' Hopkinson's library also included a collected edition of Shakespeare. In his letter Washington tells Hopkinson that he had grown accustomed to sitting for his portrait. Originally he felt considerable impatience while the portraitists painted, but now he could 'sit like patience on a monument whilst they are delineating the lines of my face'.[21]

Washington's simile comes from a speech Viola makes to Orsino in *Twelfth Night*. Describing a woman – really herself – who has never told the man she loved how she felt, Viola says:

> she pin'd in thought,
> And with a green and yellow melancholy
> She sat like Patience on a monument,
> Smiling at grief.[22]

The orders Washington wrote during the Revolutionary War reflect his knowledge of *Julius Caesar*. Every night he had to devise paroles – passwords for the inspectors of the guard – and corresponding countersigns. Sometimes the words he selected reflect the books he read. In one instance he used the name 'Brutus' as his parole. Another time he used 'Brutus' as his countersign. Whereas General Sullivan saw him as a Caesar, Washington himself more closely identified with Brutus, comparing the revolt against King George III to Brutus's attack against the king-like Caesar. Here's another word Washington used as a parole: 'tyrannicide'.[23]

From Morristown the first week of March 1777 Washington wrote to his friend and officer William Woodford to congratulate him on his promotion to brigadier general. Open-minded yet stubborn, Woodford's contrary impulses could come into conflict. Washington knew that this letter of congratulations was a delicate matter, since two men with less seniority were promoted over Woodford. After an earlier slight, Woodford had resigned his commission, which he reclaimed months later, on Washington's advice. Because of this hiatus, Woodford had lost the seniority he had accumulated before his temporary resignation. Sensitive to Woodford's feelings, Washington urged him to set aside his personal sentiments and consider the reason why they were fighting. His letter is a masterpiece of principle and persuasion:

> You may feel somewhat hurt, in having two officers placed before you (tho perhaps never to command you) who once were inferior in point of rank to you; but remember, that this is a consequence of your own act. and – consider what a stake we are contending for – Trifling punctilios should have no influence upon a mans conduct in such a cause; and at such a time as this – If smaller matters do not yield to greater; if trifles, light as air, in comparison of what we are contending for, can withdraw, or withhold gentlemen from service, when our all is at stake, and a single cast of the die may turn the

> tables, what are we to expect – It is not a common contest we are ingaged in – every thing valuable to us depends upon the success of it – and the success upon a speedy, and vigorous exertion. Consider twice therefore, before you refuse.[24]

Almost lost amidst Washington's eloquence is his allusion to *Othello*. After Iago has convinced his wife Emilia to give him the handkerchief that Othello had presented to Desdemona, he relates in soliloquy his devious plan:

> I will in Cassio's lodging lose this napkin
> And let him find it. Trifles light as air
> Are to the jealous confirmations strong
> As proofs of holy writ.[25]

The phrase 'trifles light as air' presents an interpretive problem. Was Washington deliberately alluding to *Othello*, or had the simile become proverbial? Given the presence of *Othello* in his library and the familiarity with the play Washington shows elsewhere, the simile does seem like an allusion. Washington would return to *Othello* years later. In a letter to his adopted grandson George Washington Custis, he recalls what Iago says about reputation: 'To speak evil of any one, unless there is unequivocal proofs of their deserving it, is an injury for which there is no adequate reparation. For, as Shakespeare says, "He that robs me of my good name enriches not himself, but renders me poor indeed", or words to that effect.'[26] With these words Washington evokes Shakespeare's name to reinforce the advice he gives his namesake.

While using Iago's scheming words in his advice to Woodford, Washington applies them in a positive manner. Iago takes advantage of 'trifles light as air' to destroy Othello. Washington uttered the same phrase to put the situation the Americans faced into perspective. Given the war's profound significance, rank and promotion mattered little. The greatness of their cause required a greatness of spirit that could rise above such trivialities. Washington's letter worked. Woodford accepted the promotion and joined Washington's army at Morristown, commanding the Third Virginia Brigade.

As the war progressed, Washington gradually defined the meaning of military success. By now the British had taken possession of Philadelphia as well as New York, but capturing cities did not necessarily mean success. As long as Washington could keep an army in the field, he could endure and continue to fight. He was confident the British understood this idea as well. In a letter to Henry Laurens, the new president of the Continental Congress, Washington explains: 'They well know, that it is our arms, not defenceless towns, they have to subdue, before they can arrive at the haven of their wishes; and that till this end is accomplished, the superstructure they have been endeavouring to raise "like the baseless fabric of a vision" falls to nothing.' Washington's quotation from *The Tempest* was not lost on Laurens, who also quoted Shakespeare in his correspondence.[27]

Jefferson had used the same simile from *The Tempest* to describe something he had lost, his library. Washington, alternatively, used Prospero's words to project the future, predicting that what the British hoped to achieve would fade into nothing. British troops could capture all the towns they wished, but they would not win the war unless they conquered the American forces in the field.

After the brilliant success at Trenton and Princeton the subsequent activities in New Jersey in 1777 were disappointing. By late May Washington had built up his army in Morristown to 9000 men and equipped them with arms, which the French had covertly supplied. But the manoeuvres between the British and American forces against one another in New Jersey proved inconclusive. In July Samuel Adams, then serving in the Continental Congress, wrote to Richard Henry Lee to express his frustration, arguing that their army should have pressed its advantage when it had the chance:

> I profess not the least degree of knowledge in military matters, and therefore hazzard no opinion. I recollect however that Shakespeare tells us, there is a tide in human affairs, an opportunity which wise men carefully watch for and improve, and I will never forget because it exactly coincides with my religious opinion and I think it warranted by holy writ, that 'God helps those who help themselves.'[28]

Adams serves Lee a gallimaufry of references mixing folklore and book culture. He starts with Brutus's famous words from *Julius Caesar*, which Lee knew well, having used them himself earlier in a letter to Patrick Henry. Adams then suggests that Shakespeare's words coincide with a passage he attributes to the Bible. But the words Adams quotes do not come from the Holy Scriptures, but from Benjamin Franklin, who says in *Poor Richards Almanack*, 'God helps them that help themselves.' Franklin may have put this proverb into its most memorable form, but he did not coin it. In different forms the proverb had been around for centuries. Shakespeare offers a variation in *Richard II*: 'The means that heavens yield must be embraced / And not neglected.' Perhaps Adams's attribution of the proverb to 'holy writ' should not be taken literally, either. The phrase 'holy writ' forms part of a proverbial comparison Iago uses in *Othello*, which circulated throughout Revolutionary America: 'as true as holy writ'.[29]

Parliament frequently debated the American war. Not all its members supported the continuation of hostilities. In the House of Commons Sir George Savile, the MP for Yorkshire, questioned the efficacy of the British tactics. Savile had long sympathised with the Americans. The previous decade he had voted to repeal the Stamp Act, spoken against Sir George Grenville's insensitive colonial policy and protested the Coercive Acts, finding them 'an extraordinary exertion of legislative power'.[30]

During a debate about the war in the House of Commons on 21 November 1777, Savile 'said that the idea of convincing the Americans of their errors by their swords at their throats, put him in mind of a passage in Shakespeare, where Lady Macbeth says, "I will with wine and wassel so convince, etc."'[31] John Adams, it seems, was not the only one to compare Mother England to Lady Macbeth. Savile was recalling an episode from the first act of the play, in which Lady Macbeth prepares her husband to murder Duncan. She tells him what she will do once Duncan falls asleep:

> his two chamberlains
> Will I with wine and wassail so convince
> That memory, the warder of the brain,
> Shall be a fume, and the receipt of reason
> A limbeck only.[32]

In other words, she will get them drunk enough to empty their heads, after which she would pour into them whatever she wishes the chamberlains to believe. Applying Lady Macbeth's words to current events, Savile understood that the threat of force would have no more effect on the brave Americans defending their natural rights than Lady Macbeth's wine and wassail would have on Duncan's chamberlains.

Savile had already predicted that France would enter the war on the American side. Spain would also enter the war against England, but without recognising American independence. The Americans had been working hard to persuade the Europeans to join their cause ever since declaring independence. Congress had appointed three commissioners – Deane, Franklin and Jefferson – to negotiate treaties with the European powers. Jefferson declined the position, so

Congress replaced him with Arthur Lee – Richard Henry Lee's little brother – who was already in Europe.

Upon reaching Paris, Franklin quickly got down to business and approached Charles Gravier, comte de Vergennes, the French foreign minister. In January 1777 the American commissioners formally requested aid from the French government. France soon promised the new nation the first of several substantial loans. A formal treaty would take more time. When news of General Burgoyne's defeat at Saratoga at the hands of General Horatio Gates in October 1777 reached Paris that December, it reignited American negotiations with the French, which had stalled over the course of the year.

Vergennes much preferred negotiating with Franklin over the others. Sadly, the Hamlet-like sense of hopelessness Deane had expressed earlier had metastasised into a selfish desire for personal gain. Congress dismissed Deane and appointed John Adams to replace him. Adams brought his ten-year-old son John Quincy Adams to Europe with him. They did not reach Paris until after the news of Burgoyne's defeat, which had effectively accomplished Adams's mission before his arrival.

Franklin and his fellow commissioners did not work together very well, especially after two more Americans, Ralph Izard and another Lee brother – William – joined them. Paris lionised Franklin – the scientist with a sense of humour – and ignored the others. Izard's personal jealousy prompted him to undermine the mission at every turn. He never could get over his animosity. Years later Izard called Franklin 'that d——d old rascal'.[33]

The tempers of the American commissioners did not suit one another, and they were having trouble cooperating, as Franklin informed a friend: 'You know the natural disposition of some of us, how jealous, how captious, how suspicious even of real friends, and how positive, after suspecting a while, that the suspicions are certain truths, "Confirmations strong, as proofs from holy writ".'[34] Quoting the speech in which Iago voices his plan to use Desdemona's handkerchief to fuel Othello's jealousy, Franklin demonstrates its relevance for characterising the personal intrigue among the commissioners.

William Carmichael, the American chargé d'affaires in Madrid, added another nuance as he alluded to the same motif from *Othello*. Desdemona's handkerchief symbolised Othello's obsessiveness as well as his jealousy. Carmichael wrote to Franklin to express his inability to pay the Spanish bills that had come due, given the sorry state of American credit overseas. The worry made him sick to his stomach. He told Franklin, 'These bills haunt my imagination as much as the fatal handkercheif did the jealous brain of Othello. The remembrance of them will serve as an emetic to me.'[35] Carmichael's letter to Franklin reinforces the rhetorical value that an allusion to *Othello* could have. In the coming years Franklin would continue to make creative use of *Othello* in his correspondence.

Despite their personal differences, the American commissioners worked together well enough to persuade the French to fight with them. In February 1778 the two nations signed one treaty of alliance for mutual defence and another treaty of amity and commerce. Knowledge of these treaties soon reached Great Britain. The British were shocked. Not only were they fighting the rebellious American colonists, they now had to fight their longstanding nemesis, an enemy with a powerful army and an intrepid navy.

In 1778 London publisher Daniel Browne co-published *Shakespeare's History of the Times*. A little-known publisher who would go bankrupt the following year, Browne deserves recognition for his love of the theatre. His shop was located at 6 Catherine Street at the sign of Garrick's Head. *Shakespeare's History of the Times* assigns quotations from Shakespeare works to characterise people in the news. Though most of the people featured are members of the British upper class, both George Washington and Benjamin Franklin made it into the volume. Considering Washington's role on the battlefield and Franklin's role in negotiating a military alliance with France, one might expect that the references would be critical, but they are quite complimentary.

To characterise Franklin, *Shakespeare's History of the Times* applies a passage from the speech Cassius delivers in *Julius Caesar* as he attempts to convince Brutus to rebel against Caesar, the same passage that had adumbrated Patrick Henry's Liberty-or-death speech:

> I cannot tell what you and other men
> Think of this life, but for my single self
> I had as lieve not be, as live to be
> In awe of such a thing as I myself.[36]

Ascribing Cassius's words to Franklin, the volume casts him in the role of conspirator, but the individual passage embodies a high-minded principle, that it would be better to die than to live under a king, a man no better than his subjects who nevertheless claims the right to rule them.

Shakespeare's History of the Times ascribes to Washington a fourteen-line passage that Ulysses speaks in *Troilus and Cressida*.

Though the Greeks are at war with the Trojans, Ulysses depicts a conflict within the Greek army between the military strategists and the soldiers, who have little use for theory. Ulysses's speech begins: 'They tax our policy.'[37]

The subject pronoun of this sentence comes without a referent, and the verb is ambiguous. As Ulysses uses it, the verb 'tax' is figurative. It does not mean to impose a tax but to censure. Ulysses is saying that 'they' – his soldiers – were censuring 'our' policy, that is, the policy of the military theorists. Ascribed to Washington, this ambiguous opening sentence takes on a new meaning. The subject pronoun seems to refer to the British, and the verb becomes literal. The opening sentence says that the British are unfairly imposing taxes on the Americans: one of the major causes of the Revolutionary War. Representing Washington's thought, the rest of the passage honours his military mind. Besides equating him with Ulysses, the passage portrays Washington as a keen strategist: high praise coming from his enemy.

Valley Forge, where the Continental army spent the winter of 1777-1778, is best known for the brutal weather that Washington's troops endured during that tough and trying winter. The miserable conditions gave rise to numerous conflicts among the men, some serious enough to call for courts martial. The snow melted by the first week of April, but tensions continued to flare.

The court martial of Lieutenant Abner Dunn, who had been accused of striking a fellow officer, prompted Washington to speak out against the recent spate of courts marital, most of which he found frivolous and unnecessary. As part of his general orders for 6 April 1778, Washington recommended against courts martial for minor infractions. Written in the third person, his general orders read as follows:

> The Commander in Chief confirms the sentence and orders Lieutt Dunn to be discharged from his arrest, at the same time observing that the frequent proceedings of courts-martial presented to him which seem to originate more from personal prejudice and private animosities than real intention to promote the good of the service, gives him very sensible pain; he wishes the officers of his army to consider themselves as a band of brothers cemented by the justice of the common cause, that a perfect harmony might subsist among them and that they would settle all personal disputes among themselves in an amicable manner, ever being cautious not to trouble courts-martial or the General with private dissentions or add papers to the public files which may hereafter reflect disgrace upon themselves and the army.[38]

Aware that judicial proceedings like courts martial leave a lasting paper trail, Washington essentially asked his officers if they really wanted their petty squabbles recorded for posterity. He urged them to solve personal grievances like men. Take responsibility for your actions and reconcile your differences privately. Instead of fighting one another, work together against your common enemy on the battlefield. Ideally, his men should consider themselves a 'band of brothers'.

Washington's phrase comes from King Henry's St Crispin's Day speech, which he delivers in the fourth act of *Henry V*. To inspire his men before the Battle of Agincourt, Henry tells them that afterwards a day

> shall ne'er go by
> From this day to the ending of the world
> But we in it shall be remembered,
> We few, we happy few, we band of brothers.
> For he today that sheds his blood with me
> Shall be my brother.[39]

Like King Henry, Washington used the phrase 'band of brothers' to describe something that, ideally, would happen in the future if his men would cooperate and fight together. As the Revolutionary War continued, Washington foresaw victory, provided his men would come together like a band of brothers.

Washington's use of Shakespeare's words proved prescient. He and his men fought together at the Battle of Monmouth Courthouse that summer, and they fought at the Battle of Stony Point the following summer. His soldiers fought in South Carolina during the summer of 1780, where they suffered devastating losses. And, in 1781, they fought together during the siege of Yorktown, which culminated in Lord Cornwallis's surrender and ended British hopes of a decisive land victory.

In late 1781 Washington went into winter quarters at Newburgh, New York, which would remain his base while peace negotiations took place in Europe over the next two years. In August 1783 the Continental Congress, then meeting at Princeton, New Jersey, summoned Washington to confer on the shape and size the American military should take during the postwar period. Upon his arrival Washington established himself about four miles outside Princeton at Rocky Hill, the home of Margaret Berrien.[40]

Greetings from friends and well-wishers poured into Rocky Hill. One came in the form of a poem from Annis Boudinot Stockton, the sister of Elias Boudinot, the current president of the Continental Congress. 'To General Washington', as she titled the poem, places him foremost 'on the sacred scroll / With patriots who had gain'd eternal fame, / By wonderous deeds that penetrate the soul'.[41]

Flattered, Washington responded with a letter of thanks. His thank-you letters are usually matter of fact. Writing to a poet, however, he demonstrated his own literary skill. Inviting her to dinner at Rocky Hill, Washington wrote: 'I find myself strangely disposed to be a very indulgent ghostly adviser on this occasion and, notwithstanding "you are the most offending soul alive" (that is, if it is a crime to write elegant poetry) yet if you will come and dine with me on Thursday and go through the proper course of penitence, which shall be prescribed, I will strive hard to assist you in expiating these poetical trespasses on this side of purgatory.'[42]

These words constitute the most sophisticated use of Shakespeare in Washington's collected writings. While again making use of King Henry's St Crispin's Day speech from *Henry V*, he altered the original lines significantly. Whereas Henry says, 'But if it be a sin to covet honour / I am the most offending soul alive,' Washington reversed the order of these two lines and changed the pronouns from first to second person. Washington thus calls Stockton 'the most offending soul alive', seemingly without cause. His words would appear quite rude save for two mitigating factors: he distinguished the phrase with quotation marks, and he naturally assumed she would get the Shakespearean reference. After the quote, Washington paraphrases Shakespeare's previous line, omitting what it says about sin and coveting honour in favour of a facetious remark about writing poetry being a crime.

Washington was not done with King Henry's St Crispin's Day speech. In his 'Farewell Address to the Army' he briefly recalled the hardships his men endured throughout the war but quickly dismissed them. He did not want to dwell on their suffering but to celebrate their success. The historical significance of the war far outweighed the difficulties they endured:

> Every American officer and soldier must now console himself for any unpleasant circumstances which may have occurred by a recollection of the uncommon scenes in which he has been called to act no inglorious part, and the astonishing events of which he has been a witness, events which have seldom if ever before taken place on the stage of human action, nor can they probably ever happen again. For who has before seen a disciplined army form'd at once from such raw materials? Who that was not a witness, could imagine

> that the most violent local prejudices would cease so soon, and that men who came from the different parts of the continent, strongly disposed by the habits of education, to despise and quarrel with each other, would instantly become but one patriotic band of brothers, or who, that was not on the spot can trace the steps by which such a wonderful revolution has been effected, and such a glorious period put to all our warlike toils?[43]

Repeating the phrase 'band of brothers' from *Henry V* at the end of the Revolutionary War, Washington reiterated its relevance. Even as he reuses King Henry's words, Washington reflects a much different attitude from Shakespeare's warrior king. Before the Battle of Agincourt King Henry had said that the men who fought with him would be his brothers, but such brotherly sentiment disappears by the end of Shakespeare's play. After the Battle of Agincourt King Henry asks about the number of casualties. In response he receives a list of four aristocrats, but 'None else of name'.[44] Despite King Henry's words of equality and brotherhood before the battle, ultimately the only men who count in his world are the aristocrats.

Washington's reuse of the phrase 'band of brothers' in his 'Farewell Address to the Army' seems less an echo of *Henry V* and more an echo of the general orders he issued from Valley Forge five years earlier. Then he had encouraged his men to become a band of brothers. Now, he affirmed that they had done precisely that. Their camaraderie and selflessness had helped them win a war and establish a new nation.

13

American Shakespeareans in Europe

On Saturday, 18 January 1783, Benjamin Franklin received a letter from the comte de Vergennes asking him and the other American peace commissioners to come to Versailles Monday morning to accept the British declaration of the cessation of hostilities. Vergennes's invitation came more quickly than expected. Two of the commissioners, John Jay and Henry Laurens, were out of town. John Adams was still in Paris, so Franklin informed Vergennes that he and Adams would be at Versailles on Monday, 20 January.[1]

As far as Vergennes was concerned, Adams hardly needed to come at all. After returning to France in 1780, Adams had made an enemy of Vergennes and a nuisance of himself, so much so that Franklin wrote Congress and asked to have him removed. Adams left France for Holland, where, to his credit, he obtained diplomatic recognition of the United States after two years of tough negotiations. Adams returned to Paris in October 1782 to help negotiate the peace. He and his fellow commissioners signed the preliminary articles of peace on 30 November.

Franklin and Adams reached Versailles promptly at ten o'clock Monday morning. Officials from Great Britain and Spain arrived an hour later, and together they signed the official documents. The signing ceremony seemed anticlimactic to Adams, who wrote in his diary, 'Thus was this mighty system terminated with as little ceremony, and in as short a time as a marriage settlement.' Adams told a different story to his wife, building up the ceremony with a comparison to the theatre: 'Thus drops the curtain upon this mighty tragedy. It has unravelled itself happily for us.'[2]

News of the armistice quickly spread around Paris. That evening at the Théâtre-Français, François René Molé, a popular comedian, announced that the theatrical company would perform Charles-Simon Favart's *L'Anglois à Bordeaux* the following Saturday in honour of the peace. The play the company performed that Monday evening is more significant. On 20 January the Comédiens Français premiered their production of *Le Roi Léar*, Jean François Ducis's French translation of *King Lear*. The French theatre-going public interpreted the performance of this English classic on the Paris stage as a celebration of the armistice, a reconciliation of the differences between France and Great Britain.

Ducis did not exactly do justice to Shakespeare. He took great liberties with the play's text, revising it to suit the standards of French neoclassical drama. *Le Roi Léar* confirms Voltaire's remark that bad translations prevented the French from fully appreciating Shakespeare: 'A blind man, sir, cannot perceive the beauty of a rose, who only pricks his fingers with thorns.'[3]

Whereas Garrick had begun to introduce elements of Shakespeare's original into Tate's *Lear*, Ducis's version reinforced the ongoing appeal of Tate's version. Ducis stressed the play's didacticism. In his hands *King Lear* became an object lesson in filial piety. *Le Roi Léar* lacks the high drama of the original. The storm scene is tepid, and Léar's madness is maudlin. As in Tate's version, the Cordelia and Edgar figures – Helmonde and Edgard – are lovers. In the end, Léar's kingdom is restored to him; Helmonde and Edgard are reunited; and everything ends as merry as marriage bells.[4]

After signing the documents pertaining to the cessation of hostilities, Adams remained in Paris for the time being, but he thought about going home. The next month he wrote Abigail: 'If my resignation is not accepted, but is drawn out into length, I must come home of my own head – for my family at all events I must and will join – J'ai besoin d'être pere, as King Lear says.' Emphasising Lear's need to be a father, Adams confirmed that he had attended the performance of *Le Roi Léar*. The line he quotes is the exact line Léar speaks in the second act of the play. After attending the performance, Adams remembered the line that applied to himself.[5]

Adams's ongoing presence in Paris unsettled Franklin, who thought he was undermining the close friendship that had developed during the Revolutionary War between France and the United States. The fourth week of July Franklin wrote Robert Livingston a long letter containing a 400-word paragraph critiquing Adams. Franklin does not mention Adams by name, vaguely calling him 'one of my colleagues', but it is clear he had Adams in mind. After conveying France's continuing importance to the United States and Vergennes's helpfulness, Franklin mentions a colleague who considered France a great enemy. Having made no secret of his negative attitude toward France, Adams had voiced his opinions publicly and claimed he could prove his assertions about France's animosity toward the United States, though so far, he had shown no proof.[6]

Concerned that doubts about the French could be detrimental to the United States, Franklin found it necessary to warn Livingston. The 400-word paragraph concludes:

> I write this to put you on your guard, (believing it my duty, tho' I know that I hazard by it a mortal enmity) and to caution you respecting the insinuations of this gentleman against this court, and the instances he supposes of their ill-will to us, which I take to be as imaginary as I know his fancies to be, that Count de V. and myself are continually plotting against him and employing the news writers of Europe to depreciate his character, etca. but as Shakespear says, 'Trifles light as air, etca'. I am persuaded however that he means well for his country, is always an honest man, often a wise one, but sometimes and in some things, absolutely out of his senses.[7]

In his letter Franklin had begun finishing Shakespeare's sentence – 'Trifles light as air / Are to the jealous confirmations strong / As proofs of holy writ' – but he paused partway through it, cancelled everything he had written after the word 'air' and substituted the *et cetera*. Franklin realised Livingston was a good enough Shakespearean to recall the rest of the passage from *Othello* for himself.

Livingston never received Franklin's letter. By the time it reached Congress, he had resigned his position as secretary of foreign affairs. Since the position would go unfilled until the following year when John Jay took over, Franklin's letter went to a five-man congressional committee appointed to report on the dispatches of US foreign ministers. Elbridge Gerry, a congressional delegate from Massachusetts, was one member of the committee, and the letter fell into his hands. Franklin's *Othello* reference was not lost on Gerry – yet another Shakespeare enthusiast in Congress. Gerry owned the eight-volume 1773 duodecimo edition of Theobald's Shakespeare, which he had bound in calf and elegantly gilt.[8]

Gerry was shocked to read what Franklin had written about John Adams. He transcribed the entire 400-word paragraph, complete with Iago's words, and forwarded it to Abigail Adams. Gerry's cover letter explains: 'Inclosed is an extract of an official letter from Doctor

F——— to Mr Livingston secretary of foreign affairs dated July 22d, which is calculated to give a private stab to the reputation of our friend; at least it appears so to me.'[9]

Gerry also shared the paragraph with James Warren. In a subsequent letter to John Adams, Warren refers to the paragraph:

> What shall I say about your coming home? You know that as a friend I wish to see you, – your country wants you here, – your family would be happy to have you return, – but where and in what situation should we have been if you and Mr Jay had not been in Europe? When I form an idea of it I feel like a man that has had a hair-breadth escape from a precipice ... After all I don't know that I detest any character more than that of the Old Man, who is, as you might expect your determin'd enemy, – you will before this reaches you get a paragraph of one of his letters, which if you should by an interval be in possession of your right mind will put the matter out of doubt.[10]

Warren's letter shows how thoroughly Shakespeare's words pervaded early American rhetoric. In a letter about to a paragraph quoting one phrase from *Othello*, Warren uses another phrase from the same play.

Before sending his letter, Warren shared it with Abigail Adams. She had initially decided against sending Franklin's 400-word paragraph to her husband, finding that his current situation was, as she said, 'sufficiently irritating without any thing further to add to your vexation'. Upon reading Warren's letter, Abigail decided to send the paragraph to her husband, fearing he would think it much worse than it really was. Her letter closes with a pertinent observation from a book she had read. Abigail does not name her source, and it has escaped the attention of her editors. The passage comes from Henry Mackenzie's *Man of Feeling*, the most influential novel of sentiment in English literature. Her excerpt, slightly paraphrased from the original, puts John in the role of Harley, the novel's hero. Abigail begins in her own voice but switches to her quotation partway through the sentence:

> I cannot help adding an observation which appears pertinant to me; that there is an ingredient necessary in a mans composition towards happiness, which people of feeling would do well to acquire – a certain respect for the follies of mankind. For there are so many fools whom the opinion of the world entittles to regard; whom accident has placed in heights of which they are unworthy, that he

> who cannot restrain, his contempt or indignation at the sight, will be too, often quarrelling with the disposal of things to realish that share, which is allotted to himself.[11]

Whereas Franklin's paragraph associates John Adams with a tragic hero from Renaissance drama, Abigail Adams attempts to transform her husband into a character type from the Augustan novel, the man of feeling.

The first week of September Adams, Franklin and Jay signed the Treaty of Paris, which officially ended the war between Great Britain and the United States. British troops, who had continued to occupy New York, finally evacuated on 25 November. Washington led his army into the city that same day. He said farewell to his officers the first week of December. Later that month he proceeded to Annapolis, where Congress had convened temporarily.

In a carefully arranged ceremony on 23 December Washington declared that he would never again hold public office, and then he returned the commission as commander in chief that Congress had given him in June 1775. When news of Washington's retirement crossed the Atlantic, Europeans were astonished. They could hardly believe a victorious general would volunteer to surrender his command. Washington practically underwent an apotheosis. Europe hailed him as the greatest man of his age.

There was one man in Europe who downplayed Washington's retirement from the military: John Adams. Considering what he heard about the ceremony that took place within the Maryland statehouse, Adams concluded that Washington's performance was precisely that: a performance. Speaking as if he had been present for the event, Adams said that Washington's retirement ceremony was 'in a strain of Shakespearean and Garrickal excellence in dramatic exhibition'.[12]

Adams had been urging Abigail to join him in Europe. Terrified of the ocean crossing, she resisted for years. The Rev. William Smith discouraged his daughter from the journey, preferring to keep her nearby. By autumn 1783 her father could no longer restrain Abigail. She informed John of the sad news: 'My father, my father, where is he? With humble confidence I can say; he is with the spirits of just men made perfect, become an inhabitant of that country, from whose bourn no traveller returns.' Her familiar words come from Hamlet's To-be-or-not-to-be soliloquy, which defines death as 'The undiscovered country from whose bourn / No traveller returns'.[13]

Abigail still hesitated to cross the ocean, hoping that John would return to America and thus obviate the need for her to go to Europe. But by the second week of February 1784 she finally made up her mind to brave the ocean and join her husband. She informed him that her continual hopes of his return had disappeared: 'My expectations of your return from month to month, have vanished "like the baseless fabrick of a vision."'[14]

She still needed months to prepare for the journey, but, finally, on 20 June she and her teenaged daughter Abigail – 'Nabby', they called her – boarded the *Active*, a merchant ship bound for England. A month later they found themselves safely ensconced in a London hotel. The first week of August the two Abigails were reunited with the two Johns, John Adams and their son John Quincy Adams.

Abigail was astonished by how her son John had grown. During his father's diplomatic service, the boy had attended schools in France and Holland. He had also served as his father's secretary during the peace negotiations: vital experience that helped prepare him for his own diplomatic and political career. John Quincy Adams would not remain in Europe much longer. Soon he would return home to attend Harvard.

Once reunited, the Adamses did not linger in London but proceeded to Paris, where John Adams had a new responsibility. In May Congress had appointed Jefferson, Adams and Franklin commissioners to negotiate treaties of amity and commerce with foreign powers. Jefferson had turned down two earlier diplomatic assignments, but now, after the death of his wife, he accepted the new position. Travelling with his oldest daughter Martha, he arrived in Paris in July. Adams did not look forward to working with Franklin again, but he was overjoyed to see Jefferson. Their friendship would flourish in Paris. The following year Franklin would return to Philadelphia, and Jefferson would assume his position as minister plenipotentiary to the Court of France. Adams would be appointed minister to Great Britain.

Abigail Adams had difficulty adjusting to the Paris social scene, but she fell in love with its theatre. Having grown up in Massachusetts, she had never before attended the theatre, but she liked what she saw on the Paris stage. One evening the Adamses attended a performance of Jean Racine's *Athalie*. Abigail informed her friend Mercy Otis Warren: 'The dresses were superb, the house elegant and beautiful, the actors beyond the reach of my pen. The character of the high-priest admirably well supported. And Athalia, would have shone as Sophonisba, or Lady Macbeth: if the term shine, may be applied to a character full of cruelty and horrour.'[15]

Athalie retells the biblical story of the usurper Athaliah, the villainous daughter of Ahab and Jezebel, complete with choral sections in the manner of Greek tragedy. Previously unfamiliar with the work, Abigail understood Racine's tragedy by comparing its title character with two scheming and strong-willed female characters she knew from plays she had read, Shakespeare's *Macbeth* and Thomson's *Sophonisba*.

After relocating to Britain, the Adamses found a quiet house in Grosvenor Square and settled into life in London. On Saturday, 27 August 1785, Nabby casually mentioned to her father that she had never read Shakespeare. He was shocked. That very morning he dashed out to his bookseller and bought her a set of Shakespeare, so she could fill this gaping chasm in her literary knowledge. Nabby did not wait another day: she began reading Shakespeare after dinner that Saturday. As she read, Nabby would sometimes inscribe memorable passages into a little pocket notebook. One day she inscribed part of an exchange between Valentine and Proteus, the eponymous friends from *Two Gentlemen of Verona*. In the play's final scene Valentine says to Proteus:

> I am sorry I must never trust thee more
> But count the world a stranger for thy sake
> The private wound is deepest; oh time most curst
> Mongst all foes, that a friend should be the worst.[16]

Nabby shared the little pocket book with her mother, who could see personal implications in the lines from Shakespeare. When they left America, Nabby was engaged to Royall Tyler, a young attorney who would secure his literary reputation a few years later with *The Contrast*, the first professionally produced American comedy. While living in London, Nabby broke their engagement after a mysterious slight on Tyler's part. Her mother interpreted Valentine's words to Proteus as an approximation of how Nabby felt toward Tyler. Nabby soon grew close to William Stephens Smith, who had served as aide-de-camp to George Washington during the war and was now secretary of the American legation in London.

Nabby's introduction to Shakespeare in August 1785 came just in time. The following month the London stage would begin its new season. Drury Lane reopened on Saturday, 17 September, with *Othello*, starring Sarah Siddons as Desdemona. Abigail looked forward to seeing 'this admired and celebrated actress'. The Adamses bought their tickets a week ahead to make sure they would have seats for the opening performance.[17]

The day after they saw *Othello* Abigail described the performance to a correspondent. Siddons called to mind lines from *Paradise Lost*: 'Grace was in all her steps heaven in her eye / And every gesture dignity and love.' While enjoying her performance, Abigail recognised how much seeing a theatrical performance differed from reading a play. She had read and enjoyed *Othello* countless times, but the play had a visceral quality on stage that made her uneasy. Try as she might, Abigail had trouble overcoming her deeply ingrained racial prejudice. She informed her correspondent: 'Othello was represented blacker than any affrican. Whether it arises from the prejudices of education or from a real natural antipathy I cannot determine, but my whole soul shuderd when ever I saw the sooty More touch the fair Desdemona. I wonder not that Brabantio thought Othello must have used spells and magick to have won her affections.' The character's race made it hard for Abigail to appreciate his rhetoric. She had always admired Othello's farewell to war, but, try as she might, Abigail had difficulty appreciating the speech in performance: 'That most incomparable speach of Othellos lost half its force and beauty, because I could not seperate the coulour from the man.'[18]

On Monday, 14 November 1785, Covent Garden premiered a new production of *Romeo and Juliet* starring Joseph George Holman and Anne Brunton in the title roles. The Adamses attended either this or one of the subsequent performances of *Romeo and Juliet*, which Nabby mentions in her correspondence. She calls Brunton 'a very promising actress, a little more than seventeen, and for her age really surprizing'. Brunton played Juliet 'with the greatest judgment'.[19]

The Adamses attended a performance of *The Confederacy*, a John Vanbrugh comedy, at Drury Lane the first week of December. Nabby called it 'as great a satire upon the manners, of high life, as could have been written'. Elizabeth Farren, who played the part of Clarissa, instantly became Nabby's 'favourite comic actress'. Their evening at Drury Lane turned out to be quite long – five hours total. After *The Confederacy* the theatre staged a revival of *The Jubilee*, Garrick's stage version of the 1769 Shakespeare celebration. *The Jubilee* is the theatrical equivalent of Dodd's *Beauties of Shakespeare*. It presents a series of Shakespearean characters enacting their most famous speeches. Nabby found *The Jubilee* 'well worth seeing once, the scenery is magnificent, and there is a procession of the principle characters and a representation of the principle scenes of every one of his plays, which is very well-done, and at the close, they all appear upon the stage at one time'.[20]

Abigail's correspondence shows her ongoing interest in the stage. Like her husband, she understood how to use dialogue to bring her writing alive. In a letter to their son John Quincy Adams on Thursday, 16 February 1786, she relates something that had happened the previous night when the family returned home from dining out.

'Oh Mam!' their footman said as he greeted the Adamses when their carriage pulled up outside their home in Grosvenor Square on Wednesday evening. 'There are a thousand letters come.'

'Well,' John said to Abigail as he got out of the carriage, 'now I shall see your eyes glisten, nobody ever enjoy'd a letter more than you.'

Nobody, that is, with the possible exception of Nabby: she did not wait to hear what her father said. A 'nimble footed Daphne', Nabby bounded up the stairs to see the letters first. Abigail continues: 'From that moment untill half past twelve we were all employd in reading our letters. Even the watchmans cry, of "half past ten oclock" which upon other nights puts your pappa in motion for bed, past unheeded by.'[21]

Giving her son the latest news from London, Abigail's letter contains no less than three Shakespeare references. She relates how Nabby broke her engagement with Royall Tyler: 'Let the memory of former attachments, since the recollection of them can only be attended with pain, sleep in oblivion. As they proved not to be founded upon a durable superstructure, they have properly vanishd like the baseless fabrick of a vision, nor do I think even a wreck is left behind.'[22]

She then recalls another line from Shakespeare. 'Rouchfoucault says, and Shakspear makes the same observation that a heart agitated with the remains of a former passion is most susceptable of a new one.' Abigail does not mention her specific source, but she is recalling something Proteus says to Valentine in the second act of *Two Gentlemen of Verona*:

> Even as one heat another heat expels,
> Or as one nail by strength drives out another,
> So the remembrance of my former love
> Is by a newer object quite forgotten.[23]

It does not seem coincidental that Abigail quotes *Two Gentlemen of Verona* to characterise the end of her daughter's relationship with Tyler and the start of her relationship with William Stephens Smith, her future husband. Having read a different quotation from the same play in Nabby's pocket notebook, Abigail apparently reread the play and found another apt quotation.

Pairing Shakespeare with the duc de La Rochefoucauld, Abigail reveals another way she read Shakespeare. La Rochefoucauld is best known as a moralist. His *Maximes* is packed with pithy nuggets of wisdom. Similarly, Shakespeare's works could yield numerous maxims, which could be lifted from their contexts and stand alone as incisive conduct advice.

In her letter Abigail also gave John the latest news of the royal family. She reported a rumour about the Prince of Wales and Maria Fitzherbert: 'The royal family appeard much out of spirits yesterday, the prince of Wales like Benidict the married man.' Her letter refers to Benedick from *Much Ado about Nothing*. A confirmed bachelor as the play begins, Benedick scoffs at the idea of getting married. He compares the image of his married self with a bull dehorned and transformed into a plow horse. He says, 'As they write "Here is a good horse to hire", let them signify under my sign, "Here you may see Benedick, the married man."'[24]

In eighteenth-century America the name Benedick or Benedict became a humorous *blason populaire* signifying any recently married man. On 16 February 1786, coincidentally the same day Abigail Adams wrote this Shakespeare-laden letter to her son, Light Horse Harry Lee wrote a letter to future US president James Madison. Then in New York serving in the Confederation Congress, Lee gave Madison the latest news about a fellow congressman and another future US president, James Monroe, who was getting married that very night: 'Monroe becomes Benedict this evening.'[25]

While a student at Harvard, John Quincy Adams – yet another future US president – did not neglect his Shakespeare. In March 1786 he wrote to his sister regarding one of his assignments. Each student had to recite a passage from English literature to the class and the college president. John Quincy Adams selected a popular favourite, Jaques's All-the-world's-a-stage speech from *As You Like It*. He told Nabby: 'At the description of the justice in fair round belly, with good capon lined, every person present, the president excepted, burst into a loud laugh. I was sensible it was at my expense, but I expected it, and was not disconcerted.'[26]

The London stage entertained his parents and sister throughout the theatrical season. On 2 March 1786 they attended a performance of *Macbeth* at Drury Lane with Sarah Siddons as Lady Macbeth. The performance gave Abigail Adams much to think about. She considered the importance of casting and also contrasted the differences between reading Shakespeare and seeing his plays performed. Siddons was too great to suit the role of such a detestable character as Lady Macbeth, Abigail concluded. She could now understand why his plays were altered for the Restoration stage: 'Much of Shakspears language is so uncooth that it sounds very harsh. He has beauties which are not equald, but I should suppose they might be renderd much more agreeable for the stage by alterations.'[27]

* * *

Shortly before the Adamses saw *Macbeth* at Drury Lane, John Adams dispatched William Stephens Smith to Paris with an urgent message for Thomas Jefferson. Since their joint commission to negotiate treaties of amity and commerce between the United States and other nations would expire in May, the two had the responsibility to do as much as they could before its expiration. Though any further efforts in this regard had seemed fruitless, new and unexpected opportunities for negotiating treaties with Portugal, Tripoli and possibly other nations of the Barbary Coast arose that winter. Adams remained hopeful a diplomatic agreement between the United States and Tripoli could be hammered out, provided he and Jefferson acted quickly.

Jefferson and Smith reached London on Saturday, 11 March. They met with Adams briefly that evening and rejoined him on Sunday. Jefferson's excursion to London was a disappointment in terms of official business, but in terms of pleasurable diversion, it was a rich and rewarding personal experience. He and Adams had the opportunity to spend much time together visiting England's most renowned pleasure gardens. Jefferson drafted a narrative of their sightseeing tour, 'Notes of a Tour of English Gardens', which devotes individual paragraphs to all the gardens they visited.

Adams recorded their journey in 'Notes on a Tour of English Country Seats'. The differences between the notes both men took reveal important differences in their outlook. Whereas Jefferson scrutinised the gardens with an eye toward making improvements at Monticello, Adams had no plans to improve his property in Massachusetts, at least not in terms of its aesthetics. Adams enjoyed the country estates and pleasure gardens they visited but did little beyond naming the different gardens in his notes. The only ones that called forth appreciative comments on his part were those with literary associations. For its beauty and its grandeur, he especially enjoyed the estate of Lord Lyttelton, the author of *Dialogues of the Dead*. Adams also liked the gardens of Alexander Pope and James Thomson.

One particular destination elicited lengthier comments on Adams's part than any other, Stratford-upon-Avon. His detailed description of Stratford in 'Notes on a Tour of English Country Seats' is not unusual. Numerous other Shakespeare-loving travellers made this literary pilgrimage and described their visits at length. German traveller Karl Moritz enjoyed seeing the humble, yet neat cottages that lined the banks of the Avon, but Shakespeare's house, he thought, was the worst one in town. Adams agreed. From the inn where they were staying, he and Jefferson walked three doors down to see Shakespeare's birthplace, a house, in Adams's words, 'as small and mean, as you can conceive'.[28]

Typically, the guide within the house showed visitors a dilapidated wooden chair in the chimney corner. Moritz observed, 'Shakespeare's chair, in which he used to sit before the door, was so cut to pieces that it hardly looked like a chair; for every one that travels through Stratford, cuts off a chip, as a remembrance which he carefully preserves, and deems a precious relique.' Despite the sorry condition of the chair, Moritz could not avoid whittling off a sliver for himself. Neither could Jefferson nor Adams. They, too, cut chips off the old chair, which to literary devotees were akin to pieces of the true cross.[29]

The mulberry tree Shakespeare supposedly planted had been cut down and put up for sale. The house where Shakespeare died had been taken down, too. The spot where the house once stood was preserved as a small garden. In the nearby graveyard Adams and Jefferson saw Shakespeare's gravestone and read the famous curse upon any who should disturb the bones:

> Good friend for Jesus sake forbeare
> To digg the dust encloased heare!
> Blese be the man that spares these stones
> And curst be he that moves my bones

Overall, Adams found unsettling the incongruity between the greatness of Shakespeare's work and the meanness of his home and its meagre relics:

> There is nothing preserved of this great genius which is worth knowing; nothing which might inform us what education, what company, what accident, turned his mind to letters and the drama. His name is not even on his gravestone. An ill-sculptured head is sett up by his wife, by the side of his grave in the church. But paintings

> and sculpture would be thrown away upon his fame. His wit, and fancy, his taste and judgment, his knowledge of nature, of life and character, are immortal.[30]

In contrast, Jefferson's 'Notes of a Tour of English Gardens' makes no mention of their visit to Stratford. It's not that he did not enjoy seeing Shakespeare's birthplace. His failure to mention the visit to Stratford simply shows that Jefferson wrote what he did with a specific purpose in mind, to observe and analyse the gardens they visited in terms of both practical matters and aesthetics.

Much other evidence survives to document Jefferson's ongoing devotion to Shakespeare. According to Adams family tradition, he reacted in a manner of a devout acolyte when they reached Shakespeare's house. Decades later Abigail Adams told a correspondent that Jefferson 'fell upon the ground and kissed it'.[31] Beyond her letter, no additional evidence exists to verify Jefferson's behaviour as they approached Shakespeare's house. Her story does seem out of character for Jefferson. Regardless of its veracity, the anecdote captures his longstanding passion for Shakespeare's writings.

While in London, Jefferson saw Shakespeare in performance. He, too, attended a production of *Macbeth* with Sarah Siddons as Lady Macbeth. He saw her in *The Merchant of Venice* as well. By all accounts, her performance as Portia was inspiring, especially her appealing version of the Quality-of-mercy speech. As one contemporary observed, 'Mrs Siddons spoke the speech on mercy as it certainly should be spoken – but as in truth we never heard it spoken – as a reply to "On what compulsion must I?" From every other Portia it has always appeared as a recitation, prepared for the occasion.'[32]

During his trip to London, Jefferson was in the process of acquiring a new edition of Shakespeare's works. In 1785, John Bell had begun publishing a fine-paper, petite-format edition of Shakespeare with detailed scholarly annotations. Bell issued each of the plays and all of the annotations separately. Jefferson acquired the individual numbers of the edition as Bell published them, continuing to expand his set through 1788, when Bell released the last number. Not only did Jefferson acquire the plays, he also obtained their accompanying annotations. To Jefferson's ear, these annotations had a familiar ring to them: many were written by his old friend Samuel Henley.[33]

Shortly after he returned to Paris from London, Jefferson ordered a copy of *The Beauties of Shakespeare*. He also purchased the quarto edition of Edward Capell's *Notes and Various Readings to Shakespeare*. which contained explanatory notes, variant readings, and a glossary.

The earlier work shows that Jefferson, like Abigail Adams and so many other eighteenth-century readers, saw Shakespeare as a source for locating familiar quotations. The other work reflects Jefferson's scholarly bent.

Two years later Jefferson ordered Andrew Becket's *Concordance to Shakespeare*. Published in 1787, Becket's is the first Shakespeare concordance. Some contemporary readers had trouble understanding the usefulness of this innovative reference work. The Rev. Henry Meen, though a classical scholar, saw little scholarly value in Becket's concordance. He obtained a copy for himself but could not mask his disappointment with it. Meen found a couplet from Pope's *Dunciad* suitable to describe Becket's *Concordance*. Onto the boards of his copy he wrote: 'Nonsense precipitate like running lead, / Flows through the chinks and crannies of his head.' Meen did not stop there. Onto the volume's spine Meen inscribed a clever spine title for the volume: 'A. B.'s Nonsense on Shakespeare'.[34]

Jefferson's acquisition of Becket's *Concordance* reinforces his curiosity about Shakespeare's vocabulary, but, unlike Meen, he understood the work's usefulness for writing essays, letters and speeches. In a way Becket's *Concordance* is not dissimilar to *The Beauties of Shakespeare*: it lets readers access memorable passages in Shakespeare's writings. Becket's introduction stresses the concordance's value as a reference work, quoting Dr Johnson's comment that Shakespeare's plays 'are filled with practical axioms and domestic wisdom; and that a system of civil and economical prudence may be collected from them'.[35]

The year he left Paris to return to America, Jefferson sought an accurate portrait of Shakespeare to hang at Monticello. He wrote his friend John Trumbull, then living in London, and asked if he could help him obtain portraits of such important thinkers as Bacon, Locke, Newton and Shakespeare. Bell's Shakespeare, which reproduced the portrait of Shakespeare in the possession of the duke of Chandos, let Jefferson know that the Chandos portrait was the only genuine likeness of Shakespeare available. Jefferson gave Trumbull this information to assist his efforts to find a good portrait. If Trumbull were unable to obtain a portrait, Jefferson hoped to acquire a bust of Shakespeare to decorate Monticello.[36]

Abigail Adams deepened her knowledge of Shakespeare by reading some literary criticism. In 1787 she read Montagu's *Essay on Shakespeare*. She enjoyed it so much that she shared the work with others. She sent one copy to Mercy Otis Warren. Upon learning that Elizabeth Montagu was alive and living in London, Abigail considered befriending her but decided against it. As she says in the cover letter to

Warren: 'I should have wished to have formed an acquaintance with her, if I had not learnt that she was a violent Anti American.'[37]

As Abigail Adams predicted, Warren enjoyed Montagu's *Essay* very much, so much that she addressed a poem to her, though Adams's comment about her anti-Americanism inspired the poem more than Montagu's *Essay* itself. The opening lines of 'To Mrs Montague' say that her 'critic pen adds praise, / Ev'n to a Shakespeare's bold exalted lays'. Before her first verse paragraph ends Warren implores Montagu to reconsider her anti-American feelings and appreciate the political and cultural heritage the United States and Great Britain share. 'To Mrs Montague' is a call for rapprochement. Americans recognised Shakespeare's greatness; the British should recognise what else the two nations shared:

> Will she across the Atlantic stretch her eye,
> Look o'er the main, and view the western sky;
> And there Columbia's instant drama see —
> Reflect that Britain taught us to be free.[38]

14

How Shakespeare Ratified the Constitution

On Saturday, 14 July 1787, George Washington attended a performance of the American Company's production of *The Tempest* at Southwark Theatre on the outskirts of Philadelphia. No cast list from the performance survives, but presumably David Douglass took the part of Prospero and Nancy Hallam played Miranda. Due to a state law prohibiting theatrical performances, the venue was not called a theatre but an opera house, and *The Tempest* was not called a play but an opera, which formed part of a concert. Furthermore, *The Tempest* was not Shakespeare's *Tempest* but the version of Shakespeare's play as altered by Davenant and Dryden. According to the contemporary advertisements, the music for the play was composed by Henry Purcell, but John Weldon is now generally recognised as the composer. And the wedding masque of the fourth act was replaced by a grand fifth-act masque about Neptune and Amphitrite. Despite all these exceptions, it was apparently a good show, except that Washington left no critical opinion in his diary.[1]

Washington was in Philadelphia serving as president of the Constitutional Convention. No doubt other delegates also went to see *The Tempest* that Saturday evening. It came at an opportune moment. Since convening in May the delegates had begun planning a whole new national government. Originally, the convention had been called to amend the Articles of Confederation, but, as one of their first acts, the delegates had voted to abandon the Articles altogether and draft a new constitution. In so doing, they had decided upon a bicameral system for the legislature, with equal state representation in the upper house and proportional representation in the lower house. They still had much more to decide. The Constitution would not be finished until 17 September 1787, when all but three of the delegates in attendance signed it.

According to Article VII, nine states would have to ratify the Constitution before it could take effect. Consequently, the individual states would hold conventions to ratify the document. Between the Constitutional Convention and the last state ratifying convention, heated debates took place publicly and privately throughout the nation. To convince citizens of the value of the Constitution its defenders brought all their rhetorical skills to bear. Time and again they quoted the words of William Shakespeare to defend the Constitution and argue for its ratification.

Since the Constitution created a strong national government, its supporters became known as Federalists. Americans who preferred the Articles of Confederation, that is, a form of government that largely left governing power to the states, became known as Antifederalists. *The Federalist Papers* emerged as the single most important set of newspapers essays defending the Constitution.

Written by Alexander Hamilton, John Jay and James Madison, all using the pseudonym 'Publius', the *Federalist Papers* delineated the power and strength of the Constitution and refuted the Antifederalist campaign against it. The 'Publius essays', as they were known during their original publication, sought to convince New Yorkers to elect delegates to their state ratifying convention who would support the Constitution. Publius carefully explained what the Constitution stood for and how it would work. Though written for the New York papers, the Publius essays helped readers across the nation understand and appreciate the Constitution. Many newspapers reprinted the Publius essays, which swelled to eighty-five numbers. They were collected in two volumes in 1788. The *Federalist Papers* are now recognised as the single most important American contribution to political theory.

Hamilton wrote the first number of the series, which appeared on 27 October 1787. This opening essay established a fundamental issue. Hamilton observed: 'It seems to have been reserved to the people of this country, by their conduct and example, to decide the important question, whether societies of men are really capable or not, of establishing good government from reflection and choice, or whether they are forever destined to depend, for their political constitutions, on accident and force.' 'Federalist, No. 1' set the stage, so to speak, for the essays that follow. This is no mere turn of phrase: the language of the theatre forms an important aspect of the *Federalist Papers*.[2]

John Jay wrote 'Federalist, No. 2', which appeared four days later. Speaking as Publius, he identifies the geographical continuity of the United States, which reinforces the nation's political continuity: 'It has often given me pleasure to observe, that Independent America was not composed of detached and distant territories, but that one connected, fertile, wide spreading country was the portion of our western sons of liberty.' The shared values of the American people further contribute to their unity: 'This country and this people seem to have been made for each other, and it appears as if it was the design of Providence, that an inheritance so proper and convenient for a band of brethren, united to each other by the strongest ties, should never be split into a number of unsocial, jealous and alien sovereignties.'[3]

Jay's 'band of brethren' echoes the phrase 'band of brothers' from King Henry's St Crispin's Day speech in *Henry V*. Washington had stressed the pertinence of the phrase for bringing together his men as a unified fighting force during the Revolutionary War; it was no less pertinent for bringing together the American people under the federal government. Many of the newspaper polemicists and others who spoke in support of the Constitution would reuse the phrase 'band of brothers'. Some usages may be deliberate allusions to *Henry V*, but the phrase was quoted so often after the Constitutional Convention that it entered the vernacular.

The Rev. Aaron Hall, pastor of the First Congregational Church in Keene, New Hampshire, deserves credit for the most eloquent use of the phrase among the Federalists. Hall represented Keene in the New Hampshire Convention, voting in the majority to ratify the Constitution. When the town of Keene celebrated New Hampshire's ratification of the document, it asked Hall to deliver a speech for the occasion. Afterwards, he issued his speech as a pamphlet, and newspapers throughout New England reprinted its text. Hall spoke these moving words:

> Though all cannot think alike, which is not to be expected, any more than it is that we should all look alike; yet it becomes us to unite in the common cause as a band of brothers, since we are all embarked together for ourselves and our posterity; and notwithstanding there are some who cannot rejoice to so high a degree, at present, on the ratification of the federal government, yet I presume to say, that their living under it a short time, will give them to realize the felicity that others anticipate.[4]

Jay ended 'Federalist, No. 2' with a quotation from another one of Shakespeare's history plays, arguing that the Articles of Confederation or any other loose confederation of states would doom the nation: 'Whenever the dissolution of the Union arrives, America will have reason to exclaim in the words of the poet, 'Farewell, a long farewell to all my greatness.'[5]

These words come from Cardinal Wolsey's swansong in *Henry VIII*. In the third act Norfolk bids Wolsey a facetious farewell before leaving him alone on stage. The opening line of Wolsey's soliloquy responds to Norfolk's mocking goodbye. Wolsey then turns to express his own thoughts, as he plays upon the meaning of farewell. His soliloquy begins:

> So, farewell to the little good you bear me.
> Farewell? A long farewell to all my greatness.
> This is the state of man. Today he puts forth
> The tender leaves of hopes; tomorrow blossoms,
> And bears his blushing honours thick upon him;
> The third day comes a frost, a killing frost,
> And when he thinks, good easy man, full surely
> His greatness is a-ripening nips his root,
> And then he falls, as I do.[6]

Having Americans speak the words that Cardinal Wolsey speaks in *Henry VIII*, Jay personified the nation, but he was not attributing Wolsey's personal qualities to the national character. Like so many early American writers who quote Shakespeare, Jay detached the words from their dramatic context and applied them to suit his purpose.

In October and November many state legislatures set the dates for their ratifying conventions and for the elections that would choose delegates to them. As the elections approached, the newspaper debates over the Constitution intensified. For example, 'An Instructor', a pseudonymous contributor to the *Maryland Gazette*, wrote to the newspaper urging that local voters carefully choose qualified delegates to attend Maryland's ratifying convention. Instructor suggests that voters should give delegates the freedom to exercise their judgement: 'I am satisfied, that every sensible and patriotic citizen, is desirous that the wisest and best men in our state may be elected to the convention, and left uncontrouled to exercise their judgments on this momentous occasion.'[7] These words would not go unchallenged.

Within a week 'An Old Man' wrote to the *Maryland Gazette* to refute Instructor. Like Instructor, like so many of the authors who contributed to the ratification debate, the Old Man remains unidentified. He argues that Instructor had misconstrued the purpose of the ratifying convention. It was not to frame the Constitution but to vote whether to ratify the document drafted by the Constitutional Convention. The people should elect representatives who will vote the way they wish them to vote: for or against the Constitution. To drive home his point Old Man compares Instructor with Stephano in *The Tempest* and quotes a passage from the play regarding the plan of government Stephano envisions.[8]

In the third act of *The Tempest* Stephano accepts Caliban's suggestion that they should murder Prospero in his sleep and set himself up as monarch with Prospero's daughter Miranda as his consort and Trinculo and Caliban as viceroys. Stephano says to Caliban: 'Monster, I will kill this man. His daughter and I will be king and queen – save our graces – and Trinculo and thyself shall be viceroys. – Dost thou like the plot, Trinculo?'[9] Stephano's conniving plot is the plan of a greedy and egotistical leader who wishes to establish a government not for the good of the people, but for the pursuit of his own selfish desires. The Old Man's reference to *The Tempest* in the *Maryland Gazette* casts Instructor in the role of Stephano, someone who thinks only of himself as he imagines the new government.

This Old Man is not the first author in early American literature to cite Stephano's speech from *The Tempest*. When John Trumbull published the four-canto version of his satirical mock epic *M'Fingal* five years earlier, he, too, recalled the speech. *M'Fingal* is a double-edged satire. Chronicling the political activities of Squire M'Fingal, a supercilious Loyalist, it reveals the absurdity of the British treatment of the American people. The speaker of the poem tells the story in the third person, which nonetheless reflects the consciousness of M'Fingal, whose perspective on certain aspects of American politics reveals their faults.

The third canto of *M'Fingal* identifies some drawbacks to the Articles of Confederation. During the debates over the Constitution, a South Carolina Federalist recalled Trumbull's critique, excerpted the pertinent passage from *M'Fingal* and submitted it to the *Charleston City Gazette* to help sway voters to ratify the Constitution. Severely restricting the nation's ability to govern, the Articles of Confederation put its leaders in the same position as Stephano puts Trinculo and Caliban:

> You've but pursued the self same way
> With Shakespeare's Trinc'lo in the play,
> 'You shall be viceroys here 'tis true,
> But we'll be viceroys over you.'[10]

The Carolina Federalist read *M'Fingal* as a prophecy of what would happen to the United States if it continued to be governed under the Articles of Confederation. One final sentence follows the excerpt from *M'Fingal* in the *Charleston City Gazette*: 'I sincerely hope we shall disappoint the terrible prophecy of the author by accepting the federal constitution proposed to us.'[11]

The Federalists did not have a monopoly on Shakespeare. Sometimes the Antifederalists quoted Shakespeare to lend authority to their arguments. Despite her close ties to the Adamses, Mercy Otis Warren turned out to be a staunch Antifederalist. In early 1788 she published *Observations on the New Constitution*, identifying herself on the title page of this pamphlet solely as 'A Columbian Patriot'. Warren's pseudonym suggests her devotion to the idea of American nationhood, but she argues that a strong central government would destroy the rights of the states and their people.

Her pamphlet targets many aspects of the Constitution. For one, she argues that the provision to establish a new federal district for the national government would lead to a dangerous abuse of power, forming a 'consolidated fabrick of aristocratick tyranny'. The American people, she asserts, 'wish for no federal city whose "cloud cap't towers" may screen the state culprit from the hand of justice; while its exclusive jurisdiction may protect the riot of armies encamped within its limits'.[12]

Warren's sophisticated use of Shakespeare reveals that Prospero's words from *The Tempest* – 'The cloud-capped towers, the gorgeous palaces, / The solemn temples' – had already entered the discourse of utopia. But Warren reverses the imagery. Though the creation of a new federal city may seem utopian, Warren makes it sound dystopian. Far from symbolising the new city, the clouds would mask the tyrannical injustice occurring within the towers they cap. Warren's use of Prospero's words to describe the new federal city functions as a prophecy of doom. It implies that this 'consolidated fabrick' will ultimately meet the same fate as Prospero's 'baseless fabric'. It shall dissolve and leave not a rack behind.

In a contribution to the *Maryland Journal*, a Philadelphia Antifederalist tells its readers that since Pennsylvania would almost surely vote for ratification, people in other states must speak out against the Constitution to save the country from ruin. This article closes with a quotation from 'the great Shakespeare':

> Methinks our country sinks beneath the yoke.
> It weeps, it bleeds, and each new day a gash

Is added to its wounds. – Bleed! – bleed! – poor country!
Grim tyranny erect thy basis sure,
For goodness dares not check thee.[13]

Though these words mostly come from Shakespeare, this Antifederalist appropriates both language and imagery in the same manner as Mercy Warren. These lines stem from a conversation in the fourth act between Malcolm and Macduff regarding the state of Scotland under Macbeth's rule. The first two and a half lines come from something Malcolm says, the next two and a half lines from something Macduff had said prior to Malcolm's remarks. The Philadelphia Antifederalist fuses the lines together to paint a picture of graphic violence. A few words differ from the original. Macduff says 'great tyranny,' not 'grim tyranny': another change that enhances the bleakness of the situation.

The Antifederalist also alters a few words in the Malcolm quote. Malcolm says, 'I think our country sinks beneath the yoke' in the original; but in the *Maryland Gazette* the line reads: 'Methinks our country sinks beneath the yoke.' The word 'methinks' occurs frequently in Shakespeare, but it is most often associated with Hamlet when he says, 'The lady doth protest too much, methinks'. The Antifederalist may use it to echo Hamlet or, alternatively, to bolster the authority of the quotation by making the lines sound Shakespearier.

The pseudonym of another Antifederalist reflects his identification with the most respected conspirator from Shakespeare's *Julius Caesar*: Brutus. A set of sixteen essays that originally appeared in the *New York Journal* under that pen name, the Brutus essays reappeared in many other newspapers throughout the nation. Attacking the Constitution on several grounds, they deserve recognition as the finest set of Antifederalist essays to emerge from the ratification debates.

In the face of these essays, perhaps it should come as no surprise that a Federalist would use 'Mark Antony' as a pen name for an essay refuting Brutus. An excerpt from Mark Antony's Friends-Romans-countrymen speech gives the essay its epigraph:

Here under leave Brutus, and the rest,
(For Brutus is an honourable man;
So are they all, all honourable men,)
Come I to speak.[14]

Mark Antony's speech in *Julius Caesar* is a rhetorical masterpiece. He calls Brutus an honourable man four times. The first time he seems to confirm what the Romans believe to be true. Gradually revealing what Brutus has said and done, Mark Antony continues to repeat the phrase, which takes on a tinge of irony. By its fourth and final utterance, the irony is clear: Brutus is not an honourable man.

Using the passage in which Mark Antony first calls Brutus an honourable man for his epigraph, the Federalist Mark Antony suggests that he will follow the same rhetorical strategy as his source. He does not. The Federalist Mark Antony eschews irony to avoid ambiguity. He concludes by revealing the duplicity of the Antifederalist Brutus in no uncertain terms: 'The investigation of truth is not his object; his patriotism is pretension; his zeal suspicious, and as he writes with design, we ought to read with caution.'[15]

Other Federalists refuted Brutus. One contributor to the *Massachusetts Centinel* mentions both Brutus and 'An Old Whig'. Not to be confused with the Old Man from Maryland, this Old Whig is an Antifederalist writer. The *Centinel* contributor complains about how monotonous the opposing arguments had become. The 'same cavillings and objections' keep occurring over and over: 'They spring up under the "Old Whig" – are refuted – and again spring up under Brutus – and so on through the whole; until their refuters are tired, and are necessitated to exclaim, "Patience, thou young and rose-lip'd cherubim, / We here discard thee."'[16]

These words come from something Othello says in a speech to Desdemona. In the fourth act of the play Othello tells her that he possessed patience enough to endure nearly any other iniquity, but adultery would be too much for his patience to bear. Continuing this line of thought, he depicts his marriage as a fountain that has turned into 'a cistern for foul toads / To knot and gender in!' He personifies his patience, explaining how it would turn as pale as death in the face of unfaithfulness: 'Turn thy complexion there, / Patience, thou young and rose-lipped cherubim; / Ay, there look grim as hell!'[17]

Like the 'band of brothers', the *Othello* reference applies a figurative relationship derived from Shakespeare to characterise the United States under the Constitution: a marriage, in this case. Once citizens accepted the Constitution, American society would become like the pure fountain of an ideal marriage. The *Centinel* contributor was not the only observer to draw the parallel between the Constitution and marriage – or to quote *Othello* in support.

William Stuart, who had served as an officer in the Continental army throughout the Revolutionary War, took sides with the Federalists during the ratification debates. He related his thoughts on the subject in a letter to a friend. For Stuart, the American people represent the husband; the Constitution itself symbolises the wife. Stuart's letter uses the language of the marriage ceremony to develop this metaphor:

> The great body of the people in every free government, must always be considered as the husband of the Constitution thereof, and consequently that as long as such Constitution performs the duties of love honor and obedience to her great constituent body, or political husband, she is entitled to be kept both in sickness and in health, with all possible love and fidelity by such her said husband and that on a breach of her duty she must expect to incur the pains and penalties of divorce.[18]

Stuart may take his metaphor too far. He soon shades into misogyny, depicting the Antifederalists as 'hen-pecked husbands' who cannot control their wives. By the time he finishes developing his comparison, Stuart predicts what will happen should the marriage between the American people and the Constitution fail: 'Chaos will come again.' Stuart takes his prediction from *Othello*. In the third act Othello says what would happen should he lose his love for Desdemona: 'when I love thee not, / Chaos is come again.'[19]

With the possible exception of 'band of brothers', no phrase from Shakespeare occurs more often in the ratification debates than Hamlet's famous question, the most famous question in the history of English literature: 'To be or not to be'. Perhaps the frequent occurrence of this interrogatory phrase should come as no surprise. To be sure, Provost Smith was not the only one to imitate the line or, indeed, the entire soliloquy with which it begins. From the mid-eighteenth century to the Revolutionary War it occurs time and again in American magazines, newspapers and almanacs. A brief survey of its use may recap the story of Shakespeare and the making of America.

Many colonial American schoolchildren encountered Hamlet's soliloquy before they read *Hamlet*. Dodsley's *Preceptor* includes the soliloquy among other speeches from Shakespeare for students to memorise and recite.[20] From the late 1740s schoolchildren throughout British North America recited Hamlet's soliloquy as part of their lessons. In Virginia, for example, the Rev. James Maury, whose students included Dabney Carr, James Madison (the future president of William and Mary) and Thomas Jefferson, used Dodsley's *Preceptor* at his school.[21]

Hamlet's soliloquy was often parodied in the British press, and American editors sometimes reprinted these new versions patterned on Hamlet's. Though they are typically called parodies, that term is imprecise. The intent of most is not to ridicule the original, but instead to use a familiar form and familiar language to express a new idea.

Most of the so-called parodies of Hamlet's soliloquy that appeared in the eighteenth-century press would be better termed imitations.

The subtitle of 'The Batchelor's Soliloquy', which appeared in the *Scots' Magazine* in 1744, makes its genre clear: 'In Imitation of a Celebrated Speech of Hamlet'. It begins:

> To wed, or not wed – that is the question;
> Whether 'tis happier in the mind to stifle
> The heats and tumults of outrageous passion,
> Or with some prudent fair in solemn contract
> Of matrimony join.

Though it first appeared in the British press, this imitation became a favourite among American readers. Circulating for decades, it was still being reprinted after the Revolutionary War. In 1786 the *New York Morning Post*, for example, reprinted 'The Batchelor's Soliloquy'.[22]

From 1762 a competing version of 'The Batchelor's Soliloquy' began appearing in the American press. The *Maryland Gazette* first printed this imitation with the same opening line of the British version, but the body of the poem is racier. It begins:

> To wed, or not to wed – that's the question:
> Whether 'tis better still to rove at large
> From fair to fair, amid the wilds of passion;
> Or plunge at once into a sea of marriage,
> And quench the fires?

In neighbouring Delaware, *The Wilmington Almanack for 1763* reprinted the Maryland version of 'The Batchelor's Soliloquy', which continued to circulate in the popular press. Five years later it appeared in another almanac, *The American Calender for 1768*.[23]

The outbreak of the French and Indian War inspired 'Shakespeare Parody'd', an imitation by an author who identified himself as 'An Officer in the Army'. This version of Hamlet's soliloquy appeared in the *New American Magazine*. The first magazine published in New Jersey, the *New American Magazine* was founded and edited by Samuel Nevill, one of the colony's leading politicians and a former editor of the London *Morning Post*. The officer debates whether he should say goodbye to his sweetheart and go to war. He begins:

> To part, or not to part: – that is the question?
> Whether 'tis nobler in the mind to suffer

The tears and strugglings of a fond adieu;
Or take arms and march by beat of drum,
And by avoiding, end them?[24]

The same sentiments this officer expressed during the French and Indian War would recur during the Revolutionary War. In January 1776 a Connecticut newspaper, the *Norwich Packet* reprinted 'Shakespeare Parody'd'. Even after the Revolutionary War, this imitation of Hamlet's soliloquy found favour among American readers. In 1788 the *Columbian Magazine* reprinted it, though its origins in the French and Indian War had been lost by then. It appeared under the title, 'A Parody Written during the Late War'.[25]

When Nevill first published 'Shakespeare Parody'd' in the *New American Magazine*, it captured his readers' attention enough to warrant reprinting another imitation of Hamlet's soliloquy. A few months later Nevill reprinted one from Dodsley's *Collection of Poems*. Though he published the poem anonymously, it was written by the Rev. Richard Jago, a minor British poet. Jago assumes the persona of an essayist debating whether to publish an essay he has written:

To print, or not to print, – that is the question.
Whether 'tis better in a trunk to bury
The quirks and crotchets of outrageous fancy,
Or send a well-wrote copy to the press
And by disclosing, end them.[26]

Like other favourite imitations of Hamlet's soliloquy, Jago's poem continued to circulate in the colonial press. On 14 January 1769 the *Antigua Mercury* reprinted the poem. Two months later the *South Carolina Gazette* reprinted it, and the following year Isaiah Thomas reprinted it in the *Massachusetts Spy*.[27]

In the same issue, indeed, on the same page as Jago's poem, the *South Carolina Gazette* reprinted another version of the soliloquy, 'A Parody on Shakespear'.[28] This latest imitation reflects the growing political controversy between the colonies and the British government. It begins:

Be taxt, or not be taxt, that is the question:
Whether 'tis nobler in our minds to suffer
The sleights and cunning of deceitful statesmen,
Or to petition 'gainst illegal taxes,
And by opposing end them?

This imitation had been written for the *Georgia Gazette*, which had first published the poem two weeks earlier. It, too, would circulate throughout Revolutionary America. The following year Thomas would reprint it in the *Massachusetts Spy*.[29] By the time Thomas got ahold of the poem, its Georgia origins had been obscured. That readers from Georgia to Massachusetts shared similar sentiments toward the British government shows how unified the American colonies were becoming as Revolution approached.

'To be, or not to be?': the question continued to resound from the end of the Constitutional Convention into the following summer, when the Constitution was finally ratified. Olney Winsor, a native of Rhode Island who had established himself as a merchant in Alexandria, Virginia, had an intercolonial perspective on the issue. In his opinion 'to be or not to be' a nation was the 'grand question' of the day.[30] Winsor's remarks appear in a private letter to a family member, but many of the authors who contributed to the public debates over the Constitution came to the same conclusion.

During the ratification debates, the use of Hamlet's soliloquy differed from its use during the colonial period. The playfulness of the imitations largely disappeared. Hamlet's opening line was not imitated: it was repeated. Turning away from imitations, American authors restored the serious tone of Shakespeare's original. Far from marking the start of a humorous commentary, the line reverts to a frank and forthright question. Once again, the opening line of Hamlet's most famous soliloquy becomes an existential question. Would the United States of America survive as a nation, or would the loose confederation of independent states ultimately destroy its nationhood?

The use of Hamlet's words in the ratification debates began at least as early as October 1787. The last day of that month, the same day 'Federalist, No. 2' appeared, the *Virginia Independent Chronicle* published a letter from a North Carolina contributor, which begins: 'Mr Printer, "To be or not to be" is now the question! – The moment is at hand when America will rise respected and affluent, or sink into contempt, anarchy, and perhaps a total dissolution of our short existence as a nation.'[31]

Calling on people to support the Constitution as 'the only ultimatum upon which our commercial and political existence rests', this contributor emphasises that the nation's future depends on ratification. The present crisis is 'pregnant in events the most important America has ever yet witnessed, since it not only embraces the happiness of this generation but of millions who are yet to rise out of the womb of futurity.'[32] The message appealed to readers across the nation.

Newspapers in Massachusetts, New York, Pennsylvania and South Carolina soon reprinted the article.

At least one Antifederalist asked Hamlet's existential question. William Symmes, who represented Andover, Massachusetts, in his state's ratifying convention, wrote a detailed analysis of the Constitution in a letter to a friend. Symmes thought that the individual states had the right to ask Hamlet's question for themselves: "With regard to every state, "To be nor not to be – that is the question".'[33] Symmes reflects the attitude of many Antifederalists: would the creation of a strong federal government mean the destruction of the individual states? Symmes ultimately realised that Hamlet's question, at least when applied to the states, was unfounded. He abandoned his Antifederalist tendencies and, with the majority of delegates to the Massachusetts convention, voted to ratify the Constitution.

The first week of December a contributor to the *New Hampshire Spy* published an article the day before a special session of the New Hampshire legislature was scheduled to meet. '"To be, or not to be" one solid republic, cemented by an efficient government, and supported by one federal head, against which the waves of anarchy may, foaming, spend their strength in vain, is a question which must call the attention of every individual in this honourable assembly.' The article ends:

> If a Washington, – a Franklin, and other American patriots are still dear to them, we may venture to hope, that a speedy compliance with the recommendation of the late Convention will be the effect of their meeting, and that unanimity and order, 'Heaven's first law,' will grace all the proceedings of the Fathers of the people.

To be sure, Shakespeare was not the only great English writer the Federalists brought to bear in their arguments. The phrase 'Heaven's first law' comes from Pope's *Essay on Man*.[34]

Maecenas, a pseudonymous South Carolina essayist, used the first line of Hamlet's soliloquy as his epigraph: 'To be or not to be? That is the question!' The essay then begins: 'Whether the new constitution is to be adopted is the present topic of conversation, and the doubt is whether it sufficiently secures to the citizens of America their liberties.'[35] Using the word 'whether' – the first word of the second line of Hamlet's soliloquy – directly after quoting its first line, Maecenas links his message with Hamlet's, making them seem like one continuous utterance. Maecenas does not sustain the similarity. Instead of melancholy reflection, Maecenas carefully refutes those who argued that the Constitution gives the executive branch too much power.

In April 1788 a New Hampshire writer used the first line of Hamlet's soliloquy as a motto, following it with a strong opening paragraph:

> Can you, my fellow countrymen, on a question of existence as a nation hesitate in your decision? whether to be united and powerful, each supporting the dignity of the other; or to be divided into petty states, each seeking and contending for its own local advantages; and like the bundle of twigs which separated, was easily destroyed by an old and infirm man. Unite or die has been a successful motto to this country; never was it more applicable than at this moment.[36]

In addition to Hamlet's existential question, this New Hampshire Federalist draws on other cultural references that stretch from the classical era to recent American history. 'The Bundle of Sticks', one of Aesop's fables, had long been a story illustrating strength in unity. And in the *Pennsylvania Gazette* Franklin had printed his cut-snake political cartoon when he announced the start of the French and Indian War.[37] Beneath the cartoon Franklin supplied the following caption: 'Join, or die.' In his article Franklin argued that the best way for the American colonies to defend themselves against French hostility would be to work together. Franklin's motto for the cut-snake cartoon – the first symbol of the unification of the American colonies – also applied when it came to the Constitution.

The New Hampshire Federalists were persuasive. When their state's convention met in June 1788, its delegates voted to ratify the Constitution, making it the ninth state to do so and thus making ratification official. The heated debates that had been taking place elsewhere soon cooled down, and additional states voted for ratification. As the American people had debated whether to ratify the Constitution, they had looked to Shakespeare, not for the answer but for the question. With the ratification of the Constitution, Americans had answered Hamlet's grand question for themselves, and they had answered it in the affirmative: to be.

Notes

Ever since Nicholas Rowe established the tradition of modernising Shakespeare's texts, nearly all of Shakespeare's editors have followed suit. Even in the most scrupulously prepared scholarly editions, modern conventions of spelling and punctuation determine the look of his texts. Editions of eighteenth-century American authors, on the other hand, are typically not modernised. Instead, editors present them with all the quirks of capitalisation, spelling and punctuation characteristic of the times in which they were written. To keep the numerous quotations from eighteenth-century texts in their original form would result in a strange incongruity: it would make the eighteenth-century authors look older than Shakespeare. Consequently, I tread a middle path with eighteenth-century texts. I have regularised them in terms of capitalisation, but, except for a handful of silent emendations, I have not altered them in terms of spelling or grammar.

Many passages from Shakespeare may differ somewhat from what readers may recall. There is a reason for this departure. In large part my Shakespeare quotations come secondhand. In other words, they do not come directly from Shakespeare but from the writings of early American authors who were quoting Shakespeare from memory. I quote the texts as Washington and Adams and Jefferson remembered them. Besides citing the quoted texts, my notes also provide citations for Shakespeare's texts.

Given the vast number of sources a work like the present one requires, the following notes are quite extensive. I hope they do not intimidate. Frequently cited sources are keyed to the list of abbreviations. Otherwise, the first time a source is used in a chapter, a full citation appears. Subsequent citations to that work within the chapter provide the author's last name, if known, and a short title. In other words, if you encounter a short title, you should find full publication information earlier within the notes for that chapter, except, as I said, for the sources that appear in the following list.

List of abbreviations

AFC

Butterfield, L. H., Wendell D. Garrett and Marjorie E. Sprague, eds., *Adams Family Correspondence*, 13 vols to date (Cambridge, MA: Belknap Press, 1963-).

ANB
Garraty, John A., and Mark C. Carnes, eds., *American National Biography*, 24 vols (Oxford: Oxford University Press, 1999).

DAJA
Butterfield, L. H., Leonard C. Faber and Wendell D. Garrett, eds., *Diary and Autobiography of John Adams*, 4 vols (Cambridge, MA: Belknap Press, 1961).

DHRC
Jensen, Merrill, John P. Kaminski and Gaspare J. Saladino, eds., *The Documentary History of the Ratification of the Constitution*, 29 vols to date (Madison: Wisconsin Historical Society Press, 1976-).

DVB
Kneebone, John T., J. Jefferson Looney, Brent Tarter and Sandra Gioia Treadway, eds., *Dictionary of Virginia Biography*, 3 vols (Richmond: Library of Virginia, 1998-2006).

Hayes, *George Washington*
Hayes, Kevin J., *George Washington: A Life in Books* (Oxford: Oxford University Press, 2017).

Hayes, *Road*
Hayes, Kevin J., *The Road to Monticello: The Life and Mind of Thomas Jefferson* (Oxford: Oxford University Press, 2008).

Highfill
Highfill, Philip A., Jr, Kalman A. Burnim and Edward A. Langhans, *A Biographical Dictionary of Actors, Actresses, Musicians, Dancers, Managers and Other Stage Personnel in London, 1660-1800*, 16 vols (Carbondale: Southern Illinois University Press, 1973-1993).

Johnson and Burling
Johnson, Odai, and William J. Burling, *The Colonial American Stage, 1665-1774: A Documentary Calendar* (Madison, NJ: Fairleigh Dickinson University Press, 2001).

LDC
Hubert, Paul, and Ronald M. Gephardt, eds., *Letters of Delegates to Congress, 1774-1789*, 26 vols (Washington: Library of Congress, 1976-2000).

Lemay, *Calendar*
Lemay, J. A. Leo, *A Calendar of American Poetry in the Colonial Newspapers and Magazines and in the Major English Magazines through 1765* (Worcester, MA: American Antiquarian Society, 1972).

Lemay, *Life*
Lemay, J. A. Leo, *The Life of Benjamin Franklin*, 3 vols (Philadelphia: University of Pennsylvania Press, 2006-2009).

ODNB
Matthew, H. C. G., and Brian Harrison, eds., *Oxford Dictionary of National Biography*, 60 vols (Oxford: Oxford University Press, 2004).

PBF
Labaree, Leonard W., et al., *The Papers of Benjamin Franklin*, 42 vols to date (New Haven: Yale University Press, 1959-).

PJA
Taylor, Robert J., Mary-Jo Kline and Gregg L. Lint, eds., *Papers of John Adams*, 19 vols to date (Cambridge, MA: Belknap Press, 1977-).

PGW: Colonial
Abbot, W. W., Dorothy Twohig and Philader D. Chase, eds., *The Papers of George Washington, Colonial Series*, 10 vols (Charlottesville: University Press of Virginia, 1983-1995).

PGW: Confederation
Abbot, W. W. and Dorothy Twohig, eds., *The Papers of George Washington: Confederation Series*, 6 vols to date (Charlottesville: University Press of Virginia, 1992-).

PGW: Revolutionary War
Chase, Philadern D., at al., ed., *The Papers of George Washington, Revolutionary War Series*, 24 vols to date (Charlottesville: University Press of Virginia, 1985-).

PMHB
Pennsylvania Magazine of History and Biography

PTJ
Boyd, Julian P., et al., eds., *The Papers of Thomas Jefferson*, 32 vols to date (Princeton: Princeton University Press, 1950-).

PTJRS
Looney, J. Jefferson, ed., *The Papers of Thomas Jefferson: Retirement Series*, 14 vols to date (Princeton: Princeton University Press, 2004-).

VMHB
Virginia Magazine of History and Biography

Winans
Winans, Robert B., *A Descriptive Checklist of Book Catalogues Separately Printed in America, 1693-1800* (Worcester, MA: American Antiquarian Society, 1981).

WMQ
William and Mary Quarterly. Arabic numerals preceding the abbreviation denote the series.

1. *Mr William Shakespeares Comedies, Histories, and Tragedies*

1. Kevin J. Hayes, *The Library of William Byrd of Westover* (Madison: Madison House, 1997), no. 804.
2. Martin H. Quit, 'Byrd, William', *DVB*, 1: 463-66.
3. Hayes, *Library of William Byrd*, pp. 5-12.
4. Thomas Morris, *Miscellanies in Prose and Verse* (London: James Ridgway, 1791), p. 47.
5. Nicholas Rowe, *The Tragedy of Jane Shore* (London: Bernard Lintott, 1714), unpaginated.
6. Gary Taylor, *Reinventing Shakespeare: A Cultural History from the Restoration to the Present* (New York: Weidenfeld and Nicolson, 1989), pp. 70-71.
7. Hayes, *Library of William Byrd*, pp. 25-26.
8. William Byrd II to Betty Cromwell, 4 September 1703, *The Correspondence of the Three William Byrds of Westover, Virginia, 1684-1776*, ed. Marion Tinling, 2 vols (Charlottesville: University Press of Virginia, 1977), 1: 237; Carl R. Dolmetsch, 'William Byrd II: Comic Dramatist?' *Early American Literature* 6 (1971): 18-30.
9. William Byrd II to Betty Cromwell, 4 September 1703, *Correspondence*, 1: 237; Emmett L. Avery, *The London Stage, 1660-1800 ... Part 2: 1700-1729*, 2 vols (Carbondale: Southern Illinois University Press, 1960), 1: 41.
10. Taylor, *Reinventing Shakespeare*, p. 73.
11. Hayes, *Library of William Byrd*, nos. 817-20; Jeremy Collier, *A Short View of the Immorality and Profaneness of the English Stage* (London: S. Keble, 1698), p. 50.
12. [James Drake,] *The Antient and Modern Stages Survey'd* (London: Abel Roper, 1699), pp. 201-204.
13. *Macbeth*, 2.3.46-47.
14. Jeremy Collier, *Mr Colliers Dissuasive from the Play-house: In a Letter to a Person of Quality, Occasioned by the Late Calamity of the Tempest* (London: Richard Sare, 1703), p. 15; Avery, *London Stage*, 1: 50.
15. Hayes, *Library of William Byrd*, p. 37; William Byrd, *The Secret Diary of William Byrd of Westover, 1709-1712*, ed. Louis B. Wright and Marion Tinling (Richmond, VA: Dietz Press, 1941), p. 214.
16. Hayes, *Library of William Byrd*, p. 41.
17. Ibid., no. 804.
18. Edwin Eliott Willoughby, 'The Reading of Shakespeare in Colonial America', *PBSA* 31 (1937): 48; Alden T. Vaughan and Virginia Mason Vaughan, *Shakespeare in America* (Oxford: Oxford University Press, 2012), p. 17.
19. Hayes, *Library of William Byrd*, no. 804.
20. Alfred Van Rensselaer Westfall, *American Shakespearean Criticism, 1607-1865* (New York: H. W. Wilson, 1939), pp. 32-33.
21. Georgianna Ziegler, 'The Earliest Recorded Shakespeare in America?' *Collation*, 12 July 2016.
22. Joseph Lyon Miller, 'Major Edward Dale', *1WMQ* 17 (1909): 201-202.
23. Hayes, *Library of William Byrd*, nos. 803-805, 808-810, 813, 815.
24. Byrd, *Secret Diary*, p. 202.
25. Taylor, *Reinventing Shakespeare*, p. 62.
26. Isaac Bickerstaff (pseud.), *The Tatlers* (London: H. Hills, 1710), 2: 312.
27. Taylor, *Reinventing Shakespeare*, pp. 64-66.

28. Byrd, *Secret Diary*, pp. 109-10; Sara B. Bearss, 'Custis, John', *DVB*, 3: 636.
29. *PGW: Colonial*, 6: 289, identifies 'Collier answerd' as John Dennis's *Usefullness of the Stage* (1698), but other books could suit this spine title.
30. 'Catalogue of the Library of Daniel Parke Custis from a Manuscript in the Collection of the Virginia Historical Society', *VMHB* 17 (1909): 412.
31. Hayes, *George Washington*, p. 116.
32. Ibid., p. 111; George Washington, 'Inventory of Books in the Estate', *PGW: Colonial*, p. 297.
33. Ibid., p. 348.
34. Edmund Berkeley, Jr, 'Berkeley, Edmund', *DVB*, 1: 448-49; Byrd, *Secret Diary*, p. 30.
35. 'Library of Edmund Berkeley, Esq.', *1WMQ* 2 (1894): 250-51.
36. Hayes, *Library of William Byrd*, p. 85.
37. William Byrd I to Arthur North, 13 July 1689, *Correspondence*, 1: 111; Philip Alexander Bruce, *Institutional History of Virginia in the Seventeenth Century*, 2 vols (New York: Putnam, 1910), 1: 426.
38. William Hand Browne, ed., *Proceedings of the Council of Maryland, 1696/7-1698* (Baltimore: Maryland Historical Society, 1903), p. 298; Robert K. Headley, Jr, *Wills of Richmond County, Virginia, 1699-1800* (Baltimore: Clearfield, 2002), p. 6.
39. Bernard C. Steiner, 'Law Libraries in Colonial Virginia', *Green Bag* 9 (1897): 352.
40. 'Libraries in Colonial Virginia', *1WMQ* 3 (1894): 133-34.
41. Richard Beale Davis, *Intellectual Life in the Colonial South, 1585-1763*, 3 vols (Knoxville: University of Tennessee Press, 1978), 2: 509.
42. Peter Dyson, 'Changes in Dramatic Perspective: From Shakespeare's *Macbeth* to Davenant's', *Shakespeare Quarterly* 30 (1979): 402-407.
43. [William Shakespeare,] *Macbeth: A Tragedy* (London: William Cademan, 1673), p. 1; [William Davenant,] *Macbeth, A Tragedy: With Alterations, Amendments, Additions, and New Songs* (London: P.C., 1674), p. 1.
44. Alexander Pope, ed., *The Works of Shakespear*, 6 vols (London: Jacob Tonson, 1723-1725), 1: ii.
45. Dyson, 'Changes', p. 404.
46. Avery, *London Stage*, 2: 549.
47. Joseph Addison, *Works*, ed. Richard Hurd and Henry G. Bohn, 6 vols (London: George Bell, 1888), 2: 321.
48. Hayes, *Library of William Byrd*, pp. 48-49.
49. William Byrd, *The London Diary (1717-1721) and Other Writings*, ed. Louis B. Wright and Marion Tinling (London: Oxford University Press, 1958), p. 56.
50. Ibid., p. 77; Avery, *London Stage*, 2: 482; Mark Batty, 'Booth, Barton'; and Moira Goff, 'Booth [née Santlow], Hester', *ODNB*.
51. Byrd, *London Diary*, p. 190.
52. Ibid., pp. 209, 250.
53. 'Library of Edmund Berkeley', pp. 250-51.
54. Alan F. Day, *A Social Study of Lawyers in Maryland, 1660-1775* (London: Garland, 1989), pp. 139-41.
55. Ronald Hoffman and Sally D. Mason, *Princes of Ireland, Planters of Maryland, A Carroll Saga, 1500-1782* (Chapel Hill: University of North Carolina Press, 2000), p. 92; Day, *Social Study*, p. 513.

56. Ibid.; William T. Brantley, ed., *Reports of Cases Argued and Adjudged in the High Court of Chancery* (Baltimore: M. Curlander, 1885), p. 539.
57. Day, *Social Study*, pp. 513-15; Hoffman and Mason, *Princes of Ireland*, p. 92.
58. Day, *Social Study*, p. 515.
59. Frances Teague, *Shakespeare and the American Popular Stage* (Cambridge: Cambridge University Press, 2006), p. 15.

2. *Benjamin Franklin and the Governors*

1. 'Should We Inform', *New-England Courant*, 2 July 1722.
2. Lemay, *Life*, 1: 163.
3. Benjamin Franklin, 'Silence Dogood, No. 1', *PBF*, 1: 9; *Julius Caesar*, 1.1.1-7.
4. Allan Kulikoff, 'Silence Dogood and the Leather-Apron Men', *Pennsylvania History* 81 (2014): 366.
5. *Henry VI, Part II*, 4.2.9-12.
6. Increase Mather, *A Testimony against Several Prophane and Superstitious Customs Now Practised by Some in New England* (London, 1687), sig. A2v.
7. Sidney Lee, *Shakespears Comedies, Histories and Tragedies: A Supplement to the Reproduction in Facsimile of the First Folio* (Oxford: Clarendon Press, 1902), p. 14, says Cotton Mather owned a First Folio, but Anthony James West, *The Shakespeare First Folio: The History of the Book*, 2 vols (Oxford: Oxford University Press, 2003), 2: 300, debunks this notion.
8. John Josselyn, *An Account of Two Voyages to New-England* (London: Giles Widdows, 1674), pp. 122-23; Ben Jonson, *The Masque of the Gypsies* (London: J. Okes, 1640), p. 70.
9. Samuel Gerrish, *A Catalogue of Curious and Valuable Books, Being the Greatest Part of the Libraries of the Reverend and Learned Mr Rowland Cotton ... and Mr Nathanael Rogers* (Boston: Samuel Gerrish, 1725), lot 56 (Winans, no. 9); John Langdon Sibley, *Biographical Sketches of Graduates of Harvard University*, vol. 3 (Cambridge, MA: Charles William Sever, 1885), p. 325.
10. Kevin J. Hayes, 'Cotton Mather', *American Book-Collectors and Bibliographers*, ed. Joseph Rosenblum (Detroit: Gale, 1994), p. 156.
11. Jonathan Mayhew, *The Expected Dissolution of All Things, and Motive to Universal Holiness* (Boston: Edes and Gill, 1755), p. 17.
12. Psalms, 49: 11; *Tempest*, 4.1.152-156.
13. W. H. Bond, 'Introduction', *The Printed Catalogues of the Harvard College Library, 1723-1790*, ed. W. H. Bond and Hugh Amory (Boston: Colonial Society of Massachusetts, 1996), xiii, xxiii.
14. Ibid., xiv.
15. *Catalogus Librorum Bibliothecae Collegii Harvardini quod est Cantabrigiae in Nova Anglia* (Boston: B. Green, 1723), p. 95 (Winans, no. 8).
16. Edwin Wolf, 2d and Kevin J. Hayes, *The Library of Benjamin Franklin* (Philadelphia: Library Company of Philadelphia and the American Philosophical Society, 2006), pp. 20-21.
17. Hugh Amory, 'Printing and Publishing the Catalogues', *Printed Catalogues of the Harvard College Library,* p. xxxv; Clifford K. Shipton, *Sibley's Harvard Graduates*, vol. 8 (Boston: Massachusetts Historical Society, 1951), pp. 118-20; John Dryden, *The Tempest: or, The Enchanted Island* (London:

Henry Herrington, 1676 [i.e., ca. 1692], no. 5 in a volume of plays from Samuel Browne's library; George Granville, Lord Lansdowne, *The Jew of Venice* (London: Ber. Lintott, 1701), no. 10 in same volume (Harvard University, Houghton Library *AC7.B8188.Zz711p).

18. Benjamin Franklin, *The Autobiography of Benjamin Franklin: A Genetic Text*, ed. J. A. Leo Lemay and P. M. Zall (Knoxville: University of Tennessee Press, 1981), p. 20.
19. Mark W. Brewin, *Celebrating Democracy: The Mass Mediated Ritual of Election Day* (New York: Peter Lang, 2008), pp. 18-19.
20. [William Keith,] *The Observator's Trip to America, in a Dialogue between the Observator and His Country-Man Roger* ([Philadelphia: Andrew Bradford,] 1726), pp. 19-20.
21. David Haugaard, 'Keith, William, (c. 1669-1749)', *The Bloomsbury Encyclopedia of the American Enlightenment*, ed. Mark G. Spencer, 2 vols (New York: Bloomsbury, 2015), 2: 608.
22. Jeanne M. Malloy, 'American Secular Prose Dialogues before 1790', PhD diss. (University of Delaware, 1991), p. 123; *Merchant of Venice*, 3.1.55-58; Keith, *Observator's Trip*, p. 17.
23. [William Keith,] *An Essay on the Education of a Young British Nobleman, after He Leaves the Schools* (London: A. Millar and J. Roberts, 1730), pp. 25-26.
24. William Smith, *The History of the Province of New-York, from the First Discovery to the Year MDCCXXXII* (London: Thomas Wilcox, 1757), p. 151.
25. Franklin, *Autobiography*, pp. 32-33.
26. John Wilcox, *Bibliotheca Burnetiana: Being a Catalogue of the Intire Library of His Excellency William Burnet* (London: John Wilcox, 1730?), lot 582.
27. Kevin J. Hayes, 'Benjamin Franklin's Library', *The Cambridge Companion to Benjamin Franklin*, ed. Carla Mulford (Cambridge: Cambridge University Press, 2008), pp. 11-12.
28. Smith, *History of the Province of New-York*, p. 123; Mary Lou Lustig, *Robert Hunter, 1666-1734: New York's Augustan Statesman* (Syracuse: Syracuse University Press, 1983), p. 55.
29. Jason Schaffer, 'Early American Drama', *The Oxford Handbook to Early American Literature*, ed. Kevin J. Hayes (Oxford: Oxford University Press, 2008), pp. 458-59.
30. Peter A. Davis, *From Androboros to the First Amendment: A History of America's First Play* (Iowa City: University of Iowa Press, 2015), p. 143; William C. Carroll, 'Songs of Madness: The Lyric Afterlife of Shakespeare's Poor Tom', *King Lear and Its Afterlife*, ed. Peter Holland (Cambridge: Cambridge University Press, 2002), p. 93.
31. Benjamin Franklin, 'An Account of the New Invented Pennsylvanian Fire-Places', *PBF*, 2: 425; Lois Margaret MacLaurin, *Franklin's Vocabulary* (Garden City, NY: Doubleday, Doran, 1928), p. 104.
32. *King Lear*, 1.4.116-120; Franklin, 'Poor Richard, 1739', *PBF*, 2: 223.
33. Franklin, *Autobiography*, p. 133; Malloy, 'American Secular Prose Dialogues', p. 125.

34. Oral Sumner Coad, 'Drama: The First American Play', *Nation*, 17 August 1918, p. 182.
35. [Robert Hunter,] *Androboros: A B[i]ographical Farce in Three Acts* ([New York: William Bradford], after 1714), p. 21.
36. Schaffer, 'Early American Drama', p. 458.
37. Mark Twain, *Adventures of Huckleberry Finn*, ed. Walter Blair and Victor Fischer (Berkeley: University of California Press, 1985), p. 411.
38. Alexander Pope, *Poetry and Prose*, ed. Aubrey Williams (Boston: Houghton Mifflin, 1969), p. 317; Edmund Burke to David Garrick, 16 July 1765, *The Private Correspondence of David Garrick with the Most Celebrated Persons of His Time*, 2 vols (London: Henry Colburn and Richard Bentley, 1831), 1: 190.
39. Alexander Pope, ed., *The Works of Shakespear*, 6 vols (London: Jacob Tonson, 1723-25), 5: 542.
40. Frederic B. Tromly, 'Macbeth and His Porter', *Shakespeare Quarterly* 26 (1975): 151-56.
41. Rowe, *Works of Mr William Shakespear*, 5: 2566; Pope, *Works of Shakespeare*, 6: 491.
42. Philalethes (pseud.), 'Who Steals My Purse', *Virginia Gazette*, 10 April 1746.
43. Pope, *Works of Shakespear*, 5: 593; 6: 531; Maynard Mack, *Alexander Pope, A Life* (New York: Norton, 1985), p. 420.
44. Alexander Pope, 'Fragment of a Satire', *Miscellanies in Prose and Verse*, vol. 2 (Dublin: Sam. Fairbrother, 1728), p. 84.
45. Lewis Theobald, ed., *The Works of Shakespeare*, 8 vols (London: J. Tonson, 1733), 1: xxxv, 5: 414.
46. Kevin J. Hayes, *The Library of John Montgomerie, Colonial Governor of New York and New Jersey* (Newark, DE: University of Delaware Press, 2000), p. 16.
47. William Smith, *History of the Province of New-York*, p. 173.
48. Hayes, *Library of John Montgomerie*, no. 607; Pope, *Works of Shakespear*, vol. 1, sig. f2r.
49. Hayes, *Library of John Montgomerie*, pp. 37-41.
50. 'Roll of Freemen of New York City, 1675-1866', *Collections of the New-York Historical Society for the Year 1885* (New York, 1886), p. 116; Hayes, *Library of John Montgomerie*, nos. 526, 618 and 607.

3. Franklin Redux

1. Benjamin Franklin, *The Autobiography of Benjamin Franklin: A Genetic Text*, ed. J. A. Leo Lemay and P. M. Zall (Knoxville: University of Tennessee Press, 1981), p. 39.
2. Samuel Johnson, 'Memoirs of the Life of the Rev. Dr Johnson', *Samuel Johnson, President of King's College: His Career and Writings*, ed. Herbert Schneider and Carol Schneider, 4 vols (New York: Columbia University Press, 1929), 1: 7.
3. Louise May Bryant and Mary Patterson, 'The List of Books Sent by Jeremiah Dummer', *Papers in Honor of Andrew Keogh, Librarian of Yale University by the Staff of the Library, 20 June 1938* (New Haven: Yale University Press, 1938), pp. 487, 472.

4. Samuel Johnson, 'A Catalogue of Books Read by Me from Year to Year Since I Left Yale College', *Samuel Johnson*, 1: 500.
5. Ibid., p. 501.
6. Ibid., p. 502-503.
7. Henry Fielding, *The History of the Adventures of Joseph Andrews*, 2d ed., 2 vols (London: A. Millar, 1742), 2: 151.
8. Johnson, 'A Catalogue of Books', p. 509; Nicholas Rowe, *Tamerlane, A Tragedy*, 2d ed. (London: Jacob Tonson, 1703), p. 28.
9. Johnson, 'Catalogue of Books', pp. 510, 512.
10. Ibid., p. 519.
11. Samuel Johnson to William Samuel Johnson, 23 April 1744, *Samuel Johnson*, 1: 118.
12. Franklin, *Autobiography*, pp. 39-40.
13. 'Advertisements', *Grub Street Journal*, 15 March 1732.
14. Benjamin Franklin, 'Poor Richard, 1746', *PBF*, 3: 62; Franklin, *Autobiography*, p. 37.
15. [James Ralph,] *A Critical Review of the Publick Buildings, Statues and Ornaments in, and about London* (London: C. Ackers, 1734), p. 119.
16. Ibid., p. 203.
17. [James Ralph,] *The Case of Authors by Profession or Trade, Stated* (London: R. Griffiths, 1758), p. 27.
18. Emmett L. Avery, *The London Stage, 1660-1800 ... Part 2: 1700-1729*, 2 vols (Carbondale: Southern Illinois University Press, 1960), 2: 806.
19. Highfill, 12: 240; Thomas Morris, *Miscellanies in Prose and Verse* (London: James Ridgway, 1791), p. 48.
20. Samuel Baker, *A Catalogue of the Library of James Ralph* [London, 1762], lot 260.
21. William Warburton, ed., *The Works of Shakespear*, 8 vols (London: J. Tonson, 1747), 1: xii-xiii.
22. Stephen Parks, 'Shakespeare and His Editors, 1594-1790: The Catalogue of an Exhibition in the Beinecke Library, March-May 1975', *Yale University Library Gazette* 50 (1975): 106.
23. *Hamlet*, 3.1.61-62, 65; Alfred Owen Aldridge, 'A Religious Hoax by Benjamin Franklin', *American Literature* 36 (1964): 206-207; Benjamin Franklin, *A Dissertation on Liberty and Necessity, Pleasure and Pain*, *PBF*, 1: 65.
24. Alwin Thaler, 'Shakespeare and Franklin', *Shakespeare Quarterly* 12 (1961): 478; Jane Girdham, 'Thurmond [née Lewis], Sarah', *ODNB*.
25. J. Miling, 'Oldfield, Anne', *ODNB*.
26. Edwin Wolf, 2d, and Kevin J. Hayes, *The Library of Benjamin Franklin* (Philadelphia: American Philosophical Society and Library Company of Philadelphia, 2006), no. 907.
27. Laird Okie, 'Ralph, James', *ODNB*.
28. [Alexander Pope,] *The Dunciad, Variorum* (London: A. Dob, 1729), p. 61; *Hamlet*, 1.4.51-54.
29. Pope, *Dunciad, Variorum*, p. 62.
30. Avery, *London Stage*, 2: 833.
31. Ibid., pp. 832-834, 847.

32. *The London Budget of Wit: or, A Thousand Notable Jests* (London: Walker and Edwards, 1817), pp. 271-72.
33. William Franklin to Elizabeth Graeme, 9 December 1757, *PBF*, 7: 289.
34. Ibid., p. 290; George Winchester Stone, Jr, *The London Stage, 1660-1880 ... Part 4: 1747-1776* (Carbondale: Southern Illinois University Press, 1962), pp. 613, 615, 622, 625-26.
35. George Winchester Stone, Jr, 'Garrick's Production of *King Lear*: A Study in the Temper of the Eighteenth-Century Mind', *Studies in Philology* 45 (1948): 89-103.
36. [Joshua Steele,] *An Essay towards Establishing the Melody and Measure of Speech to Be Expressed and Perpetuated by Peculiar Symbols* (London: J. Almon, 1775), p. 91.
37. Wolf and Hayes, *Library of Benjamin Franklin*, no. 3249; Benjamin Franklin to William Franklin, 14 July 1773, *PBF*, 20: 312.
38. Kevin J. Hayes, 'Prospects for the Study of Benjamin Franklin', *Resources for American Literary Study* 33 (2010): 2.
39. Kevin J. Hayes, 'Libraries and Learned Societies', *Encyclopedia of the North American Colonies*, ed. Jacob Ernest Cooke, 3 vols (New York: Scribner, 1993), 3: 129.
40. Edwin Wolf, 2nd, *The Library of James Logan of Philadelphia, 1674-1751* (Philadelphia: Library Company of Philadelphia, 1974), no. 1824. Henry N. Paul, 'Shakespeare in Philadelphia', *Proceedings of the American Philosophical Society* 76 (1936): 721, says Logan owned the 1714 edition of Rowe's Shakespeare; Wolf does not.
41. Wolf, *Library of James Logan*, no. 1301.
42. F. C., 'I Have Heard', *South Carolina Gazette*, 3 June 1732.
43. Johnson and Burling, pp. 112-17; 'Epilogue to *The Recruiting Officer*, Written by Thomas Dale, MD and Spoken by Silvia in Man's Cloaths, at the Opening of the New Theatre, in Charles-Town in South Carolina, in 1734 [sic, i.e., 1735/6]', *Gentleman's Magazine*, May 1736, p. 288 (Lemay, *Calendar*, no. 408); Roslyn L. Knutson, 'Thomas Dale (1700-1750)', *American Writers before 1800: A Biographical and Critical Dictionary*, ed. James A. Levernier and Douglas R. Wilmes, 3 vols (London: Greenwood Press, 1983), 1: 413-15.
44. William Howland Kenney, *Laughter in the Wilderness: Early American Humor to 1783* (Kent, OH: Kent State University Press, 1976), p. 183.
45. ['A Duel of Dunghill Soldiery'], *South Carolina Gazette*, 6 September 1735 (Lemay, *Calendar*, no. 379).
46. 'Lost or Stolen', *South Carolina Gazette*, 29 June-20 July 1738.
47. Lemay, *Life*, 2: 28-29.
48. Ibid., 2: 310.
49. James Parker to Benjamin Franklin, 14 June 1765, *PBF*, 12: 176; *Henry VIII*, 3.2.455-457.
50. Linda Anderson, *A Place in the Story: Servants and Service in Shakespeare's Plays* (Newark: University of Delaware Press, 2005), p. 177.
51. 'Of Anger, Envy, and Malice', *Pennsylvania Gazette*, 19 July 1733; 'Of Anger, Envy and Malice', *South Carolina Gazette*, 18 August 1733, reprinted from the *London Magazine*, September 1732, pp. 283-85 or the *Universal Spectator*, 9 September 1732.

52. 'Of Anger, Envy, and Malice', *Pennsylvania Gazette*, 19 July 1733.
53. *Henry VIII*, 1.1.132-134.
54. [Walter Chamberlaine,] 'A Tale of the Travellers', *Pennsylvania Gazette*, 11 February 1736 (Lemay, *Calendar*, no. 398 [unattributed]). For the attribution, see Alice Lefanu, *Memoirs of the Life and Writings of Mrs Frances Sheridan* (London: G. and W. B. Whittaker, 1824), pp. 42-43.
55. 'Shakespear's Plays', *Pennsylvania Gazette*, 16 February 1744; *The Charter of the Library Company of Philadelphia* (Philadelphia: B. Franklin, 1746), pp. 15-16 (Winans, no. 19).
56. *National Union Catalog: Pre-1956 Imprints*, 754 vols (London: Mansell, 1968-1981), no. S0451851; Wolf and Hayes, *Library of Benjamin Franklin*, pp. 35-39.
57. Benjamin Franklin, 'On the Candidacy of Barlow Trecothick, 8 March 1768', *PBF*, 15: 64.
58. *Othello*, 5.2.336-39.
59. *A Genuine Account of the Late Secret Expedition to Marinico and Guadaloupe under Commodore Moore and General Hopson* (London: R. Griffiths, 1759).
60. Abigail Adams to John Adams, 6 December 1794, *AFC*, 10: 288.
61. Benjamin Franklin, 'The Colonist's Advocate: VIII, 5 February 1770', *PBF*, 17: 58-61; *Hamlet* 1.2.186-87.
62. [Samuel Johnson,] *An Introduction to the Study of Philosophy, Exhibiting a General View of All the Arts and Sciences, for the Use of Pupils* (New London: T. Green, 1743), p. 28; Samuel Johnson to Benjamin Franklin, November 1750, *PBF*, 4: 74-75.
63. Benjamin Franklin, *The Idea of the English School*, *PBF*, 4: 107.
64. Lois Margaret MacLaurin, *Franklin's Vocabulary* (Garden City, NY: Doubleday, Doran, 1928), p. 15; Lemay, *Life*, 3: 178.

4. *William Parks and the* Virginia Gazette

1. Richard Lewis, *The Mouse-Trap: or, The Battle of the Cambrians and Mice* (Annapolis: W. Parks, 1728), p. 50.
2. Alexander Pope, ed., *The Works of Shakespear*, 6 vols (London: Jacob Tonson, 1723-25), 1: xx.
3. 'The *Virginia Gazette*', *Virginia Historical Register* 6 (1853): 22.
4. Richard Beale Davis, *Intellectual Life in the Colonial South, 1585-1763*, 3 vols (Knoxville: University of Tennessee Press, 1978) 3: 1446.
5. Lawrence C. Wroth, *William Parks: Printer and Journalist of England and Colonial America* (Richmond: William Parks Club, 1926), pp. 30, 51.
6. Harold Lester Dean, 'An Identification of the "Gentleman of Virginia"', *PBSA* 31 (1937): 10-20.
7. Daphne H. O'Brien, 'Dawson, William', *ANB*; Jay B. Hubbell, *The South in American Literature, 1607-1900* (Durham, NC: Duke University Press, 1954), pp. 33-34.
8. Carl Dolmetsch, 'William Byrd of Westover as an Augustan Poet', *Studies in the Literary Imagination* 9 (1976): 77; Nanette C. Tamer, 'The Poetry

of Colonial Virginia', *A History of Virginia Literature*, ed. Kevin J. Hayes (Cambridge: Cambridge University Press, 2015), pp. 58-59.

9. James Southall Wilson, 'Best-Sellers in Jefferson's Day', *Virginia Quarterly Review* 36 (1960): 227; Jeffrey J. Folks, 'William Dawson (1704-1752)', *American Writers before 1800: A Biographical and Critical Dictionary*, ed. James A. Levernier and Douglas R. Wilmes, 3 vols (London: Greenwood Press, 1983), 1: 431; Richard E. Amacher, 'William Dawson (1704-1752)', *Southern Writers: A New Biographical Dictionary*, ed. Joseph M. Flora and Amber Vogel (Baton Rouge: Louisiana State University Press, 2006), p. 100; Hubbell, *South in American Literature*, p. 34.
10. Earl Gregg Swem, Introduction to *Poems on Several Occasions* (New York: Charles F. Heartman, 1920), unpaginated.
11. Dawson, *Poems on Several Occasions*, p. 27.
12. Ibid., pp. 28-29.
13. Ibid., p. 29.
14. Ibid., p. 30.
15. Robert D. Arner, 'The Short Happy Life of the Virginia "Monitor"', *Early American Literature* 7 (1972): 130-47.
16. Ibid., p. 138.
17. 'Monitor, No. 17', *Virginia Gazette* (Parks), 31 December 1736.
18. Thomas Jefferson, *Jefferson's Literary Commonplace Book*, ed. Douglas L. Wilson (Princeton: Princeton University Press, 1989), pp. 109-10.
19. *Thesaurus Dramaticus*, 2 vols (London: Thomas Butler, 1724), 2: 91.
20. Kevin J. Hayes, *A Colonial Woman's Bookshelf* (1996; Eugene, OR: Wipf and Stock, 2016), pp. 56-57.
21. ['Grieving Immoderately',] *Virginia Gazette* (Parks), 11 March 1737.
22. Ibid.
23. Stephen Greenblatt, *Hamlet in Purgatory* (Princeton: Princeton University Press, 2001), p. 247; Andy Mousely, *Re-Humanising Shakespeare: Literary Humanism, Wisdom and Modernity* (Edinburgh: Edinburgh University Press, 2007), p. 44.
24. 'Grieving Immoderately'; *Hamlet*, 1.2.94-97.
25. Musaephilus (pseud.), 'A Tale Extracted from Shakespear', *Virginia Gazette* (Parks), 17 June 1737. Another item is signed 'Musiphilus': 'Once, Beneath a Myrtle Grove', *Virginia Gazette* (Parks), 24 November 1738 (Lemay, *Calendar*, nos. 463, 516).
26. Alan C. Dessen, *Rescripting Shakespeare: The Text, the Director, and Modern Productions* (Cambridge: Cambridge University Press, 2002), p. 175.
27. *Henry VI, Part I*, 2.2.38-43.
28. Kevin J. Hayes, 'Poetry in the Time of Revolution', *The Cambridge History of American Poetry*, ed. Alfred Bendixen and Stephen Burt (Cambridge: Cambridge University Press, 2015), p. 141.
29. Kate McLoughlin, *Authoring War: The Literary Representation of War from the Iliad to Iraq* (Cambridge: Cambridge University Press, 2011), p. 59.
30. *Henry VI, Part I*, 2.3.22-23.
31. Ronald Knowles, *Shakespeare's Arguments with History* (Houndmills, Basingstoke: Palgrave Macmillan, 2002), p. 24; Thomas Morton, *The New English Canaan*, ed. Charles Francis Adams, Jr (Boston: Prince Society, 1883), p. 285.

32. *Henry VI, Part I*, 2.3.60-61.
33. Charles Edelman, *Brawl Ridiculous: Swordfighting in Shakespeare's Plays* (Manchester: Manchester University Press, 1992), p. 65.
34. William H. Castles, Jr, 'The *Virginia Gazette*, 1736-1766: Its Editors, Editorial Policies, and Literary Content'. PhD diss. (University of Tennessee, 1962), p. 117.
35. Joseph Addison, *The Works of Joseph Addison*, ed. George Washington Greene, 6 vols (London: W. W. Gibbings, 1891), 1: 187-88.
36. Hayes, *George Washington*, pp. 104-105.
37. 'Journals of the Council of Virginia in Executive Sessions, 1737-1763', *VMHB* 15 (1908): 381-82; Alexander Pope, ed., *The Works of Shakespeare*, 8 vols (London: J. Tonson, 1735) (College of William and Mary, Swem Special Collections Research Center, PR2752.P7 1735).
38. 'We Hear the Following', *Virginia Gazette* (Parks), 3 June 1737.
39. Charles W. Nichols, 'Fielding and the Cibbers', *Philological Quarterly* 1 (1922): 278-89.
40. Ibid.
41. [Benjamin Ibbot,] 'A Fit of the Spleen in Imitation of Shakespear', *Virginia Gazette* (Parks), 22 July 1737.
42. [William Davenant,] *Macbeth, A Tragedy* (London: P. C., 1674), p. 65.

5. Dr Alexander Hamilton and the Ancient and Honourable Tuesday Club of Annapolis

1. Dr Alexander Hamilton, *Gentleman's Progress: The Itinerarium of Dr Alexander Hamilton, 1744*, ed. Carl Bridenbaugh (Chapel Hill: University of North Carolina Press, 1948), p. 189.
2. 'Among the Characters of the British Worthies', *American Magazine* 1 (1741): 33.
3. 'To Be Sold by Samuel Eliot', *Boston Gazette*, 27 December 1743; *A Catalogue of the Library of Yale-College in New-Haven* (New London, CT: T. Green, 1743), p. 44.
4. 'A Character of the Spaniards, Hollanders, Italians and French', *Independent Advertiser*, 27 March 1749.
5. John Smibert to Arthur Pond, 6 April 1749, 'Smibert-Moffatt Letters', ed. Worthington Chauncey Ford, *Massachusetts Historical Society Proceedings* 49 (1916): 34.
6. Wayne Craven, *Colonial American Portraiture: The Economic, Religious, Social, Cultural, Philosophical, Scientific, and Aesthetic Foundations* (Cambridge: Cambridge University Press, 1986), p. 165.
7. Hamilton, *Gentleman's Progress*, pp. 114, 134; Richard H. Saunders, *John Smibert: Colonial America's First Portrait Painter* (New Haven: Yale University Press, 1995), p. 125.
8. Isaiah Thomas, *The History of Printing in America*, 2 vols (Albany: Joel Munsell, 1874), 2: 104-105; 'Poor Printers', *New York Gazette*, 29 February 1748.
9. Rhodri Lewis, *Hamlet and the Vision of Darkness* (Princeton: Princeton University Press, 2017), pp. 71-73.
10. 'Just Imported from London', *Pennsylvania Gazette*, 15 December 1743; *A Catalogue of Choice and Valuable Books* (Philadelphia: B. Franklin, 1744),

lot 141 (Winans, no. 17); 'Now on Sale, by Auction', *Pennsylvania Gazette*, 5 March 1745.

11. R. Alonzo Brock, ed., 'Journal of William Black', *PMHB* 2 (1878): 46.
12. Ibid., 46-47.
13. Hayes, *George Washington*, p. 7; Alden T. Vaughan and Virginia Mason Vaughan, *Shakespeare in America* (Oxford: Oxford University Press, 2012), p. 12.
14. Thomas Jefferson, *Notes on the States of Virginia*, ed. William Peden (Chapel Hill: University of North Carolina, Press, 1955), p. 177.
15. William Stith, *The History of the First Discovery and Settlement of Virginia* (Williamsburg: William Parks, 1747), p. 179.
16. Nicholas Rowe, ed., *The Works of Mr William Shakespear*, 6 vols (London: Jacob Tonson, 1709), 1: x.
17. Hamilton, *Gentleman's Progress*, p. 191. For Henry Lee's library see the 'Legacy Libraries' section of the online database *LibraryThing*.
18. John Adams, 'Diary', *DAJA*, 1: 132.
19. Gary Taylor, *Reinventing Shakespeare: A Cultural History from the Restoration to the Present* (New York: Weidenfeld and Nicolson, 1989), pp. 65-66.
20. Lawrence C. Wroth, 'Gentleman's Progress: The Itinerarium of Dr Alexander Hamilton', *William and Mary Quarterly*, 3 ser. 6 (1949): 125.
21. Quoted in Kevin J. Hayes, 'Dr Alexander Hamilton', *The Oxford Handbook of Early American Literature*, ed. Kevin J. Hayes (Oxford: Oxford University Press, 2008), p. 240.
22. Alexander Hamilton, *The History of the Antient and Honorable Tuesday Club*, ed. Robert Micklus, 3 vols (Chapel Hill: University of North Carolina Press, 1990), 1: 125; 3: 28.
23. Ibid., 3: 29.
24. Ibid., 1: 247.
25. Heather James, 'Shakespeare's Classical Plays', *The New Cambridge Companion to Shakespeare*, ed. Margreta de Grazia and Stanley Wells (Cambridge: Cambridge University Press, 2010), p. 154.
26. Hamilton, *History*, 1: 247; *Hamlet*, 5.1.198-205.
27. Hamilton, *History*, 1: 358-59; *King Lear*, 1.4.103-104.
28. Hamilton, *History*, 1: 37.
29. Ibid., 2: 18.
30. Ibid., 2: 21.
31. Ibid., 2: 24.
32. Ibid., 2: 26.
33. Ibid., 2: 26-27
34. Ibid., 2: 27.
35. Ibid., 2: 28.
36. Ibid., 3: 214-15.
37. Robert Micklus, 'Dr Alexander Hamilton's "Modest Proposal"', *Early American Literature* 16 (1981): 109.
38. Johnson and Burling, pp. 128, 157-58, 161.
39. Joseph Towne Wheeler, 'Reading and Other Recreations of Marylanders, 1700-1776', *Maryland Historical Magazine* 38 (1943): 170.

40. Hamilton, *History*, 2: 138-39.
41. Ibid., 2: 139.
42. Ibid., 2: 141.
43. Ibid., 2: 142.
44. Ibid., 2: 144.
45. Ibid., 2: 145.
46. Ibid., 2: 393.

6. *The Colonial American Stage*

1. [Lewis Hallam,] 'This Is to Inform the Public', *Virginia Gazette* (Hunter), 12 June 1752.
2. Highfill, 7: 34, 48.
3. Highfill, 7: 37-38.
4. Hunter D. Farish, *Second Theatre Historical Report: Block 7 Lot 21 and 22* (1940; Williamsburg: Colonial Williamsburg Foundation Library, 1990), pp. 4-5.
5. 'A Morning Walk', *Virginia Gazette* (Hunter), 28 August 1752; *Much Ado about Nothing*, 5.3.24-27; David Fordyce, *Dialogues Concerning Education* (London, 1745), p. 235.
6. Joachimus Bertrand, 'Romeo and Juliet', *New York Gazette*, 23 March 1730, reprinted in George Freedley, 'An Early Performance of *Romeo and Juliet* in New York', *Bulletin of the New York Public Library* 40 (1936): 495.
7. André-G. Bourassa, 'The Rebirth of French Theatre in the Province of Québec, 1765-1825: The Role of French Actors and Directors from the United States', *Theatre Symposium* 2 (1994): 85.
8. Jonathan Swift, *Gulliver's Travels*, ed. Henry Morley (London: George Routledge, 1890), p. 278.
9. Bertrand, 'Romeo and Juliet', p. 495; Alfred Westfall, 'A New American Shakespeare Allusion', *Modern Language Notes* 63 (1948): 401-403.
10. *Othello*, 3.1.170-171.
11. Ewa Elandt, '"The Judicious Author": A Note on Possibly the First American Production of *Romeo and Juliet*', *Studia Anglica Posnaniensia* 25-27 (1991-93): 269.
12. Bertrand, 'Romeo and Juliet', p. 495.
13. Ibid.
14. Kevin J. Hayes, *The Library of John Montgomerie, Colonial Governor of New York and New Jersey* (Newark, DE: University of Delaware Press, 2000), p. 27.
15. James Alexander to Cadwallader Colden, 18 June 1729, *The Letters and Papers of Cadwallader Colden*, vol. 1 (New York: New York Historical Society, 1918), pp. 280-81.
16. 'By His Excellency's Permission', *New York Gazette*, 26 February 1750.
17. Dwayne W. Pickett, et al., *'The Old Theatre Near the Capital': Archaeological and Documentary Investigations into the Site of the Third Theatre* (1998; Williamsburg: Colonial Williamsburg Foundation, 2003), p. 7.
18. 'Observations on the Late Performance of *Othello*', *Virginia Gazette* (Hunter), 8 August 1751.

19. 'By Permission of his Honour the President', *Virginia Gazette* (Hunter), 26 September 1751; 'Advertisements', *Virginia Gazette* (Hunter), 24 October 1751.
20. Johnson and Burling, p. 151.
21. Lewis Hallam, 'The Case of the London Company of Comedians', *New York Mercury*, 2 July 1753.
22. Quoted in Jacob Larwood, *Theatrical Anecdotes; or, Fun and Curiosities of the Play, the Playhouse, and the Players* (London: Chatto and Windus, 1882), p. 26.
23. David Garrick, *Lethe: A Dramatic Satire* (London: Paul Vaillant, 1749), p. 29.
24. Johnson and Burling, pp. 150-54.
25. Hugh F. Rankin, *The Theater in Colonial America* (Chapel Hill: University of North Carolina Press, 1965), p. 55; William Dunlap, *History of the American Theatre*, 2 vols (London: Richard Bentley, 1833), 1: 16-17.
26. [John Singleton,] 'Prologue', *Virginia Gazette* (Hunter), 22 September 1752.
27. Johnson and Burling, pp. 160-61.
28. 'Williamsburg, December 8', *Virginia Gazette* (Hunter), 8 December 1752.
29. Farish, *Second Theatre Historical Report*, p. 5.
30. Pickett, *Old Theatre*, pp. 7-8.
31. Hallam, 'Case of the London Company'.
32. Ibid.
33. Johnson and Burling, p. 168.
34. Roberta Mock, 'Moody, John', *ODNB*; Jared Brown, 'Hallam, Lewis', *ODNB*.
35. Johnson and Burling, p. 187.
36. Ibid., p. 188.
37. Quoted in George O. Seilhamer, *History of the American Theatre before the Revolution* (Philadelphia: Globe, 1888), pp. 96-97.
38. Alexander Graydon, *Memoirs of His Own Time with Reminiscences of the Men and Events of the Revolution*, ed. John Stockton Littell (Philadelphia: Lindsay and Blakiston, 1846), pp. 87-88.
39. Highfill, 11: 157-58.
40. Johnson and Burling, pp. 197-205.
41. Page Life, 'Bernard, John', *ODNB*.
42. John Bernard, 'Early Days of the American Stage, Being a Selection from the Papers of One of Its Managers', ed. Bayle Bernard, *Tallis's Dramatic Magazine, and General Theatrical and Musical Review* 1 (1851): 237.
43. Johnson and Burling, p. 212.
44. John Bernard's autobiography first appeared as *Retrospections of the Stage*, ed. William Bayle Bernard, 2 vols (London: H. Colburn and R. Bentley, 1830), which contained no information about the Douglass Company. Bayle Bernard edited additional portions of his father's autobiography in a six-part series for *Tallis's Dramatic Magazine*. The last instalment, which appeared in June 1851, published Bernard's transcription of the playbill. The subsequent reprintings stem from this publication. Seilhamer, *History of the American Theatre*, gives both 1761 and 1762 as possible years. Rankin, *Theater in Colonial America*, pp. 93-94, selects 1761. Johnson and Burling, p. 227, hedge and list the year as '1762?' Robert Adger Law, 'Shakespeare in Puritan Disguise', *Nation*, 26

November 1916, p. 486, apparently the first to check a perpetual calendar, identified 1765 as the only possible year on which 10 June fell on a Monday.

45. Bernard, 'Early Days', p. 238.

7. *John Mercer, Governor Dinwiddie and the* Dinwiddianae

1. William Warburton, ed., *The Works of Shakespear*, vol. 1 (Dublin: R. Owen, 1747), unpaginated back matter.
2. J. A. Leo Lemay, 'Mercer, John', *ANB*; Bennie Brown, 'John Mercer: Merchant, Lawyer, Author, Book Collector', *'Esteemed Bookes of Lawe' and the Legal Culture of Early Virginia*, ed. Warren M. Billings and Brent Tarter (Charlottesville: University of Virginia Press, 2017), pp. 97-98; George Mason to John Mason, 13 March 1789, *The Papers of George Mason*, ed. Robert A. Rutland, 3 vols (Chapel Hill: University of North Carolina Press, 1970), 3: 1142.
3. 'On Friday the 14th', *Virginia Gazette* (Rind), 27 October 1768; C. Malcolm Watkins, *The Cultural History of Marlborough, Virginia* (Washington, DC: Smithsonian Institution Press, 1968), pp. 202, 205; Brown, 'John Mercer', p. 102.
4. 'To Be Sold by Garrat Noel', *New York Mercury*, 25 February 1754.
5. Kevin J. Hayes, *The Library of William Byrd of Westover* (Madison: Madison House, 1997), no. A17; Hunter Dickinson Farish, *Journal and Letters of Philip Vickers Fithian, 1773-1774: A Plantation Tutor of the Old Dominion* (Williamsburg: Colonial Williamsburg, 1965), pp. 227, 229.
6. Hugh Amory, 'Lennox [née Ramsay], (Barbara) Charlotte', *ODNB*; Susan Carlile, *Charlotte Lennox: An Independent Mind* (Toronto: University of Toronto Press, 2018), p. 128.
7. 'Borrowed Some Time This Spring', *New York Gazette*, 8 May 1758.
8. 'An Inventory of the Estate of Bayley Green taken October 9, 1755', *York County Estate Inventories*, is available on the Colonial Williamsburg website. 'To Be Sold', *Virginia Gazette* (Hunter), 24 October 1755; Benjamin Rush, 'The Wisdom and Experience of Mellow Old Age, 1785-1789, 1805, 1806', *Franklin in His Own Time: A Biographical Chronicle of His Life, Drawn from Recollections, Interviews, and Memoirs of Family, Friends, and Associates*, ed. Kevin J. Hayes and Isabelle Bour (Iowa City: University of Iowa Press, 2011), pp. 103-104.
9. Vol. 2 of John Mercer's copy of *The Works of John Sheffield, Earl of Mulgrave, Marquis of Normandy, and Duke of Buckingham, 4th ed, corrected* (London: D. Browne, 1753), survives at the Virginia Historical Society (Z986.M262B8).
10. Brent Tarter, 'Dinwiddie, Robert', *ANB*.
11. Ibid.
12. Edmund Randolph, *History of Virginia*, ed. Arthur H. Shaffer (Charlottesville: University Press of Virginia, 1970), p. 193.
13. J. A. Leo Lemay, 'The Colonial Virginia Satirist', *VMHB* 75 (1967): 492.
14. [William Smith,] *A Review of the Military Operations in North-America from the Commencement of the French Hostilities on the Frontiers of Virginia in 1753, to the Surrender of Oswego, on the 14th of August, 1756* (London: R. and J. Dodsley, 1757), p. 6.

15. Stephen Brumwell, *George Washington, Gentleman Warrior* (London: Quercus, 2012), p. 52; George Washington to Horatio Sharpe, 24 April 1754, *PGW: Colonial*, 1: 86.
16. [John Mercer,] 'The *Dinwiddianae*: Poems and Prose', *The Colonial Virginia Satirist: Mid-Eighteenth-Century Commentaries on Politics, Religion, and Society*, ed. Richard Beale Davis (Philadelphia: American Philosophical Society, 1967), p. 18.
17. Ibid., p. 19.
18. Thomas Jefferson to John Wayles Eppes, 24 June 1813, *PTJRS*, 6: 223.
19. Mercer, *Dinwiddianae*, p. 19.
20. Watkins, *Cultural History*, p. 202.
21. Mercer, *Dinwiddianae*, p. 20.
22. Ibid.
23. Ibid.
24. Ibid., p 21.
25. *Henry IV, Part I*, 4.2.36-37.
26. Mercer, *Dinwiddianae*, p. 17.
27. George Washington, 'Remarks', *PGW: Confederation*, 5: 520.
28. Smith, *Review of the Military Operations*, p. 48; *Henry VIII*, 5.2.77-79.
29. Mercer, *Dinwiddianae*, p. 24.
30. [William Donaldson,] *North America, A Descriptive Poem* (London: J. Shepheard, 1757), p. 19.
31. Ibid.; Julius Caesar, 4.3.268-274.
32. Mercer, *Dinwiddianae*, p. 23.
33. Ibid.
34. Ibid.
35. *Othello*, 3.3.273-277.
36. Robert Bolling, 'A Prayer', *Robert Bolling Woos Anne Miller: Love and Courtship in Colonial Virginia, 1760*, ed. J. A. Leo Lemay (Charlottesville: University Press of Virginia, 1990), p. 99.
37. Mercer, *Dinwiddianae*, p. 25.
38. Ibid.
39. *Hamlet*, 3.2.66-70; Alexander Surbanov, *Shakespeare's Lyricized Drama* (Newark: University of Delaware Press, 2010), p. 213.
40. Mercer, *Dinwiddianae*, p. 28.
41. Ibid.
42. Ibid., pp. 29-30.
43. William Smith, *Discourses on Several Public Occasions during the War in America* (London: A. Millar, 1759), p. 176.
44. Mercer, *Dinwiddianae*, p. 30.
45. J. A. Leo Lemay, 'The Rev. Samuel Davies' Essay Series: The Virginia Centinel, 1756-1757', *Essays in Early Virginia Literature Honoring Richard Beale Davis*, ed. J. A. Leo Lemay (New York: Burt Franklin, 1977), p. 160.
46. Samuel Davies, *Religion and Patriotism the Constituents of a Good Soldier* (Philadelphia: James Chattin, 1755), p. 19.
47. [Samuel Davies], 'Virginia Centinel, No. IX', *Pennsylvania Gazette*, 16 September 1756.

48. [Samuel Davies,] 'The Virginia Centinel, No. X', *Virginia Gazette* (Hunter), 3 September 1756; *Henry VI, Part II*, 3.1.300-301.
49. Lemay, 'Rev. Samuel Davies' Essay Series', pp. 131-32.
50. Mercer, *Dinwiddianae*, p. 25.
51. Lemay, 'Rev. Samuel Davies' Essay Series', pp. 132-33.

8. *The Labyrinth of Mental Nature: Reading Shakespeare, Becoming John Adams*

1. Philip Goff, 'Diversity and Region', *Themes in Religion and American Culture*, ed. Philip Goff and Paul Harvey (Chapel Hill: University of North Carolina Press, 2004), p. 327; John Adams, 'Autobiography', *DAJA*, 3: 268.
2. John Adams, 'Literary Commonplace Book', *PJA*, 1: 10.
3. John Adams, 'A Letter to William Crawford Telling "How I Live," October 1758', *The Earliest Diary of John Adams: June 1753-April 1754, September 1758-January 1759*, ed. L. H. Butterfield, Wendell D. Garrett and Marc Friedlaender (Cambridge, MA: Belknap Press, 1966), 1: 91; Caius Cornelius Tacitus, *Opera quae supersunt*, ed. Jakob Gronovius, 4 vols (Glasgow: Foulis, 1753), 1: 279; H. Trevor Colbourn, *The Lamp of Experience: Whig History and the Intellectual Origins of the American Revolution* (1965; New York: Norton, 1974), p. 7; Peter Shaw, *The Character of John Adams* (Chapel Hill: University of North Carolina Press, 1976), p. 35.
4. *Othello*, 2.3.247-249; Adams, 'Letter to William Crawford', p. 91.
5. Ibid.; Colley Cibber, *Plays*, 2 vols (London: Jacob Tonson, 1721), 1: 105.
6. Adams, 'Letter to William Crawford', p. 91.
7. John Adams, 'Letters to Three Friends on Studying Law, October–November 1758', *Earliest Diary*, 1: 65.
8. Ibid.
9. Ibid., 1: 66; *Hamlet* 1.3.115-118, 120.
10. Adams, 'Letters to Three Friends', 1: 67.
11. John Adams, 'A Letter to Richard Cranch about Orlinda, a Letter on Employing One's Mind, and Reflections on Procrastination, Genius, Moving the Passions, Cicero as Orator, Milton's Style, &c., October–December 1758', *Earliest Diary*, 1: 69.
12. Alexander Pope, *Poetry and Prose*, ed. Aubrey Williams (Boston: Houghton Mifflin, 1969), p. 127.
13. Adams, 'Letter to Richard Cranch', 1: 72-73.
14. Evelyn Gajowski, *The Art of Loving: Female Subjectivity and Male Discursive Traditions in Shakespeare's Tragedies* (Newark: University of Delaware Press, 1992), p. 67.
15. *Othello*, 3.3.348-351; Adams, 'Letter to Richard Cranch', 1: 76.
16. Ibid.; John Adams to Abigail Adams, 28 December 1794, *AFC*, 10: 326.
17. Thomas Prince, *Earthquakes the Works of God, and Tokens of His Just Displeasure* (Boston: D. Fowle and Z. Fowle, 1755), p. 20; John Adams, 'Marginalia in Winthrop's Lecture on Earthquakes, December 1758?', *DAJA*, 1: 61; Lemay, *Life of Benjamin Franklin*, 3: 124.
18. John Adams, 'Diary', *DAJA*, 1: 60.

19. Thomas Hanmer, ed., *The Works of Mr William Shakespear*, vol. 4 (London, 1748) (Boston Public Library, Special Collections, Adams 235.7).
20. John Adams, 'Autobiography', *DAJA*, 3: 278.
21. John Adams, 'Misanthrop, No. 1', *PJA*, 1: 185.
22. John Adams, 'Misanthrop, No. 2', *PJA*, 1: 188-89.
23. Ibid.
24. Ibid., p. 188.
25. John Adams, 'Shakespeare's Characters and Figurative Language', *Earliest Diary*, 1: 101.
26. Ibid., p. 102.
27. Ibid.; *Macbeth*, 5.5.22-27.
28. Adams, 'Shakespeare's Characters' p. 102.
29. Ibid.
30. Ibid.
31. Abigail Adams to Elizabeth Smith Shaw, 4 March 1786, *AFC*, 7: 81.
32. Abigail Smith to John Adams, 19 April 1764, *AFC*, 1: 37.
33. Barbara A. Mowat, 'The Founders and the Bard', *Yale Review* 97 (2009): 11.
34. Lyman C. Draper, ed., 'Journal of General Daniel Smith, Aug. 1779, to July, 1780, Running Line between North Carolina and Virginia – Tennessee and Kentucky', *Tennessee Historical Magazine* 1 (1915): 63.
35. John Adams, 'Diary', *DAJA*, 1: 66.
36. Ibid., 1: 176-77.
37. Ibid., 2: 53.

9. *The 1760s*

1. William Tudor, *The Life of James Otis, of Massachusetts* (Boston: Wells and Lilly, 1823), pp. 16-17.
2. John Adams to William Tudor, 29 March 1817, *The Works of John Adams*, ed. Charles Francis Adams, 10 vols (Boston: Little, Brown, 1856), 10: 246.
3. Ibid., p. 247.
4. Ibid., pp. 245-46.
5. James M. Farrell, 'The Writs of Assistance and Public Memory: John Adams and the Legacy of James Otis', *New England Quarterly* 79 (2006): 536.
6. John Adams to William Tudor, 29 March 1817, *Works*, 10: 247-48.
7. Joseph Towne Wheeler, 'Reading Interests of the Professional Classes in Colonial Maryland, 1700-1776', *Maryland Historical Magazine* 36 (1941): 300; Robert William Schoeberlein, 'Mental Illness in Maryland: Public Perception, Discourse, and Treatment, from the Colonial Period to 1964', PhD. diss. (University of Maryland, 2006), pp. 5-6; Charles Carroll of Annapolis, 'Inventory at Doohergan [1762]' and Charles Carroll of Carrollton to Charles Carroll of Annapolis, 7 January 1763, *Dear Papa, Dear Charley: The Peregrinations of a Revolutionary Aristocrat*, ed. Ronald Hoffman, et al., 3 vols (Chapel Hill: University of North Carolina Press, 2001), 1: 297, 304.
8. J. Bryan Grimes, *North Carolina Wills and Inventories* (1912; Baltimore: Genealogical Publishing, 1967), p. 491; Ludwick Hartley, 'The Dying Soldier and the Love-Lorn Virgin: Notes on Sterne's Early Reception in America', *The Winged Skull: Papers from the Laurence Sterne Bicentenary Conference*,

ed. Arthur H. Cash and John M. Stedmond (Kent, OH: Kent State University Press, 1971), p. 159.

9. Walter B. Edgar, 'Libraries of Colonial South Carolina', *South Carolina Historical Magazine* 72 (1971): 107; Herbert A. Johnson, *Imported Eighteenth-Century Law Treatises in American Libraries, 1700-1799* (Knoxville: University of Tennessee Press, 1978), p. 76.
10. Walter B. Edgar, 'Popular Books in Colonial South Carolina', *South Carolina Historical Magazine* 72 (1971): 175; Richard Beale Davis, *A Colonial Southern Bookshelf: Reading in the Eighteenth Century* (Athens: University of Georgia Press, 1979), p. 95.
11. Samuel Carne, 'All Persons Any Wise Indebted', *South Carolina Gazette*, 24 December 1763.
12. 'An Inventory and Appeasement of the Estate of Mr John Herbert, Dec'd', *VMHB* 18 (1910): 181; Thomas Katheder, *The Baylors of Newmarket: The Decline and Fall of a Virginia Planter Family* (New York: iUniverse, 2009), p. 162.
13. Hugh Blair, ed., *The Works of Shakespear*, vol. 6 (Edinburgh: W. Sands, 1753) (Colonial Williamsburg, John D. Rockefeller, Jr Library, Special Collections PR2752.S26 1753).
14. *A Catalogue of Books to Be Sold at the Post Office, Williamsburg* [Williamsburg, 1772.] The Library of Congress dates this catalogue '176-', but Winans, no. 81, identifies several novels from 1771 and 1772 on the list, hence the approximate date of 1772.
15. Paul Baines, 'Capell, Edward', *ODNB*.
16. 'Thomas Walter, Just Arrived from London', *South Carolina Gazette*, 17 June 1766; 'Just Imported, and to Be Sold by John Mein, at the London Book-Store', *Connecticut Gazette*, 12 September 1766; 'Coats-of-Arms in Virginia', *1WMQ* 2 (1893): 25; Samuel Johnson, ed., *The Plays of William Shakespeare*, 8 vols (London: H. Woodfall, 1768) (Princeton University, Rare Books and Special Collections, 3925.1768.2).
17. Stephen B. Weeks, *Libraries and Literature in North Carolina in the Eighteenth Century* (Washington: GPO, 1896), p. 202.
18. Clairborne T. Smith, Jr, 'Milner, James', *Dictionary of North Carolina Biography*, ed. William S. Powell, 6 vols (Chapel Hill: University of North Carolina Press, 1979-1996), 4: 279-80; Grimes, *North Carolina Wills*, p. 519; Arthur Sherbo, 'Farmer, Richard', *ODNB*.
19. 'Just Imported, and To Be Sold by John Mein', *Connecticut Gazette*, 12 September 1766; John Mein, *A Catalogue of Curious and Valuable Books* [Boston, 1766], lot 1150 (Winans, no. 59).
20. John Adams, 'Diary', *DAJA*, 1: 338.
21. *Othello*, 1.1.135-136.
22. 'To Be Sold by James Johnson', *Georgia Gazette*, 7 April 1763; 'To Be Sold Valuable Books, Neatly Bound', *New Hampshire Gazette*, 26 April 1765; 'Robert Fowle, Has for Sale', *New Hampshire Gazette*, 1 July 1768; 'The Following Collection of Books', *South Carolina Gazette*, 12 January 1768; *A Catalogue of Books, Sold by Rivington and Brown* ([Philadelphia?] 1762), p. 16 (Winans, no. 45); [Garrat Noel's Bookstore'], *New York Journal*, 3 November 1768; 'William Rind, Has Imported in the *Charming Nancy*', *Maryland Gazette*, 26 August 1762.

23. William Dunlap, *Books and Stationary, Just Imported from London* ([Philadelphia: William Dunlap, 1761]) (Winans, no. 37).
24. Johnson and Burling, pp. 215-16.
25. Andrew Auguecheek (pseud.), *Universal American Almanack: or, Yearly Astronomical Magazine for ... 1760* (Philadelphia: William Bradford and Andrew Stueart, [1759]), unpaginated.
26. Charles Evans, *American Bibliography*, 14 vols (New York: P. Smith, 1941-1959), nos. 9004-9005.
27. 'This Day Is Published, by Hugh Gaine', *New York Mercury*, 20 July 1761; Alden T. Vaughan, 'Shakespeare Discovers America: America Discovers Shakespeare', *Shakespeare in American Life*, ed. Virginia Mason Vaughan and Alden T. Vaughan (Washington: Folger Shakespeare Library, 2007), p. 15.
28. Nahum Tate, *King Lear, A Tragedy: As It Is Now Actd at the King's Theatre, Revived with Alterations* (London: C. Hitch, 1760); William Shakespeare, *The Tempest: A Comedy* (London: C. Hitch, 1761).
29. 'The Following Plays and Farces', *New York Mercury*, 24 June 1765.
30. Kevin J. Hayes, 'Libraries and Learned Societies', *Encyclopedia of the North American Colonies*, ed. Jacob Ernest Cooke, 3 vols (New York: Scribner, 1993), 3: 129-30.
31. Marcus A. McCorison, ed., *The 1764 Catalogue of the Redwood Library Company at Newport, Rhode Island* (New Haven: Yale University Press, 1965), nos. 589-590; Hunter Dickinson Farish, ed., *Journal and Letters of Philip Vickers Fithian, 1773-1774: A Plantation Tutor of the Old Dominion* (Williamsburg: Colonial Williamsburg, 1965), p. 223; Samuel Johnson, 'Preface', *Plays of William Shakespeare*, 1: lvi.
32. *A Catalogue of Books, Belonging to the Union Library Company of Philadelphia* (Philadelphia: Henry Miller, 1765), p. 37 (Winans, no. 55); *Catalogue of Books, Belonging to the Association Library Company of Philadelphia* (Philadelphia: William Bradford, 1765), p. 59 (Winans, no. 51); 'Upon a Late Examination of the Books', *Pennsylvania Journal*, 23 October 1766.
33. *The Charter, Laws, Catalogue of Books, List of Philosophical Instruments, etc. of the Juliana Library-Company in Lancaster* (Philadelphia: D. Hall and W. Sellers, 1766), p. 49 (Winans, no. 53); Charles I. Landis, 'The Juliana Library Company in Lancaster', *PMHB* 43 (1919): 231.
34. [Elizabeth Montagu,] *An Essay on the Writings and Genius of Shakespear* (London: J. Dodsley, 1769), p. 16; Thomas Morris, *Miscellanies in Prose and Verse* (London: James Ridgway, 1791), pp. 43-44; James Boswell, *The Life of Samuel Johnson* (New York: Everyman's Library, 1992), p. 368.
35. Chester T. Hallenbeck, 'A Colonial Reading List from the Union Library of Hatboro, Pennsylvania', *PMHB* 56 (1932): 333, tentatively identifies the Hatboro copy of Theobald's Shakespeare as the seven-volume 1733 first edition, but the borrowing records show it was an eight-volume edition.
36. Kevin J. Hayes, *A Colonial Woman's Bookshelf* (1996; Eugene, OR: Wipf and Stock, 2016), pp. 12-13; Hallenbeck, 'Colonial Reading List', p. 321.
37. Ibid., p. 315.
38. Ibid., p. 310.
39. Ibid.

40. Kevin J. Hayes, 'Carter, John', *ANB*.
41. 'This Day Is Published', *New York Gazette*, 4 February 1762; George Francis Dow, *The Arts and Crafts in New England, 1704-1775* (Topsfield, MA: Wayside Press, 1927), p. 39; 'The Second Part of the Celebrated Lecture on Heads', *New York Gazette*, 13 August 1767.
42. Hanford Henderson, 'Shakespeare in Marble in Colonial America', *Shakespeare Quarterly* 12 (1961): 156-57.
43. Henry C. Van Schaak, 'Captain Thomas Morris in the Country of the Illinois', *Magazine of American History* 8 (1882): 470-79.
44. Thomas Morris, 'Shakespeare on the Maumee in 1764', *The Maumee Valley through Fifty Years, 1763-1813* (Ann Arbor: University of Michigan, 1940), unpaginated.
45. For the concept of books as talismans, see Kevin J. Hayes, *Folklore and Book Culture* (1997; Eugene, OR: Wipf and Stock, 2016).
46. Morris, *Miscellanies*, pp. 16-17, 63.
47. Richard Alan Ryerson, *John Adams's Republic: The One, the Few, and the Many* (Baltimore: Johns Hopkins University Press, 2016), pp. 46-47; [Stephen Sayre,] *The Englishman Deceived: A Political Piece* (London: G. Kearsley, 1768), p. 19.
48. Ryerson, *John Adams's Republic*, p. 47.
49. John Adams, 'A Dissertation of the Canon and the Feudal Law, No. 4', *PJA*, 1: 125.
50. Ibid,; John Adams to Philip Mazzei, *PJA*, 13: 152.
51. Adams, 'Dissertation, No. 4', p. 126.
52. John Adams, 'Diary', *DAJA*, 1: 263.
53. John Adams to J. Morse, 5 December 1815, *Works*, 10: 189; Jean-Paul Goffinon, *Aux origines de la Révolution américaine, John Adams: La Passion de la distinction* (Brussels: Editions de l'Université de Bruxelles, 1996), pp. 130-31; *Troilus and Cressida*, 1.3.312.
54. Adams, 'Diary', *DAJA*, 1: 275.
55. Hugh Blair, ed., *The Works of Shakespear*, 8 vols. (Edinburgh: A. Kincaid, 1761), vol. 2, 4, 5, 6 (Boston Public Library, Adams 235.6).
56. Adams, 'Diary', *DAJA*, 1: 281.
57. Ibid., p. 286.
58. 'Looking over Shakespear', *Boston Gazette*, 30 December 1765.
59. Adams, 'Diary', *DAJA*, 1: 286; 'To the Printer', *North Carolina Gazette*, 26 February 1766.
60. Adams, 'Diary', *DAJA*, 1: 286.
61. Robert C. Waterston, 'Tea-Party Anniversary', *Massachusetts Historical Society Proceedings* 13 (1875): 192; 'Catalogue of Books Belonging to the Estate of Josiah Quincy Junr. Esq: Deceas'd', *Portrait of a Patriot: The Major Political and Legal Papers of Josiah Quincy, Junior*, ed. Daniel R. Coquillette and Neil Longley York, 5 vols (Boston: Colonial Society of Massachusetts, 2007), 5: 911, 897.
62. Josiah Quincy, Jr, 'The Southern Journal', *Portrait of a Patriot*, 3: 102; *Tempest* 1.2.3-5; John Milton, *Paradise Lost*, book 1, lines 181-182.
63. William Blackstone, *Commentaries on the Laws of England: Book the Fourth* (Oxford: Clarendon Press, 1769), p. 2; Michael Foster, 'Of Homicide',

A Report of Some Proceedings on the Commission of Oyer and Terminer and Goal Delivery for the Trial of the Rebels in the Year 1746 (Oxford: Clarendon Press, 1762), p. 264.

64. 'Josiah Quincy's Argument for the Defense: 3 December 1770', *The Legal Papers of John Adams*, ed. L. Kinvin Wroth and Hiller B. Zobel (Cambridge, MA: Belknap Press, 1965), 3: 241.

10. *Thomas Jefferson and His Williamsburg Circle*

1. 'Williamsburg, Feb. 22', *Virginia Gazette* (Purdie and Dixon), 22 February 1770; Hayes, *Road*, p. 1.
2. Thomas Jefferson to John Page, 21 February 1770, *PTJ*, 1: 63.
3. Ibid.
4. Thomas Jefferson, *Jefferson's Literary Commonplace Book*, ed. Douglas L. Wilson (Princeton: Princeton University Press, 1989), pp. 109, 114-16.
5. Ibid., p. 106; *Julius Caesar*, 2.2.32-37.
6. Thomas Jefferson, 'Thoughts on English Prosody', *Writings*, ed. Merrill D. Peterson (New York: Library of America, 1984), p. 611.
7. *Jefferson's Literary Commonplace Book*, p. 107; *Julius Caesar*, 3.1.99-103.
8. *Jefferson's Literary Commonplace Book*, p. 107; *Henry V*, 4.3.20-23.
9. *Henry V*, 4.3.28-29.
10. Paul A. Cantor, *Shakespeare's Roman Trilogy: The Twilight of the Ancient World* (Chicago: University of Chicago Press, 2017), p. 150.
11. *Jefferson's Literary Commonplace Book*, p. 108; *Coriolanus*, 4.1.4-9.
12. John Bernard, 'Recollections of President Jefferson (1828)', *Jefferson in His Own Time: A Biographical Chronicle of His Life, Drawn from Recollections, Interviews, and Memoirs of Family, Friends, and Associates*, ed. Kevin J. Hayes (Iowa City: University of Iowa Press, 2012), p. 112.
13. 'The Coles Family', *VMHB* 7 (1899): 101-102; Thomas Hanmer, ed., *The Works of Shakespear* (London: J. and P. Knapton, 1748) (University of Virginia, Special Collections, PR2752.H3 1748 v.1-7, 9).
14. Genevieve Yost, 'The Reconstruction of the Library of Norborne Berkeley, Baron de Botetourt, Governor of Virginia, 1768-1770', *PBSA* 36 (1942): 118.
15. Ibid., 116.
16. Brent Tarter, 'Botetourt, Norborne Berkeley, baron de', *DVB*, 2: 108-109.
17. John E. Selby, 'Murray, John', *ANB*; Alexander Pope, ed., *The Works of Shakespear*, 6 vols (London: Jacob Tonson, 1723-1725) (Colonial Williamsburg, John D. Rockefeller Jr Library, Special Collections, PR2752. P7 1723).
18. Arthur Sherbo, *Shakespeare's Midwives: Some Neglected Shakespeareans* (Newark: University of Delaware Press, 1992), pp. 112-13.
19. *Merry Wives of Windsor*, 4.2.24-25; Edmond Malone, ed., *Supplement to the Edition of Shakspeare's Plays Published in 1778 by Samuel Johnson and George Steevens*, 2 vols (London: C. Bathurst, 1780), 2: 688.
20. Fraser Neiman, 'The Letters of William Gilpin to Samuel Henley', *Huntington Library Quarterly* 35 (1972): 160-62.
21. Malone, *Supplement*, 2: 684.

22. Quoted in Mellen Chamberlain, 'Rev. Samuel Henley, D.D.', *Proceedings of the Massachusetts Historical Society* 15 (1878): 235.
23. Thomas Jefferson to Samuel Henley, 3 March 1785, *PTJ*, 8: 11-13.
24. Malone, *Supplement*, 2: 682-83, 689, 698-99, 709.
25. Samuel Henley to Thomas Jefferson, 18 July 1785 and 16 November 1785, *PTJ*, 8: 304, 9: 39.
26. Quoted in Chamberlain, 'Rev. Samuel Henley', p. 236.
27. Thomas Jefferson, *Jefferson's Memorandum Books: Accounts, with Legal Records and Miscellany, 1767-1826*, ed. James A. Bear, Jr and Lucia C. Stanton, 2 vols (Princeton: Princeton University Press, 1992), 1: 289, 347.
28. Johnson and Burling, p. 372.
29. [Jonathan Boucher,] 'To Miss Hallam', in George O. Seilhamer, *History of the American Theatre before the Revolution* (Philadelphia: Globe, 1888), p. 279.
30. *A Catalogue of the Very Valuable and Extensive Library of the Late Rev. Jonathan Boucher* (London: Leigh and Sotheby, 1806), lots 5344, 5348, 5992.
31. Jonathan Boucher to George Washington, 2 August 1773, *PGW: Colonial*, 9: 294; Jonathan Boucher to William Smith, 4 May 1775, 'Letters of Rev. Jonathan Boucher', *Maryland Historical Magazine* 8 (1913): 239.
32. Boucher, 'To Miss Hallam', p. 279.
33. Johnson and Burling, p. 371.
34. *Cymbeline*, 3.6.23-24.
35. *Measure for Measure*, 4.3.157; Eric Partridge, *Shakespeare's Bawdy*, 3d ed. (1968; London: Routledge, 2001), p. 288.
36. Samuel Johnson and George Steevens, eds., *The Dramatick Writings of Will. Shakspere*, 20 vols. (London: John Bell, 1788), 20: 49-50.
37. Dr Alexander Hamilton to Baillie Hamilton, August 1755, in Elaine G. Breslaw, 'A Dismal Tragedy: Drs Alexander and John Hamilton Comment on Braddock's Defeat', *Maryland Historical Magazine* 75 (1980): 139; Governor Dunmore to Lord Dartmouth, 24 December 1774, *Documentary History of Lord Dunmore's War, 1774*, ed. Reuben Gold Thwaites and Louise Phelps Kellogg (Madison: Wisconsin Historical Society, 1905), p. 376.
38. Johnson and Steevens, *Dramatick Writings of Will. Shakspere*, 8: 85.
39. *Merchant of Venice*, 2.1.4-7; Johnson and Steevens, *Dramatick Writings of Will. Shakspere*, 7: 16.
40. *Much Ado about Nothing*, 1.1.239-241.
41. Thomas Percy, ed., *Reliques of Ancient English Poetry*, 3 vols (London: J. Dodsley, 1765), 1: 129.
42. Quoted in E. Millicent Sowerby, *Catalogue of the Library of Thomas Jefferson*, 5 vols (Washington: Library of Congress, 1952-1959), no. 4538.
43. Jefferson, 'Autobiography', *Writings*, p. 5.
44. Hayes, *Road*, pp. 120-21.
45. Thomas Augustine Arne, *To Keep My Gentle Jessy: A Favourite Sons in the Merchant of Venice* ([London, 1760?]) and *The Serenade: Sung by Mr Mattocks in the Merchant of Venice* ([London, 1770?]) (University of Virginia, Special Collections, A1723.J4 no. 66, 39).
46. Robert Skipwith to Thomas Jefferson, 17 July 1771, *PTJ*, 1: 74.
47. Thomas Jefferson to Robert Skipwith, 2 August 1771, *PTJ*, 1: 78.

48. Hayes, *Road*, p. 124.
49. Thomas Jefferson to Robert Skipwith, 2 August 1771, *PTJ*, 1: 77.
50. Ibid.
51. Sowerby, *Catalogue*, no. 4712.
52. Thomas Jefferson to Dabney Carr, 19 January 1816, *PTJRS*, 9: 368-69; 'Dabney Carr's Library', *VMHB* 2 (1894): 225.
53. Thomas Jefferson to Bernard Minor, ca. 1773, *PTJRS*, 7: 629.
54. Ibid.
55. 'Inventory of Books Received by Thomas Jefferson from the Estate of George Wythe, circa September 1806', Massachusetts Historical Society Collections Online.
56. 'A Course of Lectures', *Virginia Gazette* (Purdie and Dixon), 2 January 1772; 'A Course of Lectures', *Virginia Gazette* (Rind), 6 February 1772.
57. 'Articles of the Virginia Society [1772]', *The Bland Papers: Being a Selection from the Manuscripts of Colonel Theodorick Bland, Jr of Prince George County, Virginia*, ed. Charles Campbell, 2 vols (Petersburg: Edmund and Julian C. Ruffin, 1840), 1: xxv-xxvii.
58. Johnson and Burling, p. 444; Hayes, *George Washington*, p. 146.
59. Ibid.
60. *Troilus and Cressida*, 5.2.55-56; Ebenezer Cook, 'The Sot-weed Factor: or, A Voyage to Maryland', *An Early American Reader*, ed. J. A. Leo Lemay (Washington, DC: USIA, 1988), p. 153.
61. Johnson and Steevens, *Dramatick Writings of Will. Shakspere*, 19: 71-72.
62. Ibid.; John Campbell, *A Political Survey of Britain*, 2 vols (London, 1774), 2: 95.
63. Johnson and Steevens, *Dramatick Writings of Will. Shakspere*, 19: 72.

11. *The Blast of War*

1. Colley Cibber, *The Lady's Last Stake: or, The Wife's Resentment* (London: John Bell, 1795), p. 19.
2. Odai Johnson, *London in a Box: Englishness and Theatre in Revolutionary America* (Iowa City: University of Iowa Press, 2017), pp. 191-92.
3. *King John*, 5.2.148-153.
4. *King John*, 5.7.117-118.
5. 'To the Printer of the *Pennsylvania Packet*', *Pennsylvania Packet*, 13 June 1774; *Richard II*, 2.1.61-67.
6. 'To the Printer of the *Pennsylvania Packet*', *Virginia Gazette* (Rind), 23 June 1774; 'From the *Pennsylvania Packet*', *New York Journal*, 30 June 1774; 'From the *Pennsylvania Packet*', *Connecticut Gazette*, 15 July 1774.
7. John Dickinson, *Letters from a Farmer in Pennsylvania, to the Inhabitants of the British Colonies*, ed. R.T.H. Halsey (New York: Outlook, 1903), p. 89; *An Address to the Committee of Correspondence in Barbados* (Philadelphia: William Bradford, 1766), title page.
8. Whitfield J. Bell, Jr, *Patriot-Improvers: Biographical Sketches of Members of the American Philosophical Society*, vol. 1 (Philadelphia: American Philosophical Society, 1997), p. 187; Joseph E. Fields, 'A Signer and His Signatures: or, The Library of Thomas Lynch, Jr', *Harvard Library Bulletin* 14 (1960): 220; *Official Descriptive Catalogue of Colonial and Revolutionary*

Relics Now in Possession of the Citizens of New Jersey (Trenton: Naar, Day and Naar, 1895), p. 93. For Robert Treat Paine and Richard Henry Lee see the 'Legacy Libraries' section of the online database, *LibraryThing*.

9. *Macbeth*, 1.1.1-4; William Wirt, *Sketches of the Life and Character of Patrick Henry* (Philadelphia: James Webster, 1817), pp. 156-57.
10. *The Association, etc.* ([Philadelphia, 1774]), p. 5; Bob Jingle (pseud.), *The Association, etc. of the Delegates of the Colonies, at the Grand Congress* ([Philadelphia,] 1774), p. 11.
11. Wirt, *Sketches*, pp. 7, 427.
12. Kevin J. Hayes, *The Mind of a Patriot: Patrick Henry and the World of Ideas* (Charlottesville: University of Virginia Press, 2008), no. 52.
13. *Julius Caesar*, 1.2.93-96.
14. Lloyd J. Matthews, 'Patrick Henry's "Liberty or Death" Speech and Cassius's Speech in Shakespeare's *Julius Caesar*', *VMHB* 86 (1978): 300-301; Hayes, *Mind of a Patriot*, pp. 71-74.
15. Quoted in J. Franklin Jameson, ed., 'Journal of a French Traveler in the Colonies, 1765', *American Historical Review* 26 (1921): 745.
16. *Julius Caesar*, 5.5.69-76.
17. Frank Shuffelton, 'Mercy Otis Warren', *American Colonial Writers, 1735-1781*, ed. Emory Elliott (Detroit: Gale, 1984), p. 247.
18. Josiah Quincy, Jr, *Observations on the Act of Parliament Commonly Called the Boston Port-Bill* (Boston: Edes and Gill, 1774), p. 57.
19. P. M. Zall, ed., *Ben Franklin Laughing: Anecdotes from Original Sources by and about Benjamin Franklin* (Berkeley: University of California Press, 1980), p. 97.
20. Hayes, *Road*, p. 164; Thomas Jefferson to William Small, 7 May 1775, *PTJ*, 1: 165.
21. Mark V. Kwansy, *Washington's Partisan War, 1775-1783* (Kent, OH: Kent State University Press, 1996), p. 15.
22. Janet Schaw, *Journal of a Lady of Quality: Being the Narrative of a Journey from Scotland to the West Indies, North Carolina and Portugal, in the Years 1774 to 1776*, ed. Evangeline Walker Andrews and Charles McLean Andrews (New Haven: Yale University Press, 1923), p. 190.
23. Josiah Quincy, Jr, 'The Southern Journal', *Portrait of a Patriot: The Major Political and Legal Papers of Josiah Quincy, Junior*, ed. Daniel R. Coquillette and Neil Longley York, 5 vols (Boston: Colonial Society of Massachusetts, 2007), 3: 230.
24. Schaw, *Journal of a Lady*, p. 191; *Henry IV, Part I*, 4.2.33-37.
25. Joseph Ward to John Adams, 23 October 1775, *PJA*, 3: 237-38.
26. Ibid.; *Henry V*, 4.3.24-29.
27. Philip Freneau, *A Voyage to Boston* (New York: John Anderson, 1775), pp. 8, 10.
28. Ibid., pp. 11, 14; Kevin J. Hayes, 'Poetry in the Time of Revolution', *The Cambridge History of American Poetry*, ed. Alfred Bendixen and Stephen Burt (Cambridge: Cambridge University Press, 2015), pp. 129-51.
29. Philip Freneau, 'On Devastations Committed in a Booksellers Library, by Rats, Mice, etc.', *Poems Written and Published During the American Revolutionary War*, 2 vols (Philadelphia: Lydia R. Bailey, 1809), 1: 266.
30. *Henry V*, 3.1.3-7.

31. 'Just Published, and To Be Sold by William Woodhouse', *Pennsylvania Gazette*, 15 November 1775.
32. John Adams, 'Autobiography', *DAJA*, 3: 370.
33. Silas Deane to Elizabeth Deane, 1 October 1775, *LDC*, 2: 91.
34. Revelations, 14.13.
35. *Hamlet*, 3.1.64-67.
36. Neil L. York, 'Hamlet as American Revolutionary', *Hamlet Studies* 15 (1993): 40-53.
37. Sayre N. Greenfield, 'Quoting *Hamlet* Outside Britain in the Eighteenth Century', *Shakespeare's World / World Shakespeares: The Selected Proceedings of the International Shakepseare Association World Congress, Brisbane, 2006*, ed. Richard Fotheringham, Christa Jansohn and R. S. White (Newark: University of Delaware Press, 2008), p. 243; Hamlet (pseud.), 'Alas Poor Cato!', *Pennsylvania Ledger*, 30 March 1776.
38. A. Owen Aldridge, *Thomas Paine's American Ideology* (Newark: University of Delaware Press, 1984), p. 169; [William Smith,] 'To the People of Pennsylvania, Letter IV', *Pennsylvania Ledger*, 30 March 1776; Thomas Paine, 'The Forester's Letter III', *Collected Writings*, ed. Eric Foner (New York: Library of America, 1995), p. 75.
39. Harry M. Ward, 'Knox, Henry', *ANB*.
40. Charles Lee to George Washington, 5 April 1776, *PGW: Revolutionary War*, 4: 43.
41. William Congreve, *The Way of the World*, in *Restoration Plays from Dryden to Farquhar*, ed. Edmund Gosse (London: J. M. Dent, 1912), p. 234.
42. Charles Lee to George Washington, 5 April 1776, *PGW: Revolutionary War*, 4: 43; *Richard III*, 4.4.484-485.
43. Charles Lee to Robert Howe, 5 April 1776, to Richard Henry Lee, 5 April 1776, *The Lee Papers*, 4 vols (New York: New York Historical Society, 1872-1875), 1: 375, 379.
44. Horatio Gates to John Adams, 23 April 1776, *PJA*, 4: 142.
45. *Hamlet*, 3.4.204-207.
46. Richard Alan Ryerson, *John Adams's Republic: The One, the Few, and the Many* (Baltimore: Johns Hopkins University Press, 2016), p. 98.
47. John Adams, *Thoughts on Government*, *PJA*, 4: 86.
48. Ibid., p. 87.
49. Richard Henry Lee to Patrick Henry, 20 April 1776, *LDC*, 3: 565.
50. 'Resolution of Independence Moved by R. H. Lee for the Virginia Delegation', *PTJ*, 1: 298.
51. Thomas Jefferson to Henry Lee, 8 May 1825, *Writings*, ed. Merrill D. Peterson (New York: Library of America, 1984), p. 1501.
52. Quoted in Elizabeth H. Nuxall, ed., *The Selected Papers of John Jay*, 5 vols (Charlottesville: University of Virginia Press, 2010-), 1: 402.
53. Thomas Jefferson to James Madison, 30 August 1823, *The Republic of Letters: The Correspondence between Thomas Jefferson and James Madison, 1776-1826*, ed. James Morton Smith, 3 vols (New York: Norton, 1995), 3: 1876.
54. Samuel Adams to John Pitts, ca. 9 July 1776, *LDC*, 4: 417.
55. 'Notes of Proceedings in the Continental Congress', 7 June to 1 August 1776, *PTJ*, 1: 317.

56. *Richard III*, 4.4.406-409.
57. *Richard III*, 5.3.311.

12. *'Band of Brothers'*

1. Hayes, *George Washington*, pp. 169-70.
2. Harry M. Ward, 'Knox, Henry', *ANB*; Henry Knox to Lucy Flucker Knox, 28 December 1776, *The Revolutionary War Lives and Letters of Lucy and Henry Knox*, ed. Phillip Hamilton (Baltimore: Johns Hopkins University Press, 2017), p. 66; James Wilkinson, *Memoirs of My Own Times*, 3 vols (Philadelphia: Abraham Small, 1816), 1: 128.
3. Henry Knox to Lucy Flucker Knox, 7 January 1777, *Revolutionary War Lives*, pp. 70-71.
4. David Hackett Fischer, *Washington's Crossing* (Oxford: Oxford University Press, 2004), p. 366.
5. Paul David Nelson, 'Lee, Henry', *ANB*; Henry Lee to C. C. Lee, 9 February 1817, *Memoirs of the War in the Southern Department of the United States*, ed. Robert E. Lee (London: Sampson, Low, 1869), p. 64.
6. 'Extract of a Letter from an Officer at Morris Town, Dated February 21, to the Printer', *Virginia Gazette*, 28 March 1777.
7. *Henry IV, Part I*, 5.4.118-120.
8. Agricola (pseud.), *The Squabble: A Pastoral Eclogue* (Philadelphia: Andrew Steuart, 1764), p. 7.
9. John Sullivan to George Washington, 13 February 1777, *PGW: Revolutionary War*, 8: 330.
10. Ibid.
11. Quoted in Edward J. Lowell, *The Hessians and Other German Auxiliaries of Great Britain in the Revolutionary War* (New York: Harper and Brothers, 1884), p. 227.
12. 'Gentlemen Who Wish', *Pennsylvania Evening Post*, 16 January 1776.
13. Oliver Wolcott to Laura Wolcott, 19 March 1776, *LDC*, 3: 413; 'An Inventory of the Sundry Household Goods and Chattels Found in the House of Hugh Ferguson of Graeme Park Taken This Seventeenth of September 1778', *Pennsylvania Archives*, 6th ser., 12 (1907): 657.
14. 'Brought by Mistake from Fredericksburg', *Virginia Gazette* (Purdie), 27 June 1777.
15. Kevin J. Hayes, *The Mind of a Patriot: Patrick Henry and the World of Ideas* (Charlottesville: University of Virginia Press, 2008), nos. 36, 103, 117; E. Millicent Sowerby, *Catalogue of the Library of Thomas Jefferson*, 5 vols (Washington: Library of Congress, 1952-1959), nos. 1434, 1981, 2930, 4638.
16. *Journal of the House of Delegates of Virginia: Anno Domini, 1776* (Richmond: Samuel Shepherd, 1828), p. 29; Alexander Pope, ed., *The Works of Shakespear*, 6 vols (London: Jacob Tonson, 1723-1725) (Colonial Williamsburg, John D. Rockefeller Jr Library Special Collections, PR2752.P7 1723); Blanche Adams Chapman, *Marriages of Isle of Wight County, Virginia, 1628-1800* (1933; Baltimore: Clearfield, 2002), p. 91.
17. Hayes, *Road*, p. 201; Sowerby, *Catalogue*, no. 4711.

18. Helen R. Watson, 'The Books They Left: Some "Liberries" in Edgecombe County, 1733-1783', *North Carolina Historical Review* 48 (1971): 252; 'Sale of Gov. Martin's Property', *The State Records of North Carolina*, ed. Walter Clark, vol. 22 (Goldsboro, NC: Nash Brothers, 1907), p. 885.
19. Francis's Gentleman, ed., *Bell's Edition of Shakespeare's Plays*, vol. 1 (London: John Bell, 1774) (Folger Shakespeare Library, PR2752 1774b copy 5 v. 1 Sh.Col.)
20. Hayes, *George Washington*, p. 181.
21. Johann Ewald, quoted in Charles R. Hildeburn, 'Francis Hopkinson', *PMHB* 2 (1878): 320; Henry N. Paul, 'Shakespeare in Philadelphia', *Proceedings of the American Philosophical Society* 76 (1936): 721; George Washington to Francis Hopkinson, 16 May 1785, *PGW: Confederation*, 2: 561-62.
22. *Twelfth Night*, 2.4.112-115.
23. George Washington, 'General Orders', 7 December 1775, 28 December 1778, 22 May 1779, *PGW: Revolutionary War*, 2: 503, 18: 519, 20: 567.
24. George Washington to William Woodford, 3 March 1777, *PGW: Revolutionary War*, 8: 508.
25. *Othello*, 3.3.322-325.
26. George Washington to George Washington Custis, 28 November 1796, *The Writings of George Washington from the Original Manuscript Sources, 1745-1799*, ed. John C. Fitzpatrick, 39 vols (Washington: GPO, 1939), 35: 296.
27. George Washington to Henry Laurens, 3 October 1778, *PGW: Revolutionary War*, 17: 238; Henry Laurens to William Livingston, 19 April 1779, *LDC*, 12: 353.
28. Samuel Adams to Richard Henry Lee, 15 July 1777, *LDC*, 7: 344.
29. Benjamin Franklin, 'Poor Richard Improved, 1758', *PBF*, 7: 341; *Richard II*, 3.2.29-30; Bartlett Jere Whiting, *Early American Proverbs and Proverbial Phrases* (Cambridge, MA: Belknap Press, 1977), no. H256.
30. John Cannon, 'Savile, Sir George, Eighth Baronet', *ODNB*.
31. *The Parliamentary Register; or, History of the Proceedings and Debates of the House of Commons*, vol. 8 (London: J. Almon, 1778), p. 30.
32. *Macbeth*, 1.7.63-67.
33. P. M. Zall, *Ben Franklin Laughing: Anecdotes from Original Sources by and about Benjamin Franklin* (Berkeley: University of California Press, 1980), p. 151.
34. Benjamin Franklin to [Robert Morris?], 21 December 1777, *PBF*, 25: 331.
35. William Carmichael to Benjamin Franklin, 3 March 1782, *PBF*, 36: 641-42.
36. *Shakespeare's History of the Times; or The Original Portraits of That Author Adapted to Modern Characters* (London: D. Browne and J. Murray, 1778), pp. 20-21; *Julius Caesar*, 1.2.93-96.
37. *Shakespeare's History of the Times*, p. 48; *Troilus and Cressida*, 1.3.196.
38. George Washington, 'General Orders', 6 April 1778, *PGW: Revolutionary War*, 14: 410.
39. *Henry V*, 4.3.56-62.
40. Hayes, *George Washington*, pp. 200-201.
41. Annis Boudinot Stockton, 'To General Washington', *Only for the Eyes of a Friend: The Poems of Annis Boudinot Stockton*, ed. Carla Mulford (Charlottesville: University Press of Virginia, 1995), p. 118.

42. George Washington to Annis Boudinot Stockton, 2 September 1783, *Writings*, 27: 127-28.
43. George Washington, 'Farewell Orders to the Armies of the United States', 2 November 1783, *Writings*, 27: 224.
44. *Henry V*, 4.8.108.

13. American Shakespeareans in Europe

1. Benjamin Franklin to Vergennes, 18 January 1783, *PBF*, 38: 596.
2. John Adams, 'Diary', *DAJA*, 3: 106; John Adams to Abigail Adams, 22 January 1783, *AFC*, 5: 74.
3. 'The American Peace Commissioners: Acceptance of the British Declaration of the Cessation of Hostilities [20 January 1783]', *PBF*, 38: 605-608; 'Voltaire and Shakespeare', *Players*, 14 July 1860, p. 12.
4. E. Preston Dargan, 'Shakespeare and Ducis', *Modern Philology* 10 (1912): 20-28.
5. John Adams to Abigail Adams, 26 February 1783, *AFC*, 5: 99; Jean François Ducis, *Le Roi Léar, tragédie* (Paris: P. Fr. Gueffier, 1783), p. 35.
6. Benjamin Franklin to Robert R. Livingston, 22[-26] July 1783, *PBF*, 40: 356.
7. Ibid.
8. *Catalogue of a Collection of Valuable and Scarce Books, Being Part of the Library of the Late Elbridge Gerry, Esq.* ([Boston, 1815]), lot 254.
9. Elbridge Gerry to Abigail Adams, 18 September 1783, *AFC*, 5: 250.
10. James Warren to John Adams, 27 October 1783, *PJA*, 15: 322-23.
11. Abigail Adams to John Adams, 15 December 1783, *AFC*, 5: 280-81.
12. John Adams to Benjamin Rush, 21 June 1811, *Old Family Letters: Copies from the Originals for Alexander Biddle* (Philadelphia: J. B. Lippincott, 1892), p. 287.
13. Abigail Adams to John Adams, 20 September 1783, *AFC*, 5: 253; *Hamlet*, 3.1.78-79.
14. Abigail Adams to John Adams, 11 February 1784, *AFC*, 5: 302-303.
15. Abigail Adams to Mercy Otis Warren, 5 September 1784, *AFC*, 5: 448.
16. *Two Gentlemen of Verona*, 5.4.69-72; Abigail Adams to Mary Smith Cranch, 4 July 1786, *AFC*, 7: 236.
17. Charles Beecher Hogan, *The London Stage, 1660-1800 ... Part 5: 1776-1800* (Carbondale: Southern Illinois University Press, 1968), p. 829; Abigail Adams to Elizabeth Smith Shaw, 15 September 1785, *AFC*, 6: 362.
18. Abigail Adams to William Stephens Smith, 18 September 1785, *AFC*, 6: 366-68.
19. Hogan, *London Stage*, p. 842; Abigail Adams 2d to John Quincy Adams, 22 January 1786, *AFC*, 7: 22.
20. Hogan, *London Stage*, p. 866; Abigail Adams 2d to John Quincy Adams, 5 December 1785, *AFC*, 6: 478.
21. Abigail Adams to John Quincy Adams, 16 February 1786, *AFC*, 7: 62-63.
22. Ibid., p. 63.
23. Ibid.; *Two Gentlemen of Verona*, 2.4.190-193.
24. *Much Ado about Nothing*, 1.1.247-249.
25. Henry Lee to James Madison, 16 February 1786, *The Papers of James Madison*, ed. William T. Hutchinson and William M. E. Rachal, 17 vols (Chicago: University of Chicago Press, 1962-1991), 8: 493.
26. John Quincy Adams to Abigail Adams, 2d, 15 March 1786, *AFC*, 7: 91.

27. Abigail Adams to Elizabeth Smith Shaw, 4 March 1786, *AFC*, 7: 81.
28. Karl Moritz, *Travels, Chiefly on Foot, through Several Parts of England, in 1782* (London: G. G. and J. Robinson, 1795), pp. 186-87; John Adams, 'Notes on a Tour of English Country Seats, etc., with Thomas Jefferson, 4–10 April 1786', *DAJA*, 3: 185.
29. Moritz, *Travels*, 186-87; Adams, 'Notes', p. 185.
30. Ibid.
31. Quoted in Barbara A. Mowat, 'The Founders and the Bard', *Yale Review* 97 (2009): 1.
32. Hogan, *London Stage*, p. 876.
33. Hayes, *Road*, p. 321.
34. James Mascarene Hubbard, *Catalogue of Works Relating to William Shakespeare and His Writings in the Barton Collection, Boston Public Library* (Boston: Boston Public Library, 1880), p. 73.
35. Andrew Becket, *A Concordance to Shakespeare* (London: G. G. J. and J. Robinson, 1787), p. iii.
36. Thomas Jefferson to John Trumbull, 18 January 1789, *PTJ*, 14: 467.
37. Abigail Adams to Mercy Otis Warren, 14 May 1787, *AFC*, 8: 45.
38. Mercy Otis Warren, 'To Mrs Montague, *Author of Observations on the Genius and Writings of Shakespeare*', *Poems, Dramatic and Miscellaneous* (Boston: I. Thomas and E. T. Andrews, 1790), p. 181.

14. How Shakespeare Ratified the Constitution

1. George Washington, *The Diaries of George Washington*, ed. Donald Jackson and Dorothy Twohig, 6 vols (Charlottesville: University Press of Virginia, 1976-1979), 5: 176.
2. Publius (pseud.) [Alexander Hamilton,] 'The Federalist 1: *New York Independent Journal*, 27 October 1787', *DHRC*, 13: 494; Eva Saks, 'The Staging of the Constitution: or, The Republican Masque of *The Federalist Papers*', *Theatre Journal* 41 (1989): 360-80.
3. Publius (pseud.) [John Jay,] 'The Federalist 2: *New York Independent Journal*, 31 October 1787', *DHRC*, 13: 518.
4. Aaron Hall, 'An Oration Celebrating New Hampshire Ratification, Keene, N.H., 30 June 1788'. *DHRC*, 28: 422.
5. Publius (pseud.) [John Jay,] 'Federalist 2', *DHRC*, 13: 520.
6. *Henry VIII*, 3.2.350-358.
7. An Instructor (pseud.), 'Baltimore *Maryland Gazette*, 16 November 1787', *DHRC*, 11: 57. Subsequent citations follow the format established by *DHRC* editors, who typically use newspaper and date to title individual essays.
8. An Old Man (pseud.), 'Baltimore *Maryland Gazette*, 20 November 1787', *DHRC*, 11: 60.
9. *Tempest*, 3.2.106-109.
10. John Trumbull, quoted in A Federalist (pseud.), '*Charleston City Gazette*, 16 May 1788', *DHRC*, 27: 285.
11. Ibid.
12. Mercy Otis Warren, 'Observations on the Constitution', *DHRC*, 16: 285.

13. 'Extract of a Letter from Philadelphia, 18 November, *Maryland Journal*, 14 December 1787', *DHRC*, 2: 260.
14. Mark Antony (pseud.), '*Independent Chronicle*, 10 January 1788', *DHRC*, 5: 672.
15. Ibid., p. 677.
16. '*Massachusetts Centinel*, 12 December 1787', *DHRC*, 4: 418.
17. *Othello*, 4.2.61-63.
18. William Stuart to Griffith Evans, 11 July 1788, *DHRC*, 18: 258.
19. *Othello*, 3.3.92.
20. [Robert Dodsley,] *The Preceptor: Containing a General Course of Education, Wherein the First Principles of Polite Learning Are Laid Down*, 2 vols (Dublin: George Faulkner, 1749), 1: 60-62.
21. Hayes, *Road*, pp. 32-35.
22. 'The Batchelor's Soliloquy', *Scots' Magazine*, April 1744, p. 176; 'The Batchelor's Soliloquy', *New York Morning Post*, 12 August 1786.
23. 'The Batchelor's Soliloquy', *Maryland Gazette*, 19 August 1762 (Lemay, *Calendar*, no. 1876); 'The Batchelor's Soliloquy', *The Wilmington Almanack, or Ephemeries, for ... 1763*, ed. Thomas Fox (Wilmington: James Adams, [1762]), unpaginated; 'The Batchelor's Soliloquy', *The American Calender: or, An Almanack for ... 1768*, ed. Philo Copernicus (pseud.) (Philadelphia: William and Thomas Bradford, [1767]), unpaginated.
24. An Officer of the Army (pseud.), 'Shakespeare Parody'd', *New American Magazine,* January 1759, p. 334 (Lemay, *Calendar*, no. 1553).
25. 'Shakespeare Parody'd', *Norwich Packet*, 22 January 1776; 'A Parody, Written During the Late War', *Columbian Magazine*, February 1788, p. 112.
26. Richard Jago, 'Hamlet's Soliloquy, Imitated', *A Collection of Poems* 6 vols (London R. and J. Dodsley, 1758), 5: 82-83; 'Hamlet's Soliloquy, Imitated', *New American Magazine*, May 1759, pp. 470-71 (Lemay, *Calendar*, no. 1599).
27. 'From the *Antigua Mercury*, Jan. 14', *South Carolina Gazette*, 16 March 1769; 'A Parody on Shakespear', *Massachusetts Spy*, 7 August 1770. Neil L. York, 'Hamlet as Revolutionary', *Hamlet Studies* 15 (1993): 40-41, reprints the *Massachusetts Spy* version but misattributes it to Isaiah Thomas.
28. 'From the *Georgia Gazette*, March 1: 'A Parody on Shakespear' *South Carolina* Gazette, 16 March 1769.
29. 'To the Printer of the *Georgia Gazette*: A Parody on Shakespear', *Georgia Gazette*, 1 March 1769; 'A Parody on Shakespear', *Massachusetts Spy*, 14 August 1770.
30. Olney Winsor to Mrs Olney Winsor, 10, 17 April 1788, *DHRC*, 9: 734.
31. '*Virginia Independent Chronicle*, 31 October 1787', *DHRC*, 8: 139.
32. Ibid., p. 140.
33. William Symmes, Jr, to Peter Osgood, Jr, 15 November 1787, *DHRC*, 14: 116.
34. '*New Hampshire Spy*, 4 December 1787', *DHRC*, 28: 55-56.
35. Maecenas (pseud.), '*State Gazette of South Carolina*, 6 December 1787', *DHRC*, 27: 51.
36. '*New Hampshire Gazette*, 16 April 1788', *DHRC*, 28: 291.
37. J. A. Leo Lemay, 'The American Aesthetic of Franklin's Visual Creations', *PMHB* 111 (1987): 475-77.

List of Illustrations

1. *William Byrd's Westover*, South Riverfront Elevation, photograph, Library of Congress, Prints and Photographs Division, Washington, DC (reproduction number: HABS VA,19-WEST,1-79).
2. *The Rev. Samuel Johnson,* wood engraving. From Evert A. Duyckinck and George L. Duyckinck, *Cyclopaedia of American Literature* (1856) Kevin J. Hayes Collection, Toledo, Ohio.
3. Hubert Gravelot, *And Has Not Sawney Too His Lord and W[hor]e* (1742), engraving and etching, Library of Congress, Prints and Photographs Division, Washington, DC (reproduction number: LC-USZ62-86066).
4. James McArdell, after a painting by Benjamin Wilson, *Mr Garrick in Hamlet* (1754), mezzotint, Library of Congress, Prints and Photographs Division, Washington, DC (reproduction number: LC-USZ62-115300).
5. Alexander Hamilton, *Self-Portrait*, drawing. Reproduced from Albert Bushnell Hart, ed., *Hamilton's Itinerarium: Being a Narrative of a Journey from Annapolis, Maryland through Delaware, Pennsylvania, New York, New Jersey, Connecticut, Rhode Island, Massachusetts and New Hampshire from May to September, 1744* (Saint Louis: William K. Bixby, 1907), frontispiece.
6. I. Neagle, after a painting by Henry Fuseli, *Merchant of Venice, Act 4, Sc. 4* (1803), engraving, Library of Congress, Prints and Photographs Division, Washington, DC (reproduction number: LC-USZ62-99061).
7. *Provost William Smith*, wood engraving. From Evert A. Duyckinck and George L. Duyckinck, *Cyclopaedia of American Literature* (1856). Kevin J. Hayes Collection, Toledo, Ohio.
8. *John Adams*, an engraving after a portrait by John Singleton Copley, Library of Congress, Prints and Photographs Division, Washington, DC (reproduction number: LC-DIG-ppmsca-15705).
9. *Abigail Adams*, steel engraving, after a painting by C. Schessle. From Rufus Wilmot Griswold, *The Republican Court* (1854). Kevin J. Hayes Collection, Toledo, Ohio.

10. *James Otis*, wood engraving. From Evert A. Duyckinck and George L. Duyckinck, *Cyclopaedia of American Literature* (1856). Kevin J. Hayes Collection, Toledo, Ohio.
11. Pierre du Simitiere, Redwood Library, drawing, Library of Congress, Prints and Photographs Division, Washington, DC (reproduction number: HABS RI,3-NEWP,15-1).
12. *The Stamp Act Denounced* (1913), wood engraving, Library of Congress, Prints and Photographs Division, Washington, DC (reproduction number: LC-USZ62-51563).
13. Henry Fuseli, *Lady Macbeth* (1784), mezzotint, Library of Congress, Prints and Photographs Division, Washington, DC (reproduction number: LC-USZC4-5857).
14. *The Bloody Massacre Perpetrated in King Street, Boston on March 5th, 1770, by a Party of the 29th Regt*, re-graved by Sidney L. Smith from the original engraving by Paul Revere, Library of Congress, Prints and Photographs Division, Washington, DC (reproduction number: LC-DIG-pga-12360).
15. *Thomas Jefferson*, steel engraving by H. B. Hall's Sons, New York. From Lyon Gardiner Tyler, *Encyclopaedia of Virginia Biography* (1915). Kevin J. Hayes Collection, Toledo, Ohio.
16. Sarony and Major, *The Destruction of Tea at Boston Harbor* (1846), lithograph, Library of Congress, Prints and Photographs Division, Washington, DC (reproduction number: LC-DIG-ds-03379).
17. *Carpenters' Company Hall,* photograph, Library of Congress, Prints and Photographs Division, Washington, DC (reproduction number: HABS PA,51-PHILA,229-11).
18. Currier and Ives, *Give Me Liberty, or Give Me Death!* (ca. 1876), lithograph, Library of Congress, Prints and Photographs Division, Washington, DC (reproduction number: LC-DIG-pga-08961).
19. N. Currier, *Washington at Princeton, January 3d. 1777*, lithograph, Library of Congress, Prints and Photographs Division, Washington, DC (reproduction number: LC-DIG-pga-10103).
20. *Gen. Washington Resigning His Commission to Congress, Annapolis, Md., Dec. 23, 1783*, photograph of a painting by John Trumbull in the United States Capitol, Library of Congress, Prints and Photographs Division, Washington, DC (reproduction number: LC-DIG-det-4a26395).
21. Thomas Gainsborough, *Mrs Siddons*, Library of Congress, Prints and Photographs Division, Washington, DC (reproduction number: LC-DIG-det-4a26277).
22. *John Jay* (1889), engraving after a painting by Joseph Wright, Library of Congress, Prints and Photographs Division, Washington, DC (reproduction number: LC-USZ62-95399).

Index